EVA
BRAUN

EVA BRAUN

LIFE WITH HITLER

Heike B. Görtemaker

Translated from the German by Damion Searls

ALFRED A. KNOPF · NEW YORK · 2011

This Is a Borzoi Book published by Alfred A. Knopf.

Translation copyright © 2011 by Damion Searls

www.aaknopf.com

Originally published in Germany as *Eva Braun: Leben
mit Hitler* by Verlag C. H. Beck oHG, Munich, in 2010.
Copyright © 2010 Verlag C. H. Beck, Munich.

Library of Congress Cataloging-in-Publication Data
Görtemaker, Heike B., [date]
Eva Braun : life with Hitler / by Heike B. Görtemaker ;
translated from the German by Damion Searls. —
1st American ed.
p. cm.
"This Is a Borzoi book" — T.p. verso.
Originally published in Germany as Eva Braun : Leben
mit Hitler, by Verlag C. H. Beck, Munich, in 2010.
Includes bibliographical references.
ISBN 978-0-307-59582-9
1. Braun, Eva.   2. Hitler, Adolf, 1889–1945 — Friends
and associates.   3. Hitler, Adolf, 1889–1945 — Family.
4. Mistresses — Germany — Biography.   5. Spouses of
heads of state — Germany — Biography.   6. Women —
Germany — Biography.   7. Germany — History —
1933–1945 — Biography.   I. Title.
DD247.B66G67 2011
943.086092 — dc22
[B]   2011009551

Front-of-jacket photograph: Bettmann/Corbis
Jacket design by Gabriele Wilson

Manufactured in the United States of America

First American Edition

CONTENTS

PART THREE Downfall

EVA
BRAUN

Introduction

On March 7, 1945, when Eva Braun had a chauffeur bring her in a diplomatic car from Munich to Berlin, she wanted to write the final chapter of her story herself.[1] That story had begun in 1929, in the offices of a Munich photographer, Heinrich Hoffmann, where she met the leader of a far-right political party that had not, at the time, been very successful: the National Socialist German Workers' Party (Nationalsozialistiche Deutsche Arbeiterpartei, or NSDAP). That leader's name was Adolf Hitler. Now she was driving to the capital, against his will, in order to die with him.

Hitler had ordered her to stay on the Obersalzberg, a mountain in the Bavarian Alps near Berchtesgaden, where he owned a large residence called the Berghof. Berlin was badly damaged, practically destroyed, after the Allied air strike of February 3; the air-raid sirens were sounding several times a day. The Soviet Red Army had reached the Oder River in January, while American and British forces, supported by numerous allies, were approaching from the west. As a result, no one in the Reich Chancellery expected Eva Braun to appear. Albert Speer remarked about her arrival in his memoir *Inside the Third Reich*: "Figuratively and in reality, with her presence a messenger of death moved into the bunker."[2] Be that as it may, she was also stepping out from the shadows of her existence as merely a mistress. Her name became inseparable from that of Hitler, and she herself, with their joint death, became a legend with him. Is that what she wanted?

No one, writes the British historian Ian Kershaw, shaped the twentieth century more powerfully than Adolf Hitler. The shocking experience of a "modern, advanced, cultured society . . . so rapidly sink[ing] into barbarity"[3] has undeniably had consequences down to the present day. In the process, the name Hitler has become a symbol: around the world, standing for violence, inhumanity, racism, perverted nationalism, genocide, and war. Ever since January 30, 1933, when Hitler was named Chancellor by President Paul von Hindenburg and the NSDAP legally came to power, there have been countless attempts not only to describe the structure and institutions of the National Socialist dictatorship, but also, more than anything, to explain the "phenomenon" of Adolf Hitler.[4] The debates continue even today.

Eva Braun, in contrast—the mistress for many years and eventually the wife of "evil incarnate"—has been seen as historically insignificant, as "a very pale shadow of the Führer,"[5] even as "a historical disappointment," in Hugh Trevor-Roper's words. As nothing. The reason for this was the belief that Eva Braun "played no role in the decisions that led to the worst crimes of the century," that she was nothing more than part of Hitler's private pseudoparadise, which may in fact have made it possible for him to pursue "his monstrous horrors all the more persistently."[6] Thus Eva Braun has remained a marginal figure in the biographies of Hitler. The few books that treat her own life story emphasize her allegedly tragic "fate as a woman" and refrain from presenting Hitler's girlfriend in her social, cultural, and political contexts—unless the book's author has an ideological agenda of his or her own.[7]

This disregard of Eva Braun as a historical figure is due in no small part to the dominant image of Hitler in the historical literature, because the question of whether Hitler should be portrayed as a human being at all is a controversial one even now. Some of his biographers maintain that their subject is a "nonperson"; Joachim C. Fest, for example, in the early 1970s, admitted that Hitler had apparently overwhelming power and "his own kind of greatness," but criticized the paleness of his person and his rigid, statuelike, theatrical appearance, while remarking on Hitler's "inability to lead an everyday life."[8] Decades later, Ian Kershaw said that

Hitler's "entire being" was given over to his role as "Führer,"* to the point where he lacked a "private," a "deeper" existence: the personal life of this despot who had an "extraordinary kind" of "charismatic" power consisted, according to Kershaw, of nothing more than a chain of "empty routines."[9] Even from a distance of sixty years, even while they are convinced that historical scholarship has "painstakingly taken the measure" of the "abyss," historians persist in looking at "the grotesque face of the monster" when it comes to Hitler himself.[10]

But doesn't this interpretation risk succumbing to Hitler's own self-presentation, according to which his individuality was of secondary importance? Do we not thereby dehumanize him, and as a result let him escape our critical understanding? It was Joseph Goebbels after all, Hitler's Minister of Public Enlightenment and Propaganda, who tirelessly promulgated the idea that the "Führer" had sacrificed his private life and all of his individual happiness for the German People†—that he stood "above all the daily worries and cares of ordinary mortals 'like a rock in the sea.' "[11] Are we not still creating an artificial figure when we look back at him in this way, one that only makes it harder for succeeding generations to confront their own histories and understand the nature of the Nazi dictatorship?

In no way do I mean to argue for an overemphasis on the individual in history. Nor am I suggesting that we should show "understanding" for the dictator's private side, especially since that dictator has already become an object of dubious fascination as "the devil in person." Rather, a serious, source-critical study of Eva Braun, which no one has carried out until now, offers a new perspective on Hitler, and one that can help undo his demonization.

Thus the question is: Who was this woman, actually, and what perspective does she open up onto this "criminal of the century"? The fact is

---

*Translator's note: "*Führer*," which is also the ordinary German word meaning "leader," is now known in English as Hitler's title. It should be kept in mind that calling Hitler the "Führer" was heavily ideological, the way referring to someone as "Our Dear Leader" would be in English. For that reason, Görtemaker puts "Führer" in quotes throughout her book when it is an idolizing reference to Hitler.

†Translator's note: "*Volk*," the German word for a people or tribe, also has a different connotation in the Nazi context. I have translated it as "the People" (capitalized), to emphasize its idealized, monolithic meaning, and have translated the adjective form, "*völkisch*," as "Populist," meaning "nationalist" or "xenophobic" in addition to the normal English sense of "populist."

that Eva Braun and Adolf Hitler were together for fourteen years—a relationship that ended only with their double suicide. Moreover, this relationship was one of Hitler's few close personal ties to any woman at all. She was largely concealed from the German public, and in terms of external appearance, Eva Braun—young, blond, athletic, attractive, fun-loving—absolutely did not fit Hitler with his "psychopath's face" (Joachim Fest's phrase), who looks prim, stiff, and elderly in the private photographs in which he appears. Eva Braun, it is said, loved fashion, movies, and jazz; read works by Oscar Wilde (who was banned in Germany after 1933); liked to travel; and pursued sports to excess.[12] Her life hardly corresponded to the petit bourgeois ideal of the German woman as propounded by Nazi ideology: bravely defending the husband's home and her motherhood before all else. So what did connect Eva Braun to Hitler? What were her relations like with the men in the Nazi leader's innermost circle—Hermann Göring, Albert Speer, and Martin Bormann? What light does this relationship shed on Hitler? Did he live with his lover in a kind of parallel private world that was fundamentally opposed to the official "Führer image"? Or is it in fact impossible to separate public and private in this way? Did both worlds belong together inseparably—for Eva Braun as well as for Hitler?

By all appearances, Eva Braun was a young woman of average abilities from a conventional, lower-middle-class family. She clearly did not stand out due to her background or her interests. It is often mentioned that she was noticeably lacking in any political sympathies or interest in current events at all.[13] Eva Braun was not sophisticated and glamorous like Magda Goebbels, nor was she politically influential like Annelies von Ribbentrop (daughter of the champagne manufacturer Otto Henkell), nor did she possess the fanaticism of a Gerda Bormann. But it is precisely her allegedly average ordinariness that invites us to reconstruct her historical circumstances. Her "normality" at the center of this atmosphere of "evil" is like an anachronism that brings this evil into relief and shows it in a new light.

PART ONE The Meeting

On April 30, 1945, at around 2:30 p.m., Erich Kempka, Hitler's driver since 1932, receives a phone call in the garage in the basement of the Reich Chancellery in Berlin. He is to get hold of fifty gallons of gasoline and bring it to the entrance of the "Führer bunker" in the Chancellery garden. He will be given further details there. When Kempka arrives with the men who are helping him carry the gasoline canisters, SS-Sturmbannführer Otto Günsche explains that the Führer is dead. He, Günsche, has been assigned to burn the body immediately, since Hitler did not want to end up "on display in a Russian panopticon." Günsche and Kempka enter the bunker, where Martin Bormann hands over Eva Braun's body to Kempka. She is wearing a dark dress that feels damp around the area of the heart. Kempka carries her upstairs to the exit, preceded by Heinz Linge (a valet) and Dr. Ludwig Stumpfegger carrying Hitler's corpse. Günsche, Bormann, and Joseph Goebbels follow behind. Shortly before 3:00 p.m. they lay the two bodies next to each other in the sand on level ground, pour five barrels of gasoline over them, and set them on fire. The men stand in the bunker entrance and, as the bodies burn, raise their arm one last time in the Hitler salute. When artillery shells start falling on the site, they hurry back into the protection of the bunker.[1]

1

Heinrich Hoffmann's Studio

Almost sixteen years earlier, in October 1929, Hitler and Eva Braun met for the first time in the studio of photographer Heinrich Hoffmann. Hoffmann was a press photographer and portrait photographer well known in Munich after World War I, as well as a publisher and a National Socialist from the beginning. He ran a studio, called Photohaus Hoffmann, at 25 Amalienstrasse, near Odeon Square in central Munich. From there he supplied the Munich *Illustrierte Presse* (Illustrated Press) and domestic and foreign agencies with his pictures. Hoffmann's father was a photographer as well, and he had apparently forced his son to follow in his footsteps; Hoffmann had owned a business of his own in Munich since 1909.[1] Even before 1914, Heinrich Hoffmann had made a name for himself with the public and in artistic circles with his photography service—the "Hoffmann Photoreport"—as well as by taking portrait photographs. Still, he owed his flourishing business to the NSDAP. After World War I, which he spent on the French front as a reservist in a replacement detachment of the air force, he put his talents at the service of the far-right nationalist movement that was rising to power.[2]

The Nazi Party's House Photographer

It is no longer possible to reconstruct exactly when and in what circumstances Hoffmann met Hitler for the first time. Hoffmann's daughter, Henriette von Schirach, later claimed that the Populist poet and writer Dietrich Eckart had put her father in contact with Hitler; Hoffmann himself said in his memoir that their first encounter was for purely business reasons, after an American photo agency offered him one hundred dollars for a photograph of Hitler, on October 30, 1922.[3] As early as 1947, in an unpublished written statement in his own defense, Hoffmann claimed that the "American press" had offered him "a large sum for the first picture of Hitler" at the time. In order to get this money, "under any circumstances," he contrived a seemingly chance encounter by suggesting that Hermann Esser, a good friend of Hitler's, hold the reception for his upcoming wedding in Hoffmann's house, on July 5, 1923. In this way, he planned to meet Hitler, who was to be one of the witnesses at the ceremony.[4]

In fact, Hoffmann had been a member of the German Workers' Party (Deutsche Arbeiterpartei, or DAP) since April 6, 1920—six months after Hitler had joined. Anton Drexler had founded the party in January of the previous year, in Munich, and it had recently changed its name to the National Socialist German Workers' Party (Nationalsozialistiche Deutsche Arbeiterpartei, or NSDAP). Hoffmann began to publish the weekly newspaper *Auf gut deutsch* (In Good German), edited by the radical nationalistic and anti-Semitic Dietrich Eckart, Hitler's friend, mentor, and father-figure. This failed poet used the paper to rail against the Weimar Republic, Bolshevism, and Judaism, under the motto "Germany, Awake!"[5] There is much evidence to suggest that Hoffmann became friends with this circle of like-minded men, including Eckart, Hitler, and the journalist Hermann Esser, before he began to make himself useful to the NSDAP and especially to the man who became its leader starting on July 29, 1921: the aggressive "beer hall agitator" Adolf Hitler.[6] Despite numerous requests, Hoffmann at first respected Hitler's wish not to be photographed. Hoffmann's first portrait of Hitler, in fact, appeared only after the failed Beer Hall Putsch of November 8–9, 1923, which made Hitler famous throughout Germany but also landed him in jail. (Hoffmann photographed him as a prisoner.) The following year, Hoffmann published a photo brochure titled (in German) "Germany's Awakening, in Words and Pictures." In 1926, the tireless Hoffmann, together with Hitler and Hermann Esser (their mutual friend and the first head of propaganda for the Party), founded a richly illustrated weekly Party newspaper, the *Illustrierter Beobachter.* That same year, at Hoffmann's suggestion, the *Völkischer Beobachter* (The People's Observer, the Nazi newspaper) included photographs for the first time—from Hoffmann's own studio, needless to say.

The NSDAP was thus on the cutting edge, technologically speaking. Only a few years earlier it had been common practice to illustrate newspaper stories with drawings or engravings. Even *The New York Times* started to print photographs regularly only in 1922. Photojournalism's true breakthrough, made possible by the development of the 35 mm camera in 1925, had only just begun.[7] Unlike in America—and also England and France, where the British *Daily Mirror* and French *Illustration* had set up a daily photographic exchange service between London and Paris as early as 1907—in Germany the practice of printing photographs in newspapers only slowly gained popularity.[8]

Among the pictures Hoffmann published in the *Völkischer Beobachter* was a series showing, for the first time, Hitler giving the Nazi salute with outstretched arm before a march of thousands of Party faithful on July 4, 1926, at the first NSDAP convention after it was reestablished in Weimar.[9] Already, in the earliest phase of the Nazi Party's rise to power, Hoffmann was putting his initiative and photographic skill behind the power of images—and the power of the Party's not uncontroversial leader, who was controversial even within the Party at first. For Hitler and the propaganda campaign he was waging against both external opponents and opponents within the Party, Hoffmann soon made himself indispensable. He became Hitler's "personal photographer."[10] From then on the leader of the Nazi Party almost never appeared without Hoffmann, whether on trips, on the campaign trail, or at lunch at Hitler's local Munich pub.

Hoffmann's decision to devote his career entirely to Hitler and the NSDAP paid off only in later years, however. In 1929, the Landtag (state parliament) campaigns and mass rallies provided Hoffmann's business with more and more assignments. These included the four-day NSDAP convention in Nuremburg on August 1–4, with the spectacular parade of sixty thousand SA and SS members, and Hitler's appearance on October 26 in the Zirkus Krone in Munich with Alfred Hugenberg, the press tycoon and head of the German National People's Party (Deutschnationale Volkspartei, or DNVP), in connection with the proposed German referendum against the Young Plan. That same year gave the Nazi Party its first electoral victories. In the Reichstag (national parliament) election the previous year, on May 20, 1928, it looked as though the National Socialists were sinking back into insignificance—they received only 2.6 percent of the vote—but in the Landtag and municipal elections of 1929 the trend was uniformly upward.[11] With the world economic crisis unfolding in the background, and the rise in unemployment to 3.32 million people in Germany, the NSDAP achieved gains in Saxony, Baden, and Bavaria; in Thuringia, in fact, its vote tally rose from 4.6 to 11.3 percent.

In light of these results, it is no accident that Hoffmann, then forty-four years old, was able to expand his business even in fall 1929, at the onset of the worldwide economic crash. He profited both from the increasing number of assignments from the Party and from the greater use Hitler himself made of him. Photo agencies were booming in any case, since by that time more and more newspapers were illustrating their reports with photographs. The demand throughout the world for news photographs was constantly on the rise, and a flourishing business grew from Hoffmann's small workshop in a courtyard behind 50 Schellingstrasse. It moved to 25 Amalienstrasse in September 1929, and was renamed the NSDAP-Photohaus Hoffmann. Shortly before the reopening, Hoffmann hired new employees, and one of them was the seventeen-year-old Eva Braun.[12]

"Herr Wolf"

Eva Braun's job at Photohaus Hoffmann seems to have been primarily behind the counter. In any case, the various statements about her actual duties are contradictory. For example, Henriette von Schirach—Hoffmann's daughter and a friend of Eva Braun's the same age as she, who was thus in a position to know—says at one point in her memoir that Braun was an "apprentice in [Hoffmann's] photo lab," but mentions elsewhere that Braun sold "roll films" in her father's "photo store."[13] In fact, both were true. Eva Braun, Heinrich Hoffmann later wrote, had been a "novice and shop assistant" and worked for him "in the office, as a salesgirl, and also in the laboratory." From 1933 on, after Braun was "more established" in the business, she worked exclusively "in photography."[14]

To be a photographer was a very respected and enviable career for a woman at the time. The field was new and modern and the idea of becoming a fashion or portrait photographer attracted many women. Eva Braun was especially interested in fashion. Her first task at Hoffmann's, though, was to learn how to use a camera and develop pictures. From the beginning, her duties included running small errands for Hoffmann and his clients and working behind the counter. Along with press photography, the rise in amateur photography offered a steadily growing market, so Photohaus Hoffmann not only took photographs but also sold photographic equipment, which was now readily available to the public. In addition, it sold pictures and postcards of its own, and Eva Braun was also responsible for those sales, according to Baldur von Schirach, Hoffmann's son-in-law and the future Youth Leader of the Nazi Party.[15] Hoffmann's preferred motifs and images included his fellow Party members and, especially, portraits of its leader, Adolf Hitler.

Eva Braun probably met Hitler for the first time in October 1929, a few weeks after starting her job.[16] She was apparently working late, organizing papers, when Hoffmann introduced her to one "Herr Wolf" and asked her to fetch some beer and sausages for him and his friend, and for herself as well, from a nearby restaurant. During the meal together that followed, the stranger was "devouring" her "with his eyes the whole time," and he later offered her "a lift in his Mercedes." She refused. Finally, before she left the studio, Eva Braun's boss, Hoffmann, asked her: "Haven't you guessed who that gentleman is; don't you ever look at our photos?" After she said no, Hoffmann said: "It's Hitler! Adolf Hitler."[17]

This account appears in the first published biography of Eva Braun, from 1968, by the Turkish-American journalist whose birth name was Nerin Emrullah Gün. According to Gün, Eva Braun told one of her sisters—presumably Ilse, the oldest of the three sisters—about this first meeting with Hitler, which occurred "on one of the first Fridays in October," either October 4 or October 11, 1929. But how reliable is Gün? His work is quoted extensively even today, and it tends to give the impression that Eva Braun dictated her story directly to him. From whom did he get his information, and how? And what are we to make of his own thoroughly enigmatic history?

Gün worked in the press department of the Turkish embassy in Budapest during World War II. Shortly before the end of the war, on April 12, 1945, the secret police ordered his arrest for allegedly being an enemy of the German state; he was sent to the Dachau concentration camp. Two weeks later, on April 29, 1945, he was liberated along with the other prisoners by the American Seventh Army. Gün moved to the United States, simplified his name to Gun, and later wrote a book about the assassination of John F. Kennedy. That was presumably why the CIA suspected him, as a member of the Communist Party, of being involved himself in the assassination of President Kennedy and charged him with having committed espionage and falsified documents in Europe.[18]

In the mid-1960s, on the occasion of the anniversary celebration of the liberation of Dachau, Gun visited West Germany. That was apparently when he arranged to meet Eva Braun's family and other former members of Hitler's inner circle. He tracked down Franziska Braun, Eva's mother, in her house in Ruhpolding, Bavaria, and also questioned Eva's sisters, Ilse and Margarete (who was called Gretl), as well as Eva's best friend, Herta Schneider (née Ostermayr). Gun obtained access to Eva Braun's private photographs and letters, and these were published for the first time in his book. However, Gun does not give precise details about the sources of his information, and he switches freely back and forth between invented anecdotes and factual testimony from actual witnesses in a way that makes it impossible for the reader to determine which is which.

Ilse Hess, Rudolf Hess's wife, wrote in a letter to Albert Speer on June 25, 1968, that Gun, "the author of the book about Everl [her nickname for Eva Braun]," had stayed with her, Ilse Hess, "for weeks" in Hindelang, since he was now planning to write a biography of her husband; she wrote that she now called him only by the name "Mr. I pay all" (in English), since that was his "favorite expression."[19] This remark shows the lack of respect she had for him; Gun apparently had little background knowledge and Ilse Hess did not take him seriously. Presumably, Gun likewise stayed with the Braun family the year before while he was researching his book on Eva Braun, although there is no concrete evidence either way.

Thus we cannot say that the sequence of events at the first meeting between Eva Braun and Hitler has been established with certainty, even if matters may well have played out the way Gun describes. It is certainly unclear why Hoffmann would have introduced his prominent friend and Party colleague under the fake name "Wolf."[20] (Hitler did often use that name for himself, especially when traveling.) Possibly Hoffmann was trying to forestall a nervous, or even hysterical, reaction from the young woman. In any case, nothing could stop the attraction that apparently sprang up spontaneously on both sides. From then on, Hitler, already forty years old, remembered himself to the seventeen-year-old Eva Braun with compliments and little gifts every time he visited the studio.

Such visits were not at all difficult for Hitler to arrange. Photohaus Hoffmann, on the corner of Amalienstrasse and Theresienstrasse, was directly across the street from Café Stephanie, a favorite spot for the leading Nazi politicians. Before World War I, it had been a meeting point for the bohemians of the Schwabing district, including such figures as Heinrich Mann, Erich Mühsam, Eduard Graf von Keyserling, and Paul Klee. The Party's headquarters were just a side street away, at 50 Schellingstrasse, the same street where the editorial and printing offices of the *Völkischer Beobachter* were located a few houses farther on. At 50 Schellingstrasse itself was the building where Heinrich Hoffmann and his family used to live, and Hoffmann's "workshop" was located next door. That was where he photographed Hitler, Göring, and other Party leaders.[21] Also on Schellingstrasse was the Osteria Bavaria, the oldest Italian restaurant in Munich, where Hitler and his fellow Party members often used to go; it is still there today, under the name Osteria Italiana. Henriette von Schirach described the restaurant as a "cool, small winery with a little courtyard painted in Pompeian red and a 'temple,' that is, an alcove with two columns in front of it," which was kept reserved for Hitler. However, Hitler's later secretary, Traudl Junge, said that the Nazi leader's regular table was the "least comfortable table all the way in the back, in the corner."[22]

Hitler rarely ate alone. His constant companions from the early 1920s on included not only Heinrich Hoffmann but also Ernst F. Sedgwick Hanfstaengl,[23] a German-American who was named head of the Party's Foreign Press Bureau in 1931. Ernst was the younger brother of the art publisher Edgar Hanfstaengl, who had taken over the family business, "Franz Hanfstaengl Art Publishers," in 1907; he led the New York branch of the publishing house until the end of World War I and then returned to Munich. Hitler's Munich circle in the early years also included Adolf Wagner, the powerful Gauleiter* of the Munich–Upper Bavaria region, called the "despot of Munich"; Julius Schaub, Hitler's personal assistant; Christian Weber, a "potbellied former horse trader" (in Joachim Fest's words) and good friend of Hitler's; and Hermann Esser, a found-

---

* Translator's note: "*Gauleiter*" is a Nazi bureaucratic term for a regional Party administrator, roughly equivalent to a Party "governor."

Eva Braun in Photohaus Hoffmann, posing on a desk, 1930

ing member of the NSDAP, whom Goebbels called "the little Hitler."
Later additions included the young Martin Bormann (a Party member
since 1927), Otto Dietrich (press chief of the NSDAP since 1931), SS General Joseph "Sepp" Dietrich, Max Amann, and Wilhelm Brückner (an
SA-Obergruppenführer and Hitler's chief adjutant since 1930).[24]

   Eva Braun was only occasionally invited out by Hitler—to a meal, a
movie, the opera, or a drive in the Munich region. Henriette von Schirach recalled, about the beginning of the acquaintance between her
father's friend and Eva Braun, that Hitler could "give the most thrilling
compliments": "May I invite you to the opera, Miss Eva? I am always surrounded by men, you see, so I know very well how much the pleasure of
a woman's company is worth." Who, she said, "could withstand" that?[25]
Although their relationship seemed to be a rather superficial one at first,
Hitler immediately had the girl investigated. Martin Bormann, at whose
wedding Hitler had recently been a witness, was given the assignment as
early as 1930 to determine whether the Braun family was "Aryan," that is,
had no Jewish ancestors.[26] Bormann, who had meanwhile risen to the
SA Supreme Staff, was to remain one of Hitler's closest and most trusted
friends from 1933 until Hitler's death.[27]

Eva Braun, still a minor at that point, presumably did not suspect a thing about Bormann's vetting. It is easy to imagine that this girl was impressed by her new acquaintance's prominence and was open to his political ideas. There is no evidence as to whether she herself, or her parents, held anti-Semitic views. Since Ilse Braun, four years older than her sister Eva, worked as a receptionist for a Jewish doctor who was also a close friend of hers, there seem not to have been ideological prejudices in Braun's family. Photographs of Eva Braun from her early years working in Hoffmann's photography store show a very childish-seeming girl, who obviously liked to be photographed and was not shy about striking poses in the office rooms.[28] Her relationship with Hitler is said to have remained purely "platonic" until 1932. Heinrich Hoffmann, in his memoir *Hitler Was My Friend* (London, 1955; German translation, 1974), claimed that his employee had pursued the relationship and had let it be known that "Hitler was in love with her and she would definitely succeed in getting him to marry her."[29] He did not perceive any "intense interest" on Hitler's part at first, though. In truth, what Hoffmann's observations reveal is the difference between a young woman—still a teenager, in fact—and a bachelor rather more advanced in years: while she spontaneously and enthusiastically expressed her feelings, he set store by the utmost discretion.

Trustee in Personal Matters

The mutual trust between Hitler and Hoffmann—indispensable for the long sittings in the portrait studio and attested by the countless photographs in which Hitler struck uninhibited poses—extended to their private lives.[30] Henriette von Schirach later recalled that her family moved into a "tremendously modern apartment in Bogenhausen" in 1929, "which Hitler liked" to visit. He ate spaghetti there, with "a little muscat, tomato sauce on the side, then nuts and apples," and improvised on the piano after the meal.[31] Hitler felt "at home" with Hoffmann and his family, according to Albert Speer in *Inside the Third Reich*. In the garden of the photographer's villa in Munich-Bogenhausen, Hitler could, as Speer observed in the summer of 1933, behave without the slightest formality, "lie down on the grass in shirtsleeves" or recite from "a volume of Ludwig Thoma."[32]

Hitler practicing oratorical poses, photographed by Heinrich Hoffmann, 1926

By that point Hoffmann and Hitler had been friends for at least a decade. Hoffmann's son-in-law Baldur von Schirach later reported that Hitler had come to know "family life" with Hoffmann; Hoffmann's first wife, Therese (Lelly); and their children, and that he had been taken in as a member of the family.[33] The photographer and his family were, so to speak, the core of the private circle around the unmarried NSDAP leader. After Therese Hoffmann's early death in 1928, the bond between the two men seemed to grow even stronger. During Hitler's many trips in the service of the Nazi Party's ambitions, not only Hoffmann himself but also—at Hitler's request—Hoffmann's daughter Henriette accompanied him, to bring a little youthful freshness into the company of men.[34] Family celebrations, such as Hoffmann's son Heinrich's confirmation in March 1931, his daughter Henriette's wedding the following year, or Hoffmann's remarriage in 1934, were celebrated together. Not only that, the weddings were organized by Hitler himself in his apartment on Prinzregentenplatz.[35]

In Obersalzberg and Berlin as well, Hoffmann was there as Hitler's constant companion.[36] Despite never holding an official position in the government or the Party, the photographer enjoyed a position of trust— and thus power—that important Party members such as Goebbels or Bormann envied, thanks to his practically unlimited access to Hitler until 1944. Others, such as Otto Wagener, head of the political-economic department of the Nazi Party, were annoyed that Hitler would occasionally discuss "the most secret matters in the presence of his close companions." Wagener "sometimes heard something of truly decisive importance only by complete accident from the photographer, Hoffmann."[37]

But why did Hitler choose Hoffmann in particular—someone known as a hard-drinking bon vivant, someone whose character and habits actually didn't match his at all—as his confidant and constant companion? It is an important question because the relations between Hitler and Hoffmann are analogous to the relationship between Hitler and Eva Braun. She, too, seemed not to match her lover, either in outward appearance or in inner temperament. Hoffmann and Hitler were connected by their similar experiences in World War I, their nationalistic and anti-Semitic convictions, their petit bourgeois backgrounds, and their early ambitions to be artists. Nevertheless, what was decisive for Hoffmann's status as "personal photographer" was his absolute loyalty and fidelity to Hitler himself, which he made clear from the beginning. Hoffmann followed to the letter any and all of the restrictions on photographing or publishing that were imposed upon him, and retouched his pictures according to instructions.[38] Hitler in turn ensured that the position of his personal photojournalist remained more or less unofficial to the end, so that Hoffmann remained dependent on him and under his control at all times.

In fact, Hoffmann was not only Hitler's fellow Party member, friend, and photographer, but a kind of go-between—even, in a sense, his private ambassador—in ways that crossed the boundaries between propaganda work, private life, and, later, political activities in the realm of art. It was at Hoffmann's house that Hitler could meet Eva Braun for afternoon tea or dinner, informally and out of the public eye.[39] And it was Hoffmann to whom Hitler entrusted his girlfriend when she accompanied him to Party events, unbeknownst to the uninitiated, under the guise of an "official photographer of the NSDAP." Financial transactions concerning Braun, too, such as the purchase of a house, were carried out via Hoffmann in the early years. At the same time, Hitler also entrusted him with political tasks far outside the purview of a propaganda photographer, and for which Hoffmann actually had no experience. For example, Hoffmann was allowed to select artworks for the prestigious "House of German Art" (Haus der Deutschen Kunst) exhibit in Munich in 1937, to the amazement and annoyance of several contemporaries, and was later placed in charge of the "Great German Art Exhibition" that was held yearly. Hoffmann became Hitler's personal art adviser and art buyer, in which capacity he committed art theft on a grand scale. As further signs of the position of trust he enjoyed, he was made a member of the Committee for the Utilization of Products of Degenerate Art, as established by Goebbels in May 1938, and was granted a professorship in July of the same year.[40]

During the preparations for war against Poland, and the signing of the Nonaggression Pact with the Soviet Union which Hitler pursued to that end, Hitler even promoted his friend to Special Ambassador and sent him with Foreign Minister Joachim von Ribbentrop's delegation to Moscow on the evening of August 22, 1939. Hoffmann later boasted that he was supposed not only to photograph the event, but, more important, to report back to Hitler about Stalin and his entourage.[41] The reason for this was not least that Hoffmann was indispensable to Hitler as an informer: the loyal factotum would have access to everyone in Moscow and be able to give Hitler rumors and information about the behavior of everyone there—including the Germans. "Keep your eyes and ears open" was Hoffmann's assignment. As a result, it is hardly surprising that Ribbentrop suggested, after the fact, that Stalin had objected to Hoffmann's "activities."[42] In fact, Hoffmann's presence must have displeased Ribbentrop as well, and also Friedrich-Werner Graf von der Schulenburg, the German ambassador.

It would therefore considerably understate Hoffmann's importance to describe him merely as an "interlocutor" of Hitler's, who enjoyed "the fool's freedom" to say what he wanted and who, in contrast to the "Führer," understood nothing about politics so that Hitler's conversations with him about politics were useless.[43] Hoffmann himself fostered this interpretation in his postwar memoirs by presenting himself as an apolitical person, for obvious reasons.[44] During the denazification proceedings in 1947–1948, while the press labeled him one of the "greediest parasites of the Hitler plague," and his own goal was to establish the greatest possible plausible distance between himself and the Nazi system in order to save his own life and livelihood, he cast his role in an even more modest light. In an unpublished defense attestation from 1947 he insisted that he had "avoided political topics" with Hitler, and that Hitler had come under the "bad influence" of others and was no longer receptive to "advice from familial circles." His "task," Hoffmann claimed, consisted primarily in fulfilling the wishes of other people around Hitler. He countered the charge of having been a leading propagandist for the NSDAP by pointing out that his name had never appeared in the official National Socialist registers and that the office of a "Reich Photographic Correspondent" did not even exist.[45]

That was indeed the case: no official position with this name did exist. Nonetheless, ever since 1933 when he opened a branch of his business in Berlin ("Hoffmann Press," 10 Kochstrasse), Hoffmann on his own initiative had included the title of "Reich Photographic Correspondent of the NSDAP (Member of the Reich Association of German Correspondents and News Office e.V.)" in his correspondence. In Munich, along with his Photohaus, he owned the "Brown Photo Shop" on 10 Barer Strasse as well as the "National Socialist Picture Press" at 74 Theresienstrasse.[46] With his books of photographs—vetted by Hitler—that were printed in the millions, titles such as (in German) *Hitler in His Mountains* (1935), *The Hitler Nobody Knows* (1936), *Hitler Off Duty* (1937), and *Hitler Conquers the German Heart* (1938), Hoffmann filled an important function in the "Führer propaganda" system. He single-handedly shaped the personal side of Hitler's "Führer image" with his purported insider's snapshots and cast Hitler as the "father of the nation," in his early years as Chancellor, by suggesting a closeness between the "leader" and the "fellow people" that did not exist. The fact that Hoffmann held no official government position and did not pursue his career in the Party, but rather remained directly connected to Hitler purely by loyalty and true belief, was in fact prerequisite for his unique field of operations. It obviously made sense for Hoffmann, under pressure from the denazification authorities, to describe his relationship with Hitler as having been of a purely "private nature." Hoffmann's excuse that he was merely an "employee" who "occasionally used" the title of Reich Photographic Correspondent in his correspondence must also be understood against the background of the Munich denazification court's decision of January 1947, which included him among the group of "major offenders" and sentenced him to ten years of labor camp and the confiscation of his assets.[47]

The same motives that led Hoffmann to disguise his political role within the Nazi system may also have led him to keep his knowledge of Hitler's private life to himself. Hitler's relationship with Eva Braun—which did, after all, begin in Hoffmann's photography shop—was another object of the denazification court's investigations: he was accused of having used the relationship between his young employee and the NSDAP leader "to gain political power." Thus we can hardly expect Hoffmann to shed light on the dark corners of the relationship between Hitler and Eva Braun. His primary concern was to make his lack of knowledge and distance from the events plausible to the court. Thus he spoke of a "highly unromantic acquaintance" and kept silent about his own interactions with Eva Braun and her family.[48]

In short, the question of whether Hoffmann was, as is often claimed in retrospect, finally responsible for having brought about the relationship between Hitler and Eva Braun can be answered only speculatively. It is also impossible to tell what the personal relationship was between Hoffmann and his second wife, Erna, and his prominent friend's girlfriend, who had no official existence but nonetheless played a special role in Hitler's life. Still, Braun's younger sister Gretl also worked as one of Hoffmann's employees later, which suggests that Hoffmann was to some extent responsible for the two sisters' financial security. And pictures from Gretl Braun's second wedding in 1950 show that his connection was not entirely broken off after the end of the war.[49] In any case, Hoffmann's description of the events connected to Eva Braun in his 1955 memoir remains curiously vague and incomplete, not least because the denazification proceedings against him were concluded only shortly before his death on December 16, 1957. Hoffmann's memoirs thus need to be read as fundamentally a perpetrator and collaborator's attempt to exonerate himself.[50]

2

Munich After the First World War

When Eva Braun met Hitler in Munich, in the fall of 1929, the Bavarian capital was already fast in the grip of the Nazi Party. Since the NSDAP's reestablishment in 1925, the number of Party members had more than tripled and it was no longer merely one of many Populist-nationalist movements: it had won the field from all rivals in only four years. It put forward candidates in Landtag elections throughout Germany and had achieved its first successes. But even though Hitler, the Party's leader and most successful hatemonger, had already received nationwide attention, appearing before a crowd of sixteen thousand people for the first time in Berlin, on November 16, 1928, his base of power remained Munich. There, in his favorite city, he had been an attraction for years. Every week he filled beer halls such as the Hofbräuhaus with thousands of listeners. In addition, the fourth convention of the NSDAP, in Nuremberg on August 1–4, 1929, was his first successful propaganda spectacle, one that would soon be followed by many more.[1]

A City of Extremes

Why were the National Socialists so successful in Bavaria? After Germany's defeat in World War I, what was it there that provided such a fertile breeding ground for nationalism and antidemocratic and anti-Semitic ideologies? One explanation is the way that radical political transformations were set in motion and carried out in the Kingdom of Bavaria during the final phase of the war. As is well known, the German Revolution of 1918–1919, or November Revolution, started in the Bavarian capital, Munich. It lasted longer and was more radical there than anywhere else in Germany. Even before the end of hostilities—on November 7, 1918, four days before the armistice was officially signed in a railroad car near the northern French city of Compiègne—exhaustion with the war, destitution, and the accompanying political radicalization had resulted in a speedy end to the centuries-old Bavarian Wittelsbach monarchy. King Ludwig III fled Munich after a mass rally led by Kurt Eisner, a Jewish journalist and radical socialist, two days before the fall of Kaiser Wilhelm II in Berlin and the abolition of the monarchy in the whole German Empire. For members of the radical right in Munich, this sequence of events gave rise to the so-called Dolchstoss Legend, the fabrication according to which Jews and Communists had "betrayed" their own country with a "stab in the back" and caused Germany to lose the war. Nazi propaganda would make successful use of this legend against "Jewish Bolshevism" a few years later.[2]

A provisional revolutionary government, under Eisner, took power and declared itself the "Free Republic of Bavaria" and the "Democratic Social Republic of Bavaria," with the motto "Long live peace! Down with the royal family!" Eisner took over the leadership of the hastily formed Council of Workers, Soldiers, and Farmers. However, after having, in Eisner's words, "swept away the old junk of the Wittelsbach kings," the new government proved to be completely incompetent.[3] Agrarian reform plans on the Soviet model were not in fact a suitable way to solve the economic and social problems affecting Bavaria. In addition, Eisner himself, who imagined a "society of spirits" and saw himself as representing a new, pacifist Germany, was utterly unsuited to be a politician. His revolutionary comrades—described by the German historian Hagen Schulze as "literati, chansonneurs, con artists, and psychopaths, without exception"—hardly presented a better picture.[4] Eisner's radical-left government was therefore diametrically opposed to the mostly conservative population, especially in rural areas. Yet the representatives of the upper middle class, too, generally disliked Eisner's regime. Thomas Mann, for instance, as early as November 8, 1918, came to the conclusion that Munich—and Bavaria as a whole—was now "governed by Jewish scribblers," "racketeer[s]," "profiteer[s]" and "Jew-boy[s]." He wondered, "how long will the city put up with that?"[5]

Eisner was not a native of Bavaria and from the beginning he was subject to relentless, unscrupulous anti-Semitic attacks. He received threatening letters and there were even calls for his assassination. The campaign against him ended with his being shot dead on a public street by Anton Graf von Arco-Valley, a student and former officer, on February 21, 1919, after the Bavarian National Assembly elections and shortly before he was to step down. Since there was no civil order worthy of the name, anarchy threatened after the murder. "They never understood Eisner," the writer Ricarda Huch wrote about her fellow Bavarians after the bloody deed,

> just as little as he understood them. How could they? There wasn't the slightest trace of Bavarian royalism, coziness, roughness, and sloppy good nature in him—he was an abstract moralist, who wrote perfectly good drama criticism and no doubt terrible poems. Criticism and theory, though, do not make a ruler any more than they make an artist: one needs to be able to actually do it.[6]

What followed were two Soviet-style republics that plunged Munich into political chaos once and for all. The first, under Ernst Niekisch, leader of the "Munich Central Council of the Bavarian Republic," dissolved the parliament and removed Eisner's legal successor, the social-democratic prime minister. In accordance with the Soviet ideal, the government broke off all "diplomatic relations" with the German government. It lasted only one week. The government that followed, run by the Munich Communist Party and supported by the Soviet Union, lasted all of two weeks. Nevertheless, the concomitant violence, with bloody battles between the communist revolutionaries and their opponents, were to shape the political atmosphere for years. For example, street fighting in Munich on May 3, 1919, in which the German army and specially formed Bavarian Freikorps* units defeated the so-called dictatorship of

---

* Translator's note: German paramilitary organizations, made up largely of defeated German soldiers returning from World War I and often deployed semiofficially to fight communists. Many Freikorps members later joined the SA and SS.

the Red Army, cost the lives of more than six hundred people. The leaders of the Soviet-style republic were either killed by the Freikorps or received heavy sentences for high treason, as did the writers Ernst Toller and Erich Mühsam. Thousands of supporters of the "Spartacists" ended up in jail. The Bavarian capital thereby became the main stronghold of an extraordinarily pronounced anticommunism and radical anti-Semitism.[7]

Everyday Life and the Political Environment

Daily life in Munich suffered greatly during the early days of the revolution and the "reign of terror" after Eisner was assassinated. Many stores were closed, either because they could no longer obtain any food or because they were looted. Public transportation didn't run, postal service was limited, there were curfews at times, private conversations on the telephone were prohibited, the mail was censored. During the battles between German troops and the second Munich republic, Munich was completely cut off from deliveries of food from anywhere else. Payments collapsed.

People saw these events, however, in very different ways, depending on the observer's political views, age, career, gender, and social class.[8] Thomas Mann, for example, recorded in his diary on May 17, 1919: "We're only lacking groceries now. Will have to eat lunch in the hotel. The house is cold, so afraid of catching cold, namely feeling in my teeth. But my two little rooms are cozy, total peace and quiet."[9] For large numbers of the population, in contrast, hunger, lawlessness, armed street fighting, and murder, always in the context of the lost world war, constituted traumatic experiences that turned Munich into a breeding ground for an above-average number of Populist-nationalist groups. The gradual stabilization of the economic situation throughout Germany after 1924 did little to change that.

Even so, the later rise to power of the National Socialists cannot be seen as an inevitable development. The NSDAP's political breakthrough did not take place until the start of the global economic crisis of 1929–1930, after all.[10] There is no disputing, though, that anti-Semitism had become a "firm foundation" in the Bavarian city since the turmoil of the Munich republics, whose leaders often came from Jewish families.[11] Even renowned newspapers such as the *Münchner Neueste Nachrich-*

ten spread these ideas. Klaus Mann, whose upper-class daily life was "affected . . . very little, and only indirectly," by the revolution and civil war, recalled that as a young man he saw postrevolutionary Munich as "a bore and altogether barbarous," in addition to its having "a poor reputation among liberals." He wrote:

> It was considered the most reactionary place in Germany—a center of the counter-revolutionary tendencies smoldering all over Europe. Flippant editors in Berlin used to run the dispatches from Munich under the caustic heading: "From the Hostile Countries Abroad!" The people of Munich, in their turn, stubbornly believed that Berlin was ruled by a conspiracy of Jewish bankers and Bolshevist agitators.[12]

The truth is that the right-wing Bavarian state government under Minister President Gustav Ritter von Kahr, which came to power in 1920 and followed a path opposed to the Weimar Republic, made it possible for far-right enemies of democracy to become increasingly effective. Even Hitler was seen by Kahr—a former royal official and monarchist, and now a member of the Bavarian People's Party (Bayerische Volkspartei, or BVP)—not as a political opponent but as an ally in the fight against communism. The so-called Bavarian Defense Forces, too, which grew out of the Bavarian Freikorps bands from the battle against the communist republics, were oriented in a Populist-conservative direction and laid the foundation for the rise of an authoritarian, fiercely antidemocratic power structure in Bavaria. Without this unique political environment, along with the encouragement and financial support from influential Populist-nationalist circles in Munich society, Hitler's rise would not have been possible.

The National Socialist Movement

Finally, the significance of the traditional Munich beer halls must not be underestimated as a factor in recruiting the majority of National Socialist supporters. The party life of the NSDAP played out in large part in the bars of the city. That was nothing new; pubs and inns had a long history in Germany as political gathering places. Nothing had changed in that regard since the Peasants' War in the early sixteenth century, and especially since the civil revolution of 1848, with its "saloon republicans." In Munich, too, the pubs formed a central part of the political culture. Thus it is no accident that the NSDAP was born from the "political regulars" in one of Munich's many beer halls. Its predecessor, the German Workers' Party (Deutsche Arbeiterpartei, or DAP), had been founded in the Fürstenfelder Hof hotel on January 5, 1919. Hitler joined this little group of right-wing extremists less than a year later, on September 12, 1919; the following month, they opened their first place of business in a back room of the Sterneckerbräu beer hall, which also served as a weekly meeting place. Hitler announced the first Party program of the NSDAP in the famous Hofbräuhaus, with its thirty-five hundred seats—the same place where the communists had proclaimed the second Munich republic on April 13, 1919.

This institution, in the middle of the old city and originally established to supply the royal court with specially brewed beer, was already, since the turn of the century, a sightseeing destination for visitors to Munich from all over the world. The French journalist and travel writer Jules Huret wrote that you had to go to the Hofbräuhaus to "come into contact with the true beer drinkers. . . . A horrid smell of beer and tobacco fills the hall. Hundreds of drinkers are sitting side by side at heavy oak tables on rough benches, smoking cigars or long pipes. The crowd is from the People—laborers, handymen, coachmen, next to officials young and old, office workers, shopkeepers, the petty bourgeois. . . ." The mood was "as free as could be, sometimes even boisterous": the "lack of embarrassment and the naturalness" left "nothing to be desired."[13]

With this sketch of the people who filled the Hofbräuhaus, Huret described, ten years before the NSDAP was founded, its social structure, drawn from every class of the population. Among the proclaimed goals of the Party's "25 Point Program," announced by Hitler to around two thousand people in the Hofbräuhaus on February 24, 1920, were the unification of all Germans into a "Greater Germany," the abolition of the Treaty of Versailles and the Treaty of Saint-Germain-en-Laye, the demand for "land and soil" for the German People, and the declaration that no Jew is a legal citizen and that every "non-German" who had immigrated since the day of the German army's mobilization (August 2, 1914) would be forced to leave the "Reich."[14] With this program, proclaimed in mass rallies, the NSDAP attempted to set itself apart from other German Populist factions. The "German Nationalist Protection and Defiance Federation" (Deutschvölkischer Schutz und Trutzbund), founded in Bamberg in 1919, still constituted the strongest organization of this type by far in Germany. It had 25,000 members by the end of 1919, while the NSDAP had only around 2,350 members a year later, at the end of 1920. Proof of "Aryan ancestry" was a prerequisite for membership in the Federation just as for membership in the NSDAP, and both far-right groups used the same symbol as an emblem: the swastika.[15]

But as early as 1920, Hitler was already proving himself to be a successful propagandist for his hitherto insignificant party. He made several public appearances a month, more than any other Party member—most often in Munich beer cellars or in Zirkus Krone, but also in Rosenheim, Stuttgart, and Austria—and he filled even the largest venues, flanked by his aggressive, paramilitary SA men. The truth was that his events offered the greatest "entertainment value." Still, the NSDAP's breakthrough needed more than Hitler's "hypnotic rhetoric" and his power over "the soul of the mob" in a haze of tobacco smoke. A serious "atmosphere of crisis" and supporters and patrons from the highest circles of society were necessary as well.[16]

The Populist writer Dietrich Eckart, for example, a bohemian and favorite of the salons who had lived in Berlin before World War I, put Hitler in contact with the Berlin piano manufacturer Edwin Bechstein and his wife, Helene, in the early 1920s, and this was both financially and socially valuable for Hitler. The Bechsteins lived in both the German capital and Munich, and not only were among the most important early financial backers of the NSDAP, but also arranged for Hitler to make further influential connections, such as with the family of the composer Richard Wagner in Bayreuth.[17] Ernst Hanfstaengl likewise made an effort "to work on Hitler's behalf" starting in 1922; fascinated by Hitler's "aura of someone out of the ordinary" and his "unique appearance," Hanfstaengl became a close companion with international connections. The publishers and spouses Hugo and Elsa Bruckmann also counted themselves among Hitler's numerous admirers in Munich. Rich and politically influential, they contributed in many ways and in no small degree to Hitler's social recognition.[18]

In 1923, at the peak of hyperinflation in Germany, the NSDAP was as popular as it had ever been up to that point. The number of Party members rose to over fifty thousand.[19] But after the failed Beer Hall Putsch (or Hitler Putsch) of November 8–9, 1923, in Munich—the violent, so-called

national revolution against the "Berlin Jew-government," in which fourteen members of the uprising and four policemen lost their lives—the
Party's rise came to a halt. The NSDAP was outlawed; Hitler and many
of his comrades-in-arms ended up in prison or were forced to flee. The
National Socialist movement seemed to be over, and the refounding of
the Party in the Bürgerbräukeller on February 27, 1925, did not at first seem
to make much of a difference. Financial problems, intraparty squabbles,
and sluggish recruitment of new members gave the impression throughout Germany that the National Socialists were in decline. The situation
changed abruptly in 1929. The worldwide economic depression, poverty,
and rising unemployment put the German parliamentary democracy in
an increasingly embattled position and helped the NSDAP achieve a
renewed upswing nationwide, although the center of the Party remained
in Munich. Hitler, a "howling dervish," in Carl Zuckmayer's words, was
on the threshold of his political breakthrough in the autumn of 1929
when, in the photography store of his friend Heinrich Hoffmann, he met
Eva Braun—the woman he was to die with sixteen years later in Berlin.[20]

3

THE BRAUN FAMILY

Eva Braun, baptized Eva Anna Paula Braun, was the second of three daughters of a vocational school teacher in Munich. When she was born, on February 6, 1912, troubled times lay ahead for Germany and the world. The Balkans, with its multicultural countries and border conflicts, had long been like a powder keg ready to blow up at any time. The assassination of Austrian Crown Prince Franz Ferdinand and his wife on June 28, 1914, unleashed the First World War, and Germany had to pay for its defeat with submission to the Versailles Treaty. The atmosphere within the Braun family was tense as well: Eva's parents, Friedrich and Franziska Braun, underwent a marital crisis in 1919, after eleven years of marriage, which ended in their divorce on April 3, 1921. It is not known what caused the split. Possibly, as for many couples, their living apart for years as a result of Friedrich's military service led to their estrangement. He had voluntarily enlisted in the war in 1914, and he was stationed first in Serbia, then elsewhere, finally serving in a military hospital in Würzburg until the end of April 1919. During this period, Franziska — a veterinarian's daughter who had worked as a seamstress in a Munich textile company before her marriage — mostly lived alone with her three small children. In the divorce, she was granted custody of the girls, who were thirteen, nine, and six at the time. But the separation did not last long; the following year, on November 16, 1922, Friedrich and Franziska Braun remarried.[1]

Middle-Class Normalcy

Financial reasons may well have played a large part in the Braun family's reuniting. There had been famine in Germany since the end of the war; prices never stopped rising, and in August 1922 inflation reached an initial high-water mark of 860 marks to the dollar. While foreign visitors poured into Germany to buy things cheaply, it grew more and more difficult for Germans to pay for the basic food they needed with their ever-more-worthless money.[2] The result was strikes, demonstrations, and labor unrest. Friedrich Braun himself, as a teacher, was not faced with unemployment, but in the period of hyperinflation in 1922–1923, when a pound of butter cost 13,000 marks, the fixed salaries of public employees lost an enormous amount of value. Craftsmen, small business owners, and the self-employed suffered likewise, of course. In these circumstances—inflation and reduced income—it was not possible to run two households.[3]

The economic situation improved only after currency reform was carried out in November 1923. Chancellor Gustav Stresemann, in office for only three months, managed to stabilize the currency and reorient the German approach to the question of reparations. The conflict between Germany and the Allies about the amount and method of reparations payments had escalated ever since the Versailles Treaty of June 28, 1919, in which the victors in World War I dictated the terms of the peace. Stresemann's skill in negotiating, especially with the French, resulted in a new, less strict financing program for the German Reich, which was drawn up in London on August 16, 1924, with the decisive help of American bankers. This Dawes Plan—named after Charles G. Dawes, the American lawyer and banker who played a leading role in its formulation—was intended to support the German economy in order to promote the rebuilding of Europe. Money poured into Germany from the United States in the following years—a loan of 800 million gold marks as well as private investments—enabling the economic recovery that had so long been hoped for. The so-called Golden Twenties of the Weimar Republic had begun, during which exports boomed while unemployment remained high and the national debt increased.[4]

For the Brauns, these developments meant a great improvement in their own financial situation. In 1925, they moved, with a servant, into a large apartment at 93 Hohenzollernstrasse in Schwabing, Munich's artists' and entertainment district. In the following years the family could also afford an automobile; they bought a BMW 3/15 with the money from an inheritance.[5] After the painful experiences of the inflation, they clearly preferred to convert their money into valuable property as quickly as possible. Still, despite a situation now lacking in material worries for the most part, Friedrich and Franziska Braun's marriage seems to have remained unhappy. Eva Braun's friend Herta Ostermayr later described Eva's family circumstances in that period as "not very pleasant." That is why, Ostermayr said, Eva Braun spent "almost her whole childhood at my house" and also took vacations "with me at the rural estate of my relatives." Eva Braun's ties to her school friend's parents were so close, according to Ostermayr, that she called them "Father and Mother."[6] Herta Ostermayr, or Herta Schneider after her marriage in 1936, knew Eva Braun from elementary school and was her closest friend. Later, she and her children would be regular guests at the Berghof until the end of the Nazi regime.

Ostermayr's statements are significant because they contradict the testimony of the Braun family. Franziska Braun in particular emphasized to the journalist Nerin E. Gun that her daughter grew up in an intact household. She assured Gun that "not a single cloud" had cast its shadow across her marriage, "not even a real quarrel."[7] This statement is obviously false, in light of the legal dissolution of the marriage. Franziska Braun—who, like every other member of the family, fell under pressure to justify herself after 1945, given her personal relations with Hitler—retroactively constructed a private idyll that never, in fact, existed.

At any rate, Friedrich Braun in the mid-1920s was able to offer a solid, middle-class prosperity to his family, which extended to his daughters' education. Eva attended elementary school from 1918 to 1922, then a lyceum on Tengstrasse, not far from their apartment. In 1928 she spent a year at Marienhöhe in Simbach am Inn on the German-Austrian border, a Catholic institute rich in tradition. A Merian copperplate engraving from around 1700 shows the view of Braunau from Simbach across an old wooden bridge—the same Braunau where Adolf Hitler had been born on April 20, 1889. The institute in Simbach had opened a housekeeping school only a few years earlier. The facility itself had been in existence since 1864, and was run by the Institute of the Blessed Virgin Mary, an order of Roman Catholic nuns pledged to the rules and spiritual exercises

The Braun family (left to right): Ilse, Friedrich, Franziska, Gretl, and Eva, 1942

of St. Ignatius of Loyola. Founded by the English nun Mary Ward (1585–1645), one of the most important woman of the seventeenth century, and thus also known in Germany as the "Institute of the English Maiden," this order of women was active throughout Europe and is considered even today a pioneer in women's education.[8] Along with home economics, Eva Braun studied bookkeeping and typing at Marienhöhe and was thereby trained for future office work—a path that was by no means taken for granted for girls in the middle-class environment of that time. When Eva Braun, at the age of seventeen, returned from Simbach to Munich, on July 22, 1929, she moved back in with her parents. Only a few months later, in September, she answered an ad in a Munich newspaper and found a trainee position: Heinrich Hoffmann, photographer, was hiring.[9]

The Constant Companion: Margarete Braun

Eva Braun was not to be the only member of her family to work for Hoffmann. Three years later, in early April 1932, her younger sister Margarete Berta (Gretl) followed her and was given a job as a salesgirl in the photographer's publishing house. Sixteen at the time, Gretl had just dropped out of the Franciscans' upper girls' school in Medingen near Willingen on the Danube and was entering the sphere of NSDAP activities.[10] It is highly likely that Eva Braun's recommendation played a role in getting her sister the job: by that point, Eva already had an intimate relationship with Hitler. But it is also true that Hoffmann needed more employees: his business, recast by the owner himself as the "Hoffmann National Socialist Photographic Propaganda Division," expanded its activities for the NSDAP through the start of the year of crisis, 1932.[11]

Important votes were soon to be held: for Reich President on April 10, and for the Reichstag (Parliament) in July. Unemployment was running rampant—almost six million people in Germany were jobless. In these circumstances, the NSDAP could expect an enormous increase in its vote tallies, and it ran its propaganda machine at full speed. For example, Hoffmann, shortly before Gretl Braun got a job with him, was "charged with the responsibility of carrying out the photo-reporting for the Reich President electoral campaign" on April 1, 1932, in his capacity as Hitler's "Party photographer."[12] In addition, his press was turning out massive quantities of Nazi photo-illustrated books for the first time, and in mid-1932 Hoffmann also took over a press photography illustration office in Berlin, finally ensuring his presence at the center of political events.[13] Still, it is noteworthy that both Braun sisters, who henceforth were to move in Hitler's closest private circles, worked for Hoffmann. It is not known whether Hoffmann gave Gretl Braun a position to "be helpful" to Eva Braun, and thereby indirectly do the "Führer" a favor, and the specific details about his private and business dealings with Gretl Braun remain unclear. Hoffmann himself kept silent about these dealings for the rest of his life.[14]

In any case, Eva and Gretl Braun remained inseparable in the years to follow. They left home together in 1935 and moved into an apartment in Munich, then a few months later into a single-family house that Hoffmann bought for them on Hitler's instructions. Gretl Braun accompanied her sister during their weeks-long stays on the Obersalzberg as well, and also on foreign trips, for example to Italy.[15] Starting in 1936 at the latest, she was a member of the Berghof inner circle around Hitler. She is rarely mentioned, however, in the memoirs and reminiscences from the period. Only the secretaries, Christa Schroeder and Traudl Junge, would later remark that the Nazi leader occasionally tried to marry off his girlfriend's sister. Junge, who traveled to the Berghof only starting in

March 1943, also recalled that Gretl Braun was in love with Fritz Darges, an SS-Obersturmbannführer and Hitler's personal adjutant, but that their affair was "a little too dangerous and not private enough" for him, given her close personal relations with Hitler.[16]

Whereas Eva Braun's role and her significance for Hitler have been controversial since the war, her sister's profile has remained unclear. What did she do at the Berghof? What was her relationship to Hitler, and to Eva? Only one thing is clear: Gretl Braun never stepped out from the shadow of her older sister before 1944. Her role was, it seems, organized around Eva Braun's needs: she acted in the background, as Eva's guest, companion, or chaperone. This role changed only with her marriage, on June 3, 1944, which gave her the status of wife at last. She married Hermann Fegelein, Heinrich Himmler's liaison officer in the "Führer headquarters" and — according to Albert Speer — one of the "most disgusting persons in Hitler's circle."[17] At the instigation of her sister Eva, Gretl had grown up from girlhood in a political environment that she remained attached to until the bitter end; her marriage to Fegelein only consolidated her position there.

The Distant Sister: Ilse Braun

Ilse Braun, in contrast, spent her life at some distance from her sisters, geographically at least. She was the first to move out of their parents' house, in 1929, and by her own account lived for years in the office of her Munich employer, the ear, nose, and throat doctor Martin Marx.[18] He was fourteen years older than she, likewise born in Munich, and had received his PhD from Ludwig Maximilian University in 1922 and practiced in the Bavarian capital ever since.[19] In a postwar interview, Ilse Braun did not provide further background about her residence in her employer's office, and we do not know if she had an intimate relationship with her boss or if he was merely doing the young woman a favor by putting a room at her disposal. Ilse Braun's life circumstances — standing in radical opposition to the ideas of morality prevalent at the time — certainly suggest that the Braun family ties remained problematic. Furthermore, Ilse Braun's position working for a "Jewish" doctor, as she herself stated he was, obviously led to tensions with her sister Eva, who at the time was not only working for Hoffmann (and thus the Nazi Party) but was also in personal contact with Hitler. In any case, Ilse Braun maintained after the end of the war that her sister had pointed out "the impossibility of our having two such opposite jobs" and had asked her to break off both business and personal ties with the doctor.[20] Presumably, Eva Braun was afraid that if her older sister's affair with Dr. Marx became known in her National Socialist environment, it could threaten her own developing relationship with Hitler.

Nonetheless, Ilse Braun worked as a receptionist for Martin Marx for another eight years, leaving only, on his "advice," when he was making preparations to emigrate in 1937—or so she emphasized under questioning in October 1946.[21] In fact, the discrimination against and exclusion of Jewish doctors, roughly a quarter of all the doctors in Munich, had already started shortly after Hitler came to power. In the Bavarian capital, 80 percent of "non-Aryan" doctors in the national health insurance system lost their licenses due to a new regulation announced in April 1933. The "cleansing" of the field of medicine, demanded by Hitler personally, was carried out more diligently in Munich, under Karl Fiehler (mayor, 1933–1945), than elsewhere, since Fiehler was a committed National Socialist of the first order and an extreme anti-Semite. He had doctors fired from state-run facilities, clinics, and universities for racist ideological reasons.[22]

At first, the private practice of the doctor for whom Ilse Braun worked and under whose roof she lived was not affected: Dr. Marx could continue, like many of his colleagues, to practice unhindered, despite the exclusion from government positions. The situation in Munich became more extreme only with the proclamation of the "Nuremberg Laws," with their "Law for the Protection of German Blood and German Honor," on September 15, 1935. Not only marriage but also "extramarital relations" between "Jews and citizens of German or related blood types" would now be prosecuted, likewise any work by an "Aryan" woman under forty-five in a "Jewish" household.[23] Ilse Braun's friendship with her employer and above all her remaining under his roof now meant that both of them risked arrest on charges of "defiling the race." The Gestapo carried out checks in Munich in this regard and followed up on rumors and suspicions. Nevertheless, Ilse Braun and Martin Marx apparently remained undisturbed until their business and personal relationship came to an end in early 1937.

By then, Eva Braun had become a figure of permanent importance in Hitler's life, joining the Nazi leader at his refuge on the Obersalzberg whenever he was there. She had dedicated herself entirely to Hitler and his

life and must have found her sister's living and work situation, unchanged
for years, completely unbearable. Ilse's later career developments suggest
that it was Eva who was responsible for Ilse's dismissal and who, at the
same time, helped her find a remarkable new career and place to live. For
immediately after her departure from Dr. Marx's office, Ilse Braun started
work as a secretary in Albert Speer's office in Berlin, on March 15, 1937.[24]
A month and a half earlier, on January 30, Speer had been named "General Building Inspector for the Reich Capital" by a "Führer's edict" and
was given the responsibility of remaking the architecture of Berlin into a
"World Capital Germania." The ambitious architect, just thirty-two years
old at the time, was a trusted friend of the Nazi leader and among the
frequent guests at the Berghof, where he also knew Eva Braun. He must
have been only too happy to do a favor for his "Führer's" girlfriend. That
is the only way to explain why Ilse Braun was one of Speer's first employees to move with him into his new Berlin office building at 4 Pariser Platz,
the just-requisitioned Prussian Academy of Arts.[25]

Ilse Braun's employer of many years, Martin Marx, left Germany only
the following year, in 1938, and emigrated to the United States, which
since 1936 had been the main destination for German doctors. With an
established personal practice of many years' standing, Dr. Marx, like
numerous members of his profession, decided to flee the country only
quite late. Ilse Braun stated after the war that she had "tried to intercede
for him," while it had been apparent to him that, she said, "my sister
was unable—and I was even less able—to do anything to help him." In
fact, it was Ordinance 4 of the "Reich Citizenship Law" of July 25, 1938,
which revoked the license to practice medicine of all Jewish doctors in
Germany, that was the decisive factor. Dr. Marx was officially expatriated
on April 5, 1939, according to the expatriation list published six months
later, on November 15, in the *Deutscher Reichsanzeiger*. The revocation
of his doctorate from Munich's Ludwig Maximilian University followed
on October 25 of the same year.[26]

Ilse Braun, meanwhile, had already married in Berlin, in October
1937, and she therefore gave up her job with Speer after only six months.[27]
Nothing is known about her husband, named Höchstetter. They divorced
after approximately three years. Ilse Braun nonetheless stayed in Berlin.
Her sister Eva had had a small apartment of her own in the Old Reich
Chancellery since early 1939 and occasionally stayed in the capital. In
1940, after the outbreak of the war, Ilse Braun graduated from a train-

ing program in the editorial offices at the *Deutsche Allgemeine Zeitung* (DAZ) newspaper and worked as an editor there until summer 1941.[28] This well-known conservative national paper, once owned by the Ruhr industrialist Hugo Stinnes and his heirs, was transferred to the National Socialist Deutscher Verlag only at the beginning of 1939. Thus the *DAZ*, like the vast majority of newspapers in the capital, was a part of the Nazi Press Trust controlled by Max Amann, the Reich Press Chamber's powerful president and an old comrade-in-arms of Hitler's from the early days of the NSDAP.[29]

Still, it is difficult to understand—almost incomprehensible—how and by what means a simple doctor's receptionist found a trainee position as a *DAZ* journalist. By comparison, a colleague of Ilse Braun's, Elisabeth Noelle-Neumann, who was given a trainee position there at the same time, was not only seven years younger than Ilse Braun but was highly qualified, was faithful to the Nazi regime, came from a rich, upper-middle class family, and had received a doctorate under Emil Dovifat, a well-known professor of journalism at Berlin University.[30] Of course, none of that was true of Ilse Braun. Yet Ursula von Kardorff, a member of the editorial staff of the *DAZ* from 1939 through 1945, clearly knew even back then whom she was dealing with, and knew that her new colleague's sister, Eva Braun, was "often" to be found "with Hitler at the Berghof." Still, after Ilse Braun's brief excursion into Berlin's newspaper world, Kardorff remained in contact with her "former trainee," especially since, as she wrote in her diary, Ilse Braun seemed "not particularly nazi." So it stands in Kardorff's entry from July 30, 1944, after she visited Ilse Braun and looked at photographs showing Eva and Gretl with Hitler at the Berghof: "I thought to myself, this connection could still be useful someday, if things get really bad."[31]

After Ilse Braun remarried, on June 15, 1941, she left Berlin. She moved to Breslau with her husband, a certain Fucke-Michels, and worked there as an editor for the *Schlesische Zeitung*.[32] One hint about who her husband may have been appeared in a *New York Times* article on April 12, 1998: in the context of a story about an international conference on the subject of art looted during the Holocaust, the unusual name Dr. Fucke-Michels came up. He was described as a "Nazi cultural aide" who in 1942 had told Hans Posse, director of the Staatliche Gemäldegalerie in Dresden and an art representative of Hitler's, that a valuable medieval manuscript had been confiscated in 1938 because there was a danger that the Jewish owner would leave the country.[33] Was this Ilse Braun's husband? In the memoirs and reminiscences of the members of the Berghof circle, Eva Braun's older sister is not mentioned once; there is obviously not the slightest hint about her husband. Only in the fragmentary notes of the historian Percy Ernst Schramm, who was the official diarist for the Operational Staff of the German High Command (Oberkommando der Wehrmacht, or OKW) during the war, and who was present during the questioning of Hitler's personal physicians in 1945–1946 in the course of his work for the U.S. Army Historical Division, is it stated that Ilse Braun was married to a "propaganda man" in Breslau.[34] In any case, we cannot believe Ilse Braun's later testimony that she received neither "financial support nor any other privileges" from her sister Eva, in light of her job in Berlin, at the very least.[35] Likewise, her flight from Breslau to the Obersalzberg at the end of the war does not suggest a great distance between her and Eva Braun.

4

RISE TO POWER AT HITLER'S SIDE

After 1931, the contact between Eva Braun and Hitler grew more intensive. Yet he also insisted at every opportunity, to fellow Party members, that he lived only for politics and therefore his private life belonged to the cause. Otto Wagener, for instance, the first chief of staff of the SA who spent 1929 to 1933 near his "Führer" and heard many of his personal conversations, recalled one long discussion in which Hitler explained to him that he could not ever marry: "I have another bride: Germany! I am married: to the German People and their fate! . . . No, I cannot marry, I must not."[1] Nonetheless, he met with Eva Braun more and more often, although the exact circumstances and precise development of their relationship remain unclear.

The "Führer's" Long-Distance Lover

Heinrich Hoffmann, who saw Eva Braun almost daily and the leader of the Nazi Party often, remarked that Hitler himself "did not let on" about any close relationship at the time—either because he was not interested in the young woman or because he "did not want to say anything." Hoff-

Eva Braun (undated)

mann said he was convinced that Eva Braun became Hitler's lover only "many years later."[2] His daughter Henriette von Schirach, in contrast, wrote in her memoir that the "love affair" between Braun and Hitler had already started by the winter of 1931–1932.[3] Hitler's housekeeper, Anni Winter, who lived in Hitler's apartment at 16 Prinzregentenplatz along with her husband and another subletter, likewise claimed that Eva Braun became Hitler's lover at the start of 1932.[4] This version of events, which Nerin E. Gun retold without providing any exact sources, was later confirmed by the historian Werner Maser, relying on a personal communication from Anni Winter in 1969.[5]

Thus the evidence suggests that their intimate relationship did begin in 1932. Hitler's driver, Erich Kempka, also claimed immediately after the war that he had known Eva Braun "since 1932," in which case she must have been traveling in Hitler's entourage by then.[6] Anna Maria Sigmund similarly claimed, referring to Albert Speer's *Spandau: The Secret Diaries*, that a sexual relationship between Eva Braun and Adolf Hitler started in Hitler's apartment at the beginning of 1932.[7] Yet Speer says nothing of the sort, neither in his *Spandau: The Secret Diaries* nor in *Inside the Third Reich*—with good reason, since he was not yet a close colleague of Hitler's in 1932. He was an independent architect in Mannheim and joined the

NSDAP and the SA only in the previous year; in 1932 he was receiving his first assignments from the Party.[8]

Nonetheless, in the entry of February 15, 1947, Speer recalls a private visit with Hitler eleven years in the past, in Munich, where Hitler had lived since October 1929 in the aristocratic Bogenhausen neighborhood, on the third floor of a majestic, baroquely Jugendstil corner building that today is a protected landmark.[9] While Henriette von Schirach noticed primarily the "impressive paintings" and spoke of a "perfect apartment" where the furniture was "big, dark, and severe,"[10] Speer was less impressed. He had risen during the course of Hitler's Reich chancellorship to become his most important architect and representative for urban development in Rudolf Hess's staff, and yet he noted in *Spandau: The Secret Diaries*:

> The décor was petty-bourgeois: a lot of imposing oak furniture, glass-doored bookcases, cushions embroidered with saccharine sentiments or brash Party slogans. In the corner of one room stood a bust of Richard Wagner; on the walls, in wide gold frames, hung romantic paintings of the Munich School. Nothing suggested that the tenant of this apartment had been chancellor of the German Reich for three years. A smell of cooking oil and leftovers wafted from the kitchen.[11]

Speer's contemptuous description is obviously a product of his later view of this period. Eva Braun, on the other hand, who met with Hitler here, must have admired the apartment much as her friend of almost the same age, Henriette von Schirach, did. There were hardly any other opportunities for Braun and Hitler to be together undisturbed: she still lived with her parents, as was common at the time for unmarried women, and Hitler, too, did not live alone before fall 1931. His half-sister's daughter, Angela "Geli" Maria Raubal, born on June 4, 1908, in Linz, lived with him at Prinzregentenplatz for two years after moving from Vienna to Munich in 1929. She failed to complete a course of study in medicine at the Ludwig Maximilian University, and had an affair with Hitler's chauffeur at the time, Emil Maurice, which Hitler put a stop to.[12] When she took her own life in her room, by shooting herself in the lung on September 18, 1931, rumors about Hitler's relationship with his twenty-three-year-old stepniece immediately began to circulate.[13] Incest and jealousy were spoken of as possible motives for the suicide, and there were even speculations about murder. The weapon, a Walther 6.35 cali-

*Hitler with his
stepniece, Geli Raubal,
July 1930*

ber pistol, did belong to Hitler. But the police ruled out foul play.[14] In
fact, in view of the upcoming Landtag elections of April 1932, Hitler himself and the Gauleiter of Berlin and publisher of the Nazi propaganda
newspaper *Der Angriff* (The Attack), whom Hitler named Reich Minister
of Propaganda on April 27, 1930—Joseph Goebbels—used Raubal's suicide to cultivate Hitler's public image as the un-self-interested "Führer"
and thus to conceal his private life as a human being.

Here is Hitler's declaration only six days after his niece's death, at an
NSDAP gathering in Hamburg: "What has given me the most pains
and cost me the most work is what I love best: our People."[15] And Goebbels, in his so-called "Diary"—actually a document always intended for
posterity—recorded the following about a conversation with Hitler under
the date October 27, 1931: "Then he told us about Geli. He loved her very
much. She was his 'good comrade.' There were tears in his eyes. . . . This
man, at the height of his success, without any personal happiness, committed only to his friend's happiness. What a good man Hitler is!" A few

weeks later, on November 22, Goebbels noted that the "Führer" had told him "about the women he loved very much" and "the one-and-only he could never find."[16] In fact, Hitler often said to his fellow Party members that he had no "ties to the world" anymore and belonged "only to the German People now." He repeated in this context his old credo renouncing marriage, necessary in view of the political "task" that lay before him and the National Socialist "movement." He had already stressed that he had to "deny himself" private happiness since "all his thoughts and efforts" belonged to the oppressed and despised German People.[17]

But what did Hitler's decision to remain unmarried have to do with his niece's death? Didn't such explanations only invite further speculation about the nature of his relationship with Geli Raubal? In fact, we can conclude from this pathos-laden exaggeration of Geli Raubal's role, along with Hitler's overheated explanations about the "religion" of marriage, that he was now more than ever concerned to conceal his personal life, which was starting to be discussed publicly, except insofar as he could manipulate it to his political benefit. With his followers, this trick was completely successful. Otto Wagener, for instance, a close member of Hitler's staff for three years as head of the politico-economic division of the NSDAP, believed that he could see "just the man Adolf Hitler before him" during these apparently trustworthy communications.[18] And Heinrich Hoffmann insisted, many years later, that Hitler's "whole being" had changed after his stepniece's death—that "a piece of Hitler's humanity" died with her. His work was "now an exclusive pursuit of a single goal," Hoffmann said. "Attaining power!"[19]

Hitler and Goebbels thus staged, both in Party circles and before the public, a myth of solitude and isolation intended to make the Nazi leader personally unassailable and make his self-presentation as the "savior" of the German People, standing above everyone, more plausible. It was a necessary move. In late 1931, the NSDAP was on the rise. From a radical group limited to Bavaria it had become, within ten years, a political power to be taken seriously, playing an ever-greater role on the national stage since its sensational victory in the Reichstag election of September 14, 1930. The NSDAP was the second-strongest party in the Reichstag, after the Social Democratic Party (Sozialdemokratische Partei Deutschlands, or SPD), and together with the German National People's Party (DNVP) under Alfred Hugenberg, parts of the German People's Party (DVP), and the "Steel Helmet" league of World War I veterans they formed a so-called

National Front against the Weimar state. At the same time, Hitler and
his political adviser Hermann Göring were received for a discussion with
Reich President Paul von Hindenburg for the first time on October 10.[20]
Hitler, not even a German citizen at the time, had arrived—to great public effect—at the summit of political power.[21]

Hindenburg, the eighty-four-year-old former General Field Marshal
and a celebrated war hero, had for more than a year left a so-called Presidential Cabinet in charge of state business—without the approval of Parliament, which, since the beginning of the Great Depression in 1929 and
the collapse of the German economy, was wracked with all sorts of divisions. The Weimar constitution granted Hindenburg dictatorial powers
"to restore public safety and order," and with these powers he was unable
to solve the country's problems but he was able to prevent the state from
total collapse for the time being.[22] As democracy tottered and the ranks of
the unemployed swelled from 4,840,000 in November 1931 to 6,127,000
in February 1932, the NSDAP mobilized voters from every class of society.
It won the Hessian Landtag election of November 15, 1931, and put forward its leader as a candidate for Reich President against Hindenburg in
early 1932.

Although Hindenburg decisively defeated Hitler in the second round
of voting on April 10, 1932, 53 percent to 36.8 percent, the "chess match
for power" had begun, as Goebbels strikingly put it at the beginning of
the year.[23] The Landtag elections in Prussia, Bayern, Württemberg, and
Anhalt, as well as the city parliament election in Hamburg, were coming
up. In addition, the political right forced Chancellor Heinrich Brüning,
chosen by Hindenburg two years earlier, to step down, on May 30, 1932,
and this cleared the path to dissolve the national parliament and hold new
elections on July 31.[24] In the interim, Hitler traveled tirelessly throughout the country, giving speeches, with an entourage consisting of Julius
Schaub, Julius Schreck, Wilhelm Brückner, Hermann Esser, Sepp Dietrich, Max Amann, Otto Dietrich, and of course Heinrich Hoffmann, in
various combinations. He crisscrossed Germany in spectacular fashion
on his "Germany flights" in a rented airplane, as he had done before in
the election campaign for President—a true marathon journey from one
city to the next that only strengthened his image as Germany's omnipotent "Führer" and "savior."[25]

During this period, the NSDAP and above all its head of propaganda,
Goebbels, organized the rallies and marches that accompanied Hitler,

under the slogan "Direct to the People." The Party had propaganda films
made and produced records with its leader's "Appeal to the Nation."[26]
The Propaganda head office had moved from Munich offices on Hede-
mannstrasse to Berlin by then, near the Anhalter train station in what
is today the Friedrichshain-Kreuzberg neighborhood. There Goebbels
spoke to an NSDAP rally in the Lustgarden on July 9, 1932, the same day
Hitler celebrated a so-called Day of Greater Germany in Berchtesgaden.[27]
Hoffmann's studio, too, was operating at full speed. Every election event
was accompanied by photographers, and the resulting images were used
and disseminated in Party publications. The first of what would be many
large-format photo-illustrated books published by Hoffmann appeared in
1932, photographically dramatizing the "cult of the Führer" by casting
Hitler as the "savior" and glorifying "his" movement.[28]

Eva Braun, working in Hoffmann's photo lab, could thus follow the
course of the elections and the appearances of her secret lover by means
of Hoffmann's propaganda materials, produced in huge numbers and not
yet winnowed down for publication. There was not much time for the
relationship itself, of course. Even after the Reichstag elections, in which
the NSDAP won 37.4 percent of the vote and became the strongest political force in Germany, with 230 seats in Parliament, Hitler allowed himself only a few days of rest and relaxation in Munich and Berchtesgaden.
Accompanied by Goebbels, with whom he was in constant contact, Hitler
traveled to the Tegernsee (a lake in the Bavarian Alps), went to the opera
in Munich, and then withdrew to Haus Wachenfeld, the small summer
house on the Obersalzberg that he had rented in 1928. The housekeeper
there was his half-sister Angela Raubal, mother of the dead Geli. Hitler
gathered around him the members of his innermost NSDAP leadership
circle—Goebbels, Göring, Gregor Strasser, Wilhelm Frick—and they
worked out what would be necessary if the NSDAP were to take power.[29]
It is unclear when and how he saw Eva Braun during that stay, or even
if he saw her at all. However, Otto Wagener, who said himself that he
accompanied Hitler "on the majority of his many trips," said in his memoir that during the 1932 campaign Hoffmann often brought "his little lab
girl Eva Braun" along, "whom Hitler liked to see at the table in the evening, for distraction."[30]

What is certain is that Hitler and his colleagues in the Nazi Party
were anxious to take power as quickly as possible after their electoral successes, and they feverishly schemed about how best to do so. Hitler had

not yet, after all, reached his goal of being named Chancellor. In secret
negotiations on August 6, 1932, with Kurt von Schleicher, the influential but inscrutable Minister of Defense in Chancellor Franz von Papen's
conservative-national cabinet, Hitler demanded the office of Chancellor
for himself and six additional key cabinet posts for his party, including
ministers of the interior, economy, and finance, but to no avail.[31] Hindenburg in particular was consistently opposed to the NSDAP leader's
demands. Talks between the two men at the elderly president's offices
at 73 Wilhelmstrasse—the former "Ministry of the Royal House"—on
the afternoon of August 13, 1932, did nothing to change that. Hitler was
offered the position of Vice-Chancellor and turned it down.[32]

Martyrdom or Calculation?

During this politically decisive period, there was no time for Hitler to see
his young Munich girlfriend regularly. In any case, the NSDAP leader was
often in Berlin, where since February 1931 he regularly stayed in a suite at
the legendary Hotel Kaiserhof at 4 Wilhelmplatz (formerly Ziethenplatz),
across the street from the Reich Chancellery. The hotel was the first luxury
hotel in the city, opened in 1875 and three years later one of the showpieces
of the 1878 Congress of Berlin, which took place under the leadership
of Chancellor Otto von Bismarck. Since the early 1920s, the hotel management had sympathized with the right-wing nationalist forces operating
against the Weimar state, so it was no coincidence that the top floor of the
hotel turned into the NSDAP's provisional headquarters.[33]

Despite his frequent absences, there is no evidence for the claim that
Hitler wanted "an undemanding short-term relationship" with Eva Braun
at first any more than there is for the opposite claim.[34] It is documented
in numerous sources, however, that the twenty-year-old woman tried to
take her own life with her father's gun at some point during the course of
1932. Witnesses from Hitler's circle as well as members of the Braun family reported this fact after the war, although there are differing accounts
of exactly what happened and when. Hoffmann wrote in his postwar recollections that Eva Braun did not show up at work one "summer morning" in 1932, and that he heard about her suicide attempt that afternoon
from his brother-in-law, Dr. Wilhelm Plate. Eva Braun had called Plate
in the middle of the night, according to Hoffmann, since she was get-

ting "scared" after her gunshot wound.[35] Hoffmann did not explain how she would have been in a position to make such a phone call, since her parents did not have a phone in their house at 93 Hohenzollernstrasse at that time; nor is it clear why, wounded and panicking, she would try to reach her boss's brother-in-law, of all people. Is it not far more likely that she would turn to Hoffmann himself on that night, who would then in turn reach out to his brother-in-law, the doctor in the family, for advice? Another implausible element in Hoffmann's version of events is the claim that he informed Hitler about the dramatic events only when Hitler happened to drop by the photo shop that afternoon.[36] Hoffmann's account is thus not reliable—what it shows is primarily Hoffmann's own intent to conceal the extent of his role in the relationship between Eva Braun and Hitler.

Hoffmann's son-in-law, Baldur von Schirach, has left a more plausible account, which also gives a precise date for the incident—despite the fact that he must have heard about what happened from Hoffmann or Dr. Plate. He says that Eva Braun's first suicide attempt took place on the night of August 10–11, 1932. According to Schirach, Hitler received a farewell note from Eva Braun on the morning of August 11—shortly before his planned departure from the Obersalzberg to Berlin—and immediately postponed the trip. That evening, he met with Dr. Plate in Hoffmann's Munich apartment, where Plate told him about Braun's injuries and Hitler said to Hoffmann that he wanted to take care of "the poor child." Only on the following day, Friday, August 12, did he finally leave for Berlin.[37]

These statements agree with Goebbels's notes. Under the date of August 11/12, Goebbels wrote that Hitler was on the Obersalzberg early on the morning of August 11, and that Hitler and he traveled together to a meeting in Prien on the Chiemsee (a lake nearby). "In the afternoon," the two men continued to Munich, where Hitler went to his apartment on Prinzregentenplatz; while Goebbels took the night train to Berlin, Hitler stayed in Munich. "The Führer," Goebbels noted, "will come later by car." They met up again only at 10 p.m. on August 12, in Caputh, to discuss the Nazi leader's upcoming meeting with President Hindenburg.[38]

A third, completely different version is Nerin E. Gun's, for which he gives Ilse Braun as the source. This version dates the suicide attempt to the night of November 1–2, 1932. On that night, says Ilse Braun according to Gun, she found her sister Eva by chance, alone in her cold, unheated apartment, covered in blood, on the bed in their parents' bedroom, while their parents were away on a trip. Despite her injury, Eva Braun was conscious and had herself called a doctor to take her to the hospital. "The bullet had lodged just near the neck artery," in Ilse Braun's exact words according to Gun, "and the doctor had no difficulty in extracting it. Eva had taken my father's 6.35 mm caliber pistol, which he normally kept in the bedside table beside him."[39] In this account, it is unclear (to say the least) where Eva Braun could have telephoned from; the date in early November is also significantly different from Hoffmann's and Schirach's accounts. Nevertheless, the events could indeed have played out like this, as we can see from a closer examination of Hitler's schedule.

The Nazi leader was in the middle of an exhausting campaign trip at the time, and undertaking his fourth "Germany flight" between October 11 and November 5. The Reichstag elections of July 1932 had not solved the problem of the Weimar Republic's inability to govern, but only led to a further weakening of the forces of democracy in the parliament, so that Hindenburg's Chancellor, Franz von Papen, was defeated by the second sitting of the newly elected Reichstag, on September 12. The Communist Party's motion of no confidence, supported by the NSDAP and all the other major parties, had toppled the government. The Reichstag was thus dissolved, for the second time in the space of a year; the requisite new elections were called for November 6. Now it was up to the National Socialists and their "Führer" to mobilize the masses even more forcefully and finally emerge from the election as the absolute victors.[40]

On the evening of November 1, 1932, after giving election speeches that day in Pirmasens and Karlsruhe, Hitler first flew back to Berlin, where he was to speak at a large rally in the sports stadium on the following evening.[41] He would have heard about the incident in Munich that same night, and left the capital in the early morning hours of November 2.[42] Goebbels was at a rally that night in Schönebeck, south of Magdeburg, until 1 a.m., and arrived in Berlin at around 4 a.m.; he noted curtly in his diary: "To Berlin. . . . 4 a.m. arrival. Hitler just gone."[43] Together with Hoffmann and an adjutant, according to Gun, Hitler was chauffeured to Munich so that he could visit Eva Braun in the hospital on the morning of November 2. Hoffmann accompanied Hitler to the hospital, where he expressed doubt about the seriousness of Braun's suicide attempt in the presence of the attending physician. After the physician explained that Braun had "aimed at her heart," Hitler is said to have remarked to Hoffmann: "Now I must look after her," because something like this "mustn't happen again."[44]

Although the precise details remain unknown, witnesses and historians agree that Eva Braun felt abandoned and calculatedly acted to make the perpetually absent Hitler notice her, and to tie him more closely to her.[45] She is said to have intentionally summoned Hoffmann's brother-in-law, Dr. Plate, rather than her sister's friend, Dr. Marx, to ensure that Hitler would immediately hear about the incident from his personal photographer.[46] In truth, only a year after Hitler's stepniece Geli Raubal's suicide and in the middle of his political battle for the chancellorship, whose success was closely bound up with the "Führer cult" around him, the NSDAP could not afford a new scandal that opened up Hitler's personal life to public discussion once more. He thus had to bring under control a relationship he had apparently misjudged. From then on, in this version of events, a tight bond grew out of the hitherto rather loose relationship with Eva Braun. Heinrich Hoffmann wrote after the war that Hitler told him then that he "realized from the incident that the girl really loved him," and that he "felt a moral obligation to care for her."[47] About his own feelings, in contrast, it seems that the "Führer" had nothing to say.

Alone in the Vestibule of Power

Meanwhile, only a few intimates knew about Hitler's relationship with Braun, now twenty years old. Hitler himself had erected a "wall of silence" around her. They made no joint public appearances: only once in the twelve years after 1933 were Hitler and Eva Braun seen together in a published news photo, which in fact shows Eva Braun sitting in the second row, behind Hitler, at the Winter Olympics in February 1936 in Garmisch-Partenkirchen.[48] Nothing in the picture indicates any personal relationship between her and the dictator. Officially, Eva Braun was on the staff of the Berghof as a private secretary.[49] The German public learned only shortly before the end of the war that Hitler had lived with a woman and eventually married her, and many people at the time considered this report a mere "latrine rumor."[50]

In Hitler's more immediate environment, on the other hand—among his close colleagues in the Party and their wives, and adjutants and staff members—the relationship between their "Führer" and Eva Braun could not remain a secret. For example, on January 1, 1933, a Sunday evening only a few months after her attempted suicide, she accompanied Hitler to a performance at the Munich Royal Court and National The-

ater, together with Rudolf Hess and his wife, Ilse; Heinrich Hoffmann
and his fiancée, Erna Gröbke; and Hitler's adjutant Wilhelm Brückner
and Brückner's girlfriend Sofie Stork. Hans Knappertsbusch, the musical director of the Bavarian State Opera House, was directing Richard
Wagner's *Die Meistersinger von Nuremberg*.[51] This opera had premiered
on the same stage in 1868, and its performance on New Year's Day 1933
launched the nationwide celebrations of Wagner on the occasion of the
fiftieth anniversary of his death on February 13, 1883.

At the same time, only a few streets away from Max-Joseph-Platz and
this nationalistic drama about the life and work of the early-modern
minnesingers, twenty-seven-year-old Erika Mann was celebrating the
premiere of her politico-literary cabaret, "The Peppermill," in the Bon-
bonnière, a small, somewhat dilapidated stage near the Hofbräuhaus.[52]
Erika Mann, here lashing out in supremely entertaining and successful
fashion at the main players in the dawning "new age," was as hated in
Munich's nationalist circles as her father, Thomas Mann. And in fact,
the same Hans Knappertsbusch, a prominent representative of Munich's
intellectual life, initiated a "Protest from Munich, the Richard Wagner
City" against Thomas Mann, which was published in the *Münchner
Neueste Nachrichten* three months later, in April 1933. The occasion was
a lecture the writer gave in the purview of the Wagner celebrations at the
university, with the title "The Sorrows and Greatness of Richard Wagner."
Knappertsbusch and more than forty cosigners resolutely rejected Mann's
alleged disparagement of Wagner.[53]

Hitler, too, adored Richard Wagner and his music beyond all measure,
and counted upper-class Wagnerians—such as the Munich publisher
Hugo Bruckmann and his wife, Elsa, and the Berlin piano manufacturer
Edwin Bechstein and his wife, Helene—among his early supporters.
Ernst Hanfstaengl, the publisher's son, moved in these circles as well,
and it was in his apartment on Pienzenauer Strasse, by the Herzogpark,
that Hitler and his companions concluded their Wagner evening on January 1.[54] Eva Braun visited Hanfstaengl for the first time on that night,
although he had, as he later reminisced, already noticed her a few months
earlier in Hoffmann's photography shop: "She was a pleasing-looking
blonde . . . well built, with blue eyes and a modest, diffident manner."
On the evening of January 1, he wrote, Hitler was in a "relaxed mood" and
"lively and in good spirits, the way he was in the early 'twenties." According to Hanfstaengl, Hitler said: "This year belongs to us. I will guarantee
you that in writing."[55]

Adolf Hitler and Eva Braun at the center of a group photo, 1932

This harmonious private occasion stood in stark contrast to the precarious political situation at the start of 1933, after the November election. The turnout was lower than in the summer elections and the NSDAP received two million fewer votes, losing 34 of their 230 Reichstag seats. Still, the National Socialists combined with the Communists, who gained votes, took a majority of the seats in the Reichstag, so that, as before, no governing majority in Parliament was possible without the participation of the radical parties. Chancellor Franz von Papen stepped down on November 17, after the failure of his plans to dissolve Parliament, and on December 3 Hindenburg named Kurt von Schleicher, Papen's minister of defense, the new Chancellor. While Papen and Schleicher jockeyed for power, a leadership crisis broke out within the NSDAP.[56] Gregor Strasser — Reich Organization Leader, head of the left wing of the Party, and for years Hitler's only significant opponent within the Party itself — was willing to form a coalition, as opposed to the uncompromising head of the Party, who aimed solely at exclusive power, and he negotiated with Schleicher about forming a right-wing bloc and participating in the government.[57] But he was unable to prevail over Hitler in the Party, and on December 8, Strasser stepped down from all his Party offices. Hitler, as Hinrich Lohse, the once-powerful Gauleiter of Schleswig-Holstein, recalled after the war, had shown himself "in this toughest test of the movement" to be "the master and Strasser the journeyman."[58]

In the following weeks, Hitler not only crushed Strasser's central command structure within the NSDAP but also laid out again the organizational framework for his "personal" authority based on relationships of personal devotion. The document, from December 15, 1932, is called (in Hitler's bureaucratic German) "Memorandum Concerning the Inner Reasons for the Instructions to Produce a Heightened Fighting Power of the Movement." The document states:

> The basis of the political organization is loyalty. In loyalty, the recognition of the necessity of obedience for the construction of every human community is revealed as the noblest expression of feeling. . . . Loyalty and devotion in obedience can never be replaced by formal, technical measures and institutions of any type.[59]

Hitler was here demanding from the members of his party—especially the Gauleiters, or regional leaders, who formed its foundation—absolute loyalty. Any deviation from his dogma of devotion meant for him a delegitimizing of his claim to be the "Führer," or "Leader," and therefore could not be tolerated. In fact, Hitler was laying claim to what Max Weber once categorized as "charismatic authority." In such a system of authority, according to Weber's typology, there is only the leader and the disciples, and the leader is obeyed "purely personally . . . on the basis of the leader's exceptional personal qualities," so long as his "leadership quality," his "charisma" and "heroism," can constantly be established and reestablished. Competence, expertise, and privilege play no more of a role than does reliance on traditional bonds.[60] Hitler himself spoke of the "fanatic apostles" who were necessary in order to spread the Nazi worldview.[61]

Yet what effect did such leader-disciple bonds, which certainly existed between Hitler and close associates such as Hoffmann, Hess, and Goebbels, and later Speer and Bormann, have on Hitler's relationship with Eva Braun? Was it acceptable, from the point of view of the "disciples," that their idol, transfigured into someone or something larger than life by his own propaganda, showed himself to be as incomplete as any ordinary human being by having ordinary human needs? Did the same moral commandment of unswerving submission, which Hitler described as the foundation for every human community, apply to Eva Braun as well? According to Max Weber's definition, the "charismatic leader" does not distinguish between private and public bonds, since his authority is based solely on "purely personal social relationships."[62] In this context, Eva Braun's suicide attempt may well have demonstrated to Hitler her loyalty and adoration to the utmost possible degree, and the self-sacrifice that he demanded from all his followers. By January 1933, in any case, it was clear that, despite their unavoidable geographic separation, Eva Braun had become a lasting and crucial figure in Hitler's life.

Meanwhile, in Cologne and Berlin, Hitler was in multiple negotiations about the formation of a new government with the scheming Franz von Papen, the opponent of the new Chancellor, Kurt von Schleicher. President Hindenburg was aware of these meetings and approved of them, and Schleicher suspected that the efforts to topple him were going on behind his back.[63] The Nazi propaganda machine played up the significance of an NSDAP victory in the Landtag election in the principality of Lippe-Detmold on January 15, 1933, and this gave Hitler some tactical leverage. But a decisive turn in the question of who would be chancellor came about only due to the machinations of a businessman named Joachim von Ribbentrop, in whose villa in Dahlem outside Berlin Hitler had his meetings with Papen and then, on the evening of January 22, with Oskar von Hindenburg, the President's adjutant and son. When Schleicher's government stepped down on January 28, Papen gave his unqualified support to a Hitler cabinet.[64] After conservatives such as Baron Konstantin von Neurath, the foreign minister; Count Lutz Schwerin von Krosigk, the finance minister; Baron Paul von Eltz-Rübenach, the postal and traffic minister; and Alfred Hugenberg, the head of the German National People's Party (DNVP), declared themselves willing to work in a government led by Hitler, Hindenburg named the NSDAP leader Chancellor, on January 30, 1933.[65]

Hitler had reached his goal. Immediately after his swearing in, he had himself driven the few steps from the Reich Chancellery to the Hotel Kaiserhof, flanked by cheering crowds.[66] Numerous faithful followers were already waiting there, including Göring, Goebbels, Hess, Hanfstaengl, and Hoffmann. Together they celebrated attaining the center of power in the German Reich. "Wilhelmstrasse is ours," Goebbels remarked, full of satisfaction, in his diary that would be published a year later as *Vom Kaiserhof zur Reichskanzlei* (From Kaiserhof to the Reich Chancellery).[67] Hess wrote to his wife, Ilse, that he had "not thought possible until the last moment" what had now become "reality."[68]

The first meeting of Hitler's cabinet took place at 5:00 p.m. the same day. At around 8:30, Hitler showed himself at the window to his followers, who—in an improvised mobilization from Goebbels—marched from the Grosser Stern in the Tiergarten, through the Brandenburg Gate, to

Wilhelmstrasse in a torchlit procession that included thousands of Berlin-
ers.[69] Although the conferring of power upon the head of the NSDAP was
in no way seen as a turning point at the time, the leading National Socialists immediately created the legend of a "German revolution," and they
conducted themselves like bellicose upstarts. Intoxicated by their success,
they did not leave the Chancellery until the early morning hours of January 31.[70]

Hindenburg, who had temporarily been using the official residence in
the Chancellery since October 1932, apparently saluted the masses marching past his window until after midnight. Gathered around Hitler were his
vice-chancellor, Franz von Papen, Wilhelm Frick, and Hermann Göring
as minister without portfolio and acting head of the Prussian interior
ministry, as well as Joseph Goebbels, Rudolf Hess, NSDAP lawyer Hans
Frank, Heinrich Hoffmann, and other followers. As the night progressed,
Hitler managed to withdraw to a small room next to the chancellor's ball-
room and reception hall, where he held forth in a monologue for hours
on end before his comrades-in-arms.[71] A large number of phone calls and
telegrams had already arrived from Germany and abroad, acknowledg-
ing the change of government, to the point that the telephone lines were
sometimes jammed. Nevertheless, Hitler, it is said, tried to reach Eva
Braun by phone in Munich that night.[72]

Eva Braun did not actually have her own phone. In the early 1930s,
a telephone was a luxury item that only a few private households could
afford, especially in a time of general economic hardship. Long conversations on the telephone were still rare; in general, the phone was used for
brief communications or to call for help in emergencies. There were, however, already some four hundred thousand connections in the metropolis
of Berlin, population four million. The German postal service was just
beginning to promote the purchase of telephone connections, with a brochure called "You Need a Telephone Too."[73] In any case, Hitler could
reach Eva Braun by phone only at the office of his friend Hoffmann. She
apparently spent nights at the office, sleeping on a "bench" and waiting
for her lover's phone call.[74] Only after Hitler was introduced to Braun's
best friend Herta Ostermayr at Café Heck in Munich, which was after he
had come to power, did he "always" call the Ostermayrs "from Berlin"—
as Herta later recalled—"since the Brauns didn't have a phone."[75] This
arrangement did not last long, though—the official phone book of May 1,
1934, lists Eva Braun with her own phone number at 93 Hohenzollern-

strasse. Even though the address was that of her parents' apartment, the name in the phone book was hers alone,[76] which shows that the phone line was acquired especially for her, so that she could talk on the phone with Hitler undisturbed.

On January 30, 1933, there was no such possibility. If we are to believe Nerin E. Gun, it was a nun collecting donations from the Brauns on the afternoon of January 30 who told Eva the news from Berlin. Eva Braun's first reaction was happiness; then, in the following days at Photohaus Hoffmann, she enthusiastically collected photographs of the National Socialist rally in Berlin while her father and her sister Ilse expressed reservations about the change in government. According to Gun, Franziska and Ilse Braun, who lived together in the family home in Ruhpolding in Upper Bavaria after Friedrich Braun's death on January 22, 1964, stated that Eva Braun grew very pensive after her initial reaction of high spirits, because she was afraid that she would be able to see Hitler even less often than before.[77]

PART TWO Contrasting Worlds

5

WOMEN IN NATIONAL SOCIALISM

National Socialist propaganda put forth an official image of women that implied a single standard model for women's lives. Countless brochures, textbooks, proclamations, and speeches constructed the ideal of a woman's world completely restricted to the domestic and social realms. In a speech before the National Socialist Women's League at the NSDAP convention in Nuremberg on September 8, 1934, for example, Adolf Hitler explained: "If we say that the world of the man is the state, the world of the man is his struggle, his readiness for battle in the service of the community, then we might perhaps say that the world of the woman is a smaller world. For her world is her husband, her family, her children, and her house."[1] As the speech continued, Hitler referred to "nature," "God," and the "Providence" that had "assigned women to their ownmost world" and made them, in this clearly demarcated realm, "man's helper" and his "most faithful friend" and "partner."[2]

The "Reich Women's Leader" Gertrud Scholtz-Klink, only thirty-two years old at the time, spoke to the members of her sex at the same event. Although she was to push for the *Gleichschaltung** of the women's unions

---

*Translator's note: Sometimes translated as "coordination" or "integration," this term refers to the nationalization under National Socialism of previously private or independent organizations.

and the establishment of a women's labor service in the coming years, she
implored the women in her audience to become a part of the People—
and part of History—by "being a mother." At the same time, though, she
also appealed to women working in industry or farming, by declaring:
"Clear the path from yourself to other women, and never let your first
question be what National Socialism brings us, but rather ask first, and
over and over again: What are we prepared to bring to National Socialism?"[3] Clearly the "Reich Women's Leader"—unlike Hitler himself—was
concerned not to exclude working women, who numbered more than a
million by that point, but instead to integrate them, as well as housewives,
into the Nazi "Volksgemeinschaft."*[4]

Ideology and Reality

In actual fact, the image that Hitler and the Nazi propagandists presented
of the lives of women and girls in Germany had little to do with reality.
In 1932, during the worst phase of the economic depression in Germany,
a higher percentage of women than men were fully employed.[5] After
Hitler came to power, the number of women in industry rose steadily
from 1,205,000 in 1933 to 1,846,000 in 1938.[6] The actual lives of women in
the "Third Reich" beyond the "cult of the mother" was thus significantly
more multilayered and complex than is generally assumed.

There were, however, many professions that women were no longer
allowed to practice after 1933. Hitler had personally forbidden women
from being licensed as judges or lawyers in the German Reich, and
decided that "women were categorically not to be used as high government officials." Exceptions would be made only "for positions especially
suited to women, in the areas of social work, education, and health services."[7] At the Party convention in 1936, Hitler declared once again to "all
the literary know-it-alls and equal-rights philosophizers" that there were
"two worlds in the life of a People: the world of the woman and the world
of the man."[8] However, economic constraints such as the shortage of
labor in the country, as well as Nazi political goals including the rearmament program under way since 1936 and the concomitant need for work-

---

* Translator's note: The "Volksgemeinschaft" was the Nazi social ideal of a racially unified and hier-
archically organized "People's community."

ers, made it harder to carry out a unified ideological political program for women and families based on racist/biologist principles.[9]

The realities of women's lives in the National Socialist state were increasingly studied as a topic of historical research only from the late 1970s on. Until then, scholars of National Socialism concentrated primarily on analyzing the structures of power and thus women, who were excluded from important political, economic, and military roles in the Nazi state, were typically seen as insignificant and their influence was little examined. This approach was likewise—in fact, above all—to be found in the biographical portraits of the leading National Socialists— Hitler, Speer, Himmler. The journalist Gitta Sereny was an exception: for her biography of Speer, she also made sure to talk with Speer's wife, Margarete, who had, after all, "for years seen Hitler as a private man day after day" and, Sereny believed, could hardly have "remained in total ignorance" of the Nazi crimes.[10] Joachim Fest, on the other hand, as late as the early 1990s, maintained that the cult of Hitler among his early female supporters from the "better circles of society" (for example, Helene Bechstein, Elsa Bruckmann, and Viktoria von Dirksen) had its cause in the "exuberance of feeling among a certain type of older woman, who sought to awaken the unsatisfied drives inside them in the frenzy of night-time mass rallies around the ecstatic figure of Hitler." There is no talk of these women having any possible political motives or well-thought-out antidemocratic or anti-Semitic positions, though Fest does discuss their moral decay, world-weariness, "muffled covetousness," and a "maternal concern" projected onto Hitler.[11]

The memoir literature by Hitler's more or less close collaborators, which seeks to explain his mass popularity, encourages such interpretations. Moreover, in such texts the wives, girlfriends, and female family members are usually on the margins, mentioned only as passive bystanders. "Eva Braun had no interest in politics," wrote Albert Speer, for example. "She scarcely ever attempted to influence Hitler." Speer likewise claimed about his own wife that she was "not political." In general, he almost entirely excludes his family from his postwar reminiscences, in which, as his youngest daughter complained, his wife and children are "practically nonexistent."[12] The women's own writings, in turn, retrospectively give the impression that these women were occupied exclusively in the private sphere during the twelve years of Nazi rule, casting the authors as devoted but politically passive companions to their men. They deny

any personal responsibility or guilt, since they were, they say, to a large
extent unaware of what was going on around them. Margarete Speer, for
example, kept silent her whole life about her role in the Berghof inner
circle as well as about her relations with Eva Braun and Anni Brandt (the
wife of Hitler's attending physician, Karl Brandt), and was thus described
by her children "as always completely apolitical."[13] Maria von Below's
husband, Nicolaus von Below, worked in Hitler's immediate surroundings as air force adjutant from 1937 to 1945 and developed an increasingly
close "relationship of mutual trust" with him over the course of those
years; she later said that at the time, when she belonged to the circle of
women on the Obersalzberg, she had been "not all that pleased to come
into that political world"—she and her husband were, she said, "entirely
apolitical."[14]

In fact, most women claimed after the war that they had had nothing to do with politics in the years before 1945. The widespread claim of
"feminine innocence" was, not least, part of the strategy of exoneration
in a debate about the past that took place in Germany in the 1950s. Even
decades later, the psychoanalyst Margarete Mitscherlich reaffirmed, in
a much-noticed book called *The Peaceable Sex*, that anti-Semitism is
intrinsically masculine—a "social disease" that stands in close relation
to "typical male development." Women, on the other hand, are inclined
to conform to "male prejudices" out of a "fear of loss of love." In the Nazi
period, she writes, women, "like all weak and oppressed members of a
society," thus identified with the "aggressor."[15] To this day, the fact that
a woman like Eva Braun did not take part in any of "the decisions that
led to the worst crimes of the century" is taken as proof of her exclusively
private existence, "outside of history."[16] But is uncritically sharing Hitler's
worldview and political opinions not enough to transform someone from
a victim into a collaborator? Doesn't the danger of a dictatorship consist
precisely in such blind obedience?

It has thus become more and more common to no longer see the wives
of Nazi Party leaders or functionaries as mere dependents or conformists,
but to understand them as active agents, "complicit" or even "perpetra-
tors" in their own right. This new perspective has already led to studies
centered on female propagandists of the NSDAP, or on women who were
active in the SS system. But it also illuminates the hitherto unnoticed lives
of SS men's wives, and their significance for the SS "clan-community."
The conclusions were as could have been predicted: these women actively

or passively consented to the "murderous reality" surrounding them every day, and at the very least lacked a sense of guilt. It was apparently socially acceptable "normal behavior" to support criminal activity.[17]

Despite the paucity of sources, Eva Braun's case, too, and that of the other women belonging to the closed community at the Berghof, must be investigated—and her concrete everyday life and behavior in the Nazi regime reconstructed—without letting our view of the facts be obstructed by the image of women in Nazi propaganda, later strategies of self-justification, or the myth of "male power" in the Nazi regime.[18] In the final analysis, the only way to understand Eva Braun's status and social function within Hitler's private environment, and her significance in the Berghof group, is to answer the question, What were her own motives? Until now, though, no one has seemed to suppose that she pursued any goals of her own whatsoever. The technicality that she was never a member of the NSDAP or any other Party organization has been taken as proof of her allegedly apolitical behavior; Eva Braun exists in the public eye, even today, only as a submissive victim or as someone who enjoyed the fruits of male actions without participating in them. But to what extent did she herself identify with the National Socialist state? Within the limits drawn for her as a woman and as Hitler's secret mistress, was there any room to maneuver that she actively made use of? Albert Speer, in an interview with Gitta Sereny a few years before his death, claimed that Eva Braun had been "helpful to many people behind the scenes" without ever making this known.[19] How we should take Speer's brief mention of these activities remains to be seen, but it is clear that they do not fit the common picture of an entirely unaware and uninterested mistress.

The lives of the Nazi elite's wives and lovers, kept hidden from the public, developed along lines that often contradicted the publicly proclaimed principles of the regime. For example, the diplomat and travel writer Hans-Otto Meissner criticized the "founder of National Socialism" in his postwar memoir for having disregarded "the principles of the Third Reich" at his formal events. Meissner was the son of Otto Meissner, who for many years was head of the Office of the Reich President, which in 1934 became the Presidential Chancellery of the Führer, and he grew up in the Reich President's official residence on Wilhelmstrasse. He wrote that the "official representations at the Berlin Reich Chancellery," including state ceremonies and festivities, were constantly violating Party rules; in fact, they were diametrically opposed to the behavior that Party functionaries were advocating "in the whole Reich." Meissner was intimately familiar with how the Nazi regime conducted itself on the international stage, both because he worked in the German diplomatic service in London and Tokyo from 1935 to 1939 and because his father, as the "Chief of the Presidential Chancellery of the Führer and Chancellor," was almost solely responsible for managing large, formal events. He remarked that at the state dinners Hitler held in Berlin, not only was the reactionary "kiss of the hand" in good form, but participants also enjoyed the "foreign luxury products," such as "old Burgundy" and "French champagne," that were consistently demonized in Nazi propaganda.[20] And even while the NSDAP especially targeted female cigarette consumers in their nation-wide antismoking campaigns—posting in restaurants and cafés placards that said "The German Woman Does Not Smoke!"—in the Reich Chancellery "liveried servants" offered "the ladies Egyptian cigarettes," according to Meissner. The "ladies at the Führer's table," the former diplomat revealed to his countrymen in 1951, wore evening dresses from "Lanvin and Patou" and wreathed themselves "in Chanel and Chypre perfumes."[21]

Magda Goebbels: "First Lady of the Third Reich"

One such lady who often sat "at the Führer's table," filling the function of "First Lady of the Third Reich" at Hitler's side during receptions, balls, and state visits, was Magda Goebbels. Since Eva Braun, as a girlfriend kept hidden from the public, obviously could not participate in such formal functions and thus never took part in any official meals at the "Reich Chancellor's House" at 77 Wilhelmstrasse, only the wives of the highest-ranking Reich ministers were appropriate for such duties. This was particularly true for Magda Goebbels, who was attractive, elegant, and sophisticated, in the views of the time, and had a special personal relationship with Hitler as well.[22] Ilse Hess, Emmy Göring, and Annelies von Ribbentrop were only replacements: they stood in for the Propaganda Minister's wife occasionally, when she was not available.

Hitler clearly recognized quite early on the valuable public-relations qualities of Magda Quandt, as she was named when he met her. She had divorced her first husband, Günther Quandt, a major industrialist who was worth millions, and Hitler's first meeting with her, in the spring of 1931 in the Hotel Kaiserhof in Berlin, was not an accident. Magda Quandt had arranged the encounter herself by sending her ten-year-old son Harald to the NSDAP leader's suite in a blue costume-uniform to "report for duty to his Führer,"[23] who had arrived in Berlin only that morning. The maneuver worked exactly as planned: the boy's appearance and the ensuing conversation with Magda Quandt in the café in the hotel lobby, arranged by Goebbels, convinced Hitler that this woman could "play a great role" in his life as "the feminine antipole" to him in his work.[24]

She was certainly something—or, as the saying goes in German, "you could make a country with her." Her ex-husband, who had given Hitler financial support in his election campaigns, was firmly in the German business elite.[25] She herself moved in Berlin's high-society circles, after her divorce as much as before, and she even had international connections. In addition, she was financially independent, and had been a member of the NSDAP since September 1, 1930. Immediately after joining the Party, she had made deliberate efforts to get close to Goebbels, who at the time was Head of Propaganda for the NSDAP and Gauleiter of Berlin, and only four weeks later she was in charge of his "private archive."[26] This was at a time when the National Socialists were by no means established in the German capital, despite their success in the parliamentary elections of September 14, 1930; the NSDAP remained insignificant on the national level, and Prussian Prime Minister Otto Braun was fighting to classify the Party as seditious and ban it, preferably nationwide. The Berlin chief of police, Albert Grzesinski, formerly Prussian Minister of the Interior, banned the NSDAP Party newspaper *Der Angriff* on February 4, 1931, and Goebbels had to appear before Prussian judges in several slander trials. There were, in fact, conflicts within the NSDAP in this period about whether the Party should continue to pursue legal means of coming to power or should instead unleash a civil war. And despite the political violence being perpetrated by the Party and the SA, Hitler was personally working toward recognition in upper-middle-class circles,[27] insisting again and again that the NSDAP did not intend any violent coup, or putsch, only the pursuit of its goals by legal means. The developing romance between Goebbels and the urbane Magda Quandt thus seemed more than opportune to Hitler, as a way to polish his Party's image of being a mob of working-class hooligans.[28]

When it comes to understanding the twenty-nine-year-old Magda Quandt's motives for approaching the National Socialists, the existing biographies rely to a great extent on the postwar statements of contemporaries. For example, it is claimed on the basis of a reminiscence, published in a magazine in 1952, by her mother, Auguste Behrend, that in 1930 Magda Quandt was bored and looking for "a purpose in life" until she became fascinated with Goebbels as a speaker at an NSDAP election event, and spontaneously decided to become involved in National Socialism. Goebbels as a person—his charisma and his "almost eroticizing" effect—is said to be the reason why she joined the Party; his hate and his contempt for humanity were aspects of Goebbels she supposedly did not perceive.[29] Albert Speer, too, who in later years was among her close friends, described Magda Quandt as a "very emotional woman, occasionally inclined toward sentimentality."[30] Elsewhere he claims that the wives of high-ranking Party members "resisted the temptations of power far more than their husbands" and regarded the "fantasy world" of their husbands with "inner reservations."[31]

But is this account really plausible? Especially with respect to Magda Quandt? Speer's *Inside the Third Reich* as a whole gives the impression that his worldview barely allowed for the possibility of a woman with political convictions, never mind ambitions. He does not attribute any interest in political topics to a single woman in Hitler's inner circle, including his own wife. In Magda Quandt's case, the fact that she entertained a friendship with the leftist Zionist leader Chaim Arlosoroff before meeting Goebbels indicates that she was seeking a new orientation in this period, not only in her private life but also politically.[32] In light of the increasing radicalization of the Weimar Republic, and despite her own insulation from the financial struggles and unemployment resulting from the Great Depression, she clearly shared with many members of her generation the view that democracy had failed in Germany and that in the future people would have to decide between the left and the right. Like many other Germans from all social classes, especially those under forty, she found her way to the NSDAP in 1930, the year of crisis, attracted by the cult of Hitler and the vague but attractive idea of a new society, a "Volksgemeinschaft" united in the struggle for territory and for the race, which would be the only way for Germans to once again attain national greatness.

Only rarely were women active members of the Party. They constituted just 7.8 percent of the members who joined between 1925 and 1932. But neither Magda Quandt's upper-class background and high educational level, nor the fact that her stepfather, Richard Friedländer, was Jewish, deterred her from joining the loud, militant, anti-Semitic National Socialists.[33] In contrast to the Weimar parliamentary politicians, who seemed boring and fossilized, the Nazis embodied a youthful, revolutionary dynamism. They offered simple answers to complicated questions and made it possible to "flee the gray everyday"—not the least of their attractions.[34]

As early as February 21, 1931, Magda Quandt accompanied Goebbels to a Party event in Weimar.[35] Goebbels had been named "Reich Propaganda Leader" of the NSDAP at the start of that year. At the Richard Wagner festival in Bayreuth, July 21–August 19, she was already, with Goebbels, a member of Hitler's entourage, along with Erna Gröbke and Heinrich Hoffmann; Jakob Werlin, the chairman of Daimler-Benz AG; Hitler's secretary Johanna Wolf; Julius Schaub; and others.[36] In the years before he became Chancellor, Hitler traveled to Bayreuth only with close and trusted friends; there he indulged his passion for Richard Wagner's operas and pledged friendship with Winifred Wagner. She had run the festival since the death of her husband, Siegfried Wagner, the composer's son, at the start of 1931. In other words, in less than a year after joining the Party, Magda Quandt, "Goebbels's Madame Pompadour," had reached the innermost National Socialist circle.[37]

The fact that Magda Quandt included her son Harald in her political activities from the beginning is a further sign of the depth of her engagement, and her enthusiasm for the antidemocratic, anti-Semitic, and anti-communist worldview of her new friends. She brought him with her to Braunschweig, for example, on October 17, 1931, where approximately seventy-five thousand National Socialists, including members of the SS and the SA, would parade before Hitler on the following day. During the course of the rally, violent riots broke out between the Nazis and the Communists, leaving two dead and sixty seriously injured.[38] Quandt's son, in an SA uniform, was standing next to Goebbels in the front row, next to Wilhelm Frick, the National Socialist Minister of the Interior for the state of Thuringia, and Gregor Strasser, the "Reich Organization Leader." Magda Quandt could hardly have expressed her Nazi convictions, and her trust in Goebbels, more clearly.[39]

Nonetheless, Magda Quandt's precise relationship to National Socialism, both during this period and later, remains uncertain. Did she become a passionate advocate for this ideology herself, or was she only hungry for power and launching a "career as an opportunist"[40] in 1931? Can she even be seen as the victim of a cunning psychological maneuver that she herself did not understand? Hitler, according to this argument, manipulated

*Harald Quandt, age ten, next to Goebbels during the SA march in
Braunschweig, October 1931*

both her and Goebbels in his own personal interest, even to the extent of
getting them to quickly marry on December 19, 1931.[41]

Another theory, propounded by members of Hitler's inner circle, maintains that Magda Goebbels was actually in love with the Nazi leader and
had married the "limping Goebbels" only to be able to live near Hitler. Goebbels himself, in any case, seems to have been tormented with
jealousy and mistrust in the early phase of his relationship with Magda
Quandt. A few months before the wedding, he noted in his diary that he
was "suffering greatly from" his girlfriend's acting "not entirely like a lady"
with Hitler, and he was afraid she was "not secure in her fidelity."[42] A few
weeks later, he even claimed that Hitler was the one in love with Magda
Quandt—Hitler had been "crushed" to hear the news of her upcoming
marriage to Goebbels. It is unclear, however, how much these remarks
had their basis in fact and how much they arose from nothing more than
the Minister of Propaganda's imagination, as a way of emphasizing his
own masculinity and perseverance. At least in this case, the little man
crippled with a short leg and a deformed foot was victorious, even over
the all-powerful "Führer," by winning Magda Quandt for himself; thus
he commented condescendingly of Hitler: "Has no luck with women.
Because he's too soft. Women don't like that. They need to feel their master above them."[43]

The fact is, since the 1980s much has been written and speculated about the wives of the Nazi leaders and the prominent women in the Nazi regime, often on the basis of unreliable memoirs and autobiographical sources, but there has been little research. A lack of sources has led, in Magda Quandt's case, too, to contradictory claims, false dates, and the perpetuation of myths. One thing is certain: she was no victim. She acted independently and on her own initiative. The decisions she made from 1930 on, about her own life and the life of her son, stemmed from deep convictions—of that there can be no doubt, especially after 1933 when she and her children worked hand in hand with the Nazi propaganda machine in the service of the National Socialist ideals of mother and family. Also undeniable is the fact that a "bond of friendship and respect," as Otto Wagener put it, existed between her and Hitler from the beginning.[44] The frequent private meetings between Hitler and the Goebbelses in Berlin are enough to substantiate that. And the idea that Hitler used Magda Goebbels or the other people around him for his own purposes, against their will, is groundless. Rather, we must start from the assumption that the wife of the Minister of Propaganda was a fanatical believer in both the authenticity of her "Führer" and the truth of the National Socialist ideology in general.

What was her relationship with Eva Braun? The two women spent the last weeks of their lives together, in the bunker under the Reich Chancellery; that much is certain. Already in the years before the war, the women met occasionally at the Berghof.[45] They committed suicide at their husbands' sides in spring 1945—the only wives of the Nazi leaders to do so. But can we conclude that their underlying political positions were the same? Were there or were there not points of convergence and agreement in the lives of these women before their legendary common demise? Were they even, as is so often claimed, rivals for Hitler's favor?[46] The thought suggests itself naturally enough, since Magda Goebbels was put forward as a symbolic wife and mother for the Nazi state in public appearances at Hitler's side, while Eva Braun had to live hidden from the public, but there is no actual proof of any such conflict.

Emmy Göring and Ilse Hess

Like Magda Goebbels, the tall, blond Emmy Göring, who had acted in the German National Theater for ten years in Weimar, saw herself as

Hitler in conversation with Magda Goebbels and Eva Braun, in the Kehlstein
teahouse (the "Eagle's Nest") on the Obersalzberg, October 1938. To the left,
Gerda Bormann.

the "First Lady" of the Nazi state. Her husband—who performed such
various functions as Prussian Prime Minister, Commander in Chief of
the Air Force, and a director of the national economy granted absolute,
dictatorial powers—was, in the end, far more powerful politically than the
Minister of Propaganda. And it seemed clear that Göring would become
the next Führer and chancellor of the German Reich should Hitler ever
withdraw from power or die. Göring and Goebbels were said to have been
bound by a kind of "love-hate relationship," while their wives, independently of each other, in the mid-1930s led "Berlin salons" frequented by
diplomats and politicians from the NSDAP milieu.[47]

Emmy Göring, for example, who was already forty-two years old at the
time of her marriage and was not yet a member of the NSDAP, regu-

larly invited the spouses of other important Party members, including Ilse Hess, for tea at her Berlin apartment on Leipziger Platz, or at Carinhall, the Görings' residence in the Schorfheide Forest.[48] It is likely that a greater competition existed between Madga Goebbels and Emmy Göring than between Magda Goebbels and Eva Braun, who was, after all, unable to ever appear in public. In her autobiography published in 1967, in any case, Emmy Göring emphasized that despite the frosty relations between their husbands, she and Magda Goebbels "were in perfect harmony" with each other and that she "liked [Magda Goebbels] very much."[49] She was never in contact with Eva Braun, on the other hand, even though the Görings also owned a house on the Obersalzberg. If we are to believe Emmy Göring's account, she tried many times during the war years to establish a personal connection with Hitler's young girlfriend, but Hitler immediately put a stop to her efforts.[50] In 1939 he granted Emmy Göring her wish to be allowed to join the NSDAP, giving his permission personally, but in her postwar autobiography she said nothing about this decision or what lay behind it. Rather, she presented herself to the public in the 1960s as Hermann Göring's then-naive, unsuspecting, and entirely apolitical wife, who "never gave a thought" to whether she "was shopping in an Aryan or Jewish shop."[51]

Ilse Hess—the third potential Nazi "First Lady"—was an exception among the wives of the leading National Socialists. Unlike the others, she was among the earliest supporters of the National Socialist movement and was, as she said herself, "a National Socialist from inner conviction."[52] A doctor's daughter from Berlin, she was preparing for her exams in Munich when she met Rudolf Hess in the small Pension von Schildberg in Schwabing, in April 1920. He was studying economics, history, and political science at the time, and he brought her along to a so-called discussion evening run by the NSDAP as early as spring 1920, probably June 1. Adolf Hitler, whom she didn't yet know, discussed in detail the Party's goals in a small back room and cast his spell over them both. Hitler had spoken in a language, Ilse Hess later admitted, that she "craved," because he "had the courage, for the first time since 1918," to "talk about Germany."[53] Like many women of her generation, especially as the daughter of a Prussian medical officer from the First Guards Regiment in Potsdam, she had been overwhelmed by the trauma of unexpectedly losing the First World War and the feeling of humiliation resulting from the Versailles Treaty, which had "vilified the German People before all other Peoples."[54]

Hitler, though, was starting to make a name for himself in the Bavarian capital city for his anti-Semitic agitations in mass rallies against the
"Versailles diktat." As propagandist for the NSDAP—he became its leader
only in the following year, on July 29, 1921—he appeared once or twice
a week in the city's beer cellars. While Rudolf Hess joined the NSDAP
"immediately" after their joint attendance at the "discussion evening," Ilse
Pröhl, as she was called until her marriage, first became Hess's "political
secretary" and then, in late 1920, as a student of German and library science at the Ludwig Maximilian University, his "secretary, adjutant, and
staff" in one. Hess was already, as he wrote in a letter to his parents on
September 14, in "almost daily" contact with Hitler. And Ilse Pröhl, as
she retrospectively admitted in 1955, contributed the most to her future
husband's "nearly magical" bond with Hitler.[55] Finally, in 1921, she joined
the NSDAP herself and wrote in a letter to her former grammar school
teacher:

> For there is a movement starting here in Munich now, which strongly
> attracts all the young, strong, and still thoroughly healthy forces. . . . It
> is called the National Socialist German Workers' Party. It stands—to be
> right upfront about it—completely on the soil of the German People,
> or, to put it in the clean and plain and negative terms appropriate to
> the movement: we are anti-Semites. Consistently, rigorously, without
> exceptions! The two basic pillars of our movement—national, and
> social—are anchored in the meaning of this anti-Semitism. Love of
> country and of our people above all private interests.[56]

The twenty-year-old Ilse Pröhl here formulated, unambiguously and
conclusively, her belief in the fundamental ethos of a party that at that
point was only one of many Populist-nationalist groups in Munich. And
its anti-Semitism presented, as her letter makes clear, a foundation of the
Nazi ideology with which she had no problem. She and Rudolf Hess,
convinced that striving for socialism on a national basis included "in an
entirely intrinsic way the struggle against Judaism," made their support of
Hitler, whom they called "the Tribune," their raison d'être. Ilse Hess, who
after the war insisted that she had been "always passive, as a woman," was
thus in truth an activist from the beginning. Her letters, which are now
available to researchers, offer a glimpse that is otherwise hard to come by
into the world of the wives of the Nazi leaders and their ideas at the time.

Ilse Hess at the side of her husband, Rudolf Hess, after his victory in the air race around the Zugspitze on March 10, 1934. To the left, Reich Air Sports Leader Bruno Loerzer; in the background, Colonel Erhard Milch, State Secretary in Göring's Ministry of Air Travel.

When Hitler was imprisoned in Landsberg after the failed Beer Hall Putsch of November 8–9, 1923—in which Hess had taken part as well—and started writing his book *Mein Kampf* (My Struggle), Ilse Pröhl was once again there to help him. The youthfully romantic student sent her boyfriend Hess, who was with Hitler in Landsberg prison, Friedrich Hölderlin's *Elegies* as inspiration for Hitler. Hitler, though, apparently could make little headway with Hölderlin's poetry, with its oscillations between hope and lament conjuring up the certainty of mankind's renewal. Hitler liked the "type area," Hess reported, but "he did not have much understanding of the elegies."[57] Ilse Pröhl also worked with Josef Stolzing-Cerny, the editor and cultural critic of the *Völkischer Beobachter*, as a reader of Hitler's manuscript, and helped with the final version in 1925. It is unlikely, in contrast, that Rudolf Hess took part. Hitler assigned him to work on the corrections, but Hess apparently passed that work along to his girlfriend.[58]

After her marriage to Hess on December 20, 1927—he had meantime become Hitler's "private secretary" and one of his closest friends—Ilse also corresponded with publishers and Party leaders and their wives, including the Goebbels and Göring families. The correspondence gives the impression of a very familiar, cooperative relationship, with, for example, gifts exchanged on holidays. Hess was the eccentric minister without portfolio, subordinate only to Hitler himself, and the "Deputy Führer" in Party affairs, while his wife, Ilse Hess, worked to maintain relationships and mediate any conflicts that arose. For example, she wrote to Heinrich Himmler, who took over the office of Munich chief of police in 1933, with the salutation "Most honored of all Chiefs of Police!" and continued in a humorously cryptic tone that he had "the surely praiseworthy habit" of "monitoring enemies of the Fatherland." But why was he also keeping "upstanding ministers" under surveillance and pestering them with "ridiculous surveillance noises on the telephone"? If he was not the "wrongdoer" himself, perhaps he might be able to "look into what she suspected" was happening.[59]

Unlike Emmy Göring, Ilse Hess was also in contact with Eva Braun. It cannot be determined when they met, or whether their connection included personal meetings or took place entirely by letter. It is certain, though, that Hitler's girlfriend was among those who received Christmas presents from Ilse Hess, for which Eva Braun gave warm thanks in a letter addressed "Dear Madam."[60] Like the other "First Ladies of the Third Reich," Ilse Hess also played a public role, admittedly a smaller one than that played by Magda Goebbels. Pictures of Ilse Hess and her son Wolf Rüdiger Hess, Hitler's godson, appeared in newspapers such as the high-circulation *Berliner Illustrirte Zeitung*. And until her husband flew to Scotland in a fighter plane on a wayward mission on May 10, 1941, "Madame Reich Minister" employed no fewer than two secretaries of her own to keep the flood of correspondence under control. Even after Hess's mission, as "apparently persona non grata," she maintained contacts and remained, as she told the writer Hans Grimm in November 1944, "unswervingly true to the law . . . according to which we lined up under the Führer's banner in 1920." Until the very end, the idea that her husband "would stand once more at the Führer's side as one of his most faithful followers" remained for her a "wonderful dream."[61]

Eva Braun's Role

In 1933, Eva Braun turned twenty-one and legally became an adult. The problems in her relationship with Hitler continued to be the unsettled

E. B.

Obersalzberg, den 2. Jan.

Sehr verehrte gnädige Frau!
Ich danke Ihnen herzlich für
Ihr liebes Weihnachtsgeschenk. Ich habe
mich sehr darüber gefreut.
Wir sind seit dem ersten Feiertag
auf dem Berghof und fahren fleißig
Ski. Charly (Stark) hat sich bereits
den Fuß gebrochen und muß nun 3 Wo-
chen liegen. Trotzdem haben wir, zum
Entsetzen des Führers der uns allen
das gleiche prophezeit, das Skifahren
noch nicht aufgegeben.
Hat sich der kleine Muck gut
eingewöhnt und macht er seinem würdi-
gen Elternpaar keine Schande?
Ich wünsche Ihnen gnädige Frau
und Ihrem Mann noch ein recht gutes
neues Jahr.
Herzliche Grüße!
Ihre
Eva Braun.

Letter from Eva Braun
*to Ilse Hess**

situation and their lack of time together. But it is impossible to tell when and how often she and Hitler saw each other in his early years as Chancellor, from 1933 to 1935. Nevertheless, the biographical accounts up to now, based on the contents of a diary that Eva Braun allegedly kept between February 6 and May 28, 1935, claim that they were often together during

---

*Obersalzberg, January 2
Dear Madam,

Thank you very much for your lovely Christmas present. I was very happy to get it.

We have been at the Berghof since the first day of Christmas and are hard at work skiing. Charlie (Stark) has already broken his foot and has to stay in bed for 3 weeks. Still, we have not stopped skiing, to the Führer's horror; he prophesies the same fate for all of us.

Has little Muck settled in? I hope he is not disgracing his worthy parents.

I wish you a very good New Year, madam, and your husband as well.

Best regards!

Yours
Eva Braun

these years.[62] In fact, Goebbels's notes also show that Hitler, even in the months after he was named Reich Chancellor, spent most of his time in Munich. For example, in February 1933 he spent half his time in the Bavarian capital.[63] While the "transfer of power" in Berlin was turning into what the Nazis themselves called a "seizure of power"—with Hitler immediately arranging for President Hindenburg to dissolve the Reichstag, call new elections for March 5, and impose the emergency measures "For the Protection of the German People," which led to massive limits on freedom of the press and freedom of assembly—the head of the NSDAP was flying to his favorite city for several days every week. And Eva Braun— at least according to the postwar testimony of Hitler's housekeeper, who was living with him on Prinzregentenplatz—"was there every time Hitler was there." She was "sometimes taken home at night," but occasionally spent the night "in the house too."[64]

Hitler thus largely withdrew from the electoral campaign that was actually entirely about him, and in which he was cast, more than ever before, as a kind of mythical redeemer. The NSDAP, meanwhile, especially in Berlin, was intimidating and persecuting political opponents with all of the means at its disposal, including arbitrary arrests and violent attacks by the SA.[65] Late on the night of February 3, for example, Hitler traveled to Munich after announcing to high-ranking army officers an unprecedented rearmament at a sitting of the army leadership on the Bendlerstrasse (today the Bendlerblock). On the morning of February 5, a Sunday, following the "state burial" staged by Goebbels in the Berlin Cathedral to honor the SA thug Hans Eberhard Maikowski, who had been killed on January 30, Hitler left the capital again in order to celebrate Eva Braun's twenty-first birthday with her the next day, February 6.[66] Eleven days later, on February 17, Hitler flew to Munich again after an election speech in Dortmund and spent the weekend.[67] Four days later, on February 23, after a campaign appearance in Frankfurt, Hitler left for Bavaria for five days, remaining there until February 27—on the evening of which, the Reichstag burned.[68]

Why was the Chancellor spending so much time in Munich? Was Eva Braun the reason? And how did he justify his frequent absences from the seat of government? The truth was that Hitler, despite his conspicuous political rise to power, had no intention of giving up the bohemian lifestyle that he had led up until then. Rudolf Hess's announcement of "new time management" a day after taking power in the government was somewhat premature: the "Führer," Hess enthusiastically wrote to his wife Ilse on January 31, was suddenly punctual and even "always a few minutes early," so that he, Hess, now "even had to buy a watch."[69] However, Hitler, well known for never being on time, remained restless and erratic.[70] Berlin never became the center of his life. At first, he still lived in the Hotel Kaiserhof there; later, during renovations to his apartment in the Old Reich Chancellery, he stayed in the rooms "on the second floor of the office building" of his State Secretary, Hans Heinrich Lammers.[71] In Bavaria, on the other hand, he bought the apartment in Munich that he had rented until then, at 16 Prinzregentenplatz, as well as the small Haus Wachenfeld on the Obersalzberg,[72] both in 1933. In the Reichstag election of March 5, he campaigned for the seat he needed in Parliament not in Berlin but in District 24, Upper Bavaria / Swabia[73] — although whether or not he threw himself "with all his strength into the election battle," as is usually claimed, is certainly doubtful.[74] He had his head of propaganda spread the information that he was living "simply, like any other member of the People," and that he had "no pleasures and no relaxation other than his work and his task." He himself stated in an interview with the German actor Tony van Eyck after the election, in answer to the question of whether he was happy: "Happy? How can someone be happy with such immensely difficult tasks standing before him? Hopeful, yes — that I certainly am!"[75] But the picture painted by Hitler and Goebbels of the "Führer" living a life of renunciation and hardship, overcoming "by some miracle" all "bodily and spiritual strains," bore no relation to the truth.[76] Rather, the first few months of Hitler's chancellorship already showed that Berlin was primarily the "stage" on which the Nazi propaganda would perform the "cult of the Führer," while Hitler the actual person simply disappeared unnoticed.[77] Tranquil Munich and its surroundings remained his private retreat, a fact largely kept hidden from the public.

Especially for the period after the Reichstag election of March 5, in which the NSDAP won 43.9 percent of the vote but failed to reach its goal of an absolute majority, Joseph Goebbels's diary entries document the extent to which Hitler made himself scarce: he hardly ever spent ten days or two weeks in a row in the nation's capital.[78] On the other hand, he extended his stays in Bavaria, for example spending from March 26 to April 4 there, when he drove for several days to his vacation residence on the Obersalzberg. His ministers in Berlin could reach him by telephone, and by the telex service that had just been introduced and was still under construction. Thus Goebbels, now head of the newly created "Ministry for Public Enlightenment and Propaganda," communicated to Hitler in Munich by telegram the call for a general boycott of Jewish businesses on March 27, and made "a report by telephone" the following day "about the effects of the call to boycott."[79] The geographical distance did not affect the fact that Hitler was always kept well informed, and still made all the important decisions himself.[80]

Week by week, both the social climate and the political landscape of the German Reich were changing. Regulations, laws, and decrees followed one another unceasingly, all leading in the direction of the final destruction of the state governments, the elimination of political opposition, and the removal of Jewish citizens from public life, and all pursuing the goal of making the NSDAP the only power in the Reich. In April alone, no fewer than twelve such regulations went into effect, including the "Reich Governor Law" of April 7 and the "Law for the Restoration of the Civil Service," announced on the same day, according to which politically suspect civil servants and officials of "non-Aryan heritage" were fired or forcibly retired.[81] Still, Hitler himself, as Kershaw notes, was "only minimally active" in the spring of 1933 and "took almost no personal part" in the transformation of the country.[82] In April, too, the Chancellor spent the greater part of his time in Munich and its surroundings: he traveled to Munich on April 10, after only five days fulfilling his duties of office in Berlin; then he flew to Berlin on the afternoon of Friday, April 21, only to drive back to Bavaria the next day and stay until Wednesday of the following week.[83] It was difficult, in these circumstances, to get into a "work routine." Rather, as Otto Dietrich (the "Reich Press Chief" and one of Hitler's constant companions since 1933) wrote later, Hitler had "no ability to distinguish between public and private life," and conducted "his public business in the middle of his private life and lived a private life in the middle of his official business and official duties."[84]

Hitler even sidestepped the celebrations on April 20, 1933, his forty-fourth birthday and the first time his birthday was celebrated throughout the country. While the Chancellor, as Goebbels noted in his diary, tarried "somewhere or another in Bavaria" and could not be reached, the Propaganda Minister organized the "Führer's Birthday" celebration in Berlin. Following the custom of celebrating the Kaiser's birthday, the "Führer's Birthday" was to be celebrated every year, from then until the end of the Nazi dictatorship, with nationwide Party celebrations, commemorations, and marches, becoming a major fixed point in the German holiday calendar.[85] It was Goebbels, not Hitler, who attended the ceremony to honor the dictator on that evening of April 20 in the National Playhouse Berlin (today the Konzerthaus Berlin) on the Gendarmenmarkt. There the National Socialist author Hanns Johst, head dramaturge since March 1933 of the legendary former Royal National Theater, premiered *Schlageter*, a play written by him and dedicated to "Adolf Hitler in loving devotion and unwavering loyalty."[86] A few hours earlier, Goebbels had given a radio address to the public with the title "Our Hitler," which cast the absent leader as a national hero who had taken up Bismarck's "work" and was "committed to completing" it, while at the same time remaining a "comrade" and "ordinary person like any other."[87]

What was Hitler himself doing while the glorification of his person reached this "new high point"?[88] He was strolling around Munich with his entourage, nicknamed the Chauffeureska, visiting his favorite restaurants, the opera, and the theater, and relaxing with close friends in Heinrich Hoffmann's villa. In addition, he often met with Eva Braun, without letting their relationship turn into a routine or even anything reliable. Ultimately, the existence of a lover with whom he shared "no day-to-day life and no legitimate relationship," and with whom there was no possibility of feeling a "sense of finality," the way one would with a wife, was in complete harmony with Hitler's bohemian, antibourgeois lifestyle.[89] He received Eva Braun at his apartment on Prinzregentenplatz, took her to eat at Osteria Bavaria, and invited her to his vacation residence on the Obersalzberg. The young woman spontaneously packed her bags and—officially on assignment from Photohaus Hoffmann—stepped into a chauffeured Mercedes, sent by Hitler, that was waiting on the corner of Türkenstrasse a few yards from the photo shop.[90]

There is, though, hardly any evidence for these activities aside from the statements of third parties and a few photographs from the period.[91] Still, Albert Speer, who had assisted the architect Paul Ludwig Troost ("Architect to the Führer") since fall 1933 in renovating the Reich Chancellery in Berlin, and who soon joined Hitler's innermost circle and was regularly brought along to Munich for "architectural discussions," has painted a memorable picture in *Inside the Third Reich* of the usual course of Hitler's stays in Munich. The Chancellor did not pay much attention "to state or Party business during his time in Munich," Speer wrote, but rather spent his time largely "vagabonding around" on "construction sites, studios, cafes, and restaurants." After a few days, they would all set out in several cars—convertibles with the tops down if the weather was fine—for the Obersalzberg, to "Hitler's cozy little wooden house with large overhanging eaves and modest rooms." Only hours after their arrival, according to Speer, did the secretaries Johanna Wolf and Christa Schroeder arrive, "most of the time along with an ordinary Munich girl."[92] These women's closed Mercedes was "never allowed to drive in the official motorcades." Then Hitler would stay, "with Eva Braun, an adjutant, and a servant," alone "in the small house," while the secretaries and Hitler's guests, often including Martin Bormann and Reich Press Chief Otto Dietrich along with Speer, were housed in a nearby pension.[93]

Speer's look back at the early years of his close friendship with Hitler portrays the Nazi leader in stark contrast to the way the "cult of the Führer" propaganda presented him; he describes a man in a light-blue linen jacket, in a remote, isolated mountain cabin, spending his days perusing construction plans or on long walks in the forest and his nights with his young lover.[94] Eva Braun, in turn, is described as an ordinary, nice, pretty, unassuming girl. Her relationship to Hitler is given only one brief, disparaging mention. According to Speer, Hitler and Eva Braun kept, even in this circle of close friends on the Obersalzberg, a "pointless distance from each other that came across as tense," avoiding any displays of intimacy on the one hand (to the point that Eva Braun was only allowed to walk "behind both the secretaries at the end of the procession" on their hikes), but "disappearing together into the upstairs bedroom" at the end of the night. Conflicts that arose from Eva Braun's "ambiguous position in Hitler's court," as Speer called it, are meanwhile hinted at only very briefly, such as when Speer writes that the Munich girl kept her distance from everybody and that this "withdrawn type of behavior" was held against her by many people as arrogance.[95]

This portrayal of Eva Braun, on the whole positive and even respectful, is noticeably different from the largely harsh and derogatory descriptions of her from other members of the inner circle. Only Karl Brandt, the young doctor who became Hitler's personal physician at age thirty in 1934, described Braun in similarly positive terms. Under questioning from the Americans by whom he was being held as a prisoner of war in 1945, he stated that he had "seen [Eva Braun] with Hitler for several years" before he realized "who and what she was." She had never "pushed herself into the foreground," always staying "in her place."[96] The Hitler-Braun rela-

Eva Braun with Hitler in front of the chimney stove in Haus Wachenfeld, 1935. To the left, Hitler's chauffeur Julius Schreck.

tionship seemed not to have been an "open secret," at least in the years before 1936. However, Brandt's statements and especially Speer's remarks indicate that, by 1934 at the latest, Eva Braun was a regular guest on the Obersalzberg.[97]

But is Speer, passing judgment such a long time after the fact, a reliable source? Doubts are in order—as indeed, in principle, they are in order with any eyewitness report. Numerous scholars in recent years have expressed reservations about the historical reliability of Speer's *Inside the Third Reich* and *Spandau: The Secret Diaries,* finding them to be "later, fictional constructions" in which Speer was demonstrably trying to minimize his involvement with Nazi crimes and to present the more positive, elevated image he had of himself.[98] The first of these points holds true, to a greater or lesser degree, of all of the surviving Nazis' postwar publications, the second point for most writers of memoirs in general. Nonetheless, eyewitness statements are not worthless. They only require constant critical testing and analysis.

Speer's description of the past remains informative, especially since he

spent over a decade as one of Hitler's most trusted colleagues. Speer's oldest son, also named Albert and also an architect, even told the film director and author Heinrich Breloer that there was "a very genuine, deep,
emotional relationship on both sides" between his father and Hitler.[99]
Speer himself, in a letter to his friend and former colleague Rudolf Wolters about his relationship with Hitler, wrote:

> I had a split relationship to Hitler. . . . It is probably typical of most
> friendships that they are built on contradictions. With Hitler I never
> once had the feeling that I had found a friend in him. Maybe it seemed
> different to you, from the outside. I was constantly living "in the fear
> of the Lord"—it was not easy to deal with him and stay in his favor or
> even, if possible, intensify it.[100]

In his memoir, Speer claims to have come "completely under the sway
of Hitler" but never to have known Hitler's "real face." Rather, he had
followed him "unwillingly, almost unconsciously, into a world" that was
"actually quite alien" to him.[101] Speer thereby casts himself not only as
an outsider who was led astray, but as an addict, dependent and even
possessed from without—a position he grants also to Eva Braun, seven
years younger than he was when the barely thirty-year-old architect apparently struck up a close and trusting friendship with her. In an interview
with Joachim Fest, Speer explained the reasons for his friendly relations
with Hitler's lover by saying that they were both equally prisoners of their
emotions, even enslaved: "She was, like me, under Hitler's so to speak
hypnotic spell. We both suffered under him, hated him at times, but were
still unable to break free of him."[102]

Now, does this retroactively negative account of Hitler, which elevates
him to a kind of Mephistopheles figure in the interest of Speer's own
self-justification, obstruct a clear view of Eva Braun as well?[103] Does it not
present her, like Speer himself, as less self-sufficient, more dependent,
and more passive than she really was? Did she share the political positions
and basic worldview of her lover or was she really the mere "tragic slave,"
who nonetheless profited from Hitler's power by enjoying the luxurious
life that he offered her? In any case, Speer, unlike those who continued to
hold fast to their respect for Hitler after 1945 and remained true believers
in the cult of the "Führer," had no need to minimize Eva Braun's significance. He thus remains, despite all of his strategies of mythification and

self-exoneration, a key witness, due to his extraordinary personal closeness with both Hitler and Eva Braun.[104]

The "Diary"

Meanwhile, hardly any letters or personal documents exist from the dictator himself or from his companion of many years that shed any light on the nature of their relationship, or Eva Braun's role, or how she saw her role. It is well known that Hitler rarely wrote private letters, aside from thank-you notes or birthday cards. His secretary Christa Schroeder, in fact, stated immediately after the end of the war that he had considered it "his great strength" that "even in the years of struggle he wrote no letters." Such letters might have fallen "into the wrong hands" and been "exploited."[105] He also, before his suicide, made sure to destroy the greater part of his private correspondence, of which there was presumably little to begin with. Julius Schaub, his adjutant of many years, left the bunker in Berlin for this reason at the end of April 1945, on direct orders from Hitler, in order to burn the private letters and files stored in safes at both Hitler's Munich apartment and at the Berghof.[106]

Similar testimony comes from Johannes Göhler, the former adjutant to Hermann Fegelein, the liaison officer who married Gretl Braun. In an interview with the British historian David Irving, who for years spared no effort in tracking down Hitler's letters to Eva Braun, Göhler said that he had flown from Berlin to Berchtesgaden in Hitler's airplane, a Ju 290, at the end of April 1945, in order to destroy all of Hitler's private correspondence there. Several hundred handwritten letters to and from Eva Braun were said to be included there, in a footlocker.[107] Irving's interest was piqued and so, years later, he questioned Göhler's wife, who told him that she had worked for the U.S. Army Counter Intelligence Corps (CIC) from August 1945 until February 1946, during which time she helped "an American CIC officer pack up Eva Braun's aforementioned diaries from 1933–1945 as well as her correspondence with Hitler"; she also said that she herself was in possession of letters that Eva Braun had written to Gretl Braun between 1930 and 1932. Finally, she claimed that Eva Braun's private papers stored at the Berghof were not destroyed in 1945, but rather were in the hands of Robert A. Gutierrez, the former head of the CIC team in Stuttgart. Irving, sensing a sensational find, went to the United

States and succeeded in tracking down Gutierrez. He did not, however, discover any private letters of Hitler's or Eva Braun's there.[108]

Eva Braun had actually instructed her sister Gretl in her last letter from Berlin, on April 23, 1945—a week before the double suicide—to take all of "the letters from the Führer" as well as "the copies of [her] replies" to him, which she had bequeathed to her sister in a will of October 26, 1944, and "make a water-resistant packet" and "bury them if need be." She explicitly insisted: "Please don't destroy them." The other private correspondence and "above all the business papers," on the other hand, Gretl should get rid of immediately. Eva Braun emphasized that "on no account must Heise's bills be found"—she had remained to the end a regular client of the well-known Berlin fashion designer Annemarie Heise.[109] In contrast to Hitler, who tried at the end to completely wipe out any trace of his private life, Eva Braun was trying, with her sister's help, to ensure that posterity would learn about her relationship with the "Führer" and her life at his side. Her letter from April 23, 1945, reveals a woman who, faced with death, was concerned about her image for posterity. In any case, none of the documents she asked her sister to preserve have been found to this day. It seems reasonable to suppose that Julius Schaub, who arrived at the Berghof on April 25—two days after Eva Braun had written her last letter to her sister—destroyed this correspondence together with Hitler's papers before Gretl Braun could bring them to safety. The final truth, however, remains unknown.

Nerin E. Gun also reported later that Gretl Braun and Herta Ostermayr had hidden "photograph albums, amateur films, letters, jewelry, and other mementos" in the park of Fischhorn Castle in the Pinzgau region of the state of Salzburg, near Zell am See. In fact, the former SS office of Fischhorn, a subcamp of the Dachau concentration camp, was used around the end of the war as a storage depot for stolen art and other "estates" of the Nazi elite who were going into hiding. There, supposedly, Gretl Braun took into her confidence a "German refugee," who turned out to be an American "agent," and Eva Braun's estate was confiscated by the U.S. Army and sent to Washington. Gun said that he had later "chanced to find" the documents again "in a corner of the American archives."[110] These are primarily the papers, photo albums, and films shot by Eva Braun that are now stored in the National Archives in Washington. There are no letters from Hitler to Eva Braun among them.

It is therefore necessary to turn to other sources to gain insight into the relationship that existed between Hitler and Eva Braun, and any details about that relationship. But there are not many other sources. Hitler's statements that shed light on his views of women in general, for example, are found mostly in the published postwar memoirs of his former followers or, for the years after 1942, in the records of conversations induced by Martin Bormann. Occasional hints can be found in various other diaries and correspondences. Eva Braun, though, is not mentioned. It is thus difficult to reconstruct their relationship, and the question of what actually attracted Hitler to this young woman can be addressed chiefly by means of his behavior with third parties. It is said of Speer, for example, that Hitler deliberately chose him to be his architect because he was modest, "normal" compared to his other followers, young, and easily influenced, and the notoriously suspicious Hitler could be assured of admiration from Speer, who was sixteen years younger.[111] Would these motives not also apply to Hitler's choice of Eva Braun, the youngest member of the inner circle around him? By reason of her youth alone, and her lower-middle-class background, even aside from the intimacy of their relationship, she must surely have been more pliable than the other members of his retinue.

In this context, only the twenty-page diary fragment in Eva Braun's papers, written in old-style German handwriting, sheds light on the character of their relationship. It is still controversial, however, whether it was actually written by her or not. While Nerin E. Gun had Ilse Fucke-Michels, Eva Braun's older sister, check the handwriting to confirm the authenticity of the document in 1967, the editor of Christa Schroeder's memoirs, Anton Joachimsthaler, claims that the handwriting of the document proves that it is a forgery.[112] The historian Werner Maser, meanwhile, maintains that it reveals "more about Hitler's relationship to women" than most of the interpretations of the "supposedly well-informed biographers."[113] Despite these doubts, or because of them, the "Diary," as it is called, has inspired all sorts of flights of fancy since its discovery and has been not only the object of scholarly studies but also material for fanciful stories.[114]

Anna Maria Sigmund has described these jottings as "a mirror of Eva Braun's psyche," but what are they actually about? In truth, they are the thoughts of a young woman of twenty-three, usually written down some three weeks after the events described and primarily circling around the irregular comings and goings of her much older lover. We learn that Eva

Braun celebrated her birthday, February 6, 1935, in Munich without Hitler. The Chancellor spent the day in Berlin but had Wilma Schaub, the
wife of his personal assistant Julius Schaub, send "flowers and a telegram"
to his girlfriend at Photohaus Hoffmann.[115] At the same time, Hitler
apparently continued to play the role of the solitary bachelor in the capital, with the support of his Minister of Propaganda. Goebbels, in any case,
who never tired of emphasizing his close friendship with the "Führer" in
his "Diaries," noted down after a conversation with Hitler on February 3:
"Big discussion with Führer. Personal. . . . Talks about women, marriage,
love, solitude. He talks that way only with me." Three days earlier, after
a meeting in Hitler's apartment in the Chancellery, Goebbels recorded
that Hitler had told him "about his lonely and joyless private life," without
"women, without love, still filled even now with the memory of Geli."[116]

We can infer from Eva Braun's "Diary" that she herself had never yet
been to Berlin. But a visit to the capital, and to see Hitler's renovated office
and living space at the Old Reich Chancellery, did seem planned for the
near future.[117] Paul Ludwig Troost, with his wife, the architect Gerhardine "Gerdy" Troost, and his colleague Leonhard Gall, had started work
on the new design for the "Führer apartment" in 1933 and had moved the
formal reception rooms from the second floor to the ground floor so that a
private office room for Hitler, a bedroom with bathroom, and, later, living
quarters for Eva Braun, could be set up on the second floor.[118]

According to the "Diary," Hitler did not see his girlfriend until February 11, and then again on February 18, when he apparently told her that
he did not want her to work at his friend Hoffmann's photography business anymore and that he wanted to give her a "little house." It would be
"marvelous" not to have to "play the part of a shopgirl" anymore, Braun
remarked.[119] Twelve days later, on the evening of Saturday, March 2,
their next meeting took place in Hitler's apartment at 16 Prinzregentenplatz.[120] If we are to trust the entry, she spent "two marvelously beautiful
hours with him until midnight" there. Afterward—with, she emphasized,
Hitler's "permission"—Braun amused herself alone until 2 a.m. at the
Munich city "ball": the great masquerade ball in the German Theater
that took place every year for Fasching (Mardi Gras). It was the most glittering event of the season.[121] On Sunday, Hitler suddenly took the train
back to Berlin "without saying goodbye," so that his lover and his personal
photographer, who had hurried to the train station after him, arrived "just
in time to see the rear lights of the last coach." Eva Braun had waited in

Eva Braun in blackface, dressed as the American singer and entertainer, Al Jolson, ca. 1930

vain for word from Hitler, despite calling the Osteria Bavaria and spending the afternoon waiting at Hoffmann's "like a cat on hot bricks" and hoping that Hitler would accept Hoffmann's invitation to "coffee and supper."[122]

While the young woman "rack[ed her] brains" over why her lover would have hurried off so early without saying goodbye to her, Hitler was awaiting British Foreign Secretary Sir John Simon's upcoming visit to Berlin, planned for March 7. Germany had been isolated internationally after Hitler's government had come to power and had unexpectedly withdrawn from the League of Nations. England, France, Austria, and even Italy under Benito Mussolini had protested the aggressive German foreign policy toward Austria and the unconcealed rearmament efforts of the National Socialists. The British government did, however, seem amenable to negotiations, although it announced an increase in military spending shortly before the meeting, with the justification that the German rearmament could "lead to a jeopardizing of the peace."[123] As a result, Hitler postponed the planned meeting with Simon on the spot and

announced over all the German radio stations, on March 16, a reintroduc-
tion of the general draft and the raising of thirty-six divisions—in other
words, the recruiting of more than half a million German soldiers.[124] This
was in open defiance of the Versailles Treaty.

That same day, Eva Braun wrote that it was "normal" that Hitler
"shouldn't take a great interest in [her] at the moment with everything
that's going on in politics." Hitler had spent the whole week leading up to
March 15 in Bavaria, but had returned to Berlin without, as he usually did,
seeing her.[125] She had waited desperately for him, and even stood watch
on Monday in the middle of a crowd of curious onlookers in front of the
Hotel Carlton in Schwabing to see him congratulate the movie star Anny
Ondra, wife of the German boxing idol Max Schmeling, with a bouquet
of flowers, for Schmeling's victory over the American Steve Hamas in
a qualifying match for the world championship.[126] Eva Braun had met
Ondra the previous year, when Hitler invited her and her husband to
have a coffee in Franz Xaver Schwarz's house on the Tegernsee over
Pentecost weekend, presumably on May 20, 1934. Schwarz, the powerful
National Treasurer of the NSDAP, cultivated familiar relations with Hitler. So on this occasion, Eva Braun, too, along with Hitler, Hoffmann (a
friend of Schmeling's), Schaub, and Brückner, sat in the garden around
the coffee table. Schmeling wrote in his *Erinnerungen* (Autobiography)
that he noticed this unknown young woman because she "spoke entirely
naturally and obviously very familiarly with Hitler, despite all her outward
modesty." When he tried to find out from Hoffmann who she was, Hoffmann was secretive at first but then told Schmeling her name, nothing
more, and said that she was an employee of his.[127]

Hitler and the Nazi leadership made considerable propagandistic use
of Schmeling's sports successes; for his part, after his knockout win in
Hamburg on March 10, 1935, Schmeling gave the Hitler salute in the
ring in front of twenty-five thousand spectators.[128] The "dream couple"
of Schmeling and Ondra had already shot a film together—*Knock-out—
Ein Junges Mädchen, Ein Junger Mann* (Knock-out—A Young Girl, A
Young Man)—that had premiered in German theaters a few days earlier,
on March 1. Hitler quite consciously made use of their popularity—just
a few days before the coup with its foreign-relations risks—to promote
the identification of the masses with the Nazi state. He thereby satisfied
German society's need for national greatness and at the same time demonstrated to the world Germany's renewed strength and readiness to fight,

which Schmeling had so impressively proven. The decision, made by Hitler alone, to defy the military limitations of the Versailles Treaty and thus "thumb his nose at Versailles," as the American foreign correspondent William L. Shirer put it, won enormous popularity for the National Socialist government. Unhappy Eva Braun, jealously fearing the end of her relationship, had no idea about any of this.[129]

Two weeks later, when she was among the group of Munich friends whom Hitler invited to dinner at the posh Four Seasons hotel on March 31, 1935, the event itself did not warrant a single line in her diary. She and Hitler had not met in private even once in the intervening month, so she would hardly have felt honored by a semiofficial group invitation to the hotel that Hitler liked to use for celebrations, and where the Populist and anti-Semitic Thule Society had its offices as well.[130] On the contrary, she felt oppressed by the need "to sit beside him for three hours without being able to say a single word to him." Her tenacious waiting for "a line of greeting or a kind word" from him was also to be once again disappointed: when Hitler said goodbye, he merely handed her "an envelope with some money inside as he had already done once before."[131] In the years that followed, too, Hitler occasionally supplied her with cash in this way. Speer told Joachim Fest that Hitler, after dining at the Four Seasons on another occasion in 1938 with "members of the Berghof crowd and upper-level Party members," had given Eva Braun an "envelope," "in passing" and "more businesslike than anything else." Speer seemed "openly outraged," even decades later, at the low opinion of Eva Braun that this behavior of Hitler's expressed, especially the contrast between it and Hitler's "Viennese" manners with women in general; the gesture reminded Speer of something you would see in "American gangster films."[132]

Hitler, meanwhile, had every reason to be in a celebratory and generous mood at the end of March 1935. The visit from British Foreign Secretary Simon and Lord Privy Seal Anthony Eden on March 25 and 26 had been a gratifying success, despite Germany's open violation of the Versailles Treaty. Hitler had confidently given long explanations to his patiently listening guests, justifying the necessity of German rearmament, a topic that had been "absolutely taboo for years" at the meetings of the League of Nations in Geneva.[133] The aristocratic and reconciliatory restraint of the British, who even declared themselves open to a naval treaty in later negotiations, gave the Nazi leaders another great foreign-policy success and gain in prestige, as had the plebiscite of January 13, 1935, in which

*Hitler on the
Obersalzberg, purportedly
receiving the news of
the official results of the
Saar plebiscite over the
telephone, January 1935*

91 percent of the population of the Saar had voted for reunification with
Germany. Hitler's ruthless foreign policy was rewarded with Great Britain's acknowledgment of a de facto revision of the Versailles Treaty.[134]

In his private life, though, Hitler's mercilessness had led to another
catastrophe. For three long months, from early March to late May, Eva
Braun had waited for her lover to spend time with her as usual, or even for
a "good word" from him, as she wrote in her diary. But Hitler wouldn't see
her. He was working feverishly on an "alliance with England," to fracture
the existing international treaties and end Germany's international isolation. "Love seems not to be on his agenda at the moment," Braun noted
on April 29.

But there seemed to be, or actually were, personal reasons keeping Hitler in Berlin as well: a "love affair" with Baroness Sigrid von Laffert was
imputed to him, and he was in poor health. The rumor of a romance (pla-

tonic, however) with Sigrid von Laffert, a young relative of Viktoria von
Dirksen, was circulating in Berlin throughout the spring.[135] Von Dirksen,
the widow of Willibald von Dirksen, secret legations counsel under the
Kaiser, was an avowed Nazi and a supporter of Hitler's for many years; her
salon on Margaretenstrasse, in the late 1920s and early 1930s, was the most
important meeting point where the old nobility and prominent National
Socialists made contact. Her brother, the Mecklenburg landowner Karl
August von Laffert, was among the many aristocrats who joined the elite,
cultlike SS in spring 1933, and he provided the organization with financial
support and trained managerial staff.[136]

It is thus hardly surprising that Viktoria von Dirksen provided access to
the Nazi elite to the nineteen-year-old relative living with her in Berlin.
The young woman had herself spent the year 1932–1933 in the "Alliance of
German Maidens" (Bund Deutscher Mädel, or BDM), the girls' branch
of the Hitler Youth—which was not yet obligatory—and she would join
the NSDAP in 1938.[137] The young blonde was, the servant Heinz Linge
later said, one of the "most beautiful women" around Hitler, and Hitler
invited her to "all festive occasions." For example, she appeared amid the
Nazi leadership on May 1, 1934, when a "National Day of Celebration
of the German People," designed by the government to allude to a German popular spring festival, was conducted in an enormous propaganda
spectacle at Tempelhof Field. As one of the women who represented the
government in public, she did have a certain importance, a fact of which
Hitler was clearly aware: he selected such candidates personally, with an
eye to their visual effect.[138] As late as March 1939, Laffert was among the
guests invited to a state dinner in the Chancellor's residence.[139] It is certainly possible that Eva Braun in Munich, forbidden from such appearances, heard about the rumors going around Berlin in early 1935.

In addition, Hitler's health was in poor shape. Since the start of the year
he had suffered from nervous tinnitus at night and hoarseness, and was
afraid of dying of throat cancer, as the German emperor Friedrich III had
in 1888. On May 23, 1935, only two days after his second so-called Peace
Address in the Kroll Opera House in Berlin, which had attracted attention abroad as well (in it, he finally paved the way for German-English
alliance talks), he underwent an operation in the Reich Chancellery. The
doctor who treated him, Carl Otto von Eicken, a professor at the Charité
in Berlin and an expert on throat cancer, removed a polyp from the vocal
folds and recommended four weeks of recovery. Years later, an article

*Adolf Hitler and Sigrid von Laffert with Joseph and Magda Goebbels in the
dignitaries' box at the German Opera House in Berlin, December 1935. To the
left, Hitler's personal assistant Wilhelm Brückner.*

in *Time* magazine dated November 14, 1938, reported an interview with
Eicken, who was at a convention in Philadelphia, and stated that the simple medical procedure had given rise to great concern at the time. Hitler,
after being given anesthetics, had slept for fourteen hours straight.[140] Hitler waited three months before he spoke again in public, in Rosenheim
on August 11, 1935.

Under political stress and in impaired health as he was, it is hardly
surprising that Hitler did not find time for the young Munich girl. But
Eva Braun clearly took his behavior personally. On May 28, five days after
his operation and while the Chancellery was working full steam preparing for the upcoming German-English arms negotiations, Eva Braun, for
the second time in three years, attempted suicide in Munich. This time
it was not her father's revolver but an overdose of sleeping pills that was
supposed to, as her diary-fragment put it, "make 'dead sure' " of the situation.[141]

Did Braun really want to die? Was it an act of despair or a blackmail
attempt? She had, if we believe the "Diary," sent Hitler a "decisive" letter
on the day of the attempt, but the question of whether the letter told him

of her suicide must remain unanswered since the letter no longer exists and there is no other evidence for its having existed. In any case, the events of May 28, 1935, remain unclear. The suicide attempt is attested to only in Nerin E. Gun's account, based on an interview with the Braun family but not documented with a historian's thoroughness. According to Gun, Ilse Braun, as in Eva's first suicide attempt, found Eva unconscious that night. She gave first aid and called a doctor. It was also Ilse Braun who found her sister's diary on this occasion and removed the relevant pages, in order to keep the second suicide attempt and its causes secret. There is no mention of this incident in the memoir literature. Whether Hitler himself, who was in Munich at the time, ever even heard about it is not recorded.[142] The events of the following months, however, suggest that he did.

6

THE MYTH OF THE "FÜHRER," OR HERR HITLER IN PRIVATE

The first piece of circumstantial evidence in this regard is the fact that Eva Braun moved out of her parents' house on August 9, 1935, and with her sister Gretl and a Hungarian maid moved into a three-bedroom apartment at 42 Widenmayerstrasse, rented for her by Heinrich Hoffmann. Hitler, whose apartment on Prinzregentenplatz was only five minutes away, had suggested the arrangement and paid for the apartment via his agent, Hoffmann.[1] By giving Eva Braun material support and thereby giving her a clear sign of his affection, Hitler was obviously trying to avoid wider attention and especially the scandal that would certainly have been unavoidable after a successful suicide attempt on his lover's part. He also allowed her closer contact with him. She was even permitted to appear at public events, which until then she had been strictly forbidden to attend.

At the 1935 Party Convention in Nuremberg

For example, in September 1935, four months after her second suicide attempt and four weeks after moving into the apartment of her own that Hitler paid for, she attended an NSDAP convention for the first time, in Nuremberg.[2] This annual event, with its marches, torchlight processions at night, parades, and roll calls, had no purpose other than propaganda and was centered from start to finish on Hitler, whom hundreds of thousands of supporters welcomed and celebrated like a messiah. In 1935, the convention lasted from September 10 to September 16 and had as its motto "Convention of Freedom," in reference to Germany's (at least partial) liberation from the Versailles Treaty and regaining of room to maneuver militarily.[3] In addition, the session of Parliament that Hitler convened during the convention and summoned specially to Nuremberg passed, on September 15, the so-called Nuremberg Laws, hastily drawn up the previous day, which expelled Jewish citizens from the "Volksgemeinschaft" and robbed them of their civil rights.[4]

There is no authenticated information about the extent to which Eva Braun knew of these proceedings, or even when exactly she arrived in Nuremberg. There are, however, suggestions that she traveled to Nuremberg together with her boss, Heinrich Hoffmann, and Hoffmann's wife and son, along with other employees of his firm, "Heinrich Hoffmann: Publisher of National Socialist Pictures."[5] Hoffmann's business had turned into a major concern, with sales in the millions, and since he was obviously at the convention from the beginning, in his capacity as "Reich Photographic Correspondent of the NSDAP," we can presume that Eva Braun was there on the first day as well, when Hitler was driven through the city in an open car and was welcomed in the Nuremberg Historical City Hall by the mayor.[6] Ernst Hanfstaengl, who had the task of welcoming the international press in the great hall of the Cultural Union building on the afternoon of September 10, recalled that Braun had come to the convention "inconspicuously," but in an "expensive fur."[7] She probably also saw the impressive propaganda spectacle staged by Albert Speer on the zeppelin field located five kilometers southeast of the city center, where, on September 12 at 10 a.m., a roll call of the Reich Labor Service took place with an accompanying march "past the Führer"; on the following day came the roll call of the political leaders; and on the last day, September 16, starting at 9 a.m., the presentation of the armed forces, ending that night with a ceremonial tattoo.[8] In 1935, though, the zeppelin field was still bare—the well-known monumental stone architectural features, including the gigantic gilded swastika, were built only two years later. The tribunals, speaker's platform, and colossal eagle lit with several spotlights were still made of wood in 1935; Speer's

idea of a "cathedral of light," created from the beams of antiaircraft spotlights, was tested out for the first time this year, but not yet put into full
effect.[9]

For Eva Braun, meanwhile, the convention meant a further development in her relationship to Hitler. For the first time, she was allowed
to take part in an official NSDAP event along with the wives of leading
Nazis—Ilse Hess, Margarete "Marga" Himmler, and Gerda Bormann,
among others. Her presence apparently met with resistance from some
of the women, though, especially Hitler's energetic half-sister, Angela
Raubal, who kept house for him in Berchtesgaden. Herbert Döhring, the
later manager of the Berghof household, recalled after the war that "Frau
Raubal and Frau Goebbels and all these ministers' wives" were "completely shocked" that "this young, capricious, and dissatisfied-looking girl
was sitting there on the VIP rostrum."[10] Döhring, twenty-two years old
at the time and thus slightly younger than Braun, was a member of the
"Führer protection command" stationed in the Deutscher Hof hotel and
responsible for Hitler's personal safety; he could hardly have learned anything of the conflicts among the women on the VIP stage from his own
experience. He had possibly not even met Eva Braun by that point in
time. His judgment must therefore have been based partly on rumors,
partly on his later experiences at the Berghof.

Still, Julius Schaub, Hitler's personal adjutant and close associate of
many years, who followed the Nazi leader "like a shadow," in Christa
Schroeder's words, also claimed that there was "a rather tense relationship" between Raubal and Braun at the convention.[11] Schroeder herself,
a secretary in the "Führer's personal staff" in the Reich Chancellery since
1933, remarks that Angela Raubal could not stand Eva Braun from the
beginning, and that Raubal expressed to her brother her disapproval of
Braun's, in her view, "very conspicuous" behavior in Nuremberg. Schroeder said that Raubal later had to "leave the mountain"* on Hitler's wish,
and "all the other ladies" who made themselves noticeable "with disparaging remarks" were not permitted "to enjoy" the "hospitality of the house"
for long.[12]

Angela Raubal did in fact leave the Obersalzberg on February 18, 1936,
after more than seven years there, but she returned, it seems, for occasional visits. In any case, on May 22, 1936, she wrote in a letter to Rudolf

* Translator's note: "Mountain" is *Berg* in German, a pun on *"Berghof"* ("mountain estate").

Hess from Dresden that she was planning to accompany her husband on a study trip at the end of June that would pass through Munich and Berchtesgaden. She added: "Especially since my brother was here in Dresden and I spoke to him again after such a long time and he promised to come over to see us for coffee soon, I have been so wildly happy, I am afraid the gods will envy me."[13] Apparently Hitler had reestablished contact with his half-sister after only a few months. It is no longer possible to ascertain whether Eva Braun was the only reason for Raubal's departure.[14] The recollections of the members of Hitler's personal staff clearly show, however, how dramatic Eva Braun's rise seemed from the point of view of the staff and the servants. The sudden departure of Hitler's half-sister clearly showed them that anyone who dared to criticize Eva Braun or her relationship with Hitler would have to reckon with being laid off. As a result, the young woman's position in the inner circle became practically untouchable.

The Unnoticed Climb

Nonetheless, even in Nuremberg, only a few initiates knew who Eva Braun actually was. On the record, she remained invisible, and she did not stay at Hotel Kaiserhof like the wives and other female guests, such as Hitler's architect Gerdy Troost, Marga Himmler, and Gerda Bormann. (Like all lodgings in the city during the convention, Hotel Kaiserhof could be entered only with a "residence pass" given out by the management.) Instead, it is very probable that Braun, along with Marianne (Marion) Schönmann, a friend she had brought along from Munich, moved in Heinrich Hoffmann's circle as his colleague.[15] So it cannot be ruled out that she, like her boss, stayed with Hitler's entourage in the Deutscher Hof on the Altstadtring, across from the Opera House, where Hitler occupied the second floor of the hotel, as per tradition, during his stay in this "most German of all cities." Hitler had personally prohibited the wives of other Party members from being housed there, so he may well have presumed that Eva Braun, accompanied by Hoffmann, would arouse the least attention there.[16]

A photograph taken on the occasion of Hoffmann's fiftieth birthday on September 12, 1935, in Nuremberg, shows that Hoffmann's circle at the time included not only Braun and Schönmann, his family, and

other colleagues, but also Max Schmeling and the photographer Atto
Retti-Marsani.[17] Presumably, Braun also received complimentary tickets
to the various events at the convention through Hoffmann. In general,
tickets for the convention, which were sent out from the Braune Haus
(Brown House) in Munich in the "Führer's" name and signed by Rudolf
Hess, were extremely sought-after and hard to come by. Ilse Hess, loyal
to the Party line as always, decisively rejected a relative's request in the
run-up to the convention as follows: "Unfortunately, the tickets are in
such short supply that even many old comrades-in-arms in the movement
are having to stay away. In these circumstances, it is even less possible for
me to give preference to a relative who is not among the long-standing
Party faithful."[18] Eva Braun, meanwhile, was able to remain discreet, with
Hoffmann's help, even though she became a fixture in Hitler's innermost
circle from then on. Within a year—with or without a suicide attempt—
she had managed to decisively change the circumstances of her life with
Hitler, entirely to her benefit.

Eva Braun now lived in her own apartment, and a few months later
would move with her younger sister Gretl into her own house, with a
garden, in Bogenhausen, a neighborhood in Munich filled with aristocratic villas. In addition, she was a constant presence at the Berghof from
1936 on, and received Hitler in his refuge on the Obersalzberg, which
became her second residence along with Munich. She even occasionally
traveled abroad with him. Since she was concealed in his retinue as a "private secretary," outsiders had no idea that this young blond woman might
be the lover of the unmarried dictator. Eva Braun's "constant presence,"
which made such an impression on Hanfstaengl, was apparent only to
those who themselves had, or had once had, close personal contact with
Hitler.[19]

A "Lost Life"?

It is true that the formal status of lawfully wedded wife remained unat-
tainable for Braun, but did that make her life a "lost" one, as the British
biographer Angela Lambert put it right in the title of her book *The Lost
Life of Eva Braun?*[20] What was the actual difference between Braun's own
mode of existence and that of other wives or girlfriends of high-ranking
National Socialist politicians? Did it correspond to the typical role of

women in her time and social class, or had she taken on, with her tie to Hitler, an "undignified courtesan's role"? Is it true that she lived like a slave and was allowed to leave Munich only with Hitler's or Bormann's permission?[21]

Ernst Hanfstaengl, who made these claims after the war, was himself strongly under Hitler's spell and had, despite his upper-middle-class family background and education at Harvard University, supported the NSDAP as early as 1922. After his failed putsch on November 8–9, 1923, Hitler fled first to a house in Uffing am Staffelsee in the Upper Bavarian Alpine foothills some forty-five miles from Munich owned by the Hanfstaengl family. And during Hitler's following yearlong prison term in Landsberg am Lech, Hanfstaengl was among the faithful supporters who visited him many times in jail.[22] Hanfstaengl's intimate knowledge of Hitler's personal relationships was limited, though, to the 1920s and early 1930s. By the 1935 convention, he had been cut off from personal contact with Hitler for more than a year. Having fallen into disgrace, he flew to Great Britain in 1937 and tried, unsuccessfully, to achieve rehabilitation with Hitler as a "patriot and Party comrade," via Hans Heinrich Lammers, head of the Reich Chancellery, and Julius Streicher, Gauleiter of Nuremberg.[23]

Years later, the fact that Hanfstaengl had once been in close personal contact with Hitler unexpectedly turned out to work to his advantage. During the war, he was set free from the Canadian prisoner of war camp where he was being held as an enemy alien deported from Great Britain, and promoted to a position working for the Office of Strategic Services (OSS), the American secret service. Under the name "Dr. Sedgwick," he provided John F. Carter, President Roosevelt's adviser and news analyst, with information about how it would be possible to break the political power of the National Socialists in Germany.[24] Hanfstaengl's later assessment of Hitler's relationship with Eva Braun reflects, first and foremost, the cultural norms current in the 1930s, along with the church practices and civil laws, according to which extramarital sexuality was considered unnatural and immoral. Hanfstaengl's characterization of Braun's presence in Hitler's inner circle as shameful and disruptive also testifies to his unbroken perpetuation of the myth of a "Führer" who could not be judged by human standards, and whom Hanfstaengl (himself a notorious ladies' man) did not want to see undermined by a relationship that was inappropriate on any terms.[25]

Hitler and the Braun Family

In the context of the restrictive sexual morality reigning in Germany, and
Eva Braun's education by Catholic nuns, it is no wonder that Eva's parents,
Friedrich and Franziska Braun, disapproved of their daughter's lifestyle at
first. We do not know when and in what circumstances they first learned
of her relationship with Hitler. It does seem rather implausible, however,
that they learned of it only in the late summer of 1935, after Eva Braun
moved out into her own apartment, and after they met her with Hitler,
supposedly by accident—and still less plausible that they knew of their
daughter's connection to the Chancellor only in 1937.[26] The only way the
idea of such a relationship could have failed to occur to her parents was if
they attributed their daughter's unbourgeois habits and behavior of many
years—the sudden appearance of a phone line; the irregular coming and
going; the nights spent out—to her work for Photohaus Hoffmann.

   Braun's parents' first meeting with Hitler allegedly took place in the
Lambacher Hof, an inn (which still exists today) on the north shore of
the Chiemsee approximately halfway between Munich and the Obersalzberg. Hitler, who used to travel on the old road along the lake before
the Munich–Salzburg autobahn was finished, often stopped in there
with his companions. The Nazi leader was allegedly introduced to his
girlfriend's parents there for the first time on a Sunday in late August
1935, or perhaps on September 1, after returning from the dedication of
an "Adolf-Hitler-Koog" land reclamation in the Dithmarschen region of
Schleswig-Holstein. Nerin E. Gun reports that the Brauns had gone for a
Sunday outing to Lambach, and that there, totally unexpectedly, they ran
into their daughter, who was in the Chancellor's retinue as a colleague of
Heinrich Hoffmann's. Apparently nothing more than a short but friendly
greeting took place, and the Brauns are said to have known nothing about
their daughter's relationship with Hitler at that time.[27]

   Henriette von Schirach, on the other hand, claims that Friedrich
Braun intentionally traveled the more than sixty miles from Munich to
visit the inn in Lambach on that occasion and bring about a discussion
with Hitler, because he saw in Hitler's connection to his daughter "a
chance for his favorite child." She says that Hitler described this conversation as "the most unpleasant [conversation] of his life," but it nonetheless
resulted in Hitler's supporting Eva Braun with a monthly sum of money
and a house.[28]

   In fact, given the few and variously transmitted postwar statements by the family, we can only speculate about what Friedrich and Franziska Braun actually knew and thought, and what roles the two sisters, Ilse and Margarete (Gretl), might have played in the situation.[29] Whenever it is a matter of looking back from a great temporal distance—twenty years in this case—we must always keep in mind that people's perceptions, subjective to begin with, may be discussed, whitewashed, rearranged, and corrected many times over as the years go by. With the Braun family, where the issue is direct proximity to Hitler and thus knowledge of, even perhaps participation in, Nazi crimes, we can presume a certain amount of keeping silent, out of either shame or fear of criminal prosecution.[30] Would the Brauns not have had good reason, in their conversations with the journalist Gun after such a long period of silence, to play down any early knowledge of Braun's relationship with Hitler and even claim to have been opposed to it?[31]

In fact, Friedrich and Franziska Braun had already had to answer such questions in 1947, before a Munich denazification court. These appointed German trial and appellate tribunals and public prosecutors were given the responsibility of "denazifying" Germany under the "Law for Liberation from National Socialism and Militarism" imposed by the American military authorities in 1946. People were classified into the categories of Major Offenders, Offenders (activists, militarists, and profiteers), Lesser Offenders (probationers), Followers, and Persons Exonerated.

The public prosecutors in this case, according to an article called (in German) "Hitler's In-laws Before the Judge" in the newspaper *Die Welt* of August 2, 1947, put the "high-school business instructor Fritz Wilhelm Otto Braun and his wife Franziska Katharina" into the category of "Offenders," that is, according to the law, "activists, militarist, and profiteers." Eva's parents were threatened with prison sentences, confiscation of property, and—especially for the father—a ban on employment and the loss of his pension. Fritz Braun, it was claimed, had known about his daughter's relationship with Hitler, approved of it, and was in fact proud of it. Eva's mother, too, although never a Party member, was labeled an "activist" by the official prosecutor.[32] In the indictment from July 9, 1947, it was stated that the investigations had shown that "the person in question had been proud that daughter Eva was permitted to be the Führer's lover for all those years. The persons in question felt at home on the Obersalzberg. Since she was a member of the family, she didn't need to be a member of the Party."[33]

Threatened in this way, their very existence under attack—Fritz Braun, fired from public service as a teacher, was struggling along as a carpentry assistant at the time—the Brauns were obviously making every effort to minimize before the judge the intimacy of their daughter's relationship with Hitler. They stated that Eva Braun had become the dictator's "house-keeper" in 1933, and that he had "maintained a love affair with her" ever since, on terms that were "never entirely clear, but seemed to be purely platonic."[34] And at a public sitting of the Munich denazification court, on December 1, 1947, Fritz Braun stated:

> I do not know when the relationship between my daughter Eva and Hitler started. I first heard about it in 1937, from a Czech newspaper. Until then I had thought she was his secretary.[35]

The Brauns told *Die Welt* through their Munich lawyer, Otto Gritsch-neder, that they planned "to offer proof that they had always been opposed to the relationship between their daughter and Adolf Hitler." For example, they had allegedly even written a letter to Hitler, explaining that this "sleazy relationship" was not to be endured any longer.[36] The letter was, however, "suppressed and never presented" to him. Fritz Braun testified before the denazification court that he had "written a letter to the Führer and pointed out to him that I did not approve of his simply taking my daughter out of our family circle without notifying us." Braun was, he said, "furious about Hitler."[37]

It is doubtful that any such document, which would have exonerated Friedrich and Franziska Braun from the claim that they had been "activists" in the Nazi state or "profiteers" in Hitler's inner circle, ever existed. The only document that has been supplied as proof comes from the family: a copy, if we believe Gun's account, of a letter that Friedrich Braun wrote to the Chancellor on September 7, 1935—about a month after his daughter had moved out—and wanted to give to Heinrich Hoffmann so that he could pass it along to Hitler.[38] Hoffmann was visiting and pho-tographing the construction projects on Königsplatz in Munich at the time; in accordance with the plans drawn up by Paul Ludwig Troost, who had died the previous year, more than twenty thousand granite slabs were being laid and Nazi emblems being affixed to create a parade square.[39] Hitler himself was spending a few days on the Obersalzberg before the start of the NSDAP convention in Nuremberg, as he usually did; he regu-larly retreated there weeks before such conventions to write his speeches,

Eva Braun in Florence with her travel companions. From left to right: Franziska Braun, Margarete Speer, Anni Brandt, Eva Braun, Marianne Schönmann (undated).

and he was due to give no fewer than seventeen speeches at the upcoming convention.[40]

It is therefore entirely possible that Friedrich Braun gave Hoffmann this letter in Munich—a letter in which he asked Hitler "to see to it" that his daughter "return to the family." But to treat this document, even if it existed, as retrospective proof of a rebellion against Hitler is nonsense. It can only be interpreted as an act of despair. First of all, it never reached its intended recipient, either because it never in fact existed or because Hoffmann and Braun made sure that Hitler never learned about it. Second, the relations between Eva's parents and Hitler in the years to follow cast serious doubt on the claim that they felt her relationship with Hitler to be a "bitter disgrace."[41]

In fact, Eva Braun's departure from the parental home at the beginning of August 1935 did not mark a break with the family. Rather, Franziska Braun was a welcome guest on the Obersalzberg in the following ten years, and she accompanied her daughter on numerous trips, especially to

Italy, but also, in 1938, to Vienna. No conclusions about Franziska Braun's own personal relationship with Hitler can be drawn—both contemporary witnesses and third-party reports from after the end of the war are lacking. She was, however, the only member of Braun's family whom Hitler mentioned in his last will and testament, personally dictated on April 29, 1945, a day before his and Eva Braun's suicide in the bunker. He instructed Martin Bormann, the secretary to whom he gave full powers of executor, to leave everything "that possesses any personal sentimental value, or that is necessary to supporting a petit-bourgeois life," to his siblings and "likewise especially the mother of my wife" and the "faithful staff." Franziska Braun thus ranked ahead of Hitler's blood relatives, on the same level as his loyal companions who had "supported [him] for years through their work." This emphasis on Eva's mother is especially noteworthy in that neither of Eva's two sisters, nor her father, is mentioned in the testament.[42]

Can we derive from this fact a broken relationship between father and daughter, or Friedrich Braun's opposition to the Nazi regime itself? The reasons for Hitler's last instructions remain mysterious. For one thing, Friedrich Braun joined the NSDAP on May 1, 1937. For another, he testified before the court in 1947 that he had believed "to the end" in the "Führer." He also said in his statement of December 1, 1947, that his daughter would "never have entered a relationship with Hitler . . . if he had been a bad person."[43] However, his daughter's personal relationship with Hitler cannot have been the actual reason for his joining the Party. In fact, it is well known that Hitler strictly kept his relatives away from any political activity. For example, according to a statement by his sister, Paula Wolf, he invited every member of the family to the 1929 NSDAP convention in Nuremberg, where they had to promise not to join the Party.[44] It therefore seems reasonable to assume that Eva Braun was held to similar rules of conduct and that her not being a member of the Party can be traced back to Hitler's instructions. This strategy of forestalling any possible private interference in his political activities was typical of Hitler, although the case of his half-sister, Angela Raubal (later Angela Hammitzsch), shows that it clearly did not always work. She seems to have interfered even after her removal from the Obersalzberg, as is clear from a letter to Ilse Hess, and she sent "repeated requests" to government officials and Party organizations—including Interior Minister Wilhelm Frick—to inform them whenever, in her opinion, "something was not proceeding properly."[45]

In this context, it is hard to imagine that Hitler especially advocated the entry of his girlfriend's father into the NSDAP, never mind required it. Rather, it seems as though Friedrich Braun, like many teachers in the "Third Reich," merely accommodated the National Socialist regime at first before eventually, not least out of opportunism, making his turn toward the new worldview official. More than 80 percent of the members of this profession became members of the NSDAP only after January 30, 1933, and thus had the reputation among the Party leaders of being "opportunists."[46] To prevent such people from joining, a ban on new members was put into effect starting in 1933 and cancelled only on April 20, 1937, after which point all "Party aspirants" had to fill out an additional two-page questionnaire with their applications, describing in detail their efforts to date for the "movement." All of these new members, no matter what date they filed their application, were given a membership acceptance date of May 1, 1937.[47]

In addition, the Nazi educational politics since 1935 had moved in the direction of turning all teachers into "National Socialist People's educators." Especially in Bavaria after late November 1936—when Adolf Wagner, the powerful Gauleiter and Interior Minister known for his fanatical anti-Semitism, took over the additional title of Bavarian State Minister for Education and Culture, a post that had been vacant for two years— those who were not Party members were given considerably less leeway. Since that was precisely when Friedrich Braun submitted his application, according to his own testimony, Adolf Wagner could well have played a crucial role in prompting Friedrich Braun's entry into the NSDAP, along with Braun's own personal reasons.[48]

Still, Braun's membership was not merely a formality. On November 8, 1939, shortly after the war began, he took part in the memorial event for the failed Hitler putsch of 1923, in Munich's Bürgerbräukeller—among the "old fighters," no less.[49] Friedrich Braun was not actually a member of the "old guard": he had been a Party member for only two years, and he is not known to have been particularly active in Munich NSDAP circles. Thus he actually should not have been admitted to this event at all—it was an occasion reserved for "Party fanatics," according to Ian Kershaw. But it is possible that Eva Braun—perhaps through Heinrich Hoffmann— arranged for an invitation for her father so that he could hear the "Führer." In any case, he ended up in the middle of the dynamite attack against Hitler that took place on that night, leaving eight dead and sixty-three wounded. Friedrich Braun survived, though he was wounded, while Hitler, after an hour-long speech that "decisively broke with England" (as Goebbels recorded), had left the hall a quarter of an hour before the detonation.[50] The episode shows that there was certainly no unbridge-able chasm between father and daughter, or distance between Friedrich Braun and the Nazi state.

7

The Mistress and the Inner Circle

Eva Braun's rise from anonymity into the inner circle around Hitler necessarily brought with it new acquaintances and new relationships that were very demanding for the socially inexperienced young woman from Munich. She thus stayed extremely reserved at first with all the other guests on the Obersalzberg, who were the Nazi leader's close staff members. Instead, she surrounded herself primarily with her younger sister and friends she invited to the Berghof herself or brought with her from Munich. She came into contact with Hitler's confidants exclusively on the Obersalzberg (with a few exceptions). In any case, her contact there was limited at first to a few people whom Hitler selected personally and considered trustworthy.

Albert and Margarete Speer

Albert Speer was a central figure in Hitler's inner circle. And Speer's presence, and that of his wife, in what he himself called "Hitler's court" was of great importance to him and his position in the regime. His presence and "human" proximity to Hitler offered unique access to power and success

Margarete Speer on the Berghof terrace (undated)

to this architect who had lived until 1932 with, for all practical purposes, no income. As a result of this proximity, he suddenly had "the most exciting prospects" for professional success, at not even thirty years of age, and in 1937 he rose to be General Building Inspector for the Reich Capital, appointed by and reporting directly to Hitler. He now had sole control over the planning and carrying out of all municipal construction projects.

Social life on the Obersalzberg, on the other hand, was described by Speer as a "waste of time": it was "agonizing" for him, he said, and "what remain[ed]" of it "in [his] memory" was only "a curious vacuity."[1] Still, he worked assiduously to fit in with this community and included his wife, Margarete, from the start as well. Margret Nissen, Speer's younger daughter, said that her mother's role on the Obersalzberg consisted in "being there to perform official duties at her husband's side."[2] Whenever they were wanted, the Speers took part in lunches, dinners, afternoon diversions, or parties, at the Berghof or elsewhere. They also made particular efforts to include Eva Braun, who, like them, was athletic and enthusiastic about sports. They took her skiing, for example, even though Hitler "didn't like to see" such outings for fear of injuries.[3] In a private document written a few years before her death, from which her daughter published excerpts, Margarete Speer described how drastically their daily activities were curtailed by Hitler's needs. Here is the usual procedure for "lunch with the Führer":

> The phone rings. It might be two, three, sometimes even four o'clock. A friendly male voice: "The Führer requests your presence at the table." I've been ready for a long time, sitting around waiting. Albert and I are fetched. . . . [4]

While Margarete Speer—after waiting in her apartment for the summons, sometimes for hours on end—is served her food at the Berghof, a governess and a housekeeper take care of the six Speer children. The youngest daughter later said, looking back on her childhood on the Obersalzberg, that she had "grown up basically without parents in those years," since her mother and father were "more often traveling" than at home.[5] Margarete Speer's activities were thus not limited, as one might have expected, to her own household. Rather, she apparently neglected her family to support her husband's career, based as it was solely on his personal ties to Hitler. To that extent, Margarete Speer may not have been acting in a political sphere, but in a "private" sphere she was no less significant and professionally useful. And she enjoyed such a life. Unlike her husband, who later made derisive comments about it, she described "living in that circle" around Hitler as "heady" to the journalist Gitta Sereny,[6] and even before the appearance of her husband's memoir *Inside the Third Reich*, she criticized his view of the past to Joachim Fest, complaining that Albert Speer never remembered "for one second that we were happy then." After reading the book itself, which became a best seller, she is said to have told her husband: "Life hasn't left me much, but now you've ruined the little I had left!"[7]

In any case, the Speers' conduct leaves no doubt that they made every effort to be included at the Berghof. Albert Speer paints the picture in his memoir that the "bustle" there was "ruinous" for his work, the daily

Eva Braun, ice-skating (undated)

routine "tiring," and the circle of acquaintances collected there "boring." Nonetheless, he "spent endless time" with Hitler, as he himself said, and was "almost at home in his private circle." He and his wife "stayed longer at the Berghof with Hitler than in our old frame house."[8] Speer, always acutely conscious of power, records very precisely who was enjoying Hitler's favor at any given time, so it is surprising and noteworthy that he took Eva Braun to be the indicator of how much influence a person around Hitler had.

For example, in Speer's account it was a "privilege" to escort "Eva Braun to the table; she usually sat at Hitler's left." "From about 1938," only Martin Bormann enjoyed this distinction, a fact that "in itself," according to Speer, "was proof of Bormann's dominant position in the court."[9] Speer never offers an explanation of why the Führer's girlfriend—whom he later portrays as despised, humiliated, draped in cheap jewelry, and entirely uninterested in politics—possessed such importance at the Berghof. But as early as the summer of 1945, under interrogation by Allied officers at Kransberg Castle in the Taunus, he had hinted at Eva Braun's "possibilities, i.e., using the power she had within the inner circle," according to Speer. She had, Speer said, "been able to exploit . . . her position just like A.H.'s prominent colleagues."[10] Even this comparison with Hitler's "prominent colleagues" shows what a leading role Eva Braun played, in

*Eva Braun and
Albert Speer on the
Obersalzberg, 1941*

Speer's view. His statements justify the assumption that Eva Braun, not
long after stabilizing her relationship with Hitler, took on a central position within the Berghof circle.

In this context, Eva Braun's relationships with the other guests at the
Berghof, the staff, and not least the Speers, takes on a whole new significance. The question arises whether Speer's kind treatment of Braun
actually arose, as he later claimed, solely "out of sympathy for her pre-
dicament," and whether he struck up friendly relations with the young
woman for entirely selfless reasons.[11] Were their outings together and the
increasing intimacy of their interactions actually calculated on his part?
Was she not a way to cement an even tighter and more personal bond
of friendship with Hitler? For even though there was apparently a deep
emotional connection between Speer and Hitler "from the first moment
on," as Joachim Fest writes, the young architect occupied a position that
was in "constant danger."[12]

Margarete Speer, in any case, seems not to have shared her husband's connection with Hitler's girlfriend. Looking back, she does not attribute any shyness or unassuming modesty to Braun, as her husband did, but rather claims that Eva Braun was "thoroughly aware of her position" among the women and had the most say. On trips she always conducted herself "very much as the hostess": what she wanted to do was what was done "and that was that."[13] There is disapproval audible in these lines of Margarete Speer's, in spite of all the evenings, excursions, and ski vacations spent together. She absolutely did not consider Eva Braun—nor, for that matter, Magda Goebbels—as one of her personal friends, but rather as a member of her husband's "team," to whom he gave precedence over even his own children when it came to leisure time.[14] Margarete Speer thus does not, in her own retrospective judgment of Eva Braun, follow the line of explanation that her husband laid out after 1945 and stuck to in his later publications. Clearly, we can see from her account, no one dared to oppose Eva Braun's wishes at the time or call into question her preeminence within the Berghof hierarchy.

Karl and Anni Brandt

Another woman in the sporty "circle of friends" around Eva Braun and Margarete Speer was Anni Brandt, the wife of Hitler's personal physician, Dr. Karl Brandt. In *Inside the Third Reich*, Albert Speer lists the Brandts as in his "closest circle of friends."[15] Karl Brandt had joined the NSDAP in February 1932, and apparently met Hitler the same year, in Essen; he was a member of the dictator's inner circle for ten years, from 1934 until he was fired in 1944.[16] His wife, the former Anni Rehborn, famous nationwide as the SV-Bochum swimming champion, came into contact with Hitler as early as the 1920s, since she won the German championship in the 100 meter backstroke six times between 1923 and 1929 (among other championships), and the ambitious right-wing politician always liked to publicize his connection with important German athletes who fit his, and his Party's, racial ideal of strong, healthy, pure, "Aryan" bodies.[17] Conversely, the young athlete's family—in which physical health and beauty were also of great importance, in accord with the modern cult of the body in the 1920s—had supported the National Socialist movement even before 1933. Both Anni Rehborn and her father joined the NSDAP in

1932.[18] It thus seems likely that it was actually the young swimmer who introduced her then fiancé to the NSDAP leader, and brought him to the Berghof no later than summer 1933.[19]

Karl Brandt was working at the time as an assistant doctor in a casualty hospital in Bochum, and had already joined the SA in spring 1933. A few years earlier, he had dreamed of following the Protestant theologian, doctor, and philosopher of culture Albert Schweitzer, whom he admired, to his hospital in sub-Saharan Lambaréné, Gabon. But now he used the opportunities that his bride's personal connection with Hitler opened up to him. It is not entirely clear why Brandt underwent this transformation, turning away from Schweitzer and toward National Socialism; the ideological contrast between Schweitzer's Christian "worldview and philosophy of honoring life" and Hitler's deeply inhuman and racist ideas of a "struggle to the death between Peoples" and the "annihilation of the weak" could not have been any greater. If there is any point of connection between the two ideologies, it lies in Schweitzer's critique of modernity, his disapproval of the "acquisition of scientific knowledge" which had brought forth "the machine," and spiritually damaged and depersonalized mankind. Schweitzer diagnosed the political fragmentation and material suffering of modern states in similar terms. But he saw the solution to all these problems in the will to come to greater understanding between peoples and the establishment of a "culture state" that, led by a "cultural ethos," would come into existence "not according to the dictates of nationalism and national culture."[20]

Brandt, in contrast, who shared the disorientation and aimlessness of many men and women of his generation after Germany's loss of World War I and obviously was on the lookout for a charismatic savior-figure, took the nationalist path. In a document he drew up after the end of the war to provide intellectual "clarification" (his term) about what had happened, he wrote that Hitler had "opened the eyes" of the German People, "showed it its soul again and restored its faith in itself." Thanks to Hitler, Brandt wrote, "old names and values" had been "brought back to life" and "Germany's own spirit shone forth again . . . in the present."[21] The young, ambitious, not unadventurous doctor had only waited until the right moment, in 1933—or so his biographer Ulf Schmidt claims—to approach Hitler through his fiancée Anni Rehborn and attract his attention. In fact, the career of the barely thirty-year-old doctor had been steeply on the rise since the summer of 1933. In November 1933, he transferred from

Bochum to the recently reopened, well-known University Surgical Clinic
on the Ziegelstrasse in Berlin as the Party physician.[22] At his wedding,
on March 17, 1934, Hitler and Hermann Göring appeared as witnesses.
The reception took place in Göring's Berlin apartment.[23] After that, it
was probably already easy to predict that Brandt would soon be given a
position in Hitler's immediate retinue. In any case, he himself laid the
groundwork for such a position by submitting an application to the SS
in April 1934. Two months later, he received the offer to accompany the
Reich Chancellor as a specialist for accident injuries on his foreign travels.[24] From then on, Brandt and his wife were among the constant guests
on the Obersalzberg.

The close friendship between the Brandts and the Speers—Margarete
Speer called Anni Brandt her best friend—seems in retrospect to have
been anything but fortuitous. The parallels between the two men's careers
are unmistakable. Speer and Brandt, almost the same age, did not belong
to the generation of the "old fighters" from the early days of the NSDAP
but entered Hitler's inner circle only after he came to power. Both owed
their sudden career successes, and their growing political power, to Hitler
personally—not to the Party. For Brandt no less than for Speer, it must
have been of vital importance to stay within reach of the "court," even
though he was not actually a personal physician and his services as an
escort surgeon were, in the strict sense, necessary only while traveling,
primarily in case of an accident or assassination attempt.[25]

The privileged position that Brandt soon enjoyed alongside Speer can
be seen from the fact that both men, who lived and worked in Berlin,
moved onto the Obersalzberg in close proximity to Hitler during the
course of 1935. While preparations were under way to fence off the area
in a radius of fourteen kilometers, they and their families were housed in
the Bechstein Villa that already lay within the "Führer Protection Zone."
Bormann had bought the villa at the end of 1935 and repurposed it as a
guesthouse;[26] Goebbels lived there, too, when he visited the Berghof, and
it was enormously prestigious for these two men on the rise, still largely
unknown within the NSDAP, to be among Hitler's personally chosen
neighbors. In addition, Speer and Brandt were permitted to accompany
Hitler every year to the Wagner festival in Bayreuth—an honor given to
few people, according to Speer. Winifred Wagner, who ran the festivals,
formed close ties with Brandt, whom she later used, during the war, to
transmit letters to Hitler when she wanted to bypass Martin Bormann.[27]

What did it mean to be "preferred" like this by the most powerful man in Germany, over the majority of one's other colleagues and compatriots — in fact, to be promoted thanks to "the Führer's friendship"? Speer's later confession that he was "happy" then is only the barest hint of the elation and ecstasy the two men must have felt as a result of their proximity to power. Would Hitler not have been able to expect lifelong gratitude, loyalty, and tractability under those circumstances? And in fact, Brandt, after his arrest in 1945, declared in a written statement that his relationship to Hitler had been a "bond for better and for worse." Speer, too, found himself obliged to make what Joachim Fest called the "monstrous confession" decades later, in September 1974, that he, Speer, had felt himself bound to Hitler until their last encounter in the bunker with bonds of unbreakable personal loyalty and friendship.[28]

Karl Brandt, in any case, never left Hitler's side until the end of the war, gradually turning into Hitler's general factotum. Like Speer, he had direct access to the Nazi leader, who lived predominantly shut away from others, and he accompanied him on almost every occasion: at state visits, the Party conventions in Nuremberg, exhibition openings, balls, concerts both in and outside of Berlin, and, after fall 1939, on travels to the various "Führer headquarters." Brandt fulfilled all sorts of duties and shared Hitler's passion for art and architecture. There was thus hardly any time left over for his own medical responsibilities at the university clinic in Berlin.[29]

Even if Hitler's friendship with Brandt seems to have been less sensitive than that with his architect, the young doctor still fulfilled an analogous function. Largely unknown to the public and at the same time shielded against the influence of leading lights in the Party, he was, as the "Führer's" intimate friend, active in various areas of medicine, including the new construction plans for Berlin's university clinics.[30] Once the war started, Hitler gave his ambitious friend "special assignments" — that is, to murder the sick and crippled — and granted him far-reaching "special legal authority" over the health system for that reason.[31] Then, together with Philipp Bouhler, "Chief of the Chancellery of the Führer of the NSDAP" and a member of the Party for many years, Brandt, by then thirty-five years old, was promoted to head of the euthanasia program. It has also been proven that he conducted human medical experiments in concentration camps.

Brandt carried out what Hitler commanded and as a result found himself, along with Speer, Hoffmann, and Bormann, in the highest "Berghof society." Unlike the other members of this private entourage, however, who also received assignments from Hitler, usually verbally, Brandt and Speer were among the "Führer direct special representatives," of which there were only a few in the National Socialist regime. In the army of representatives, special representatives, authorized representatives, general inspectors, and Reich commissioners so characteristic of the inner structure of the Nazi regime, Brandt and Speer were thus exceptional. They occupied—Speer in construction and Brandt in medicine—next to traditional official positions in the Reich, their own spheres of power, established by "Führer's edict," in close consultation with Hitler so that they could most effectively translate certain core elements of the National Socialist worldview into reality. Both men took an active part in the racial politics of the regime as well: Brandt by killing the sick and conducting human experiments; Speer by filling the shortage of labor for his construction plans in the capital with concentration camp prisoners, as well as robbing Berlin Jews of their apartments before having them deported.[32] It is impossible to determine how decisions were taken precisely within Hitler's innermost private circle, and how they were communicated. But it is indisputable that the position and actions of these two "charismatic young men" were due not only to great personal closeness to Hitler, but also to their ideological agreement with him. There can be no question here of any "willed unconsciousness" about what was actually happening.[33]

Speer disputed these implications for the rest of his life. He insisted to the end that he had been a fundamentally apolitical architect, far removed from any ideological concerns, who at most suspected the crimes taking place around him. No anti-Semitic propaganda from him survives; he justified himself in retrospect by saying he saw Hitler's "insane hatred of Jews" as "a rather vulgar minor detail" of his otherwise convincing vision. Speer's statements on this topic about the other members of the "Führer circle," as he put it—especially about his friend Karl Brandt and about Eva Braun, whom he vigorously defends—must therefore be taken with a grain of salt at the very least. His alleging, about himself, "Politically I counted for nothing!" also casts doubt on his appraisal of Eva Braun as apolitical and lacking in influence.[34]

Since Brandt and Speer stood in an extraordinary relationship of loyalty to Hitler, the question further arises whether they might therefore have

*Karl Brandt and Eva
Braun on the Berghof
terrace, ca. 1937*

had a special relationship with Eva Braun. It is striking, in any case, that after the war both men, unlike almost everyone else in their environment, neither disputed the intimate nature of Eva Braun's relationship with Hitler nor dismissed her as insignificant in Hitler's inner circle. A U.S. Army military news service report from April 1947, summarizing Brandt's statements on the topic, maintained that the relationship between Hitler and his girlfriend was marked by openness and sincerity. Eva Braun, abrupt and severe by nature rather than feminine and compliant, had developed over the years from an average girl into a stylish lady. Hitler occasionally liked to remark, "The more important the man, the less important the woman," but this did not apply to Eva Braun.[35]

During his first interrogation in summer 1945, Brandt was trying to make a good impression on his American and British interrogators. Obviously, he denied his involvement in the murder of the sick and crippled. But his statements were saturated with unbowed admiration for Hitler. It is therefore surprising that he expressed even mild criticism of the "chosen one" at Hitler's side. Brandt said that Eva Braun's rise into the world of the rich and powerful was too much for her at first, and that in the years before the war she had made "certain guests" of the Berghof suffer under her changeable moods.[36] This statement of Brandt's, revealing for the later judgments of Braun, especially by Hitler's former staff members, corresponds with the notes that Percy Ernst Schramm, German historian and member of the U.S. Army Historical Division, made during the interrogation of Hitler's doctors in summer 1945. According to those notes, Eva Braun had caused "trouble" among those around Hitler and "put people off."[37] Who exactly her "victims" were remained unstated, however. In particular, Brandt said nothing about whether he himself, or possibly his wife—who smiled at the camera together with Eva Braun in September 1937, during the ninth Party convention, on a stage on the Nuremberg Hauptmarkt—had suffered under her.[38]

Martin Bormann

Martin Bormann played a special role in regard to Hitler's relationship with Eva Braun. Son of a postal official and former military musician, he had joined the NSDAP on February 27, 1927, and within a few years had risen to be one of the most powerful figures around Hitler. He started, though, at the bottom of the Thuringian Party hierarchy in Weimar. Since he had been found guilty as an accomplice to grievous bodily harm in 1924 and spent a year in jail, he could not afford to be choosy, and he carried out duties of all kinds for the Party, including those of bookkeeper, cashier, and driver. For example, he chauffeured the NSDAP-Gauleiter of Thuringia, Fritz Sauckel, to events and functions in the country in his own car, a small Opel. Bormann later became managing director of the Thuringia Gau press office, and in this capacity he met both Hitler and Rudolf Hess, who often traveled together to Thuringia for appearances before 1933.[39]

Within a year and a half of his joining the Party, in mid-November 1928, the conspicuously devoted and obliging Bormann was in the NSDAP headquarters in Munich. Franz Pfeffer von Salomon, commander of the SA, had asked him to take charge of managing insurance for the SA. Bormann succeeded in transforming the expensive and problematic insurance of SA members into a profitable "NSDAP Assistance Fund," and thereby helped reduce the National Socialists' notorious shortage of money. Bormann had made his reputation as a financial and orga-

Eva Braun in conversation with Martin Bormann, 1944

nizational talent, and he impressed Hitler with his unswerving business sense.[40]

This young man on the rise from the provinces further solidified his position by marrying Gerda Buch on September 2, 1939, in Munich. She was the daughter of Walter Buch, a Party member for many years and an "old fighter" in the National Socialist movement; Hitler had been a regular guest at the Buch house for years and on this occasion served as a witness at the wedding, along with the father of the bride. When the Bormanns' first son was born, seven months later, the "Führer" and Ilse Hess were the child's godparents.[41] Gerda Bormann, aged twenty, much taller than her husband and a kindergarten teacher by occupation, had been raised by her parents in a staunchly anti-Semitic "Nationalist" spirit.[42] Moreover, the family's personal contact with Hitler and his ideas had shaped her even in her youth. In a view that is consistent with this background, Joachim Fest attributed to her "unembarrassedly radical prejudices" and called her the "purest expression" of the "ideal type" of the

National Socialist woman.[43] She joined the NSDAP shortly before her wedding and, over the next thirteen years, bore nine children. She played no role, however, in the public self-presentation of the Nazi regime.

The trained farmer Martin Bormann, though, succeeded in gaining Hitler's trust and making himself indispensable to the leader. From 1933 on, he dependably managed Hitler's personal property. He also supervised the "Adolf Hitler Fund of German Trade and Industry," launched by Gustav Krupp von Bohlen und Halbach, which guaranteed the Party—and Hitler personally—an annual income in the millions from German businesses. These donations, which eventually became mandatory, added up to more than 700 million reichsmarks through 1945. The hardworking Bormann took care of all of Hitler's financial interests. He handled purchases and paid all the bills, whether for personal acquisitions, staff expenses, monetary gifts to Party colleagues, or Eva Braun's financial needs. It is thus no wonder that Bormann was able to expand more and more the scope of the position he held starting in July 1933, as chief of staff in the offices of the "Deputy Führer," Rudolf Hess. While Hess, the ardent follower of the "tribune"—Hitler—with the reputation of being the spotless "conscience of the Party," was increasingly kept away from Hitler's inner circle after 1933, Bormann and his wife soon became the dictator's substitute family at the Berghof.[44] Only a few people outside the Nazi leadership knew about him, but he was the man who was always there at Hitler's service, with unfailing discretion and reliability— qualities that he shared, of course, with Eva Braun. Bormann owed his rise to a position of power almost invisible from the outside to this close personal relationship of trust with Hitler.[45]

In this he was in no way different from the other functionaries in the Berghof circle, including Speer and Brandt, although they, unlike Bormann, occupied positions near Hitler that could also be perceived from the outside. They owed their careers just as much, however, to the patronage of the Nazi leader. Apparently, there was a ruthlessly competitive relationship between them and Bormann. Brandt, immediately after the end of the war, described Bormann as the most powerful figure in Hitler's circle, and said that the later "secretary to the Führer" (his title starting April 12, 1943) acted ruthlessly, brutally, and with such influence that having him as an enemy could endanger one's life.[46] In the autobiographical literature as well, Bormann is with few exceptions portrayed negatively. For example, Richard Walther Darré, Reich Minister of Food and Agriculture, described him as a heartless "player in his own interest," for whom Hitler was "the alpha and omega of his efforts." "Support from other circles, except for alliances of convenience within the Party," held no interest for him.[47] Only Hitler's secretary Christa Schroeder complained in her memoir that the "worst characteristics" had been attributed to Bormann unjustly, when he was one of "the few pure National Socialists" and was merely "working—often ruthlessly, sometimes brutally, too—to carry out the orders and commands Hitler gave him."[48]

What about the relations between Martin Bormann and Eva Braun? According to Otto Dietrich, the Reich Press Chief, who was among Hitler's constant companions by virtue of his position alone as early as 1931, it was Bormann who worked to make sure that the relationship between Hitler and Eva Braun, and the young woman's continual presence at the Berghof, remained secret. He was thereby able to consolidate and expand his influence in Hitler's close environment, Dietrich said, since the Nazi leader was indebted to him for his support in this matter.[49] Robert Ley, the head of the German Labor Front (Deutsche Arbeitsfront, or DAF)—the unified National Socialist trade union and a "gigantic propaganda machine," according to Ian Kershaw—who took his own life on October 25, 1945, after five months in prison at Nuremberg, left behind a similar assessment of Bormann. Ley, notorious in the "Third Reich" as a "Reich-drunkard," remained an uncritical, devoted henchman of Hitler's to the end. His last words—"But to be considered a criminal, I can't bear that"—reveal the extent of his involvement and his intellectual limitations.[50] He said of Bormann, in his "notes" that were written down in the Nuremburg military prison in 1945, that he was a "brutal, ruthless, hulking peasant." He "never left the Führer's side," made himself "liked with all sorts of little services that the Führer appreciated," and forced his way "unheard and unnoticed into the intimate affairs of a great and overburdened man." According to Ley, "Ask Bormann" was "heard all the time." Bormann fulfilled the Führer's every wish and took care of everything, including "putting through calls to Frau Braun in Munich."[51] We must keep in mind, though, with all these retrospective characterizations, that Ley as well as Bormann's other former antagonists, such as Brandt and Speer, would seem more harmless the more powerful and dangerous they could make Bormann out to be.

The mediating role that Bormann played between Hitler and the outside world applied to Eva Braun as well. She embodied, after all, the

private life of the Nazi leader, which was protected as a state secret. It is
thus natural to assume that Bormann followed Hitler's orders not only in
arranging her financial affairs but also in monitoring the young woman's
lifestyle on occasion. Heinrich Hoffmann, in his later apologia, even
claimed that "any wish of Eva Braun's was always carried out by Bormann," especially during the war years.[52] In any case, Bormann would
have known how important she was and would have been painfully aware
that she was not to be turned into his enemy. Bormann made sure of
"every person around the Führer," if we believe Robert Ley's remark.[53]
Eva Braun, in turn, was dependent on the bustling functionary, especially
in the period after 1935, when both were installed on the Obersalzberg in
immediate proximity to Hitler and regularly ate meals together. If she did
in fact hate him, as her family and Albert Speer claimed after the war, she
never showed it openly and avoided any confrontation.[54]

8

LIFE ON THE OBERSALZBERG

In January 1937, Reinhard Spitzy, adjutant and personal aide to Joachim von Ribbentrop, the German ambassador in London, accompanies his boss for the first time to a meeting with Hitler on the Obersalzberg. For Spitzy, a former Austrian fighter pilot from an upper-middle-class background, member of the NSDAP, SA, and SS since 1931, and only twenty-four years old, setting foot in the Berghof, that "legendary place," is an overwhelming experience that makes an "enormously great impression" on him. He idolizes Hitler beyond measure, "worships" him. Rigid with reverence, Spitzy stands "like a statue" with his briefcase against the wall in the great hall while Hitler and Ribbentrop, deep in conversation, walk back and forth in front of him for two hours. Suddenly a young woman with blond locks pokes her head in the doorway and tells Hitler to "finally" come eat with his guests "already." It's "high time," she says, they can't wait any longer. Shocked, Spitzy wonders who would dare "to speak to the Führer like that." After the meal, Hitler's adjutant Brückner explains to him that even the "Führer" has "a right to a private life." Spitzy should keep quiet about everything he's seen and heard—the best thing would be to forget it entirely. The young follower is devastated to learn that Hitler, whom he "believed lived the life of an ascetic, exalted above the level of sex and lust, had taken unto himself an ordinary female."[1]

Refuge and Center of Power

The incident Spitzy describes sheds light on Eva Braun's changed position within Hitler's personal circle, which had grown ever more clear
in the period after late 1935. The Obersalzberg, where she could "find
her footing" only after Angela Raubal left (as Henriette von Schirach
remarked), became her second home, along with Munich.[2] During this
period, renovations were moving full speed ahead to turn Wachenfeld,
the small country house, into the large, formal Berghof. A terrace and
veranda had been added in 1932. But after Hitler bought the house,
which he had only rented up until then, on June 26, 1933, and the
once-almost-unknown locale had become the second power center of the
German Reich, construction and technical modernization of the modest
"Alpine-style vacation home" began in earnest in 1934.[3] Before the official
opening on July 8, 1936, a new main wing that included the old country
house and several additional buildings was built. Eva Braun now had a
small apartment, adjacent to Hitler's bedroom, on the second floor of the
main house.[4] Albert Speer later told the historian Werner Maser that a
Tegernsee architect undertook the extensions "following sketches of Hitler's." The interior construction and renovations were left "in the Troost
Atelier's hands." He himself had "not been asked for advice" at the time.[5]

The rural mountain village on the Obersalzberg had meanwhile
turned into a kind of pilgrimage site. Encouraged by the cult of Hitler and
the marketing of his residence in Heinrich Hoffmann's illustrated publications, tourist travel to the region underwent an unexpected upswing.
Followers, or the merely curious, made pilgrimages by the thousands to
the Wachenfeld house to see the "Führer." As soon as they caught sight
of him, Bormann said, "the People [stood] at the fence."[6] While Nazi
propaganda used the hysteria to reinforce the legend of Hitler's closeness
to the People and to nature, the entire Obersalzberg was actually fenced
off in 1935. The region was quickly declared a "Führer Protection Zone"
and Bormann, on Hitler's orders, forced the remaining house owners and
innkeepers there to sell their property to the NSDAP. "Fief by fief, plot
by plot," he bought them up and had, as he himself said, "all the old
houses . . . torn down."[7] Now only registered groups of visitors from various Party organizations were allowed entry, and their processions past Hitler had to follow strict rules and a rigorous schedule. Spontaneous crowds
of ordinary tourists were no longer permitted.

Hitler on the Obersalzberg, 1934. As soon as they caught sight of him, Bormann said, "the people [stood] at the fence."

Thus whenever Eva Braun stayed at the Berghof, she disappeared into a heavily monitored, sealed domain, surrounded by six-foot-high security fences whose inner rings were kept under observation by Reich security forces. Admittance was permitted only to those with a special pass issued by the "Obersalzberg Administration" under Bormann.[8] Unlike in Munich, Eva Braun here lived cut off from the outside world. The same was true of everyone else who lived at the Berghof, their staff, and their servants. Christa Schroeder, who came to "the mountain" regularly as Hitler's secretary starting in August 1933, stated in her memoir that from then on she "led a life behind barriers and guarded fences," almost completely cut off "from everyday civilian and normal existence."[9] Therese Linke, on the other hand, a cook who worked on the Obersalzberg in Clubheim/Platterhof (Hoher Göll Inn), a guesthouse for the Party that the owners had been forced to sell, recalled the changes from 1936–1937 in particular: "There had been a fence around the Berghof and the rest of the area for a while. At every guard post we all had to go through the gates. . . . By then the farmers and peasants were long gone. Everything was bought up and leveled."[10]

Meanwhile, Hermann Göring, Albert Speer, and Martin Bormann had also settled on Obersalzberg in houses of their own. The construction of additional guesthouses and hotels followed, along with an SS barracks for the so-called Führer Special Security Force—Obersalzberg; the erection of an "Obersalzberg Estate" with a residential building and stables; several administration buildings; and finally the construction of two "teahouses": one beneath the Berghof and another, the so-called "Eagle's Nest," on Kehlstein, a 1,885-meter peak in the Berchtesgaden Alps. All this construction necessitated in turn the laying of new roads and the building of new tunnels and fences. Hitler himself drew up plans for a Berchtesgaden vacation destination, where a spacious "Party Forum" was to arise, but that never came to pass. Instead, during the war, construction began on air-raid bunkers and caves, which it turns out could not all be completed either, despite uninterrupted construction on Hitler's "mountain" and its surroundings until the end of the war.[11]

Despite all these changes and renovations, the house on the Obersalzberg remained Hitler's home, probably his most familiar place of residence. Life there was "to a large extent organized around him personally," as Speer stated to Allied interrogators in the summer of 1945.[12] He surrounded himself exclusively with absolutely loyal (and usually longtime) followers and their families and friends. And he lived there with Eva Braun, whenever he was there. It was always "the same limited circle," as Christa Schroeder remarked in a letter to a friend in August 1941.[13] Eva Braun and Hitler continued to meet in Munich or Berlin as well, but at the Berghof, despite the constant presence of staff and servants, a certain familial domesticity ruled, which neither the Munich apartment nor the Chancellery in the capital could offer.

Fritz Wiedemann, in connection with his time as Hitler's personal adjutant, wrote in 1938 that the dictator had felt "like the head of a household in his own domain" on the Obersalzberg and had enjoyed "comfort and a kind of family life." There were "always ladies present" as well, according to Wiedemann, "the wives of his colleagues, such as Frau Hoffmann and Frau Speer, and also the wives of the military adjutants." In the Reich Chancellery, in contrast, visits from women were "rare," he wrote.[14] As Wiedemann described the daily routine at the Berghof, Hitler woke up late, at one or two in the afternoon, then went to lunch and took "a stroll in the fenced-off area," in summer typically preceded by a "march-past" of two to three thousand visitors, and then afterward there was "a get-together on the terrace, then dinner at seven inside, and finally a movie."[15]

The Berghof after the 1935–1936 renovations

Eva Braun—who, among other things, usually took care of selecting and screening the movies that were provided by the Ministry of Propaganda in Berlin—is mentioned not even once in the adjutant's account.[16] Wiedemann, who left Germany in January 1939 and became the German consul general in San Francisco until 1941, himself explained the reason why: on the very first page of his remarks, he notes that a diplomat has to be discreet.

> So descriptions that could only come from me or another trusted source will not appear here. That would discredit me, in any age and any country. With respect to trusted details known only to a small circle, the whole world would know that the information came from me. . . .[17]

Hitler's relationship with a much younger lover obviously counted as a fact that everyone present had to maintain strict silence about, at least in public. Thus Wiedemann expresses himself only in very general terms about Hitler's relations with women in connection with life at the Berghof. He emphasizes Hitler's "deep personal regard for women" and mentions that he was "loyal and continuously kind" whenever he showed anyone his favor. All the "stories and rumors of ambiguous character," Wiedemann emphasized, were "lies": Hitler's relations with women were "probably the purest that anyone could imagine."[18]

In truth, though, the fact that the "Führer" himself was living in an "irregular" relationship made for whispers and rumors outside the fenced-in zone. Nicolaus von Below, for example, recalled almost forty years later how he had visited the Berghof for the first time in 1937, "fully ignorant" of the circle around Hitler; how he met Eva Braun and was so struck by the events there that it was still of "vital" interest to him after his return to the capital—Hitler's private lifestyle was a constant "topic of conversation" at social gatherings in Berlin.[19]

Meanwhile, the Reich Chancellor himself continued to turn his back on the capital, often for weeks at a time. Especially in the summer, he spent long periods on the Obersalzberg. To make sure that government business could be kept running smoothly, even from there, the head of the Reich Chancellery, Hans Heinrich Lammers, stayed in Upper Bavaria as well during this period, with a small staff. For months at a time, private residences across all of Berchtesgaden had to be rented for the purpose, even though the security requirements, if nothing else, were inadequate. Lammers himself, who, he wrote, took up "official residence" there every year "at the express wish of the Führer," was housed in a "large country house." But the summer tourist traffic limited the availability of the necessary housing.[20]

In early 1936, Hitler therefore ordered the establishment of a "Reich Sub-Chancellery" in Berchtesgaden. It was very important to both sides that the head of the Chancellery could be in Hitler's easy personal reach. Lammers—a fifty-seven-year-old judge, member of the NSDAP since 1932, and summoned by Hitler personally on the day the Nazis took power to be state secretary in the Chancellery—coordinated the government business. After dissolving the state governments, stripping power from Parliament, and combining the offices of President and Chancellor of the Reich after Hindenburg's death in 1934, Hitler had concentrated the duties of the state in the "Führer's" hand, and thus in the Chancellery. Lammers passed along Hitler's decisions to the appropriate departments, translated his ideas into laws, and controlled access to Hitler within the scope of his area of operation. Since cabinet meetings took place only rarely after the proclamation of the Enabling Act (or "Law to Remedy the Distress of the People and the Reich") on March 23, 1933, and not at all after 1938, Lammers functioned as the connection—often the sole connection—between the various ministries and the Chancellor. Every edict, Hitler decreed, had to pass through Lammers.[21] Often it was Lammers alone, not the Reich ministers, who advised the head of state. By weakening the government in this way, Hitler prevented the rise of any further opponents within the Party—like, most recently, SA-Führer Ernst Röhm—and, in the words of Ian Kershaw, made himself the "pole star and center of the apparatus of state."

This style of leadership, which favored the role of "chancelleries" in the political decision-making process, meant an enormous increase in power for Lammers, since he was responsible for setting the business of the day—not Otto Meissner, now head of the Presidential Chancellery; nor Philipp Bouhler, who had received the "Blood Order" (a prominent Nazi decoration) and reported directly to Hitler as head of the "Chancellery of the Führer of the NSDAP." It was among Lammers's duties to report to Hitler every morning, about situations in progress and tasks on the agenda.[22] In addition, Hitler assigned Lammers to manage his—the "Führer's"—bank accounts, and to run a "disposition fund" from which ministers and important Party members were remembered with tax-free gifts. Lammers himself, for his sixty-fifth birthday, received a gift of 600,000 reichsmarks along with a hunting lodge in the Schorfheide. Lammers also settled bills for the purchase of artworks meant for the "Führerbau" dedicated in Munich in September 1937, or the art museum in Linz that was planned, but never completed.[23] Lammers was thus Hitler's "right-hand man" and a powerful and influential figure for years within the National Socialist hierarchy.

This is the context in which a branch of the Reich Chancellery was established in 1937 in Stanggass-Bischofswiesen, northwest of Berchtesgaden and a little less than four miles from Obersalzberg. At the roofing ceremony on January 17, 1937, with Lammers present, Hitler made a short speech in which he said that he was "bold and gained trust and confidence" only at the Berghof, which was why his state secretary also had to "be here with the Reich Chancellery."[24] Already during the planning phase of the new service buildings, in September 1936, Lammers remarked in writing to Lutz Graf Schwerin von Krosigk, Minister of Finance, that Hitler was planning to stay in Upper Bavaria "even more often and for even longer periods in the future."[25] There was already a "Reichenhall-Berchtesgaden Government Airport" to provide a transportation connection with the capital.

Hitler now preferred to govern from the Berghof and carry out official functions there. There, and not at the actual seat of government in Ber-

On the terrace of the Berghof (undated)

lin, was where he sketched out his decisive political and military plans in the years to come, and passed laws and decrees. The Berghof also served to receive foreign guests and gave Hitler the chance to present himself as a statesman: British Prime Minister Neville Chamberlain and, after his scandalous abdication, the Duke of Windsor (formerly King Edward VIII of Great Britain and Ireland) were among his most prominent visitors. The question arises whether Hitler was thereby simply escaping the prescribed course of official business, or whether his changed relationship with Eva Braun played a role as well. She was always at Berchtesgaden whenever he was. In the final analysis, Berlin was a turbulent and uncontrollable environment, where it would hardly have been possible to avoid inconvenient people and burdensome duties. On the Obersalzberg, in contrast, an atmosphere of a "closed society" held sway. In truth, Hitler's residence after 1937, logistically as well as due to the installation of the most modern communications technology, was perfectly connected with the outside world—there was no question of "mountain solitude" in virgin nature, as the Nazi propaganda liked to claim.[26] Nevertheless, many Party members and representatives of the Nazi government did have the experience of finding that the "Führer" was unreachable on the "mountain" when he did not want to be reached. After the new Berghof was finished, Fritz Wiedemann claimed, the Reich Chancellor had less and less to do with day-to-day government business. "Work hours," previously "regulated to a certain extent," grew shorter and shorter, so that it was "harder and harder" to "get decisions [from Hitler] that he alone, as head of state, could make." On the Obersalzberg this situation was "even worse" than in Berlin.[27]

For example, Lammers, residing in his second seat of government a few miles away, often tried in vain to be admitted to see Hitler. Daily meetings between the two men, which had been the rule in the early years of the Nazi government, no longer took place, and the head of the Reich Chancellery, despite having risen to the rank of Reich minister, now had to seek audience through Hitler's personal adjutants, Wilhelm Brückner and Fritz Wiedemann. In 1938, after the signing of the Munich Agreement and the entry of German troops into the Sudetenland (the region of western Czechoslovakia occupied primarily by ethnic Germans and already carved off from the Czechoslovakian state), Lammers was often unable to see Hitler for weeks at a time. He wrote to Brückner on October 21 that he had not been able to give the "Führer" a "detailed report" since September 4, but now had to present to him "several laws to execute," which "could not be postponed." Lammers begged Brückner "most humbly to give the Führer this information" and to "communicate [to Lammers] a time when he might be received as soon as possible." In a second letter the same day, Lammers attempted to get an appointment for Economic Affairs Minister Walther Funk,[28] who had returned earlier that week from an extended trip to Yugoslavia, Turkey, and Bulgaria and now wanted to report on his successfully concluded foreign trade offensive in the southeast. SA-Obergruppenführer Brückner replied on October 24, however, that "the Führer was not prepared" to "receive" the report from Funk "on the Obersalzberg," and that he would see the minister "only after his eventual return to Berlin."[29]

In his own regard, Lammers followed up with a further request to the adjutant, informing Hitler that a meeting was "urgently necessary."[30] Now that so-called Reichsgan Sudetenland had been "annexed," its administration had to be reorganized, and that included among other matters the "administrative persecution" of its Jewish population.[31] The corresponding "Law Concerning the Reunification of the Sudeten-German Region with the German Reich," prepared by the Chancellery, was awaiting his signature. Even then, Wiedemann recalled, Hitler was "not in the mood to see Lammers." And so "Herr Reichsminister" waited another week, less than four miles away at the base of the Obersalzberg, before finally being permitted to set foot in the Berghof and give his "report" on October 31, 1938.[32]

This incident reveals more than an "unmethodical, even negligent style" of governing. The claim that Hitler was interested only in foreign politics by that point, and considered domestic matters inconsequential, is also incorrect,[33] since Lammers and Funk simply tried to promote Hitler's aims by implementing Funk's trade agreements concerning the Balkans, which were a preparatory step to carry out the policy of foreign expansion.[34] What we see here is how the Nazi leader, surrounded by his personal staff and his closest social circle, repeatedly created a distance between himself on the Obersalzberg and his leading political associates. Hitler postponed decisions or simply refused to make them. This in no way implies that he was weak in his exercise of power, or inefficient— such was not the case.[35]

But why, then, did he entrench himself on the Obersalzberg? Was it a psychological way to strengthen his aura of an inapproachable, absolute ruler? Or did he simply sometimes want to avoid any confrontation with the world outside the "Grand Hotel" (Eva Braun's name for the Berghof)?[36] Wiedemann, whose memoir gives the impression that Hitler neglected his political duties after 1936, even claimed that Hitler "absolutely never" received less "important personalities" than Lammers anymore after that time.[37] The truth was exactly the reverse. Speer, for example, questioned in August 1945 about Hitler's mode of working, stated that "when [Hitler] had important decisions to make" he went to the Obersalzberg and tried "to clarify things . . . for himself" by means of hours-long "conversations, repeated many times over," with his military adjutants.[38] Hence, the supposedly "unimportant people" such as adjutants, secretaries, doctors, Martin Bormann, and not least Eva Braun (still largely unknown to the public), had "access to the dictator" that well-known political figures in the Nazi elite, including Göring and Hess, were denied.[39]

The "Royal Court"

Who were the men and women of this exclusive society, who made up Hitler's private environment on the Berghof and met with him daily whenever he was there? Were they really, as is often maintained, normal, "simple" people, uneducated and without any political influence? How did this circle of individuals form? What were their relations with each other? And what role did Eva Braun play in the group?

Joachim Fest has argued that Hitler continued to prefer "the uncritical, dull milieu of simple people" around him, such as he had known from childhood on. Guido Knopp, too, said with respect to "everyday life . . . on the mountain" that the dictator's "substitute family" consisted of obsequious "personal physicians, personal photographers, personal bodyguards, secretaries, and adjutants."[40] But this way of looking at things has since been superseded. In fact, Hitler's close environment in no way consisted of a homogenous group of people. It remains the case that, aside from Goebbels and Speer, most of the "great and powerful men" of the Reich were not among this group. Hermann Göring—the power-hungry, second-most-powerful man in the Nazi hierarchy, commander in chief of the air force and "General Plenipotentiary for the Four-Year Plan," thus a major influence on the development of the rearmament economy— owned a house of his own on the Obersalzberg, but there was no private contact between him and the Reich Chancellor. Any social invitation of Göring and his wife Emmy to the Berghof was, Speer says, "completely out of the question."[41]

Heinrich Himmler, as "Reichsführer-SS and Chief of the German Police" after June 1936, reported directly to Hitler and was responsible for terror, persecution, and genocide, but he likewise appeared in Hitler's Alpine residence only for meetings. Himmler's unquestioning loyalty and belief in the leader's convictions ensured him Hitler's favor, which he used to expand his power and define his role entirely in terms of his own personal principles of military tradition and racial selection. No connection to his "Führer" on a personal level is known, however.[42] Joachim von Ribbentrop, too, whom Hitler apparently described as a "second Bismarck," appeared on the Obersalzberg only for meetings and official occasions such as the visit of David Lloyd George, the former British prime minister, on September 4, 1936. Ribbentrop, the ambassador to London starting in that year and Foreign Minister from 1938 on—thus "the greatest warmonger other than Hitler himself"—was hated by most of the other high-ranking Party members for his high-handed manner.[43] Rudolf Hess, the "Deputy Führer" who ran the Party headquarters in Munich, was also excluded from Hitler's private circle. He had been among Hitler's constant companions until 1933, with the reputation of being "the high priest of the Führer cult," but by the time Hitler moved into the "new Berghof," Hess was already estranged from the center of power. One important reason for this exclusion was probably that the former "private secretary" was seen to be a difficult person, an eccentric loner with obscure interests, unsuited to harmless diversions with others.[44]

Thus prominent representatives of the government and the Party were denied access to Hitler's private sphere, however, there were at least three distinct groups with distinct functions around Hitler at the Berghof: (1) personnel, such the doctors, personal adjutants, secretaries, servants, chauffeurs, and bodyguards; (2) military adjutants and representatives of the government, the military, and the Party, including Albert Speer, Martin Bormann, Karl Brandt, Sepp Dietrich, Hermann Esser, and Franz Xaver Schwarz; and (3) a social circle, including Hitler's lover, her family, and her friends as well as Heinrich Hoffmann and his family.[45] Only Speer and Goebbels, among the Nazi Party leadership, can be considered "friends" of the otherwise unapproachable Hitler, who was "cut off from real human contact."[46]

But was this circle on the Obersalzberg actually purely private in nature, as Speer claimed to his interrogators in 1945? Speer stated that Hitler had chosen a group of people there "apolitically," out of purely personal sympathy; that he included only those who "would not disturb his thoughts with political discussions."[47] Speer's early statements about the composition and significance of the Berghof circle thus give the impression that the people who were regularly present—including himself—were merely the dictator's personal friends, who had nothing, or an insignificant amount, to do with the regime's politics, at least until the start of the war. Politics, Speer said, was not a topic of discussion within the so-called private circle—a claim that everyone involved who survived the war stubbornly stuck to as well. But was it even possible to so sharply distinguish private life and politics, in a place that was the regime's second center of power, along with Berlin? And how does this testimony fit with the widespread belief that Hitler had no private life at all?

The various people at the Berghof were not, of course, all equal in status—or of the same gender—but the boundary between the social circle and the two official groups was extremely fluid. Hitler was the center around whom everyone revolved, and the dividing lines would dissolve and be redrawn according to the various degree of favor and trust each person found himself or herself in. Once the Alpine residence was sealed

off in 1935, a kind of community of purpose developed, in which everyone ate lunch together, spent the evenings with one another, went on
excursions, celebrated holidays, and—in changing permutations—could
be seen on the VIP platform at Party conventions.[48] There were also
trips together: Joseph Goebbels, Heinrich Hoffmann, Karl Brandt, and
their families flew to Greece in fall 1936, for example, for a semiofficial
eight-day visit; they were received by George II, the reinstated king, and
his prime minister, Ioannis Metaxas. Eva Braun, meanwhile, had joined
Heinrich Hoffmann Jr. and others on a purely private trip to Italy a few
weeks earlier, visiting Venice and Milan, among other places.[49]

Among the regular guests on the Obersalzberg, who considered spending time with Hitler to be an "exciting experience," were to be found,
after 1937–1938, Nicolaus von Below, a twenty-nine-year-old colonel of
the Luftwaffe assigned to Hitler as an adjutant, and his nineteen-year-old
wife, Maria. Below later recalled that he had entered the Chancellor's
private circle as early as four weeks after his first assignment on June 23,
1937. His explanation of how this was possible so quickly was that they had
immediately discovered a common interest in classical music. Certainly
Hitler's appointments outside of work hours did not lie within Below's
purview. The four military adjutants, one from each of the four branches
of the armed forces, unlike the personal adjutants, were on call in alterna-
tion and scheduled meetings pertaining only to military matters, in the
broadest sense, including "petitions and pleas for clemency from soldiers
and their family members."[50] Still, we may presume that Hitler developed
a certain sympathy for the strapping young air force adjutant from the
first moment he saw him, since the Belows were included on his personal
invitation list to the Wagner festivals in Bayreuth as early as July 27.[51]

Nicolaus von Below was around the same age as Brandt and Speer, and
was friends with them as well.[52] Like them, Below accompanied the Nazi
leader not only officially but also on personal trips. Ever since Hitler had
disenfranchised the previous commanders of the military and taken over
sole command of the armed forces in early February 1938, he required
constant accompaniment by military adjutants. Thus Below went regularly with Hitler to his private apartment in Munich, as well as to the
Obersalzberg, from then on. At 16 Prinzregentenplatz, the adjutant later
recalled, the housekeeper was "in constant contact with Eva Braun" and
had "a telephone connection to her ready for Hitler" immediately upon
his arrival.[53] Then, in summer 1939, Below went along to the "Reich The-

Soirée in the great hall at the Berghof, 1944

ater Week" in Vienna, an event organized by the Ministry of Propaganda that since 1934 had taken place in various cities of the Reich, including Linz. Afterward, at the Berghof, Below (alternating with Speer) followed Hitler in "long walks up and down the great hall" and was impressed by the "Führer's" thoughts circling around the "extermination" of "Jewish Bolshevism." As he later confessed in his memoir, the argument that "the German People could not live in peace . . . under this constant threat" had convinced him.[54]

Maria von Below, a landowner's daughter whom Hitler first invited to the Berghof for Easter 1938, stated in 1985, in very similar terms, that Hitler did not win the "loyalty" of those around him "by telling them his plan was murder." Rather, he persuaded everyone "because he was fascinating." "Even the early years" at the Berghof were in no way "horribly boring," she said in this interview with Gitta Sereny; Hitler held everyone in his grip by means of his personality, and his "phenomenal" "knowledge of history and art." Thus Maria von Below presented herself as unable to understand the retroactive dismissal of the Berghof society in Speer's publications. How could he have forgotten "how exciting it was for all of us? And how often we were happy there?"[55]

We can see here that Maria von Below, by far the youngest member of this half-private, half-official group of people around Hitler in 1938, defended her time in this circle more than forty years later just as forcefully and in almost the same words as Margarete Speer. How are we to comprehend this attitude, in light of the monstrous misdeeds of the Nazi regime, which these women must have learned about at least in later years? Why did they stubbornly insist on this description of a supposedly ideal world at the Berghof? Is it because they—unlike their husbands— were under no pressure from a prosecutor or a court to justify themselves after the collapse of the Nazi state? The fact remains that, to whatever greater or lesser degree they may have known about the crimes that were committed, they barely connected their life at the Berghof with the actual political events of those years.

Nicolaus and Maria von Below met Hitler and his close circle shortly after the entry of German troops into Austria on March 12, 1938, and Austria's "annexation" to the German Reich—in other words, at a time when Hitler was more powerful and more popular than ever. Not only his immediate followers but the overwhelming majority of the population celebrated this new coup, which was explicitly recognized by the Great Powers in Europe, and considered him a genius as a statesman. Air force adjutant Below, one of the many people to accompany Hitler on his "triumphal procession" to Vienna, wrote later that on this trip he understood "more and more" why the Nazi "Führer" "had won his followers, and the love of the people."[56] Maria von Below's enthusiasm looking back at this period likewise reflects the then-widespread mood, and certainly gives us insight into the emotional world of the Berghof.

Her relationship with Eva Braun, meanwhile, is difficult to judge after such a long time. Her husband's memoir gives very few hints of any possible friendly contact. In a chapter called "Peaceful Life at the Berghof," it says that in spring 1944 Hitler thanked Maria von Below "many times" for having "found such a nice relationship with Miss Braun."[57] And to Traudl Junge, Hitler's last secretary, who moved from his headquarters in East Prussia onto the Obersalzberg with Hitler's staff in early 1943, it seemed that Anni Brandt and Maria von Below were "close friends" with Eva Braun.[58] Christa Schroeder, on the other hand, states that Eva Braun had always had only one "favorite" and the others were always "careful and reserved" around her.[59] It is certainly striking that Maria von Below never appears with the other women in the Berghof group in Heinrich Hoffmann's photographs. The explanation must be that, as the wife of a military adjutant, she came along to Berchtesgaden only when her husband was on duty. In addition, the Belows seem to have attained a position of trust with Hitler, and also with Eva Braun, only in the last years before the end of the war.

From the beginning, that is to say since 1933, the Munich artist Sofie Stork was also in the circle of those around Hitler and Eva Braun. A trained sculptor and painter, and a beautiful, dark-haired woman of thirty whose father owned a well-known company that manufactured and sold fishing tackle (the "H. Stork Fishing Tackle Factory"), Sofie Stork was involved with Wilhelm Brückner, Hitler's personal adjutant, nineteen years older than she was. In the course of their acquaintance she had joined the NSDAP on December 1, 1931, and entered farther and farther into Hitler's private circle.[60] Brückner himself, a university-educated economist and an officer in the First World War, was among the "old campaigners" from the early days of the NSDAP. He was a member of the Party going back to late 1922, led the Munich SA regiment in the following years, and in that capacity took part in the Beer Hall Putsch of 1923. As a result, the State Court in Munich sentenced him to fifteen months prison and a fine of 100 reichsmarks for abetting high treason,[61] although Brückner, like all the others who took part in the putsch, actually served only part of this already mild sentence. Later, he made a living for many years with all sorts of different activities, including as a tennis coach, before again joining Hitler's circle when Hitler chose him as his personal adjutant in 1930. Otto Wagener, named chief of staff of the SA in the previous year and one of Hitler's closest confidants in the "period of struggle" until 1933, did not approve of the choice: the forty-five-year-old Brückner's whole life history, without a real career or contact with the SA, seemed dubious to Wagener. But Hitler, Wagener wrote in his autobiography while a prisoner of war in England in 1946 (it was published posthumously in 1978), justified his decision by saying that he wanted someone around him who offered "a certain security simply by virtue of his sturdy build and size," and would prevent anyone from daring to approach him.[62]

Personal adjutants were traditionally assigned to princes, army commanders, ministers of war, and Reich chancellors; they always had an officer grade and usually came from the nobility. They handled writing and business duties, received phone calls, transmitted orders, and occasionally even undertook diplomatic missions. Hitler's naming a personal adjutant at a time when he was still years away from becoming Chancellor revealed not only his concern with security and inclination to an egocentrically staged leadership style—more importantly, it revealed that Hitler was creating a further distance between himself and his fellow National Socialists. He was consciously fostering the "nimbus of the unapproachable," as Ian Kershaw formulated it, in order to both concretize to the outside world and defend from competitors within the Party his persona as the inaccessible, solitary Leader.[63]

Wilhelm Brückner remained at Hitler's side for ten years. A bearer of the Blood Order, he rose to be chief adjutant, while three additional adjutants arrived in 1933, 1935, and 1938, respectively: Julius Schaub, the longtime servant; retired Captain Fritz Wiedemann; and Albert Bormann, Martin Bormann's younger brother, trained as a bank teller and head of Hitler's "Private Chancellery," which was integrated as Chief Department 1 into the "Chancellery of the Führer of the NSDAP" under Philipp Bouhler.[64] Brückner became an honorary citizen of the city of Detmold on January 15, 1936 (an honor revoked in 1945); became a member of the NSDAP's parliamentary party for two years in 1936; and, inevitably, took part in Hitler's entire political and private life, in Berlin, Munich, and on the Obersalzberg. For example, on August 1, 1934, the day before Reich President Paul von Hindenburg died, Brückner was apparently the only person to accompany Hitler to see the elderly head of state on his deathbed.[65]

Without a doubt, the head of "the Führer's Personal Adjutant Staff" gained a power not to be underestimated. Nicolaus von Below even claimed that Brückner had attained a "paramount position," with his "authority" recognized by both the personal and the military adjutants.[66] Furthermore, it was the adjutants, especially Brückner, who had direct and practically unlimited access to Hitler. They were the link to the outside world for a "Führer" concerned to keep his distance; they supplied him with all sorts of information and contacts. In addition, the personal adjutants coordinated visits, such that even the head of the Reich Chancellery, Hans Heinrich Lammers, was obliged in 1938 to submit his request for an audience with Hitler to Brückner in writing. There were clearly also wide-ranging financial opportunities for the adjutants—Fritz Wiedemann later wrote:

> If you needed money, Brückner sent word . . . to Bormann and got 50,000 marks. He took the lion's share for himself and then passed the rest along to Schaub and to me, in decreasing amounts based on seniority and position.[67]

When Martin Bormann, who managed the fund that was at Hitler's personal disposal, complained about the large outlays of money, the Nazi leader dismissed the complaint and forbade the Party to interfere in "his spending."[68] Either Brückner or Schaub paid Hitler's private bills in restaurants and on trips—or, as it was called, managed his "petty cash." Brückner stated under questioning in August 1947 that only Schaub paid Eva Braun's bills.[69] Brückner's own role in Hitler's private milieu, meanwhile, is not easy to determine. Albert Speer—concerned, as he always was after the fact, to imply the greatest possible distance between himself and the supposedly wretched "Führer circle" on the Obersalzberg—emphasized in May 1967, in response to a question from Joachim Fest, that he had had "nothing in common with Schaub, Brückner, and Morell." Who, Speer asked his interlocutor, "could have been more different from me?"[70] His friend Nicolaus von Below, on the other hand, recalled "especially good and friendly contact" with SA-Obergruppenführer Brückner, which took on "a private character quite quickly."[71]

Brückner's girlfriend Sofie Stork seems to have been introduced into the Berghof society just as quickly and to have made close friendships there. Heinrich Hoffmann's photographs show her at parties, such as New Year's or birthdays, but also on excursions alongside Hoffmann's wife, Erna; Eva Braun; and Anni Brandt.[72] In the process of transforming Haus Wachenfeld into the Berghof, the young artist even received assignments from Hitler—and from his girlfriend. For example, Stork decorated the chimney stove in the living room and painted the tiles of the sideboard and the tea table, as well as porcelain for Eva Braun, complete with her monogram.[73] She was obviously in Hitler's good graces. Her separation from Brückner, who left her around the beginning of 1936 and married another woman a short time later, did nothing to change that: she remained a member of the most intimate inner circle at the Berghof even after the separation, along with Karl Brandt, Heinrich Hoffmann, Eva and Gretl Braun, and the secretaries Christa Schroeder and Gerda Daranowski.[74]

Brückner, on the other hand, left four years later. On October 18, 1940, Hitler fired him from his position as personal adjutant. In fact, there had been at least one departure or removal from the dictator's private realm every year since 1935: in 1936, his half-sister and housekeeper Angela Raubal was dismissed and his driver, Julius Schreck, died of natural causes; in 1937, the foreign press secretary, Ernst Hanfstaengl, fled to England; in 1938, Fritz Wiedemann was transferred to the German consulate in San

Francisco; in 1939, the servant Karl Krause was fired. Thus the idea that Hitler moved in an entirely unchanged environment of servants and adjutants from 1933 on is false. The reasons for Brückner's removal, meanwhile, are still difficult to understand today. In Below's memoir it says that the reason was a difference of opinion between Brückner and Hitler's majordomo Arthur Kannenberg, concerning "petty trifles."[75] Kannenberg, a corpulent Berlin chef and restaurant owner, was responsible with his wife for the "Führer household" in the Chancellery starting in 1933. He organized the state dinners in Berlin and on the Obersalzberg, and even went along every year to the Wagner festivals in Bayreuth, where he and his staff tended to Hitler and his guests in a house put at his special disposal by the Wagner family—the "Führerbau." Kannenberg was famous, or infamous, for his solo interludes on the accordion at the Chancellor's artists' receptions. Winifred Wagner later described him as "a little part of us"—it was impossible to imagine Hitler's private circle without him.[76] Nicolaus von Below, meanwhile, regretted the "removal" of his friend Brückner. He had always hoped, he said, that Brückner would "one day return," whereas others, such as "Bormann and Eva Braun, were happy to see him go." Christa Schroeder described an "intrigue" of Kannenberg's; she considered him to be a "shady character," and even suggested a connection between Hitler's "disfavor" toward Brückner and the end of Brückner's relationship with Sofie Stork.[77] In truth, all these retrospective judgments, expressing the speaker's own sympathies or antipathies, amount largely to hearsay. They do, however, make clear that the group of people at the Berghof was by no means a "sworn society." Jealousies, power struggles, and nepotistic favoritism were the order of the day there as well.

Politics and Private Dealings

The business interests pursued by individual members of Hitler's inner circle constitute a special chapter in the history of life at the Berghof. They show above all that Hitler looked after the personal circumstances, too, of the members of his Berghof society and was prepared to support them financially when necessary. The files of Albert Bormann, who handled and archived Hitler's personal correspondence in the "Private Chancellery of the Führer," show, for example, that Sofie Stork's personal and business contact with Hitler lasted until at least 1941. A "correspondence diary" that indicates the incoming and outgoing letters for the years 1939–1940, predominantly within a narrow circle (including Schaub, Brückner, Heinrich Hoffmann, and Hermann Esser), along with, less often, private letters such as those to or from Hitler's nephew Leo Raubal, his half-sister Angela's son, or Sigrid von Laffert, contains numerous entries on the "Stork matter," revealing Hitler's energetic business assistance. Already in September 1936, Hitler had arranged for Sofie Stork to receive 45,000 reichsmarks—an astronomical sum at the time—so that she could carry on her deceased father's fishing-tackle business in Munich, which had apparently run into financial difficulties.[78] On top of that, Hitler hired, and paid the salary of, a financial adviser who looked after the company for years "on the orders of the Führer." The auditor regularly sent annual reports to the "Private Chancellery of the Führer" from then on.[79]

In later years as well, Albert Bormann's entries show that Sofie Stork turned directly to the dictator whenever she ran into business problems. For example, in the early summer of 1940 she asked him for help in procuring Tonkin bamboo (a special type of bamboo reed used to manufacture fishing poles), which had become increasingly difficult to import from the Far East, Australia, or the United States since the start of the war. In September 1940, she put in another request directly to Hitler, for a travel permit to, and purchase approval within, Belgium and France, which had been occupied by the German army a few months earlier. The northern half of France, with its major industrial regions, came under the jurisdiction of the German military administration and was thus a coveted trading center for businesspeople from the German Reich. Sofie Stork received her concession, too, as Albert Bormann's bookkeeping proves: on October 13, 1940, she appeared in the files again, with a new request. Could her commercial representative use certain airplanes belonging to Hitler's fleet?[80]

But why would Sofie Stork have been granted such an enormous amount of assistance, financial and otherwise? Christa Schroeder, Hitler's private secretary, later claimed that Hitler so resented Wilhelm Brückner's separation from this woman that he decided "on his own accord" to compensate the ex-girlfriend financially "and very generously."[81] But is this account plausible? What would explain such an emotional reaction on Hitler's part? It seems likely that Sofie Stork's close friendship with Eva and Gretl Braun could have been one possible cause of Brückner's gradual loss of Hitler's favor and eventually his expulsion. For the young artist, in contrast, the Braun sisters' friendship and thus her belonging to Hitler's personal sphere was enough to give her extraordinary advantages. This was not the only case in which Hitler rewarded political allegiance, and above all personal loyalty, with material contributions of all kinds.[82]

Another friend of Eva Braun's was Marianne Schönmann, from Munich. Thirteen years older than Braun, she first arrived in the Berghof circle thanks to her long-standing acquaintance with Erna Hoffmann, Heinrich Hoffmann's second wife.[83] Erna Hoffmann and Marianne Schönmann both came from artist families; Schönmann's aunt, Luise Perard-Petzl, a soprano well known in Vienna and Munich, had had successes before the First World War in, among others, Wagner operas—as Sieglinde in *Die Walküre* and as Elsa in *Lohengrin*. Marianne Schönmann met Hitler, according to her own statement, around 1934 in Hoffmann's apartment in Munich. Her relationship to the world of opera, and to Wagner, probably played an important role in forming this acquaintance. They were in harmony politically as well: she had already joined the NSDAP three years previously, in December 1931.[84] She was then unmarried and still named Petzl.

When and how Schönmann met Eva Braun is not known. The statements she gave in this regard in her denazification proceedings after the war were vague: she stated before the court in 1947 that she was merely one among several "female acquaintances" who "repeatedly" invited Braun to her house in Munich. She herself first visited the Obersalzberg, she said, sometime during 1935.[85] However, Schönmann very quickly became one of the regular visitors there after Eva Braun's position at the Berghof became unassailable in early 1936. Within a few years, Marianne Schönmann was one of the women around Hitler. When she married the Munich building contractor (and NSDAP member) Friedrich "Fritz" Schönmann on August 7, 1937, at age thirty-six, Hitler and Eva Braun were among the select few guests.[86]

Marianne Schönmann and Eva Braun were apparently in regular contact in Munich as well as at the Berghof. The Schönmanns' villa near the Herzogpark was located not far from the Braun sisters' residence in Bogenhausen. After the war, when it was necessary to play down such close connections to Hitler and those near to him in order to save one's own skin, Marianne Schönmann stated that Eva Braun must have been "so obliging" to her only because of Braun's interest in opera. She emphasized, too, that her acquaintance with Eva Braun and Erna Hoffmann did not lead to any "political activity" on her part; there was "never any politicizing" between them. Neither acquaintance had "ever told [her] about the actions or any other affairs of Hitler or Heinrich Hoffmann," she said.[87]

In reality, Schönmann was extremely well informed, since the "actions" and "affairs" about which she claimed to know nothing were ones she had close and direct experience of during her numerous visits on the Obersalzberg. And she must have heard from other members of the inner circle, in one form or another, at least some details about the events taking place around Hitler—events that all those who had anything to do with him were as burningly interested in as the curious general public. Karl Brandt later stated that he was a "very close" friend of Schönmann's,[88] and Nicolaus von Below still remembered precisely, decades later, Schönmann's confident manner in Hitler's presence: he described in his memoir how Eva Braun's friend even dared to disapprove openly of one of the Reich Chancellor's decisions.

During a four-day stay on the Obersalzberg over Easter 1938, which played out "informally, in a private atmosphere" according to Below, Hitler, surrounded by his guests (including Eva and Gretl Braun, Marianne Schönmann, the Bormanns, the Speers, and the Brandts), spoke "frequently about Austria during meals and during the long nights." It was only five weeks since German troops had occupied the country and Austria had been "integrated" into the German Reich.[89] Many of the people present at the Berghof had been at Hitler's triumphal entry into Linz on March 12, 1938, and into Vienna on March 14, and had seen how their "Führer" had been frantically, jubilantly greeted by crowds of cheering Austrians for fulfilling the dream of a "Greater German Empire." Walter Schellenberg, who worked in the Reich Main Security Office and was responsible at the time for Hitler's personal security during his drives through Vienna, described a "true carnival of flowers,"[90] and Christa Schroeder later recalled the "almost hysterical outbursts of joy," which she described as "nerve-shattering."[91] Bormann, Below, and Brandt were also among those accompanying Hitler. Eva Braun, in contrast, had traveled to Vienna unofficially and separate from the others.[92] In a move that his followers did not expect, Hitler immediately chose Josef Bürckel, a schoolteacher from the Rhineland and an "old campaigner" in the movement, to take over the Austrian NSDAP and the Gleichschaltung of Austria. This was the decision that Marianne Schönmann, a native Viennese, criticized at the Berghof. His naming a non-Austrian as the "Führer's Representative for the Building Up of the Party in the Eastern Region" clearly displeased her very deeply.[93]

Bürckel's nomination must indeed have shocked the Austrian National Socialists if they were expecting to regain power once more, after the prohibition of their party on June 19, 1933, and years of political powerlessness. Simultaneously with the entry of German troops, they began to mercilessly persecute political opponents and members of religious minorities and drive them out of office. Nonetheless, Hitler chose Bürckel, an outsider, to reorganize the disorganized Austrian NSDAP and review the existing membership. Bürckel, previously the "Reich Commissioner for the Reintegration of the Saar Region," was now to ensure a successful "annexation" in Austria as well. He reported directly to Hitler and saw himself as a kind of "Gau-Prince" with dictatorial powers intended solely to enforce "the will of the Führer."[94] He peremptorily disregarded the aims of the traditional institutions, going so far as to declare that he wanted to stem the tide of "a number of candidates who consider themselves qualified to take up certain positions in the state and Party offices," in fact, "to render such office-seekers harmless."[95] With measures such as the immediate closure of all associations and organizations in Austria—which was now to be referred to only as Ostmark, "the Eastern Region"—Bürckel made himself so disliked even among Party members that his behavior gave rise to a "lively" discussion, even at the Berghof, about whether "the mentality of the Austrians [ought to be] taken into account."

But Marianne Schönmann's efforts on behalf of her homeland's Party members were in vain. A week later, on April 23, 1938, Hitler named Josef Bürckel "Reich Commissioner for the Reunification of Austria with the German Reich." Still, Schönmann brought up "several proofs of Bürckel's missteps in office over the course of the following years" in conversations with Hitler, Below recalled. On the other hand, Baldur von Schirach, who two years later would relieve Bürckel and take over the office of Gauleiter and Reich Governor in Vienna, stated that Schönmann had plied Hitler "with rumors about his predecessor," to the point where the Nazi leader had held him responsible for the "mood inimical to the Reich in Vienna."[96] Below leaves open whether, and in what way, he or others there, including Eva Braun, may have taken part in the discussion. His remarks show, though, that even in the years leading up to the war, political topics were certainly discussed at the Berghof, and not merely, as Speer would later claim, "questions of fashion, of raising dogs, of the theater and movies, of operettas and their stars."[97]

The persecution of Jews was no secret in the Berghof circle, either. Eva Braun and her friends, as well as the Speer and Brandt families, spent most of their time living in the major cities of Munich or Berlin, after all, not in any way shut off from the outside world as they were on the Obersalzberg. As but one example, they could hardly have been unaware that the mayor of Munich, Karl Fiehler, a long-time Party member who had taken part in the putsch of 1923 and served time in Landsberg prison with Hitler, had imposed radical measures against the Jewish residents of the city from very early on. Even before 1938, Jews in the Bavarian capital were forbidden to visit public baths, parks, and restaurants. They could shop only at a few shops.[98] Announcements in all German newspapers openly offered for sale Jewish businesses that had been forcibly expropriated "by reason of Aryanization." The second biggest department store in Munich underwent numerous boycotts and acts of terror at the hands of the National Socialists before being looted on the night of November 9, 1938—the so-called Night of Broken Glass—and set on fire.[99] It will probably never be possible to determine exactly how much each individual member of the Berghof group knew about such activities involving the persecution of Jews and the elimination of political opponents. As Speer said, "Hitler's private circle" was in any case not "sworn to silence"— Hitler "considered it pointless to attempt to keep women from gossiping" anyway.[100] They all were not only witnesses but believers. The survivors from this circle thus had good reasons after the war to stay quiet about what they had seen and heard around Hitler.

In Austria, meanwhile, Bürckel and his staff were busy transforming Austrian organizations into "Reich-German institutions" and restructuring the Austrian NSDAP. The currency reserves of the Austrian national bank—some 1.4 billion reichsmarks—fell into German hands as well. In addition, they pressed ahead with the "reduction of non-Aryan personnel in private companies,"[101] which in practice meant brutally stripping members of the Jewish population of their rights and property. Thousands of Austrian Jews, mostly from Vienna, had fled; their property, declared to be the property of "enemies of the Reich," was confiscated by the SS.[102] Valuable art collections and libraries changed hands in this way, with the "Führer" claiming for himself the right to make final decisions about their ultimate destinations. He decided in June 1938, for instance, that he would personally decree where the art works confiscated in Vienna would go. Heinrich Himmler, who had hurried to the Austrian capital with a company of Waffen-SS soldiers on March 12, received instructions from the Reich Chancellery that Hitler intended "primarily to put [these art objects] at the disposal of the smaller cities of Austria."[103] In the following months, it became clear that Hitler thereby meant predominantly the Upper Austrian provincial capital of Linz on the Danube, Hitler's "hometown," which he had planned since the summer of 1938 to redesign architecturally and where he intended to build an art museum of international stature. His goal was to make Linz a "world city."[104]

For the construction of the art museum in Linz, which was to show primarily German and Austrian painters of the nineteenth century, Hitler purchased pictures from art dealers as well as confiscating them from Jewish collections. Among the experts advising him on his purchases and fulfilling his "special wishes" was first and foremost the Berlin art dealer Karl Haberstock, who owned a gallery on the Kurfürstendamm.[105] The bustling Heinrich Hoffmann, worth millions by then, acted as a broker as well, along with possibly Marianne Schönmann. Even though Hoffmann was no art expert, Hitler had had him as an adviser on art for years. The "personal photographer's" obvious access to Hitler the passionate art-lover ensured that dealers would propose all sorts of sales to him. As a result, a flourishing art market developed in the dictator's immediate environment. Not only was Hitler offered, and often simply given, valuable art objects, but so were his girlfriend, his adjutants, and even his secretaries.[106] In addition, Hoffmann used his contacts to build up an extensive painting collection of his own over the years. In 1946 he confirmed under questioning from Allied interrogation officials that he had received pictures as a broker from Marianne Schönmann among others, including a work by Anton Seitz.[107] This nineteenth-century German painter of the Munich School, who portrayed the everyday life of "ordinary people," was one of the artists Hoffmann privately preferred to collect.[108] Karl Brandt also stated in 1946 that he had received pictures from Schönmann.[109]

The extent of Marianne Schönmann's activities remains in shadow, however. Officially, she was not in the art business around Hitler. A friend of hers, the Munich gallerist Maria Almas-Dietrich, in contrast, can be proven to have worked together with Karl Haberstock and Heinrich Hoffmann as a supplier for the "Linz special assignment." Heinrich

Hoffmann introduced Hitler to Almas-Dietrich in 1936; her daughter was apparently friends with Eva Braun.[110] A year later, in August 1937, Maria Almas-Dietrich already found herself, along with Hitler, Eva Braun, and Braun's Munich circle of friends, among the wedding guests in Marianne Schönmann's apartment. Working partly with Hoffmann, she would sell Hitler more than nine hundred paintings in total and thus be one of the most important art brokers for the Linz "Führer Museum."[111] She conducted her business via Martin Bormann, or directly with the Nazi leader, who then instructed his personal adjutant to pass along her invoices to Hans Heinrich Lammers, head of the Reich Chancellery.[112] Despite the evidence that Maria Almas-Dietrich worked with the Operational Center for the Occupied Territories (Einsatzstab Reichsleiter Rosenberg, or ERR), which stole property from Jewish owners throughout the regions occupied by the German army during the war, the accusation that she had dealt in stolen art has never been proven, even today, due to lack of sales documents. It is also uncertain how close her friendship with Hitler and his private circle actually was, and whether she ever received an invitation to the Berghof. It is certain, however, that she made an enormous financial profit from her dealings with Hitler. Between 1940 and 1944, she apparently took in more than 600,000 reichsmarks with her business for the "Linz special assignment."[113]

In general, there was a close intertwining of private and business relationships within the dictator's innermost circle. In this context, Heinrich Hoffmann in particular skillfully exploited his friendship with Hitler and his quasifamilial relationship with Eva Braun. And in 1936, he introduced another person into Hitler's private life who would exert a sizable influence on Hitler's mental and physical state until the end: Dr. Morell.

Dr. Morell

Dr. Theodor Morell, a ship's doctor before the First World War, had a private practice on Berlin's chic Kurfürstendamm that included artists, politicians, and Hitler's personal photographer Hoffmann among its patients. When Hitler—who didn't smoke, drank no alcohol, and kept to a strict diet—was suffering from increased stomach pains and eczema on his legs in 1935–1936, Hoffmann arranged a meeting with Morell—presumably at his house in Munich.[114] Morell apparently succeeded right away in con-

The Morells with Eva Braun at the last NSDAP convention in Nuremberg, in September 1938

vincing the hypochondriacally inclined Chancellor of his medical abilities, because from then on he invariably treated Hitler and was on call for him at all hours.

By 1937–1938 at the latest, the "personal physician" and his wife, actress Johanna "Hanni" Moller, had also joined the inner circle around the dictator. Already in January 1937, when Hitler spent as usual, the beginning of the New Year at the Berghof, Morell was present as well. Together with Hitler, Hoffmann, and the adjutant Brückner, he went to see the site where the teahouse on the Mooslahnerkopf, a mountain nearby, was to be built. In August 1937, Theodor and Hanni Morell were among Marianne Schönmann's wedding guests. And at New Year's 1937–1938, the Berlin doctor once more found himself, alongside Albert Speer, Sofie Stork, and others, on the Obersalzberg.[115] Starting in 1938, Morell seems to have taken up a permanent place among Hitler's companions. Photographs by Hoffmann show him with Karl Brandt and other faithful followers in the Reich Chancellor's special train on the way to the Austrian city of Klagenfurt, where on April 4, 1938, Hitler gave one of his many propaganda speeches leading up to the plebiscite on the "annexation" of Austria. In early September, Morell appeared in Party uniform between his wife and Eva Braun on a VIP platform at the last NSDAP Party convention ("Greater Germany Reich Party Convention") in Nuremberg;

that same month, he appeared at the conferences in Bad Godesberg and Munich.[116]

Morell was thus personally on site when Hitler, under threat of war and clearly suffering from extreme nervous tension, dramatically negotiated the cession of the Sudetenland to the German Reich. The "personal physician" accompanied Hitler to the discussions with British Prime Minister Neville Chamberlain that took place on September 22–24 in the posh Rheinhotel Dreesen, and to the Munich Conference with Chamberlain, Mussolini, and French Prime Minister Édouard Daladier in the "Führerbau" on Königsplatz on September 28–30.[117] In private, the Brandts, Speers, Bormanns, and Morells formed as it were the core of the Berghof group around Hitler, Eva Braun, and Braun's sister and friends.[118]

However, it seems—at least in retrospect—that Morell was greatly disliked there by everyone except Hitler, and was little respected as a doctor. Speer, for example, tears him apart in *Inside the Third Reich*, calling him "a bit of a screwball obsessed with making money," whose treatment methods "we never felt entirely easy about" and who was "the butt of humor" whenever Hitler was not present.[119] Franz von Sonnleithner, the Foreign Office liaison officer at the "Führer headquarters" during the last years of the war, described Dr. Morell as an irritating personality, "portly in stature, with a brownish skin color and fat fingers loaded with rings," who "did not [correspond to] the ideal image of the time."[120] Even the Wagners in Bayreuth considered him "a slob" and so unacceptable that, by order of his "Patient A," he had to avoid coming near them after 1938.[121]

Having attained a position of trust and thus a position of power with remarkable speed, he awakened suspicion and disapproval both in the private "Führer circle" and among high-ranking political associates. It did not fit into the public image of the bold and infallible "Führer"—a man who was trusted "blindly" and whose foreign policy triumphs had given him the aura of a kind of superman; a "real man" who could pull off whatever he wanted—that Morell was constantly supplying him with pills "in gold foil" and giving him injections. The public was not permitted to find out about these occasional indispositions of Hitler's, in any case, since his popularity in the country as a whole depended on his uninterrupted success.[122] The very idea of a man like Morell holding the fate of Germany in his hands by making daily decisions about the health of the mythical "hero" was suspect. Göring, for instance, allegedly called him "Herr Reich Injection Master [Spritzenmeister]," while Himmler, head of the Gestapo, secretly put him under surveillance after the war started in 1939 because he felt Morell had grown too powerful.[123] Morell himself complained about the snubs he received from all sides, and the fact that he had to fight hard to keep his position "near the Führer."[124]

Meanwhile, a practically codependent relationship developed between Hitler and Morell, especially during the war years. At first Morell used primarily digestive and vitamin pills to improve his patient's productivity and relieve, at least temporarily, his fear of becoming seriously ill, but in the last four years of his life, Hitler's intake of medicines rose to eighty-eight different substances, mostly stimulants and sedatives. Solving bodily problems by popping a pill seemed to satisfy the Nazi leader's desire for a treatment that was as discreet as possible—he did not, apparently, allow medical exams in which he would have to get undressed. Ernst Hanfstaengl later went so far as to describe Hitler's "practically spinsterish aversion to being seen without clothes on."[125] In fact, ever since the beginning of his political rise, Hitler was always concerned to minimize any access to his private life. Especially at the height of his power, the laboriously constructed legend of the "Führer" was not to be endangered by revealing any private needs and weaknesses. Hitler therefore swore by the discreet Morell; named him professor on December 24, 1938; remembered him with a tax-free endowment of 100,000 reichsmarks "on the occasion of January 30, 1943"; bestowed the "golden Party insignia" on him in February 1943; and helped in every imaginable way the pharmaceutical business that Morell ran in Hamburg and the Czech city of Olmütz. In brief: Hitler made him a very rich man.[126]

Moreover, there seems to have been hardly anyone around Hitler whom Morell did not also treat. Hitler personally made every member of his staff, and Eva Braun as well, go to see the personal physician at the least sign of any illness, apparently out of fear of catching it himself.[127] Speer, Ribbentrop, Hess, Lammers, Below, and the secretaries, as well as members of the Wagner family in Bayreuth, Hitler's longtime admirer the British aristocrat Unity Valkyrie Mitford, and the film director Leni Riefenstahl, were among Morell's patients at Hitler's behest.[128] Air force adjutant Below admitted to having agreed to an examination from Morell only "unwillingly" in early 1938, but said that he came to know Morell as a "conscientious and passionate doctor" and could "better understand" why "Hitler trusted him."[129] Speer visited Morell, according to his own account, as early as 1936, shortly after Morell had come into contact with

Hitler. At times Speer had even been, in his words, "Morell's showpiece," since "after a superficial examination" and the prescription of "intestinal bacteria, dextrose, vitamin, and hormone tablets," he spread the word about the successful treatment, even though he had in fact been treated by another doctor in Berlin. Speer lied, in other words, in order to, as he put it, "avoid offending Hitler."[130]

Eva Braun, who is not known to have suffered from any sickness more serious than the occasional cold, supposedly told Speer after an exam by Morell that Morell was "disgustingly dirty" and that she would "not let Morell treat her again."[131] We cannot know whether this corresponds to the truth, or whether Speer was retroactively making Eva Braun the star witness of his own argument against Morell. But why *would* she tell Speer—a man who himself zealously courted Hitler's favor and had misled Hitler about having been healed by the personal physician—that Morell disgusted her? Once again, Speer's explanations seem implausible and ultimately untrue.[132] Ilse Hess, in a letter to the wife of Hess's adjutant Alfred Leitgen, wrote on February 3, 1938, that the personal physician had "really helped" her husband and others "even with the heart issue." "Miss Braun," too, had had "very similar symptoms" but was now, thanks to Morell, "fit as a fiddle again."[133] Moreover, Morell's few remaining files show that Eva Braun was still his patient in January 1944.[134] She seems, in fact, to have joined Hitler when he underwent digestive cures during the war years.[135] We can only assume that by virtue of her special position she was even more concerned than the others at the "court" to placate the notoriously suspicious and standoffish Hitler—even by involving herself in his physical ailments and showing her solidarity by taking part in Morell's treatments.[136] If only because of this closeness, she could never openly express disapproval, even if she did dislike the doctor and revealed to one of the secretaries in spring 1944 that she "didn't trust him and hated him."[137]

Not the least impressive example of how dangerous it was to oppose Morell was Karl Brandt, who, along with his team of accompanying physicians, flatly rejected Morell's treatment methods. There was tension between the doctors from the beginning, with Brandt considering Morell a swindler and a quack.[138] After a bitter but surreptitious competitive struggle lasting many years, Brandt finally claimed, in October 1944, that Morell's pills were poisoning Hitler. He could not supply any proof, however, and so his intention to end Morell's career backfired and

Brandt himself was dismissed on October 10, 1944. Hitler saw the attack on Morell as a conspiracy and a betrayal of a man he trusted. And Brandt, who owed his rise entirely to Hitler's good graces, now learned for himself what it meant to stand outside the "court."[139]

Hermann Esser

In the broader Berghof circle must also be included Hermann Esser, an "old campaigner" and for many years a close friend of Hitler who used the familiar *"du"* with him. Esser was a member of the NSDAP since 1920, and already the editor in chief of the *Völkischer Beobachter* and *Der Nationalsozialist*, two Party newspapers, in his early twenties. In 1923 he rose to be the first head of propaganda in the Party, and from 1926 to 1932 he worked, again as editor in chief, for the weekly *Illustrierter Beobachter*, which was lavishly illustrated and which reported mainly on meetings, rallies, and marches of the NSDAP and the SS. Hitler's rise to Chancellor brought the trained journalist, known as an aggressive speaker and radical anti-Semite, into office as the Bavarian Commerce Secretary from 1933 to 1935. Ernst Hanfstaengl, who described Esser as his friend, called him the "enfant terrible of the Party" and also probably its "most talented orator after Hitler."[140] Hitler met with Esser whenever he was in Bavaria; as Nicolaus von Below remarked, Esser was among the Nazi leader's "Munich crowd."[141] He was a "mercenary type," like Ernst Röhm and Max Amann, and belonged to the "hard core" around Hitler going back to the early days of the NSDAP. The phrase "Germany's Mussolini is called Adolf Hitler"[142]—with which the cult of the "Führer" was born in 1922, taking Italian fascism as its model—comes from Esser. Hitler, in turn, held fast to his friendship with Esser, despite political as well as personal differences of opinion and even though Esser's brutal, boorish personality had been controversial for a long time among many Party members.[143] Albert Speer, too, remembers only reluctantly "those Bavarian vulgarians in Hitler's retinue" whom he himself "always kept . . . at arm's length."[144]

After the war, when questioned about his National Socialist career, Hermann Esser stated (in Nuremberg on December 6, 1946) that there were arguments between himself and Hitler in 1934, resulting in his stepping down as minister and withdrawing from political life. He was not politically active anymore after 1935, he said, and also stopped attending the Party convention events in Nuremberg. He had merely accepted the nonpolitical position of "President of the Reich Tourism Association" in 1936.[145] In addition, Esser claimed, he had disapproved of and criticized the Aryanization measures and other violent steps against Jews. When questioned about his book, first published in 1927 by the Party's own press, Eher Verlag, and bearing the infamous title *Die jüdische Weltpest: Kann ein Jude Staatsbürger sein? (The Jewish World Plague: Can a Jew Be a Citizen?)*, Esser talked his way out of it by saying that Alfred Rosenberg had given him all the content for the book. Even though Rosenberg was one of Esser's fiercest opponents within the Party, at least in the 1920s, Esser now tried to suggest that the chief ideologue of the Party—who by that point had already been hanged as one of the main Nazi war criminals— was the actual author of the book.[146] As for the new edition of the book that came out in 1939, shortly after the November pogrom of 1938, with the title *Die jüdische Weltpest: Judendämmerung auf dem Erdball (The Jewish World Plague: Twilight of the Jews Across the Globe)*, Esser claimed not to know a thing about it. He had, he said, neither written the book nor ever seen it.[147] The American interrogator summarized Esser's testimony in his report by saying that he had been opposed to the Nuremberg Laws of 1935 and that the "Jewish question" represented one of the reasons for his differences with Hitler.[148]

In reality, Esser had every reason to distance himself from his hate-filled screed, which among other things explained the allegedly evil "racial character" of the Jews using falsified passages from the Old Testament and the Talmud. Right in the introduction, it declared that it was time to say "Enough" to "certain more or less intellectual types with their tear-jerker morality always talking about the 'poor,' 'persecuted' Jews." The Jews were actually "enemies of the world and of humanity," and a "Reich under National Socialist government" would necessarily "stand against the Jewish world plague as a deadly enemy."[149] Esser's book was thus among the early works of National Socialist literature justifying the murder of the German and European Jews, whom Esser stigmatized as the true originators of racism. Esser claimed in Nuremberg—of course—to have heard about the "gassing" of the Jews only after the end of the war.[150]

With this testimony, Esser was trying, like so many of Hitler's close followers after the collapse of the Nazi state, to escape responsibility and save his own life and livelihood in the new era. Two months before his interrogation, the International Military Court in Nuremberg had passed sentence on the twenty-two main war criminals of the Nazi regime and condemned ten of them to death. Numerous other organizations and groups were still under suspicion, including the leadership of the NSDAP, ministers, and high government officials. The trials would drag on into the spring of 1949. Esser, who was in Nuremberg only as a witness, therefore went underground until September 1949, just to be safe.[151]

In truth, Esser absolutely did not withdraw from politics or distance himself from Hitler after 1935. The old comrade-in-arms continued to be among the regular guests on the Obersalzberg.[152] On January 10, 1937, for example, he inspected a model of the House of German Tourism, together with Hitler, Goebbels, Reich press chief Otto Dietrich, Fritz Todt (later General Commissioner for the Regulation of the Construction Industry), and Albert Speer. The foundation stone for the building was laid on June 14, 1938, in Berlin,[153] and it would be the first and only construction project to be mostly completed from the "World Capital Germania" as conceived by Hitler and Speer. Hermann Esser's posh seat of office was to have been in the center of Berlin (approximately where the New National Library [Neue Staatsbibliothek] is today), if the course of the war had not necessitated the halting of construction projects in 1942; his offices were therefore located in the nearby Columbus House at 1 Potsdamer Platz, one of the last buildings from the era of "New Construction."[154] Esser's position was not, it is true, a particularly political one like that of Max Amann (president of the Reich Press Chamber) or that of Alfred Rosenberg (Reich Minister for the Occupied Eastern Territories), but there is no question of his having disappeared from Hitler's environs.[155] Rather, he remained quite close to Hitler personally, and his later important positions—president of the National Tourism Committee after 1936, and state secretary for tourism in the Ministry for Public Enlightenment and Propaganda—show no signs of any distance between Esser and the Nazi regime, nor of his departure from its inner circle of power.[156]

By the time Esser rose to join the National Tourism Committee, all private tourist organizations had already been "coordinated" and nationalized—that is, placed under the Ministry of Propaganda's direct control—as per the "Reich Law Concerning the National Tourism Association" of March 28, 1936. Three years later, Esser was one of three state secretaries under Goebbels in charge of the tourism division in his ministry. His responsibilities included deciding who would fill the top management positions of all the state tourism associations. The Nazi regime

wanted to ensure what they called "tight, goal-focused conduct" in the
encouraging of foreign tourism. Above all, vacations and leisure time
were to be instruments of propaganda, playing no small part in the legiti-
mization of National Socialist rule. In the interest of creating a "nation of
workers united in a Volksgemeinschaft," individuals were to be channeled
into groups and managed as groups, even during their leisure hours. In
short, the regime promoted politically organized People's Tourism and
Social Tourism.[157]

Following government orders, tourism within the borders of the German Reich was given an increasingly anti-Semitic bent. The goal was
to create "Jew-free sites." Jewish and non-Jewish guests were ordered to
be separated in spas, especially in the popular vacation spots that profited from group tourist trips organized by the German Workers' Front
(Deutsche Arbeitsfront, or DAF): Bavaria, the North Sea baths, and the
Baltic Sea baths, where so-called spa anti-Semitism was widespread even
before 1933.[158] "Power Through Pleasure" (Kraft durch Freude, or KdF),
the extremely popular leisure organization of the DAF, made it possible
for the first time for the lower social classes to take vacations, thereby
winning enormous prestige for the Nazis.[159] The annual spectacle of the
Party convention in Nuremberg, destination for up to 450,000 visitors a
year between 1933 and 1938, was another tourist gold mine. The management of domestic tourism continued even during the early years of the
war, although accommodations were increasingly used for military purposes. Finally, in September 1944, the Tourism Department of the Ministry of Propaganda ceased operation. Until that point, Hermann Esser had
pursued the politics of tourism according to Nazi ideology; his office was
in no way merely an apolitical management position.

More important, however, Esser continued to have high personal status in Hitler's eyes. Otherwise it would be very difficult to explain how his
private problems—a divorce from his first wife—could have turned into
a fairly major political issue.[160] Esser's separation was extremely complicated, and it occupied not only Hitler's time and attention in 1938 but
also that of Justice Minister Franz Gürtner and Reich Minister Lammers,
head of the Reich Chancellery. Hitler, to whom it was apparently very
important to bring the chaos of his friend's family life to an end, ordered
Lammers in fall 1938 to report to him on the Obersalzberg about the
state of Esser's divorce proceedings. Lammers asked the Justice Minister for the files concerning Esser's divorce, which filled seven volumes

by that point, and had them sent to Berchtesgaden on October 29, 1938. Gürtner added, in explaining Esser's difficult situation to Lammers, that Esser's wife, whom he had married on July 5, 1923, and with whom he had two children, did not agree to the divorce that he had been pushing for for years. Esser had already tried in vain more than once to dissolve the marriage—in 1933 and again in 1935—but all of his efforts came to nothing, since, according to the divorce laws then in effect, from the Civil Law Code (Bürgerliches Gesetzbuch, or BGB) of 1900, divorce was permitted only by reason of culpable matrimonial offenses on the part of a spouse.[161] Divorce required the innocent party to file proceedings against the guilty party, and at least one of four "findings of fact"—adultery, intention to kill, malicious abandonment, or grave dereliction of marital duties—had to be proven. In this case, Hermann Esser had been living with another woman for many years and had another two children with her.[162] So he himself was guilty of adultery under the law and could not win a divorce.

Even in the Weimar Republic there had been efforts to change these regulations. But the Nazi regime was in fact the first to carry out a fundamental reform, along National Socialist lines and unopposed by the Church. It used the "annexation" of Austria as the occasion to pass a new divorce law on July 6, 1938, making the former justifications for divorce invalid and creating a system whereby a marriage was judged by its significance for the "Volksgemeinschaft." It was entirely in this sense that "refusal to propagate" and "infertility of the spouse" now counted as valid reasons for divorce. In addition, the National Socialist legislators introduced for the first time, into Section 55 of the BGB, a general concept of irreconcilable differences, according to which a marriage could be dissolved after three years of separation without a finding of guilt. The spouse who did not want the divorce could file an appeal, but the judges would decide whether sustaining the marriage was "morally" justified.[163]

The new law seemed to betoken a breakthrough in Hermann Esser's deadlocked private situation. Two days after his files arrived in Berchtesgaden, on October 31, 1938, Lammers presented the situation to Hitler at the Berghof. It was hard to predict, he said, which way the judge would rule, because the principle of determining the guilty party had not been entirely abolished by the new law, and adultery still qualified as a reason for divorce that weighed heavily. As a result, there were particular problems with remarriage, since according to Section 9 of the BGB a marriage "could not take place between a person who was divorced by reason of

adultery and the individual with whom that person had had the adulter-
ous relationship, if this adultery is determined in the divorce proceedings
to have been the reason for the divorce."[164]

Lammers remarked to Gürtner—in confidence, he wrote—that in the
discussions about the new marriage law the issue had been, above all, how
to make a divorce possible "as a consequence of the objective collapse of
the marriage . . . without it coming down to declaring one or the other
spouse guilty." In these discussions, "the Führer . . . had Esser's case in
mind." If the judges refused to follow this interpretation of Section 55,
Lammers threatened, "the only remaining course of action would be to
consider revising the law."[165] Hitler's interpretation was, Lammers wrote,
"of special significance," since he, as "Führer and Reich Chancellor,"
was in the final analysis "the sole lawgiver of the Third Reich." If the state
court's decision was not in favor of a divorce, Lammers wrote to Gürtner, "a second hearing of the case would have to be worked toward in as
expedited a manner as possible, on the Führer's instructions."[166] Clearly
law and justice had little meaning at this point for the fifty-nine-year-old
jurist, who had been educated before World War I and was an undersec-
retary in the Interior Ministry by the early 1920s. Lammers was prepared
to put himself outside any legal framework as long as the "Führer's" wish
demanded it—no matter how personal that wish might be. As in an absolute monarchy, Hitler alone embodied the law, in Lammers's view.[167]

The district court in Berlin could not resist this pressure from the very
highest places. It decided in favor of the party who was actually guilty,
and put the party who was legally and morally innocent in the dock. The
court's opinion of December 23, 1938, found that the defendant—that
is, Esser's wife—lacked "the true marital attitude," since she could not
show that she had "a serious will to sustain a true marriage."[168] Esser duly
thanked Lammers for his "support in the matter" in a letter that same day,
and reported that the district court had "announced the expected decision . . . today." As a result, he said Christmas would be "a celebration of
joy" for him, too, this year.[169] Still, the decision was not fully legal, since
Therese Esser filed the appeal to which she was entitled. Once again,
the Minister of Justice intervened. Gürtner wrote to Lammers to assure
him that on January 24, 1939, he had insisted in a meeting with the Lord
Justice of Appeal "that the sociopolitical and population-policy considerations which the Führer put into effect by issuing this decree . . . be
impressed upon the judges involved in the matter of this divorce."[170] The

Superior Court of Justice of Berlin finally rejected Therese Esser's appeal on March 17, 1939.

Less than three weeks later, on April 5, Hermann Esser remarried. Among the wedding guests were Adolf Hitler and Eva Braun, the Bormanns, the Morells, and Reich Treasurer Franz Xaver Schwarz and his wife.[171] The presence of Hitler and Braun shows that Esser had in no way fallen into disfavor, much less been banned from the inner circle. Rather, it indicates a special, almost familial bond. Eventually, on November 10, 1940, Eva Braun would become the godmother of Esser's daughter, who was given the name Eva.[172] Hitler himself had long attended his closest followers' weddings—those of Goebbels, Göring, Bormann, and Brandt, among others—and had been their children's godfather. Now Eva Braun was likewise serving as the godparent of one of those followers' children.[173]

"Lady of the House" at the Berghof, 1936–1939

It is not known whether Eva Braun, in her new and practically unassailable position at Hitler's side, undertook to be anyone else's godmother. There are suggestions, though, to indicate that Martin Bormann also named one of his daughters after her. Now, how significant was this act of becoming a godparent within the inner circle, that is, in a nonpublic sphere? Taking on duties as a godparent actually played a significant role in the Nazi regime's propaganda campaign to increase the birthrate in Germany. Hitler himself had said about mothers: "Every child [a mother] brings into the world is a victory in the battle for the life or death of her People." He thereby equated motherhood with being a soldier. For publicity, he personally became the godfather of every demonstrably "Aryan" family's tenth child.[174] In Esser's case, Hitler was once again taking on the role of patron of the families of his old Party comrades. The role of patron and protector allowed him to cast himself as the keeper of the German People, in private as well as according to his public code of conduct that he exaggerated to an almost religious level and that was given widespread publicity: "I serve him with my will, I give to him my life."[175] The question arises, of course, how he could justify to himself and to those who knew his circumstances the fact that he remained unmarried and childless despite obviously living with Eva Braun.

For the National Socialists, "boosting and facilitating the will to propagate within the Volksgemeinschaft" was one of the "most pressing tasks of the rebuilding of the People." Nazi doctors who worked in the field of "political biology" explained "intentional birth control" as a "misguided attitude in the area of character," or even went so far as to describe it as an expression of "moral decay."[176] Hitler's relationship with Eva Braun must therefore have caused some astonishment even in the trusted circle at the Berghof. In the Nazi regime, the personal needs of the individual were subordinated to the requirements of the "Volksgemeinschaft"; rogue actions taken for individual reasons were propagandistically condemned as embodying a "Jewish-liberal" outlook on life, and Hitler himself publicly declaimed that "of all the tasks before us, the most exalted and thus most holy human task is the preservation of the species defined by the blood given to us by God." But he clearly judged his own private life by entirely different standards.

Hitler absolutely refused to get married and explicitly wanted no children of his own; neither, as is said, did Eva Braun.[177] But why? On Hitler's part, was it from the politically calculated wish to "visibly stand apart" from those around him, as their "Führer"?[178] Did Hitler play, as Ian Kershaw claims, the roll of an "idol" within his closest circle of friends as well?[179] And what effects did this attitude have on Eva Braun and her position within the Berghof group? Here is where we have to distinguish between the propaganda assertions and the actual rationales. The first thing to point out is that Hitler's political style of promoting a cult of the mother while remaining an unmarried heartthrob was not his own invention. Historian Brigitte Hamann has shown that Hitler was merely copying the propaganda pose of Karl Lueger, the popular anti-Semitic mayor of Vienna (1897–1910) whom Hitler idolized, and who likewise used his bachelor status for political purposes. Like Lueger, who told his lover that he could not marry because he needed "the women" in order to "achieve anything" politically, Hitler said: "Lots of women are attracted to me because I am unmarried. That was especially useful during our days of struggle. It's the same as with a movie actor; when he marries he loses a certain something for the women who adore him. Then he is no longer their idol as he was before."[180]

Hitler accordingly emphasized, in a speech at the 1936 Party convention to the elite National Socialist Women's League (Nationalsozialist-ische Frauenschaft, or NSF), that he "never would have been able to lead the Party to victory without women's constancy and truly loving devotion

Hitler between Eva and Gretl Braun in the obligatory group photograph on New Year's Eve on the Obersalzberg, 1939

toward the movement." He knew, he said, that "women stood with the movement from the depths of their hearts, steadfast and true, and are bound together with me forever." Their children were in fact what gave his work meaning, and they belonged to their mothers "in exactly the same way . . . that they belong, in the same moment, to me."[181] Hitler drew women to him by linking the concepts of devotion, eternal bonds, and children to his own person. He thereby cast himself as the husband of every German woman and the father of every German child — in accordance with the well-known motto of the cult of the "Führer," "Hitler is Germany! Germany is Hitler!" — and satisfied their deeply rooted desire for a "messiah of the People."[182]

Out of the public eye, Hitler gave deeper insights into the real reason for his remaining unmarried over tea one night in January 1942 at his East Prussian "Führer headquarters." With respect to his private life, he said there that it was a "lucky thing" he had never married, since the time commitment of a wife would have been a burden on him. He explained further: "That's the bad thing about marriage: It establishes legal rights! So it's much more proper to have a lover. The burden drops away and everything remains a gift." If we believe this account, Hitler's confession "disturbed" the secretaries who were there, Christa Schroeder and Gerda Daranowski, so that Hitler added jokingly that "of course" this was true "only for great men."[183]

Hitler's refusal to marry Eva Braun thus apparently had nothing to do with her, nor with the assertion that, according to Albert Speer, he "obviously" thought of his girlfriend as "socially acceptable only within strict limits."[184] Rather, he seems to have been afraid to expose himself to the possibilities of a wife's power and influence, and to make himself vulnerable in the private sphere. The fact is that he always kept everyone in this sphere who could get too close to him, including all of the members of his real family, at a distance. He saw his sister Paula every year between 1929 and 1941, for example, either in Munich, Berlin, or Vienna, but demanded that she live "under the name Frau Wolf and strictly incognito."[185] Even back in 1924, when Rudolf Hess suggested to him while they were in prison together at Landsberg that Hitler could have his sister come from Vienna to Munich, Hitler reacted with panic. Hess wrote to his future wife that Hitler dismissed the idea

> with every sign of horror. He became nervous, shifted back and forth in his chair, ran his hands through his hair—"For God's sake no!" That would be, with all his love for her, a burden and a constraint—she could try to influence him before an important decision, or plead with him. He won't get married, for the same reason, and he even—he implied—avoids any serious attachments with a female. He must be able to face all dangers at any time without the slightest human or personal considerations, and be able even to die, if necessary.[186]

Given the propaganda and cult of personality that cast him as a godlike superfather, a relationship like the one he had with Eva Braun was not allowed and had to be kept in the strictest secrecy from the outside world. His girlfriend could not appear in public, so as not to damage his aura. At the Berghof, too, when official visitors or foreign guests were there she remained out of sight, withdrawing to her room the whole time. The same was true not only for Eva Braun but for all of the private guests, who, according to Speer, "were banished to the upper floor" on such occasions.[187]

Given all of these constraints upon her, can we describe Eva Braun as "Lady of the House" at the Berghof at all? After 1936, she did take

Eva Braun on the Berghof terrace, photographed by Walter Frentz, ca. 1943

on the role of the hostess more and more within their private circle at least. Unlike everyone else except Hitler, she invited friends and their children or other family members to the Obersalzberg. She also, Speer commented in August 1945, suffered from an "inferiority complex" and so "often" came across as "conceited and dismissive" to outsiders.[188] At no point, in any case, did Eva Braun act as "housekeeper" at the Berghof: other people were there to worry about the housekeeping, including a married pair of house managers as well as, for special occasions, Hitler's majordomo Arthur Kannenberg.[189] Presumably, in any case, she inter- vened in developments from time to time and tried to put her own ideas into effect. Especially among the housekeeping staff, but also among the professional colleagues and several female regular guests, she seems to have made enemies for a variety of reasons. At the end of 1945, Hanskarl von Hasselbach (a surgeon, SS-Obersturmbannführer, and the Nazi lead- er's third accompanying physician along with Karl Brandt and Werner Haase—part of Karl Brandt's team since 1934) expressed a deeply critical opinion of Eva Braun's conduct on the Obersalzberg. She called herself "Lady of the Berghof" in recent years, he reported, but only laid claim to the privileges of that position without fulfilling the attendant duties. Everyone in the house except Hitler had to do what she wanted, he said, while she hardly cared about the well-being of the service personnel. Has- selbach also held Eva Braun responsible for the makeup of the Berghof circle, and for its low "intellectual and moral level."[190]

In any case, the people in Hitler's immediate environment did not demand any explanation, much less justification, of Eva Braun's existence and presence in closest proximity to him, even in the context of the reign- ing morality of the time or Hitler's ideological stipulations. Especially in his refuge on the Obersalzberg, Hitler was surrounded by true-believing followers who not only shared his political convictions but saw in him a heroic figure of historical greatness.[191] Robert Ley—not actually in the Berghof circle but one of Hitler's earliest henchmen and uncritical of him to the very end—recorded for posterity in his cell in Nuremberg, in 1945, that Hitler's life was "a single act of sacrifice for his People right up to his sacrificial death," and claimed: "Nothing, absolutely nothing—not even the woman he loved—had any influence on him, except for his duty."[192]

Emmy Göring, in her memoir, illustrates how unwilling Hitler was to allow this image to be tarnished. She complains that she was not allowed to meet Eva Braun no matter how hard she tried to arrange it: Hitler kept Braun "under lock and key" on the Obersalzberg, she said, and when she invited the ladies of the Berghof (Anni Brandt, Hanni Morell, and Eva and Gretl Braun) to tea at her own Obersalzberg country house one day, in the "second year of the war" (1940), they all said yes but Hit- ler summoned Hermann Göring late that night and told him that Eva

Braun couldn't attend. The reason he gave was that Braun was "so bash-ful, she was even afraid" of Göring's wife.[193] In fact, Hitler had kept the second-most-powerful man in the "Third Reich" at a distance for years, in his private life. He had served as a witness at the ostentatious wedding of Hermann and Emmy Göring on April 11, 1935, at the Berlin Cathedral, and three years later had agreed to be their only daughter's godfather; politically as well, he had helped Göring reach a unique position of power and named him his successor in a secret decree as early as December 1934. But despite, or because of, Göring's popularity and growing politi-cal power—he had already started to present himself as "successor to the Führer and Chancellor" to foreign diplomats—Göring was not among the inner circle of Hitler intimates.[194] Instead, the Nazi leader avoided personal closeness, probably so as not to let his designated successor's lust for power and fame get out of hand and ultimately grow uncontrollable. Emmy Göring's attempt to get close to Eva Braun and thus to Hitler's private life must therefore have been extremely unwelcome to him.

This episode does not, as Emmy Göring put it, reveal "the tragedy of this woman [i.e., Braun] in such a moving way"; rather it shows the nature of the relationship between Hitler and Hermann Göring.[195] Furthermore, the question naturally arises: Why did Emmy Göring invite Hitler's girl-friend over for the first time only in "the second year of the war"? Why not in 1937 or 1938? Hermann Göring's loss of political power, which had already begun in 1939 and accelerated starting in September 1940 due to his military errors in the air war against England, suggests that his wife invited Eva Braun only as a means to an end: an attempt to compensate for fading political and military significance by getting closer on a per-sonal level.[196]

Hitler's inapproachability and standoffishness, meanwhile, were not simply the "Führer's" personal proclivities; they also protected him from needing to reveal anything about his personal life and thus from becom-ing humanly vulnerable. As a result, Eva Braun's "socially unclear posi-tion" can also be attributed to the fact that Hitler lived outside the bounds of his own ideology of the "Volksgemeinschaft," and claimed for himself the status of an exception.[197] In fact, it was not only Eva Braun's social sta-tus that was questionable among the "Führer's" close circle; the character of her relationship to Hitler itself remained completely mysterious. Pub-lic displays of affection or even the slightest hint of any physical closeness, at least in the years leading up to the outbreak of war, remained nonex-istent at the Berghof. Both Hitler and Braun were "thoroughly prudish,"

Speer reported to Joachim Fest in 1978. Even in his intimate circle, Hitler avoided any move in that direction. He was always careful to maintain a certain distance from his entourage, and he valued conventionality and traditional behavior. Even in his relations to Speer and Goebbels, he remained above all a "father figure."[198]

Every guest was left on his or her own to decide what the connection between Hitler and Braun might be. And so, even after the end of the war, opinions differed drastically about whether the couple had an actual love affair or merely a "relationship for show." Speer, in any case, Hitler's young close friend, had no doubt that Eva Braun was Hitler's lover. Under questioning from Allied officers in Kransberg in the summer of 1945, he stated in writing that Eva Braun meant "very much" to Hitler. Hitler had spoken of her "with great respect and inner admiration"; she was "the woman whom he loved." A mere quarter-century later, in *Inside the Third Reich*, there was no longer any talk of "love" as what Hitler felt for Eva Braun. Twenty years in prison and the influence of his editorial advisers Joachim Fest and Wolf Jobst Siedler had changed Speer's way of seeing things. The once-powerful Minister of Armaments, who remained obsessed with power to the end, was now concerned to emphasize his political and personal distance from the man whom he had served with unswerving conviction to the last moment. Now he described Hitler as cold and always unapproachable, a man who "had no humor" and acted ruthlessly, suspiciously, and cynically toward his lover.[199] Twenty-five years earlier, however, in Kransberg, when his statements had been less calculated, the same Speer had drawn a distinction between Hitler's public conduct and his dealings with people in "private life." According to Speer's earlier account, Hitler acted chilly and "rarely like a 'person'" when working, but in private he had "a soul" (that is, he was capable of feeling), "like every other human being."[200]

Max Amann, who knew Hitler since their service together in World War I, described Hitler's relation to women as "normal" in his interrogation by the U.S. Seventh Army on May 26, 1945. The only woman with whom Hitler had had "occasional intimate relations" was Eva Braun, Amann said. The literal record runs as follows: "Amann describes Hitler as a sexually normal man. Hitler's only woman friend, with whom he had occasional intimate relations, was Eva Braun, a former employee of the photographer Hoffmann. . . . During the last month she was constantly around Hitler."[201]

Two months later, Franz Xaver Schwarz, another fellow traveler of many years, "old campaigner," and friend who used the familiar "*du*" with Hitler, said diametrically opposite things about Hitler and Eva Braun. Schwarz was an anti-Semite "in every fiber of his being" and "from an early age," according to Richard Walther Darré after 1945, and in Hitler Schwarz had found the man who "saw things politically and expressed them the way Schwarz felt them to be."[202] A member of NSDAP since 1922 and its treasurer from its reestablishment in 1925 to the end, as well as a Reichsleiter, SS-Oberstgruppenführer, SA-Obergruppenführer, and member of Parliament, he—along with his wife, the former Bertha Breher—was among the Nazi leader's and Eva Braun's Munich circle of friends. Both Schwarzes were welcome guests on the Obersalzberg.[203] Under questioning from Allied officers on July 21, 1945, Schwarz stated that Hitler had had a "platonic relationship" with Eva Braun since 1931. He said Hitler himself had told him that he lived only for his work: "A woman gets absolutely nothing from me. I can't pay any attention to any of that."[204] We should note in evaluating the former Reich treasurer's reliability on this topic that he had absolutely no reason to reveal anything about Hitler's carefully concealed private life to his American interrogators. In Nuremberg at the end of 1945, Schwarz gave the impression of being a "sincere fanatic, who still professes unbound personal admiration for Hitler."[205]

Then again, Christa Schroeder, Hitler's longtime secretary, was also convinced that the erotic side of the relationship between Hitler and Eva Braun was a false pretense. It is true that, on May 22, 1945, three weeks after Hitler's and Eva Braun's demise, during an American officer's interrogation in Berchtesgaden, she answered the question of whether "Hitler saw Miss Braun as his wife" with the words "That's how he treated her." And to the follow-up question, "Did he see her that way?" she replied: "Yes, of course."[206] Meanwhile, in the memoir she published later, she claimed, like Franz Xaver Schwarz, that the entire relationship of her "leader" to the female sex had been purely platonic in nature. His stepniece Geli Raubal was the only woman he "loved," and he "would definitely have married her later," she wrote. Eva Braun, on the other hand, was in Hitler's life only to protect him "from further threats of suicide." With "her presence" he had also, she said, constructed a "protective shield against all the other pushy women."[207]

Christa Schroeder felt, as she wrote in her memoir, that this assess-

ment was corroborated by statements from Heinrich Hoffmann, Julius
Schaub, and Ada Klein, an acquaintance of Hitler's from the 1920s. In
truth, however, neither Hoffmann nor Schaub ever expressed himself in
these terms. Both men knew Hitler and Eva Braun as closely as could be
and were involved, in one way or another, in the couple's everyday life.
And neither of them argued that the relationship was not an intimate one.
Hoffmann did claim in 1947, in a written statement, that the relationship
started, in his opinion, as "merely platonic in nature." But he added that it
"took a definite shape . . . many years later," and that Hitler indulged Eva
Braun "in the usual way": "the way anyone indulges a lover."[208] He dated
the start of this development to around the time when he bought her the
house in Munich, namely 1935–1936. Hitler's former personal photographer also explicitly pointed out that he was eager to "clarify" the situation,
given the upcoming appearance of his case before the Munich denazification court. He intended to refute before the court the accusation that
he had gained any influence or "political power" in Hitler's circle from
the love affair between his employee and the Nazi leader, or that he had
even fostered the relationship for that reason. If this suspicion were to
be confirmed, it could lead to unpleasant consequences for him, since
he denied ever having had anything to do with Nazi politics or National
Socialist propaganda. It was thus in his interest to emphasize that Eva
Braun was not a "serious relationship" for Hitler in the first six years of
their acquaintance.[209]

Meanwhile, Julius Schaub, SS-Obergruppenführer and Hitler's personal adjutant, questioned on the topic in Nuremberg on March 12, 1947,
by Robert Kempner, the assistant U.S. chief counsel, gave no information
at all about the nature of the relationship between Hitler and Eva Braun.
Kempner asked whether Hitler "loved [Braun] very much" and Schaub
answered: "He was very fond of her [*Er hat sie sehr gern gehabt*]." When
Kempner followed up and asked what exactly that meant, Schaub, Hitler's
longtime close confidant who had been near him at all times for twenty
years, replied: "He liked her [*Er hat sie lieb gehabt*]." Schaub added that
Hitler had told him he would "never marry" because he "didn't have
time for it" and was "constantly away," although this "view" had met with
incomprehension from those around him: "We often wondered why, we
didn't understand. After all, we were married and not with our wives."[210]
Schaub, a simple soul, apparently knew nothing about Hitler's fears of
family ties. He also misjudged the compulsions bound up with Hitler's

categorical self-idealization, nor the fact that the power of the National Socialist system depended in large part on the myth of a "Führer" standing above all everyday politics and problems.[211] Even aside from these limitations, Schaub's statements after the war were generally questionable or downright false. Schaub seems to have remained, after Hitler's death, an uncritical admirer and loyal protector of his leader's secrets.[212]

Herta Schneider, in contrast, the friend of Eva Braun's who had perhaps the most intimate knowledge of her relationship with Hitler, stated in June 1949: "As a person, in private, Hitler was perfectly nice. Braun loved him very much and he loved her, too."[213] In the end, therefore, it seems that despite all the prudery Hitler and Eva Braun displayed, their relationship was basically like a marriage, and that they conveyed this fact to their immediate circle.

Still, Hitler certainly set the terms of the relationship and Eva Braun had to adapt to them. As for the question of why she did it, what feelings she harbored or what intentions she might have been pursuing, opinions differ. On the one hand, she has been described as an unhappy, frustrated, entirely passive and patient woman who uncomplainingly endured her "fate." On the other hand, she is portrayed as happy and cheerful, with a lust for life, and not particularly feminine. Clearly, the secrecy surrounding her person and the fact that she played an unmistakably important yet undefined role in Hitler's life, led to conflicts within the private circle and among the Nazi leader's staff, so that not all the members of this largely closed society on the Obersalzberg and in Munich liked her. These facts may explain the widely differing views of her.

Officially, Eva Braun remained a member of the staff and an employee of Heinrich Hoffmann's after 1936. She obviously did not have to show up at the office in Munich every day, but she did become a passionate photographer and home-movie maker during this period. She "often" made "photographs" and color movies of the Berghof's private circle "available" to her boss, Hoffmann, as he himself stated after the war. Eva Braun even shot movies with a 16 mm Agfa-Movex camera. She took "valuable photographs" that he apparently bought from her for enormous sums of money: for example, according to Hoffmann himself, the astronomical sum of 20,000 reichsmarks for "a piece of photography work" in 1940, though he said he could no longer remember whether the money "was paid directly to Eva Braun or handed over to her sister." It is also not known whether or how Hoffmann used these photographs.[214] But it is certainly impos-

Eva Braun photographing Hitler in conversation with Morell, 1937

sible to claim that Eva Braun no longer worked for Photohaus Hoffmann after 1936. Alfons Brümmer, an employee of Hoffmann's company, was still depositing money into her savings account at Munich's Bayerische Vereinsbank on September 15, 1943: 5,000 reichsmarks for the "secretary" on that particular day—a sum comparable to an annual income at the time.[215]

Thus there is no sign of any professional distance between Hitler's personal photographer and Hitler's girlfriend. And so it is not surprising that Hoffmann, in a written statement for his denazification proceedings of 1947–1948, says not a word about his continued professional ties to Braun after 1936. In the public denazification hearing against her, he stated only that Eva Braun had "offered her things to the business" while he himself had had "nothing to do with it."[216] In light of the amounts of money changing hands, this claim is worse than dubious. The real question is why Hoffmann might have wanted to keep Eva Braun well-disposed to him by means of these huge payments. Was he thereby ensuring that she would speak well of him to the man in charge? In any case, the "Führer's" lover seems to have been part of the nepotistic practices that were common in National Socialist circles, over and above the financial benefits Hitler accorded her personally.[217]

So as not to stand out among Hitler's entourage, Eva Braun held the official position of a private secretary. Speer later claimed that whenever the Nazi leader spent time on the Obersalzberg, she likewise had to be there—only once, he wrote in *Inside the Third Reich*, had Hitler given her "a week's vacation."[218] The insinuation here, that Eva Braun's presence at the Berghof was a kind of duty or work for her, is unfounded and in fact attributable only to the special character of Speer's memoirs. Speer himself often emphasized elsewhere the loyalty, devotion, dedication, and love Eva Braun felt for Hitler. Her constant access to the Berghof was a privilege, not a duty, which no member of the "inner circle" would ever have voluntarily gone without.[219]

In any case, Eva Braun lived in Munich most of the time. In summer 1935, when she was still living with her younger sister Margarete (Gretl) on Widenmayerstrasse, Hoffmann bought her a small house built four years earlier, at 12 Wasserburger Strasse (today Delpstrasse) in Bogenhausen. A Munich businessman, Adolf Widmann, had offered it for sale, and he said after the war that Eva Braun had visited the building to take a look and Hoffmann paid the asking price (35,000 reichsmarks) a few weeks later, with a "private check." Hitler appeared at no point in the transaction, Widmann stated.[220] Only when Widmann delayed supplying a receipt for the transfer fee that he had requested for various items in the house did Hoffmann and his attorney "verbally request" that he draw up the document "as urgently as possible," "because Hitler wanted the receipt."[221] Three years later, on September 2, 1938, ownership was transfered to Eva Braun, "private secretary in Munich."[222]

Hoffmann made contradictory statements in this regard as well. In his defense document from 1947, he first claimed that Hitler had bought Eva "a little house." In the public denazification court proceedings against Eva Braun, on July 1, 1949, in Munich, he then said that he "could no longer recall how the purchase of the house" had come to pass; he might have acquired the property for his son-in-law Baldur von Schirach. He also no longer knew whether he "had been repaid by Hitler." Finally, he added: "The end result was that I did not pay for the house. The cost was reimbursed, I don't know by whom, and I also don't know in what form."[223]

Hoffmann's sudden forgetfulness is not credible, nor is it conceivable that National Youth Leader Baldur von Schirach would ever have considered a residence as modest as the little house in Bogenhausen for himself and his family. In fact, Schirach became the owner of a seventeenth-century castle, Schloss Aspenstein, in Kochel am See (about forty miles from Munich), on March 12, 1936, around when Eva Braun and her sister Margarete moved to Wasserburger Strasse (March 30, 1936).[224] Hitler's girlfriend's new domicile was located not far from where other prominent Party members lived—on the same street, for example, as Max Amann, president of the Reich Press Chamber and director of the Central Publishing House of the NSDAP. Heinrich Hoffmann's villa was a few streets over. Heinrich Himmler (the Reichsführer-S), Hermann Giesler (architect and "General Building Inspector of the Capital City of the Movement"), and Martin Bormann lived in Bogenhausen as well, the latter at 26 Maria-Theresia-Strasse, in a villa confiscated from the painter Benno Becker.[225]

While Eva Braun was arranging her move in Munich, Hitler was in his "electoral struggle." He had just presented the Western powers with a fait accompli by having the German army march into the Rhineland demilitarized zone on March 7, 1936. His generals as well as the diplomats in the foreign service had advised against the step, since breaking international agreements—both the Treaty of Versailles and the Locarno Pact, signed in 1925—threatened to increase Germany's political isolation in Europe and possibly even risked starting another war. Nevertheless, Hitler brought off his coup and as the army marched into the Rhineland he called a sitting of Parliament in Germany, where, amid the frantic cheering of his supporters, he announced that German troops were "at this very moment occupying their future peace garrison." He swore "to never retreat, from any power or any violence, in the reestablishment of the honor of our People," and said that "with this day today," the "struggle for Germany's equality among nations" had been brought to a close. In the same breath, he made far-reaching offers to Germany's European neighbors to collectively "ensure the peace," even proposing a return to the League of Nations. Although Hitler was actually steeped in a racist imperialism that burst all bounds and left absolutely no room for a reconciliation or balance of power among nations, he said in his speech that he hoped from then on "to resolve any tensions on the path of slow, evolutionary development in peaceful collaboration."[226]

After the speech, the national parliament was dissolved and new elections were called for March 29, 1936. Once again, Hitler's recklessness—he apparently told Albert Speer later that this was "his riskiest undertaking"[227]—was rewarded: England and France protested Germany's infringement but did not take military action, and the League of Nations in Geneva confined itself to a formal condemnation of the German violation of the treaties.

Hitler, meanwhile, made the most of his success. The parliamentary elections turned into a national triumphal celebration for him, as he crisscrossed the country, appearing as an orator in Berlin, Munich, Karlsruhe, Frankfurt, Königsberg, Hamburg, Breslau, Ludwigshafen, Leipzig, Essen, and Cologne. Goebbels, the Minister of Propaganda, had planned the three-week "election campaign," in which no reelection was actually at stake, to whip up "the German People into a violent frenzy of enthusiasm."[228] It was in truth a publicity campaign on the regime's part, solely and exclusively seeking the public's approval for Hitler's policies: the NSDAP put forth a single-party list of candidates under the slogan "Reichstag for Freedom and Peace." The official results were that 98.9 percent of voters cast their votes for Hitler; the nationwide fanning of the flames of "Führer"-euphoria knew no bounds. Whether the results correctly matched the votes as actually cast is both unknowable and irrelevant: Hitler was incontestably at the peak of his popularity, being in a position to do what all the political parties during the Weimar Republic had tried to do in vain—wipe out the hated Versailles Treaty.

And Eva Braun? Would Hitler's political victories and the increasing adoration he received from the German population have meant nothing to her? It is almost impossible to imagine that Braun, then twenty-four years old, would not have felt her companion to be a kind of demigod, to whose wishes and needs she and everyone else had to submit. She may well have felt herself chosen by a higher power, since these foreign-policy successes only strengthened Hitler's own view of himself as fulfilling a higher mission and being guided by destiny. "Providence" determined the path he walked on "with the instinctive certainty we have in dreams," he had announced in front of three hundred thousand people at the Theresienwiese in Munich on March 14, 1936. And this was not just propaganda for public consumption. In his close circle as well, Hitler made no

*Eva Braun, concealed in the entourage sitting behind Hitler, at the Olympic
Winter Games in Garmisch-Partenkirchen, February 1936*

secret of his belief in "God's Providence." His sister Paula, for example,
reported that he had told her of his "absolute conviction that our Lord
God holds his protective hand above me."[229] Similarly, in 1941, during
one of his nighttime teas in the East Prussian "Führer headquarters," he
remarked that an "omnipotent power," which created "worlds," had "certainly assigned every individual creature its task." "Everything," he said,
"goes the way it has to go!"[230]

Travels

Travel was an important aspect of life in Hitler's circle. While the staff
of employees who worked closely with Hitler, such as the doctors and
secretaries, were his constant travel companions up until 1939 and after
the start of the war as well, Eva Braun seems to have been allowed to go
along only rarely. Since she never traveled as part of Hitler's official retinue, however, and her name therefore never appeared on any list in the
record, unlike the names of the wives of other high-ranking Nazi officials,
it is difficult to determine which events she actually was present at and

which not. Thus, a single photograph taken by Heinrich Hoffmann is the only evidence we have that she attended any event at the Olympic Winter Games in Garmisch-Partenkirchen, whose opening ceremony took place on her birthday, February 6, 1936.[231]

These games must have held a special attraction for Braun, herself a passionate skier; here, for the first time, Alpine skiing was among the competitions. Hitler, in contrast, avoided taking part in any sport personally. His refusal had less to do with fear of injury than with his conviction that he would present "a laughable figure every time" he took part. "When people are very famous, a lot is expected of them," he told his inner circle during one of his "table talks" in August 1942. Referring to Bismarck, he explained that "there would be demands" he would "not be able to meet." As a result, there was never any question of the Nazi leader "skiing" or "going swimming."[232] He had not forgotten the photograph that appeared on the front page of the *Berliner Illustrirte Zeitung* three days after the inauguration of President Friedrich Ebert in 1919, showing Ebert with Minister of Defense Gustav Noske shirtless in bathing trunks on the beach of the Baltic Sea spa Haffkrug. The picture had been a blow to the image of the new Weimar Republic from which it never recovered.[233] Mussolini, too, who enjoyed appearing before the Italian public as an athlete in various capacities, including as horseman, pilot, and swimmer, only opened himself up to ridicule, in Hitler's opinion, since he "couldn't actually do" all those things. Il Duce, in Hitler's view, would have been better off "piloting his Italy."[234]

Hitler arrived for the Olympic opening ceremonies in Garmisch in a special train. Officially accompanied by Reich Minister of the Interior Wilhelm Frick, Bavarian Minister of the Interior Adolf Wagner, Reich Sports Leader Hans von Tschammer und Osten, and the mayor of Garmisch-Partenkirchen and members of the German Olympic Steering Committee, he stomped through the snow on foot and entered the Olympic ski stadium. Frick had asked Hitler during the run-up to the games to prohibit the "increasing anti-Semitic propaganda" in the Garmisch area for the course of the games; he was afraid that the festivities, destination for a half a million visitors through February 16, and especially the even more prestigious Summer Olympics due to take place a few months later in Berlin, could be endangered "if there were any incidents in Garmisch."[235] As a result, the placards stating "Jews Unwelcome Here," which were common everywhere in Garmisch, temporarily disappeared.

Hitler attended the Winter Games in Garmisch several times, with

various escorts and usually with prominent Party members such as
Göring and Goebbels at his side. It is unknown at precisely which event
on which day he had Reich press chief Otto Dietrich, Eva Braun, and
other friends from Munich including Helene Bechstein, Erna Hoffmann,
and Sofie Stork with him, sitting directly behind him in the second row.
The only photograph of this group, taken by Hoffmann, gives no hint
of the time of day or the sport event. In any case, Hitler's presence in
Garmisch-Partenkirchen was largely kept from the public, and representatives of the press were permitted to be there only under strict condi-
tions. Heinrich Himmler, head of the Reich Security Service, personally
ordered the Bavarian Political Police in writing that it was "strictly forbidden" for "photographers to accompany the Führer."[236]

At the 1936 Summer Olympics in Berlin—the great international
media event of the National Socialist state—journalists and photographers were likewise subjected to severe restrictions, of course. The propaganda mission of the Nazi regime was to show the world a new, strong,
and at the same time peace-loving Germany, and to that end the com-
municative power of a picture far outweighed that of the written word.
Thus only 125 carefully selected German photographers, called "official
photojournalists," were allowed, and the 1,800 members of the press from
fifty-nine other countries were supplied with preselected material by the
photo press office of the organizing committee.[237] This fact did nothing
to dampen international enthusiasm, however. Heinrich Hoffmann's
firm took countless pictures and movies of the games and the Olympics
became a major propaganda success, not least because of photo reports,
radio reports, and, for the first time, broadcasts on television.[238]

Meanwhile, there is no photographic evidence of Eva Braun's presence.
She may not have been allowed to see for herself what Rudolf Hess called
the "first great public appearance of the new Reich."[239] In the autobiographical literature, there is not a single hint of her presence at the Summer Games. The same is true for other major public events in the prewar
years. The information that Eva Braun, accompanied by her mother and
her school friend Herta Schneider, traveled to Vienna according to Hitler's wishes on March 14, 1938, to see her lover's triumphal entry into the
city late that afternoon after the "annexation" of Austria to the German
Reich—information that allegedly comes from the family itself—is not
confirmed anywhere else in the literature.[240] Neither Nicolaus von Below
nor Otto Dietrich nor Christa Schroeder, all of whom were part of Hit-

ler's entourage together with the secretary Gerda Daranowski (who had started that spring), mentioned Eva Braun in the context of these events in their later memoirs, even though she allegedly stayed with Hitler and his staff in Vienna's Hotel Imperial. All of the autobiographers, in fact, avoid mentioning any names or giving any details of their own experiences in this matter. Von Below, for instance, refers merely to the "retinue" or the "numerous companions," and speaks of having been "witness to a historical moment." Christa Schroeder makes do with mentioning the military escort and the factotum Julius Schaub, and remarks vaguely that "back then everything was overwhelming" to her. Reich Press Chief Dietrich even gives the impression that he witnessed what he called the "ardent glow of the enthusiasm" of the Austrian masses as an entirely uninvolved bystander. Speer, perhaps the only one who would willingly have gone into any detail, was not among Hitler's entourage this time, claiming that it was only "several days later" that he learned "via the newspapers" what had taken place.[241]

In general, a similarly noticeable silence reigns supreme among the main players' memoirs concerning the exact makeup of the group around Hitler in Linz and Vienna. What might this silence mean? After all, all the members of the inner circle—Brandt, Below, Hoffmann, Dietrich, Brückner, Schaub, the secretaries, and Eva Braun—were at the center of the maelstrom of events. But why did they keep their collective observations and experiences to themselves? First and foremost, we see here again that the solidarity of this group, through to the end of the war and into the years of denazification, must not be underestimated.[242] These individuals were not ordinary observers, not part of the masses burning with enthusiasm outside the hotel who had no way to reach Hitler; rather they constituted, together with the regime's public officials there, the circle of loyal intimates, accomplices, and accessories around the Nazi leader. As a result, none of them reveal the most salient fact: the extent to which they too cheered the entry of the German army into Austria at the time, and how strongly they themselves identified with the National Socialist worldview.

In fact, it is difficult in general to determine how deeply the members of the inner circle shared Hitler's long-term political goals and vision of a Greater German Reich.[243] Their knowledge varied by how close they were to Hitler as well as by their functions. Still, the immediate effects of the Nazi expansion, beginning with Austria, were clear to see. For exam-

ple, there is a photograph in the partially preserved archive of Hoffmann's
photographs that shows Vienna Jews scrubbing the street with brushes,
watched by SS men.[244] The racist anti-Semitism that was for Hitler the
"central law of the movement" (in the words of Klaus Hildebrand), the
foundation of National Socialist propaganda, and the official dogma of
the Nazi state, certainly did not remain hidden from those close to Hitler. Rather, we must assume that Hitler's adjutants, secretaries, servants,
and, not least, Eva Braun shared without reservation the Jew-hatred of
their "boss," as they all called him. All of the later protestations like that
of Julius Schaub—that he never heard anything about the "Jewish question," much less the extermination of Jews, until after the capitulation
of 1945—must therefore be rejected, or rather understood as stemming
primarily from their fear of judicial punishment after the war.[245]

The Nazi leader's first personal will, written by hand and dated May 2,
1938, shows how tight the bonds were between Hitler and his circle. That
afternoon, Hitler set out from Berlin for a one-week state visit to Italy;
Paul Schmidt, head translator in the foreign office, later recalled that
"half the government" took part in the visit.[246] Hitler, who for years had
been suffering from premonitions of death and apparently was afraid of
being assassinated in Italy, set his private matters in order before the trip
and bequeathed all of his belongings to the NSDAP in the case of his
death.[247] At the same time, he made sure that his close relatives and colleagues, including the adjutants Schaub, Brückner, and Wiedemann,
would be financially set for life. And the first person he mentioned was his
girlfriend, twenty-six years old at the time, stating that "Miss Eva Braun,
Munich" should receive from the Party "1,000 marks a month . . . that
is, 12,000 marks a year for the remainder of her life" in the case of his
death.[248] This is the only surviving document in Hitler's hand, apart from
his testament of April 1945, that mentions Eva Braun by name. Her family claimed, after the war, that Eva herself did not know about the testament.[249] Surely not many people did know about it. Among the initiates
were, in any case, Lammers, head of the Reich Chancellery, to whom the
document was given for safekeeping, and Franz Xaver Schwarz, "Reich
Treasurer of the NSDAP," whom Hitler intended to be his executor.
Schwarz was not only the "Plenipotentiary of the Führer" in all of the Party's legal property matters, but also, as Richard Walther Darré expressed it
later, the "uncrowned king of the NSDAP," with whom no "leader of the
movement" dared "to have a falling out."[250]

Eva Braun was allowed to join this trip to Italy, and she documented it on film. More than five hundred people made the journey, in three special trains from the Anhalter station in Berlin through Munich to the Italian capital. The foreign office organized a special Ladies' Program for the spouses of the high-ranking Nazi politicians, with group outings. This glittering company included Annelies von Ribbentrop, wife of the new Reich Foreign Minister, as well as Ilse Hess, Magda Goebbels, and Marga Himmler; only Emmy Göring was missing, since her husband, the Reich Minister for Air Travel, had been declared Hitler's successor a month earlier, by "Führer edict," and had to remain in Berlin as his deputy.[251] The women stayed in Rome at the Grand Hotel (today the St. Regis Grand Hotel), built in 1894 as the first luxury hotel in the heart of the city, while Hitler and his retinue were housed in the Quirinal Palace, the residence of Italian kings.[252] Indeed, it was King Victor Emmanuel III, not Mussolini, who was the Germans' official host. Hitler, to his great annoyance, felt that Mussolini, the Prime Minister and thus subordinate to the head of state, had merely "tagged along" for their visit, as the Nazi leader complained years later.[253] The wives, in any case, were permitted to attend the dinner arranged by the King in the Quirinal on May 4—the "stiffest event imaginable," according to adjutant Wiedemann—as well as a dinner hosted by Il Duce at the Palazzo Venezia three days later.[254]

Eva Braun was excluded from all of these activities. She boarded one of the three special trains only in Munich, joining Karl and Anni Brandt, the Morells, and Maria Dreesen, wife of the Godesberg hotelier, with her son Fritz. It is nearly certain that Braun traveled in a sleeping car in the same train as Hitler. The train was put into service by the German railroad only in July 1937; called "Amerika," it consisted of two locomotives, Hitler's salon car, a conference car with a radio station and telex, a dining car, and several cars for the military escort, staff, and guests.[255] No one saw Eva Braun's face outside her immediate circle. In Rome, too, she stayed separate from the others, although no less luxuriously and no less centrally, at the Hotel Excelsior, a "white palace" built around the turn of the century on Via Veneto, the most famous street in the city. Thus cut off from her fellow travelers, she explored the city with the women in her group in particular, while Karl Brandt joined Goebbels, Himmler, Hess, Ribbentrop, and Otto Dietrich in Hitler's entourage on May 4, to visit, together with Mussolini, the enormous Victor Emmanuel Monument with its Tomb of the Unknown Soldier.[256] After an extensive program of celebrations in

Rome and Naples, Hitler and his group stayed a short while in Florence and then returned from there to Germany in the German special trains on May 9, 1938.

Hitler, who was determined to follow up the "annexation" of Austria by occupying Czechoslovakia with its Sudeten-German minority, had achieved the purpose of his visit: Italy would remain neutral in case of war.[257] Eva Braun, who did not take the train back to Germany but rather traveled onward with her companions to the island of Capri, presumably knew as little of Hitler's warlike intentions at this point as most of the others on the Italian trip. She had taken part in none of the official events and saw the maneuvers of the Italian fleet in the Gulf of Naples only from afar, while Hitler observed them from onboard a battleship, together with the King and Mussolini.[258] It is not even known whether she spent any time at all with Hitler during the trip. She was, however, ceaselessly taking photographs and shooting films. If we believe Henriette von Schirach, Eva Braun showed her movies at the Berghof in the autumn of that year and remarked to Hitler that now he would see the "real Italy" for once.[259]

After this state visit, Hitler withdrew to the Obersalzberg again and turned his attention to putting into action his idea of "Lebensraum"* in the east and his specific battle plans against Czechoslovakia. He gave the orders for war to Ribbentrop, Göring, and the highest generals of the army and their adjutants in Berlin, on May 28, 1938, and thereby caused the destruction of the European order that had been established in the Peace of Paris treaties of 1919. Hitler's path to war, and his statement that it was his "unshakeable will that Czechoslovakia disappear from the map," met with no fundamental objections.[260]

While Hitler was personally pushing ahead to war in the summer of 1938, drawing up operational plans and busying himself with the details of the Siegfried Line (a defensive structure 390 miles long on the western border of the Reich), he was simultaneously relieving his mental strain by fantasizing about retreating into private life. Linz, the capital of the state of Upper Austria—the city he envisioned as a European art capital, "a kind of German Rome," and which he styled as his "hometown" even though he had spent only two years of his youth there—was where he

---

* Literally, "living space." This concept of Hitler's was a major component in the Nazi ideology, referring to the German population's need for land and raw materials and the availability of this land in the east after the Slavic peoples were killed or deported.

planned to retire after achieving all of his political goals.[261] Linz's renovation, including a giant industrial and port district, was planned to last until 1950, and Hitler wanted to spend his twilight years there and eventually be buried there. Speer recalls that the construction of a residence "on a height," with a view over the city, was planned. Even before the war, Hitler had occasionally described his imagined farewell from politics to the assembled company at table on the Obersalzberg, for example by saying: "Aside from Fräulein Braun, I'll take no one with me. Fräulein Braun and my dog. I'll be lonely. For why should anyone voluntarily stay with me for any length of time? Nobody will take notice of me anymore. They'll all go running after my successor!"[262]

At the high point of his power, in other words, Hitler began to think about taking his leave of politics. The reason for such reflections may have been his health problems, but possibly also, in secret, the fear that his military ambitions would fail. Speer thought such talk might have been an attempt to call forth the loyalty of his colleagues in the large group, but this latter speculation is doubtful. The extensive plans for Linz were a sensitive subject for Speer in any case, since, as he told Joachim Fest in the autumn of 1974, he had not been asked for advice about them despite having offered his "cooperation."[263] It was primarily other architects who drew up the plans, even if it remained Speer's responsibility to authorize the plans in consultation with Hitler.

Thus the Linz city planning office under the Austrian architect Anton Estermann, which had submitted a design plan, became the central planning site for the project in July 1938. Then, in March 1939, came Roderich Fick, a professor at the Munich Technical College whom Hitler named "Reich Construction Adviser for the Redesigning of the City of Linz." Fick had already designed several buildings on the Obersalzberg, including Villa Bormann and the teahouse on the Mooslahnerkopf. On May 9, not long after being appointed, Fick presented a model of Linz on the Berghof terrace, in Speer's presence.[264]

Around fall 1940, Hitler appointed the architect Hermann Giesler to assist Fick. Giesler, the "Master Builder of the Capital City of the Movement," came from an architect's family in Siegen; his brother, Paul, rose in the NSDAP to be the Gauleiter of Munich–Upper Bavaria, while he himself was also a member of the Party and attended Hitler's dinner parties in Munich. Until his death in 1987, Hermann Giesler would remain an avowed supporter of Hitler.[265]

It is thus no wonder that Giesler managed, in the end, to win the unavoidable power struggle between himself and Fick, in which August Eigruber, the Gauleiter of Oberdonau Linz, played a role as well. Until the end of the war, all the monumental construction plans of what was now called the "Führer Capital" of Linz, including the "Danube River-bank Development" and Hitler's house on the Freinberg, were assigned to Giesler. The residence, sited on a "rocky plateau above the Danube," was designed in the "strictly cubicform structure typical of the Austrian country house—the Vierkanthof, built around a square courtyard." According to Giesler's apologia, Hitler apparently compared it to Holy Roman Emperor Friedrich II of Hohenstaufen's mystical Castel del Monte in southeast Italy.[266] In fact, the Castel del Monte, built in the thirteenth-century and a UNESCO World Heritage Site since 1996, is similarly situated on a small hill and is not only a symbol of power but also, due to its eight-sided ground plan with eight octagonal towers at the corners, a symbol of eternity. Friedrich II designed the "Hohenstaufen Acropolis" himself, immortalizing himself as architect and city founder. He used architecture as a way to recuperate from politics and his numerous military campaigns; wherever he stayed, his master builder was required to report to him.[267]

The National Socialists had projected themselves onto Friedrich II's life and works for a long time and in many ways. They used the legendary emperor of the Holy Roman Empire of the German Nation as a legitimating figure for their own "Third Empire" by reinterpreting him as a German hero and manufacturing a historical connection with his "First Empire," which in fact never existed. Hitler also sought out personal points of connection with Friedrich II and cast himself as a renewer of the Empire along the same lines as his historical forebearer. For example, in 1942 he had Oskar Hugo Gugg—a professor of landscape painting in Weimar and friend of Paul Schultze-Naumberg, the architect working with Hitler—execute an oil painting of Castel del Monte for the planned residence in Linz. The previous year in Rome, at Ribbentrop's instigation, a model of the Friedrich's building was made and given to Hitler in Berlin in late 1941.[268] This fantasy of a link between his place of retirement and the "castle of castles" of the Hohenstaufer emperor suggests the role that "Linz" played in Hitler's imagination and how he saw himself there. Courtly ceremonies, such as those that took place during the state visit in Italy, always called forth feelings of inferiority in him, and now he

Hitler, in raptures over a model of the city of Linz, 1943

dreamed of an old-European, princely existence for himself in the middle of the future economic and cultural center of the "Third Reich."

During the next few years, Hermann Giesler traveled to the Berghof or to Hitler's various other headquarters again and again to discuss blueprints and models of the project with him. Sometimes, according to Giesler, he stayed "for weeks."[269] In fall 1942, he even traveled to Hitler's headquarters, which had temporarily shifted east. Named "Wehrwolf" (a pun on the German for "werewolf" and "*Wehr*," meaning "defense"), the headquarters was near the Ukrainian city of Vinnytsia, where he discussed "further details of his house" with Hitler. When he asked the Nazi leader for details about the "kitchen area" and the "garden," Giesler recalled three decades later, Hitler told him that this was "Miss Braun's affair": he should discuss the matter "with her first," since she would be "lady of the house." Once he had "installed his successor and stepped down," Giesler reported, Hitler was planning to "marry Miss Braun."[270]

The postwar statements of Giesler and Speer, the "court architects," show that Hitler's dream of "Linz" was clearly not his alone. But whether

he involved Eva Braun in his plans as early as 1938 or only during the
course of the war is not known. The fact remains that these exalted visions
offered his young companion a prospect she longed for: that of a glittering, fairy-tale future at Hitler's side. Henriette von Schirach later claimed
that Eva Braun "clung to Hitler's personal vision of the future."[271] And
more and more over the course of the years to come, he expanded the
role that he imagined for her in this vision. Speer, ambitious and irritated
at the time that "my dear Giesler" was preferred over him for the project, ended by being annoyed over the precedence given to Eva Braun.
His biographer Fest reports that "Linz" was a topic of discussion even on
the day of Speer's very last meeting with the Nazi leader in the bunker
on April 23, 1945. "Miss Braun" had already made "very personal suggestions," Hitler told Speer in their last conversation, and would be responsible for the look of the business district and promenades in Linz.[272] With
their downfall imminent, it seems that Hitler and Eva Braun had fled
reality into irrationality together.

9

ISOLATION DURING THE WAR

Hitler's fantasy of someday retiring to Linz with Eva Braun and abdi-cating leadership of the Party and state to a younger man first mani-fested itself at the same time as the concretization of his war plans in Eastern Europe. He was tormented by the thought of not yet having solved crucial foreign policy problems: revising the cession of territory imposed on the German Reich by the Versailles Treaty and gaining "Lebensraum in the East." The decision for a war of aggression that he made in fall 1939 may also have been influenced by economic considerations, but the real-ization of the "Lebensraum" ideology represented the core of National Socialist foreign policy from the beginning. Already in his autobiogra-phy and political platform *Mein Kampf*, published in 1925, Hitler had announced his goal: "We will finally end the colonial and trade policies of the prewar period and transition to the soil-politics of the future. But when we speak of new soil and ground in Europe, we can only think in the first place of Russia and the border states subordinate to it." The fight against the Soviet Union was raised to a "historical mission of national socialism."[1]

On February 3, 1933, immediately after the National Socialists came to power, Hitler declared in a speech after a dinner with high-ranking military officers that the "expansion of Lebensraum" for the Germans, toward the east, would have to be carried out militarily, and the "soil" conquered in this way would have to be "Germanized." Hardly anyone present, including Hitler's personal adjutant Wilhelm Brückner, comprehended at the time the new Reich Chancellor's absolute desire for war. After all, he went on to proclaim his readiness for peace and negotiation in public speeches.[2] In addition, neither the concept of "Lebensraum" nor the idea that such space must be conquered for the German People originated with him—both belonged quite generally to the repertoire of the Populist-nationalist right. But four and a half years later, in early November 1937—when Hitler emphasized, this time in a meeting with the heads of the Wehrmacht (armed forces), that "only the path of violence" would provide the "solution to the German problem"—the domestic and foreign political situations of Germany had changed fundamentally. The National Socialist dictatorship was established; rearmament was moving full speed ahead; the Rhineland had been occupied, without any resistance from the Western powers; the "annexations" of Austria and Czechoslovakia were already decided upon. There could no longer be any doubt within the leadership of the Wehrmacht that Hitler's unchanged intent to win "agriculturally useful space" in Eastern Europe by military means, for the "protection and support of the mass of the People and its reproduction," was meant seriously.[3]

When Hitler withdrew to the Obersalzberg in late January 1939, Goebbels recorded the following for posterity in his "Diaries": "The Führer now speaks almost solely of foreign politics. Again he is turning over new plans in his mind. A Napoleonic nature . . ."[4] In truth, however—as the Minister of Propaganda knew perfectly well—these plans were neither new nor unknown. The racial-ideological genocidal intent of the Nazi regime had already shown itself, not least in the pogrom against German Jews on November 9, 1938, initiated in part by Goebbels himself.[5] And Hitler was, as always, working—though now more driven than ever—toward realizing his "vision" of the "next struggle": "a deliberate war between Peoples and between races," as he declared in early February 1939.[6]

The Outbreak of War

Is it possible that Eva Braun, intimately familiar with Hitler's sense of being on a mission and his racist ideology, could have suspected nothing of his preparations for war in the spring and summer of 1939? This seems highly unlikely, especially after the Nazi leader had given a speech before the "Greater German Reichstag" in the Kroll Opera House in Berlin, on January 30, 1939, that gave rise to "more discussion" than practically any other public statement, as Nicolaus von Below recalled.[7] In it, Hitler lamented the "warmongers" in England and America who wanted "at all costs to start a war," and he proclaimed that nothing could "influence [Germany] in the least in the resolution of its Jewish question." At the same time, Hitler threatened that should it come to war, "the result would not be the Bolshevization of the globe and thus the victory of the Jews, but rather the annihilation of the Jewish race in Europe."[8] These "foreign policy passages," Below admitted in retrospect, "depressed" him, since it was "not difficult to conclude" from these "warnings directed at the English and the Jews" that Hitler "was coming to new and far-reaching decisions."[9]

Since Hitler's unexpectedly combative appearance before Parliament attracted such wide public attention, we can assume that every member of the private "inner circle" around Hitler heard about these utterances as well. His words came close to being a declaration of war. In particular, the wives of the Nazi leaders obviously also "talked about the daily news," as Margarete Speer admitted to Gitta Sereny.[10] For Eva Braun, the events involving Hitler in Berlin over the course of 1939 must have been the focus of her attention to an even greater extent, because her life with him was no longer limited merely to Munich or the Obersalzberg: after the New Reich Chancellery in Berlin, designed by Speer, was finished and dedicated on January 9, 1939, Braun was given rooms of her own in the "Führer apartment" in the Old Reich Chancellery, with furniture personally designed for her by Speer.[11] Clearly, this new residence for Eva Braun was possible because all the official public events now took place in Hitler's new, specially built, monumental seat of office on the corner of Wilhelmstrasse and Vosstrasse.

With its 65-foot-high exterior facade, interior hallways sometimes exceeding 320 feet in length, and central marble gallery, 480 feet long, it surpassed anything that had ever been there. The New Chancellery thereby corresponded to Hitler's conception of an awe-inspiring architecture of power, enabling him to impress especially "the smaller dignitaries."[12] But even though the building included a private wing for Hitler's use, he continued to stay at his apartment at 77 Wilhelmstrasse, refurnished four years earlier by the Troost architecture office. Eva Braun, during her stays in Berlin, now no longer spent the night at the Hotel Adlon but instead, in the guise of a private secretary, could go to their common place of residence largely unremarked. Speer wrote in *Inside the Third Reich* that she "came in through a side entrance and up a side staircase." She didn't even linger in the downstairs rooms, formerly the public reception halls, "when only old friends were in the house." Instead, the architect sometimes "kept her company during her long hours of waiting."[13]

Hitler's girlfriend seems not to have remained entirely unobserved in the capital city, however. The American newsmagazine *Time*, for example, in an article published December 18, 1939, reported that "a blond Bavarian girl named Eva Helen Braun" had moved into "Hitler's official residence in Berlin, the great Chancellery on Wilhelmstrasse," during the last days of August.[14] The article referred to various sources in Germany and to an article published in *The Saturday Evening Post* two days earlier. This was not entirely true, but the magazine gave enough biographical details to indicate that the Nazi leader's private life was not a secret anywhere in the capital city, and that rumors about it had reached the ears of American journalists, too.

As early as May 15, 1939, *Time* had speculated about Mussolini's and Hitler's girlfriends, under the title "Spring in the Axis," and named Eva Braun: the young woman from Munich had her apartment paid for by her "old friend in Berlin, who always comes to see her when he is in town."[15] One of *Time*'s informants was presumably Bella Fromm, the Berlin society columnist who had immigrated to the United States in 1938. She had worked for the *Vossische Zeitung* newspaper, among others, and had excellent contacts in Berlin political society. In her best-selling diaries published in London in 1943 as *Blood & Banquets*, she mentions "Eva Helene Braun" as early as her entry of September 16, 1937, describing her as the former assistant of "Court Photographer" Heinrich Hoffmann who had possibly conquered Adolf Hitler's heart. Fromm was relying on off-the-record information from Louis Paul Lochner, an American journalist in charge of the Associated Press bureau in Berlin who had ties to the National Socialist leadership.[16] Obviously, the German public learned nothing about such overseas news reports—censorship of the press was in effect in the National Socialist state, and foreign newspapers, magazines, and books were not even permitted to be sold.

Eva Braun did, in fact, stay in Berlin in late August 1939. And she had already learned of the worsening international situation while at the

Berghof. Hitler's expansionist goals in the east—first "taking care of what remained of the Czechs" (in defiance of the concessions of the Western powers in the Munich Agreement of September 1938) and "taking possession" of the formerly East Prussian "Memel Territory" belonging to Lithuania, then reconquering the other territories lost in the First World War—meant war.[17] The Nazi regime had decided to use force as soon as any neighboring Eastern European government stood in its way, and indeed it moved closer to war when Polish Foreign Minister Józef Beck at a meeting with Hitler on the Obersalzberg on January 5, 1939, in which the Nazi leader demanded the return of Danzig to the German Reich as well as access routes to East Prussia, rejected the German ideas in the name of his government.

The Polish position did not change even after German troops marched into Prague on March 15, with Hitler declaring Czechoslovakia "the Reich Protectorate of Bohemia and Moravia" in Hradschin Castle there, nor after March 23, when the Germans occupied the Memel Territory.[18] Three days later the Polish government again rejected the National Socialist dictator's demands. Hitler then ordered concrete preparations for a war on Poland "beginning 9/1/1939." He was never interested in a diplomatic solution to the conflict, since, as he remarked to his generals in May 1939, Danzig "is not the real concern. The issue is an expansion of Lebensraum in the east."[19] As in the case of Czechoslovakia, the Western powers failed here, too—as did the League of Nations, which had been founded to collectively ensure world peace. The British government gave merely a halfhearted guarantee to Poland and worked to sign a neutrality pact with the Soviet Union, without success. Hitler's and Stalin's realpolitik calculations prevented this agreement, as did the Poles themselves, who did not trust the Soviets as a protective power. The Soviet dictator sought a rapprochement with Hitler, despite their ideological enmity, because his country was not ready for war and he was not willing to be drawn into a conflict by the capitalist powers England and France. Hitler, in turn, must have been afraid of a war on two fronts.[20]

In late June on the Obersalzberg, Hitler paced back and forth in the great hall of his estate night after night, with either Albert Speer or Nicolaus von Below, "giving his thoughts free rein" as Below recalled later. During these evenings, the Nazi leader explained that he had to lay the groundwork for the Greater German Reich's future "work of peace" by seizing the opportunity "to create a foundation for the unavoidable fight with Russia by solving the Polish problem." The English would "certainly stay completely quiet if he managed to bring about a pact with Russia," and the Poles would "come down off their high horse on their own" since they were "even more afraid of the Russians . . . than they are of us."[21] In other words, Hitler laid out his worldview and war plans with brutal clarity to the air force adjutant on duty. Nicolaus von Below's account shows, first, how great the Nazi leader's tension was with respect to the military conflicts he had planned, so that he needed to seek psychological relief in his trusted circle, far from Berlin. Second, it reveals that Hitler felt no need to exercise caution or discretion around his loyal followers on the Berghof.

The fact is, there were no ideological differences within the "inner circle." Nicolaus von Below later admitted that he had been impressed with Hitler's "thoughts" about "Jewish Bolshevism" as a constant threat to Germany and Europe; Hitler's "clear-sighted judgment of the situation" convinced him.[22] Speer, meanwhile, the "Führer's" special favorite who was on the Obersalzberg through most of the summer of 1939, kept quiet after the war about the political discussions that took place then. He answered the American interrogators' questions on the subject in September 1945 by evasively claiming that any information from him would merely be "the intuitive impressions of a man at the edge of the circle where foreign-policy questions were decided." Speer gives the impression in his later memoirs, claiming, for example—unlike Below—that he heard about the negotiations with Moscow for the first time on August 21, 1939, during dinner at the Berghof, after Stalin had sent a telex expressing his willingness to receive the Reich Foreign Minister on August 23 and sign the Nonaggression Pact that had already been drawn up.[23]

By this point at the very latest, the supposedly apolitical ladies at the table were let into the picture of the looming developments. Speer nonetheless stresses that the women were "still excluded" from discussion.[24] But Eva Braun's photographs tell another story. On August 23, 1939, in the middle of the extremely tense environment reigning at the Berghof in connection with Joachim von Ribbentrop's departure for Moscow— accompanied by, among others, Heinrich Hoffmann—she captured on film Hitler restlessly awaiting news of the progress of the negotiations in the Soviet capital. Surrounding him in the Berghof hall that afternoon were Goebbels, Bormann, Otto Dietrich, Walther Hewel (head of the Foreign Minister's personal staff), Karl Bodenschatz (Göring's adjutant and head of the ministerial office in the Reich Ministry of Air Travel), and Julius Schaub. Speer and Below were there as well, but like many others did not appear in the photographs. Goebbels notes in his "Diaries" that they waited "for hours" for "news from Moscow," until finally, "at one in the morning," the communiqué was transmitted. "The Führer and all of us are very happy," he wrote.[25]

Reich Press Chief Otto Dietrich, on the other hand, in his reminiscences published in 1955 under the title *12 Jahre mit Hitler* (Twelve Years with Hitler; published in English as *The Hitler I Knew*), passes over this day of waiting on the Obersalzberg. He writes that he had not known at the time that Hitler was "launching an attack" on Poland "but wanted to avoid war with England."[26] Dietrich presumably did not suspect the existence of Eva Braun's photographs. These are not posed pictures but snapshots that reveal the general tension. She later pasted them into a photo album and added typewritten captions pasted under the pictures— for example, " . . . and then Ribbentrop left for Moscow"; " . . . and the Führer hears the report over the radio."[27]

The Minister of Propaganda had already, on the evening of August 21, arranged for the announcement of the upcoming German-Soviet Pact over German radio, and instructed the editors of all the newspapers "to publish [news of the pact] on the first page, very large."[28] On the morning of August 22, Goebbels held a press conference in Berlin for foreign journalists, while Hitler, at the same time, informed fifty officers, including the commanders of the various armed forces, in his Alpine residence that he was definitively resolved to go to war, a war that he would be "hard and ruthless" in waging.[29] The Nazi leader spent the following days getting constant reports about the domestic and foreign reactions. The announcement of a Nonaggression Pact between the two powerful dictators, which Goebbels described as a "worldwide sensation," did not, however, produce the desired reaction in either England or Poland. Both governments immediately announced that their positions were unchanged; Britain in fact strengthened its mutual assistance pact with Poland (it was formally signed only on August 25), and the Polish government refused further discussions with the Nazi leadership.[30]

As we would therefore expect, Eva Braun's photo diary contains the following entry: " . . . but Poland still does not want to negotiate." This comment was not "naive"; it matched the view of many Germans who thought that Poland would not risk a military conflict with its powerful neighbor in these circumstances.[31] Moreover, Poland's refusal to accede to Germany's demands, withdraw from Danzig, and permit passage to East Prussia was criticized outside of Germany as well: the demands were seen as perfectly legitimate outside of National Socialist circles, too. In addition, Nazi propagandists had succeeded in imputing their own country's war intentions to the Western powers. Goebbels, for example, in an address to the Danzig population on June 17, 1939, accused "Polish chauvinists" of wanting "to smash us Germans to pieces in an upcoming Battle of Berlin," while England had "given them a blank check" to do so and was trying "to encircle the Reich and Italy." Right up to the invasion of Poland, the Minister of Propaganda constantly repeated the basic ideas of Hitler's conspiracy theory, in which Hitler wanted peace but the "encirclers" in London, Paris, and Washington wanted war. As a result of the effectiveness of the German propaganda, the Nazi leader, apparently successful at everything, enjoyed the widespread reputation in Germany of being a savvy politician on the international stage, outwitting Western powers who acted moralistic but ultimately did nothing.[32]

Was Eva Braun aware of the historic significance of these days that she spent at the Berghof, days whose drama she clearly was trying to capture on film? There is no testimony on the subject, contemporaneous or later. No information from any of the women present—who included Margarete Speer, Anni Brandt, and Gerda Bormann—has been preserved. Eva Braun's photographs themselves, however, imply that she was well aware of what was happening, as does the fact that she went along to the capital immediately afterward. She presumably rode to Berlin via Munich in one of the ten Mercedes that left the Obersalzberg on August 24, 1939. The "court," as Speer said, had repaired to the Chancellery.[33] Hitler's "situation room" was in the great hall of the Old Chancellery, and it became the center of the "Führer headquarters" in Berlin after the start of the war.[34] Eva Braun was living in her rooms on the upper floor of the Old Chancellery, but it is unclear how well informed she was about the developments. On September 1, though, she apparently witnessed in person, along with her sister Ilse who was then living in Berlin, the session of Parliament hurriedly called by Göring in which Hitler declared war on Poland. His justification was: "This night for the first time Polish regular soldiers fired on our territory. Since 5:45 a.m. we have been returning the fire, and from now on bombs will be met by bombs."[35] No one knew at the time that the alleged Polish attack on a German radio station in Gleiwitz in Upper Silesia, which German propaganda cast as "the cause of the outbreak of the war," was a fabrication by the SS, along with all the other "border incidents" that had allegedly taken place in the previous days.[36]

In the former Kroll Opera House near Brandenburg Gate in Berlin, closed since 1931 and housing the National Socialist sham-parliament since the Reichstag fire of February 1933, there were several hundred seats available for visitors and journalists, in the two tiers of boxes. According to Ilse Braun's description as relayed by Nerin E. Gun, Eva Braun cried when Hitler, dressed in battle dress with the SS insignia on his left sleeve, announced:

> My whole life, from this moment on, belongs to my People. I want nothing more than to be the first soldier of the German Reich. I have therefore put on this tunic, which was been the holiest and most price-less to me, and will take it off only after our victory, or not live through its end.[37]

The members of Parliament stood up at these words, as per protocol, and "a thunderous cry of Heil" resounded in the chamber. Eva Braun, though, according to her sister, said: "If something happens to him, I'll die too."[38] Christa Schroeder, Hitler's secretary, expressed herself in similar terms two days later, on September 3, shortly before 9 p.m., when she set off for the Polish front with Hitler in the special train (still bearing the code name "Amerika") from Berlin's Stettin station. Great Britain and France had declared war against the German Reich that day. Hitler's—and his entourage's—hope that England would continue its wait-and-see policy was thus shattered; the Nazi regime had unleashed a great war. Suitably depressed, Christa Schroeder wrote to her friend Johanna Nusser: "In a few hours we will leave Berlin. . . . For me it means going with the leader through thick and thin. As for the worst case, I don't want to think about that yet, but if it happens—my life is over."[39]

The Berghof as "Führer Headquarters"

With the start of the war, Hitler's Alpine residence became a "Führer headquarters" whenever the commander in chief of the Wehrmacht was staying there. Only the military adjutant on duty was with him at all times; Wilhelm Keitel, head of the Supreme Command of the Armed Forces (Oberkommando der Wehrmacht, or OKW) and Alfred Jodl, Hitler's most influential military adviser and Chief of the Operations Staff of the Armed Forces High Command in the OKW, were housed a couple of miles away in the "Sub-Chancellery" in Berchtesgaden. The Wehrmacht command staff, meanwhile, worked in a special train in the Salzburg train station until the end of 1942.[40] Briefings on the military situation, however, took place at the Berghof every afternoon and evening. As a result, Otto Dietrich recalled, the women had to stay in their rooms "until the 'noon briefing' ended, around 2 p.m., and the generals drove off again." The same procedure was repeated after dinner, when the "OKW gentlemen" arrived once more. Eva Braun, her friends, and the secretaries repaired to the downstairs rooms of the Berghof most of the time, where there was a bowling alley and where they could watch movies.[41]

In any case, Hitler no longer showed up on the Obersalzberg several times a month, as he had in the past. There were still extended stays, up until the end of the war, but they were less frequent and also could not happen at will, since they depended on the military situation. Spontaneous trips with a few close friends were a thing of the past, since traveling now required that the whole "Führer headquarters" be moved, including the orderlies and the security personnel, namely an SS military escort and a "Führer escort battalion." Hitler's whole way of life changed. He had now become, as Speer remarked, "a slave to work," whereas before he had "never let himself be pressured by work."[42] Especially in the latter half of the war, he stayed away at the front for months at a time.[43]

Hitler had no fixed headquarters when the war started. As a result, Hitler and his whole staff, including Schroeder and Daranowski, the secretaries; Wilhelm Brückner; Julius Schaub; Karl Brandt; Nicolaus von Below; Martin Bormann; Heinrich Hoffmann; and Otto Dietrich slept in the "Führer train" for the first three weeks of September 1939, during the so-called Eighteen-Day War against Poland. This train consisted of two locomotives, two special cars with antiaircraft guns, two luggage cars, a "Führer car," a command car, a military escort car, two dining cars, two guest cars, two sleeping cars, and a press car.[44] The train's locations in Eastern Pomerania and Upper Silesia were declared military protection zones, guarded by military police and defended with antitank and antiaircraft cannons. An airplane was kept at the ready for Hitler; it was monitored by a soldier carrying a machine gun.[45] The commander of a given

"Führer headquarters"—in this case Major General Erwin Rommel—
was responsible for all security measures.[46]

Christa Schroeder, in a letter to her friend Johanna Nusser dated September 11, 1939, described how the situation appeared from the point of
view of the secretaries accompanying the Nazi leader:

> We've been living in the train for ten days now, always changing our
> location, but since we—Daranowski and I—never leave the train, it all
> stays monotonous (for us, *very* monotonous). The heat is almost unbear-
> able, just horrible. The sun beats down all day long on the compart-
> ments and you're simply powerless against the tropical heat. . . . The
> Boss drives off with his men in the morning and we are condemned to
> wait and wait and wait some more.[47]

Meanwhile, Hitler visited various sectors of the front. His accompanying physician Karl Brandt occasionally availed himself of a field military
hospital and performed operations along with the other doctors.[48] Heinrich Hoffmann as well as employees of his company photographed the
whole campaign, producing among other things aerial shots of burning
buildings, destroyed Polish tank convoys, and the bombing of Polish bunkers and bridges.[49] Hoffmann, himself in uniform, also staged the commander in chief in his photos, taking pictures of Hitler on his "Ride Along
the Front in the Corridor" on September 4, saluting to marching soldiers,
and used this for the cover of the illustrated book he published that year,
Mit Hitler in Polen (With Hitler In Poland). He also photographed Hitler
at situation briefings in the train, in the field kitchen, talking to wounded
soldiers, and during his triumphal entry into Danzig on September 19.[50]
By the time Hitler returned to Berlin a week later, Poland, which lacked
modern military equipment, had been defeated and divided up between
the German Reich and the Soviet Union. Seventy thousand Polish soldiers
had fallen and another seven hundred thousand were prisoners of war.

In addition, Einsatzgruppen, or task forces of the secret police, part of
the SS, had marched in behind the German army and were carrying out
mass shootings, primarily of Jews. Hitler had issued a "special order" for
the ethnic "cleansing" of Poland and named Heinrich Himmler the Reich
Commissioner for the Eastern Territories.[51] We have no photographs by
Hoffmann and his associates of the murders committed, although there
are images that reveal the discrimination, violence, and persecution. They

Heinrich Hoffmann taking a photograph during the western campaign, June 1940

show, for example, members of the security service (Sicherheitsdienst, or SD) arresting Polish Jews and cutting off their beards. Hoffmann and his team also photographed transports to the ghetto and Jewish forced laborers.[52] In truth, the march of German troops into Poland was the start of a horrific program of "Germanization," deportation, and extermination. Around 3.2 million Jews were kept imprisoned in ghettos. Hitler's racial mania and hatred of the people in Poland—who were, he said, "more like animals than human beings"—found full expression for the first time during the Poland campaign.[53] It is unlikely that Eva Braun ever saw any of the thousand photographs of the Poland campaign that Hoffmann kept, but she presumably knew Hitler's stereotypical racial views and in fact may have, like many other Germans, shared them. The extermination of Jews, on the other hand, was never discussed openly in the innermost private circle; the topic was never allowed to be mentioned in Hitler's presence.[54]

Eva Braun also never joined Hitler at his garrison near the front. None of the women from the Berghof (except the secretaries) were ever brought there. Instead, Eva Braun remained in her house in Munich, drove up to the Obersalzberg with her family and friends, or traveled to Italy, escorted by several of the ladies of the inner circle. Whenever Hitler was in Berlin for a longer stay, Eva Braun also stayed in her small apartment in the Old Chancellery. For example, on the evening of November 8, 1939, she and her friend Herta Schneider found themselves with Hitler in his special train on the way to Berlin while a bomb went off in Munich's Bürgerbräu beer cellar, which the Nazi leader had just left. Eva Braun learned only the following day, in a conversation with her younger sister, who had stayed in Munich, that their father was among the many injured in the blast.[55]

Meanwhile, the war in Poland had little tangible effect in Germany. Life went on, despite the introduction of food and clothes rationing. Most people believed that the victory would be quick and then celebrated it with corresponding enthusiasm when it came. When Hitler returned to the Obersalzberg on December 27, 1939, he did so as a celebrated war hero.[56] The enthusiasm for the "blitzkrieg" in the east among the German population knew no bounds, and people hoped, as Nicolaus von Below recalled, that "England and France would be reasonable" and that it would not come to war with the Western powers. No one suspected the existence of preparations, already under way in secret, for the German army to attack in the west.[57]

During the next three months, until the invasion of Norway on April 9, 1940, Hitler traveled back and forth between Berlin, Munich, and the Obersalzberg as he had before the war. On the Obersalzberg, he passed the time with Eva Braun and the other guests. Heinrich Hoffmann, in his postwar work *Hitler Was My Friend*, writes that he "gave [Eva Braun] time off, at Hitler's request," for the occasion.[58] But this, like many of Hoffmann's other later statements, seems to be excessive bluster. In any case, the start of the war did not yet bring about any fundamental changes to the situation at the Berghof, as Hitler did not abandon his bohemian lifestyle from one day to the next. However, apart from continuing to be busy with his architectural plans, he now devoted himself primarily to the war that he had been working toward for so many years. Thus the perception that the successful Poland campaign was never discussed within the trusted circle on the Berghof is less than credible. So are the claims made after the war by the surviving main players that Hitler's further war plans—the invasion of the Netherlands, Belgium, and Luxembourg on May 10, 1940, and the attack on France—came as a complete surprise to them.

Hoffmann, for example, maintained that on the evening of May 9, while the usual company was taking the special train from Berlin via Celle and Hannover to Cologne, they had no idea where they were going, and thought they were going to Norway. Otto Dietrich similarly stated that he realized the "great offensive" had begun only on the morning of May 10, when "the first squadron of airplanes flew in the cloudless sky" overhead over the Eifel mountains "toward the west."[59] Since Hoffmann and Dietrich were both always at Hitler's side, if only because of their jobs, and since they had various channels for receiving information even aside from their proximity to Hitler, these accounts are not very convincing. In fact, Hitler's legendary obsession with secrecy often seems to be nothing more than a self-protective claim of his inner circle, invented after the war. Nicolaus von Below, who spent Easter 1939 at the Berghof with his wife, also doubts that Hitler's camouflage of the journey "was believed." In fact, every person traveling along had "his own private ties with the 'initiates,' "[60] that is, Schaub, Bormann, and Below himself, who as Hitler's military adjutant and conversation partner had precise knowledge about what Hitler was considering. Speer, too, busy since December 1939 with the construction of the first fixed "Führer headquarters" (the "Rocky Eyrie" or Felsennest, on a mountain peak near Rodert, a village near Bad Münstereifel), was clearly in the loop about Hitler's further plans.[61]

The blitzkrieg against France, justified as a preventive strike, ended on June 22, 1940, with the signing of a German-French ceasefire in Compiègne, a site rich with symbolism since it was where the armistice ending World War I was signed. In the space of a few weeks, roughly one hundred thousand French and twenty-seven thousand Germans had fallen in battle. Hitler, who had carried out the western campaign over the objections of the army's high commander, Generaloberst Walther von Brauchitsch, and wiped clean the disgrace of World War I with his victory, was now regarded as the "greatest military leader of all time."[62] It is easy to imagine how this new highpoint of Germany's "Führer" euphoria would have affected the circle on the Obersalzberg. Wolf Speer, a nephew of Albert Speer's, recalled that there were photographs in his grandmother's drawing room "of her successes in the highest society, and at the time that meant the Obersalzberg," including pictures of Hitler with Eva Braun. Luise Mathilde Speer, who herself had been invited to the Berghof several times in the spring of 1939, later remarked, according to her son Albert, that she "did not want to see any of the people gathered there in her own house." Still, she had apparently admired the "great Führer," and added, "Who knows how evenings went with Bismarck or Napoleon!"[63]

As early as July 11, 1940, five days after his grand reception in Berlin

Hitler's arrival on the Obersalzberg, Eva Braun in the foreground, 1940

where hundreds of thousands had wildly cheered him, Hitler arrived back on the "mountain." Through late October he again traveled back and forth between his refuge at Berchtesgaden and the Chancellery in Berlin; Eva Braun sometimes accompanied him to Berlin as well.[64] A twenty-two-year-old member of the Waffen-SS named Rochus Misch, part of the "Führer military escort" since early May, stayed on the Obersalzberg for the first time in summer 1940, and Eva Braun was introduced to him as a "housekeeper." She changed her outfits several times a day, he later reported, and always wore makeup. Thus she did not, in Misch's judgment, fit the "ideal of a German girl": "naturalness and rootedness in the soil" were "not her style."[65] In fact, these two qualities had nothing whatsoever to do with Hitler's personality, either. Misch also observed that Eva Braun's behavior changed "lightning fast" as soon as Hitler left the Berghof: "You could still see the limousines driving down the winding roads and already the first preparations were being made for various amus-

ing activities. Proper as a governess a moment before, now she was turning everything upside down. And she was cheerful, happy and relaxed,
almost like a child."[66]

On October 21, 1940, after Hitler departed to meet with acting French
Prime Minister Pierre Laval, the Spanish dictator Francisco Franco, and
French head of state Marshal Philippe Pétain, Eva Braun threw a party
the same evening with the Berghof staff.[67] She was dancing on the vol-
cano's edge, since Hitler failed to bring France and Spain into the war,
nor could he knock Great Britain out of the war on his own. The air war
against England was in full swing and British bombers had struck Berlin
for the first time on August 26. With these events in the background, the
lifestyle — even the very existence — of this young, sometimes effusive girlfriend must have seemed like an anachronism in the life of the idolized
"Führer and Reich Chancellor."

Until the attack on the Soviet Union, on June 22, 1941, Hitler conducted his war in large part from the Berghof. In fact, he spent the first
few months of 1941 at the Berghof almost without interruption.[68] This was
where he considered his next steps, talked them out in the presence of his
highest military officers, and formulated the goal of destroying Russia. At
no point since the 1920s had he lost sight of his declared main ideological
enemy, "Jewish Bolshevism." Only when Soviet Russia was cast down "in
a quick campaign," he believed, would the English give up their struggle
against Germany.[69] He estimated that the blitzkrieg in the east would
take about three months to reach victory. There were neither battle plans
nor any thought of supplies and reinforcements for the period after that;
everything was staked, literally, "on the first strike."[70]

In summer 1941, for the first time, Hitler stayed for months at a time
in his perfectly camouflaged, permanent headquarters, the "Wolf's Lair,"
near Rastenburg in East Prussia.[71] In light of the earlier victories, most of
the military officers, the Nazi leadership, and especially the members of
the Nazi leader's private circle were absolutely convinced that this was
another masterstroke. For example, Below, deeply familiar with the dictator's worldview and war plans from their many conversations together,
admitted in his memoir that at the time he thought "Hitler was sharply
and soberly calculating." On top of everything, Below "in that period"
often "marveled at [Hitler's] calm demeanor" and found him "humane
and sympathetic."[72] Given such uncritical acclaim, it is no wonder that
Hitler barricaded himself at the Berghof for months in the lead-up to the

Eva Braun on the Obersalzberg, ca. 1937

campaign—he clearly needed this seclusion and blind agreement from his selected entourage. When and to what extent he revealed his war plans to Eva Braun during these months remains unknown to this day. But there is no doubt that, in one form or another, he let his loyal girlfriend in on the facts at some point before he left Berlin on the special train to East Prussia. Maria von Below, in a private (and apparently tapped) telephone call with her relatives, is said to have communicated weeks earlier the exact date of the upcoming German attack on the Soviet Union. Admiral Wilhelm Canaris, head of the military secret service, later complained to Hitler about the incident during a visit to the "Wolf's Lair," at which point Hitler, to everyone's surprise, "brushed it aside with a wave of his hand."[73]

From the start, Hitler showed no political restraint or secretiveness around his two young secretaries, either. They had accompanied him to his headquarters at the front, and while eating breakfast or having an afternoon coffee with them, he explained "what a great danger Bolshevism posed to Europe" and that, if he had waited another year, "it would probably have already been too late." Christa Schroeder wrote in a letter to a friend that the women "first heard what the boss had to say about the state of affairs" over breakfast. Then, "around one o'clock," they went with him "to the general briefing" that took place in the map room, where either the chief-adjutant of the armed forces, Colonel Rudolf Schmundt, or Hitler's army adjutant, Major Gerhard Engel, gave his "situation report."

These "briefing lectures," in which Bormann, Morell, and Schaub also took part, were "extremely interesting" to Christa Schroeder.[74] The military officers, in contrast, disliked such loose conduct on the part of their commander in chief, and put a stop as soon as they could to Hitler's bringing his secretaries along to military meetings. Nonetheless, Christa Schroeder described "evening discussions with the leader" in July 1941, which "always [went on] insanely long."[75] And on August 20, after nine weeks in the "Wolf's Lair," she put Hitler's raw and unadulterated views, as she had internalized them, in a private letter:

> There is nothing I want more deeply than for the English to propose peace once we've taken care of Russia. . . . I just can't understand why the English are being so unreasonable. Once we've spread out to the east, we won't need their colonies. It's much more practical, too, to have everything nice and contiguous, it seems to me. The Ukraine and Crimea are so fertile, we can grow what we need there, and get everything else . . . in trade with South America. It's all so simple and makes so much sense. Please God, let the English come to their senses soon.[76]

The goals of this deliberate war of exploitation and annihilation against the Soviet Union, in all its contempt for humanity, could not have been formulated any more clearly and unambiguously. Incidentally, this contemporaneous letter from Schroeder also proves something else: the claim made later that Hitler never touched on political topics in the presence of women was merely another self-protective lie.

The Beginning of the End

Presumably, Eva Braun and Hitler did not see each other during the next five months. Only twice—in October, shortly after the start of the great offensive against Moscow, and in November—did he leave his wooden barracks in the Rastenburg swamps, and only for one day each time, to travel to Berlin and Munich. In early December 1941, he stayed for about a week in Berlin.[77] The New Year's party that always took place at the Berghof, with its accompanying group photograph, did not happen for New Year's 1941–1942: Hitler stayed in East Prussia. He apparently phoned Eva Braun in Munich every night at around ten.[78] The blitzkrieg had meanwhile failed; the air war against England was lost; and Hitler had declared war on the United States after the Japanese attack on the American Pacific fleet in Pearl Harbor, without being forced or even obliged by treaty to do so. By late April 1942 when he once again traveled to the Bavarian capital and the Berghof for a few days, more than a million German soldiers had fallen in battle. The SS murdered almost as many civilians in mass shootings in the occupied territories by the end of the year. In spite of the enormous losses, lack of reserve troops, and shortages of matériel on the German side, a new summer offensive was supposed to reach Stalingrad and bring about a final decision in the war.[79]

In Munich and on the Obersalzberg, however, there was not yet any sign of the war in spring 1942. While Lübeck, Rostock, Cologne, Essen, Bremen, and other major German cities had already undergone nighttime carpet bombing from the British Royal Air Force, the "capital city of the movement" had not experienced a single air attack. Hitler thus met undisturbed with August Eigruber, the NSDAP Gauleiter of the Upper Danube, on April 27 and 28 to discuss the "construction of an operetta theater" in Linz and to determine the "street profile of the grand boulevards" there, which were to have arcades and upscale businesses on all sides. "The most ideal stroll in the world will be in Linz," he enthused, stressing to Eigruber that he, Hitler, was first and foremost an architect and master builder. Even his "military operations" would not have succeeded had he "not [remained] primarily an artist": that was the only way it had been possible "to survive this winter and emerge victorious." Hitler believed that he alone had prevented a military disaster in the winter of 1941–1942, by managing everything himself;[80] in fact, to his generals' annoyance, he had constantly interfered in operations despite having hardly any insight into larger strategic considerations. In the First World War, after all, he had been only a private.

The world of the Upper Bavarian Alps seemed just as intact as Munich. As before, streets and estates were being built on the Obersalzberg under the aegis of Martin Bormann. Bormann's instructions were even declared to be a "war-critical construction program of the Führer"; unlike everywhere else in the Reich, there were no shortages of labor or restrictions on construction materials, food, or objects of daily use there. This was true first and foremost for Hitler and his entourage—their stay on the "mountain" continued to be idyllic.[81] What's more, in the early summer of 1942 Eva Braun posed Hitler in front of her camera as a devoted paterfamilias

Hitler and Eva Braun with her friend Herta Schneider's children, at the Berghof, 1944

and sympathetic private person. She even asked Walter Frentz, a young photographer who had worked as a cameraman for Leni Riefenstahl and had accompanied Hitler as a photographer since the start of the war, to take photographs of herself as well as her friend Herta Schneider's young daughter, and Hitler.[82] Since Eva Braun preserved these pictures in a separate photo album she started specially for them, it is reasonable to assume that she was thereby recording her own desire for a normal family life, and that, during the long periods of separation caused by the war, she took as much delight in her fantasy world on celluloid as Hitler did in his models of Linz. In addition, she herself often photographed and filmed Hitler with her school friend's children, or the children of other visitors to the Berghof.[83] Another reason she did this was apparently that it made the "Führer" appear the way she wanted him to be: pleasant, relaxed, private. At the same time, though, she sold these pictures to Heinrich Hoffmann, who then published them in his propaganda photo books. The assertion that Hitler knew nothing about her fake-family pictures is thus hard to believe.[84] If nothing else, he was obviously willing to make himself available to pose for her in this way. Eva Braun, for her part, clearly got vicarious satisfaction from this constant filming, which Hitler always put up with since he could not offer her a fulfilling private life in other ways.[85]

In the meantime, Eva Braun's currency at Hitler's court continued to rise. Christa Schroeder, who had no domestic life of her own since she had constantly been on call for Hitler for years, commented in her memoir that Eva Braun grew "more certain of her influence over Hitler" during the war years. She became "more self-confident," Schroeder wrote, took a greater part in mealtime conversations, and often expressed her displeasure "when Hitler continued to discuss one of his favorite topics after the meal was over, rather than getting up from the table." As soon as Eva Braun intervened, by loudly "asking the time" or looking rebukingly at Hitler, he brought "his monologues" to an end "on the spot."[86] Eva Braun thus seems to have been the only person who dared to put a stop to his well-known talkativeness; no other member of the mealtime group at the Berghof would have done so. But it did not gain her any sympathy from the others; it only emphasized the intimacy of her relationship with Hitler and showed up the obsequious behavior of everyone else. Not a few of them held it against her that she dimmed the "Führer's" radiant glow by treating him like a longtime husband.

This is not the least significant reason why Eva Braun was later called capricious, spoiled, and "very much focused on trivialities." Baldur von Schirach, for example, a member of Hitler's inner circle from the age of eighteen who continued to visit the Obersalzberg occasionally until 1943 with his wife, Henriette, said after the war that Eva Braun sometimes supplied the people at the table "with the latest gossip and scandal from the film world for hours on end." And if she "couldn't get a word in with her gossip stories," Schirach said, "she acted bored and complained about migraines, and Hitler worriedly patted her hand again and again while he was talking with his associates."[87] They now addressed each other with the informal "*du*," and the rest of the guests could relax from the "formal fireside gatherings" only when Hitler and Braun withdrew upstairs together at night.[88]

Eva Braun and Martin Bormann were the only people in Hitler's private world who became more and more important to the Nazi leader in these years. Bormann had taken over for Rudolf Hess after Hess's bizarre

Hitler and Eva Braun at the dining table in the teahouse on Mooslahnerkopf,
1940

flight to Scotland on May 10, 1941, and now ran the "Party Chancellery
of the Führer." Hess had apparently intended to conduct negotiations on
his own in order to secure peace in the west for Hitler's upcoming war
against the Soviet Union in the east, but he was now regarded as a traitor.
For months, Bormann mercilessly pursued every suspected "collaborator
in this act of insanity," on Hitler's orders.[89] But while Hess's adjutants and
others in his circle were arrested, his wife, Ilse Hess, was more or less left
alone, notwithstanding a lot of harassment from Bormann. She owed this
consideration in large part to her National Socialist attitudes, about which
no one had any doubt. But Eva Braun, too—nicknamed "Everl" in a postwar letter of Ilse Hess's—seems to have spoken up for her and supported
her.[90] It is doubtful that she did so without Hitler's knowledge—"behind
Hitler's back," as Albert Speer later claimed—since Ilse Hess continued to
be in direct contact with Hitler. For example, she wrote to a friend in early
August 1941 that "the Führer" had permitted her to write to "the big" (as
she called her husband) in England.[91] Hitler's paranoid suspicions thus
seem to have remained within limits in the case of his fugitive deputy's
wife.

Even though it was possible to get around Bormann in this case, Bormann became, with Hitler's increasing isolation in his various headquarters, Hitler's primary connection with the outside world. He was almost

Hitler in his airplane,
1942/1943

entirely unknown to the German public but was constantly with Hitler, as the most influential relayer of his orders and a liaison whom no one could bypass—not even Eva Braun.[92] Still, she apparently found her own way to get a hearing with Hitler from afar. From time to time in the head-quarters, according to Speer, "letters from Eva Braun gave rise to the most annoying interruptions." She wrote from Munich about, among other things, "cases of blatant stupidity on the part of officials," which "would send Hitler into a fit" every time until he finally ordered Bormann to investigate her accusations.[93]

Hitler left the Berghof again for several months on June 20, 1942, to command the planned summer offensive against the Soviet Union—"Operation Blue"—and Eva Braun left the next day for her last trip to Italy.[94] It is no longer possible to reconstruct how she traveled, and with whom. Christa Schroeder later claimed that at any given time Eva Braun had always had only one "favorite" among the women at the Berghof who then also accompanied her on her annual trip to Portofino.[95] This time, as in previous years, Eva Braun stayed in Italy for almost four weeks, returning to Germany only on July 17.[96] In the middle of the war, such long pleasure trips abroad were unusual and, above all, expensive. They had to be reported to the authorities in advance, and approved; a passport, visa, and travel permit were all needed, and so was foreign currency, since it was forbidden to take German currency out of the country—in the case of normal tourism, the limit was set at only ten marks, a measure that made it impossible to leave the country unchecked. The German Workers' Front, which organized Mediterranean cruises on its own KdF steamships (for example, a "cruise around Italy" from January 22 to February 1, 1939, on the *Wilhelm Gustloff*), allowed its guests to bring up to 100 reichsmarks in coins, but it was "absolutely forbidden" to bring paper money.[97] Eva Braun, in contrast, kept all her travel privileges intact, and she could hardly have realized at the time that she would never again visit the south in her life.

For in the summer of 1942, Hitler continued to be confident, even optimistic, about the progress of the war. While his girlfriend enjoyed the Italian sun, he ordered Army Group B to march on Stalingrad with the Sixth Army under General Friedrich Paulus. But on November 22, the Sixth Army, with more than 250,000 soldiers, was trapped in Stalingrad by Soviet troops. Paulus capitulated in late January 1943, and ended up as a Soviet prisoner of war along with more than 110,000 soldiers. Hitler then withdrew to the Obersalzberg in spring 1943, for three months in total, through late June.[98] The young secretary Traudl Humps experienced "the decampment and relocation of a massive organization in the last days of March, 1943," and recalled: "We were supposed to arrive in Munich around noon. It was nine. I quickly got dressed and went to breakfast. People were talking about the Berghof and about Eva Braun. I was curious to meet her. She was going to get on the train in Munich and come with us to Berchtesgaden." Humps's future husband, Hans Hermann Junge, an SS member since 1933 and one of Hitler's orderlies, explained to her that Eva Braun was "the mistress of the Berghof and tacitly recognized as such by all the guests." She went on: "I needed to prepare myself for the fact that this was the Führer's private household, that we all had to see ourselves as his guests, and that everyone would eat meals together. But all this was true for only a very small circle."[99]

The mood at the Berghof was entirely different than it had been in the previous year. After the "catastrophe on the Eastern Front" as Joseph Goebbels noted, premonitions of downfall and death began to spread on the "mountain" for the first time.[100] Meanwhile, Munich, too, had been bombed. Eva Braun's house at Wasserburger Strasse and Hitler's private residence at 16 Prinzregentenplatz were damaged. Hitler continued to present himself to others as certain of victory, but he barely ever appeared in public anymore. Even the "Führer Address" that took place every year on the anniversary of his having been named Chancellor was omitted in 1943, for the first time in ten years. Hitler was already contemplating a possible catastrophe and the "ending of his own life" that would then be necessary. Bormann, too, unsure what "turn" the war was going to take, discussed the consequences of his own possible death in a letter to his wife, Gerda. According to Hitler's orders, Bormann wrote, the widow of a Reich minister or Reich chancellor was not permitted to keep her husband's official residence. Thus, in the case of his own death, she would have to leave the house in Pullach immediately—their formal villa in the neighborhood of the Party elite, built in 1938. She would also need to vacate the house on the Obersalzberg, since she would have to reckon with harassment from Eva Braun.[101] This letter reveals how strong the rivalry was between Braun and Bormann, and how poisoned the atmosphere in Hitler's innermost circle must have been with suspicion and enmity.

Goebbels, on the other hand, who had proclaimed "total war" in a fanatical speech in the Berlin Sportpalast on February 18, 1943, painted a positive picture of Hitler's girlfriend in his "Diaries." He mentions Eva Braun there for the first time in an entry dated June 25, 1943, noting that she was "extraordinarily well read, extraordinarily clear and mature in her judgment on aesthetic questions," and made "the best impression" on him. She would certainly be, he wrote, "a valuable support for the Führer."[102] Apparently Eva Braun's status had risen so high that Goebbels finally could refer to her by name in the document he was preparing for posterity, after having kept silent about her existence until then. Ultimately, the Minister of Propaganda was trying to expand his own position and power in the immediate environment of the shattered leader.[103] Thus his diary returned to Eva Braun again, six weeks later, in the course of recording his judgment on everyone in the Nazi elite in view of the military "crisis."

Allied troops landed in Sicily in July 1943, and Mussolini was deposed and arrested. At almost the same time, the last army offensive on the Eastern Front, ordered by Hitler, failed.[104] Now, according to Goebbels, the Nazi leader was "generally thinking about who could replace whom, if someone should fall." In this context, Goebbels recorded Hitler's dissatisfaction, even indignation, with Baldur von Schirach and his wife, who were said to be attending "a social gathering" in Vienna that was "anything but National Socialist."[105] In fact, the break between Hitler and the Schirachs had come in June, when Baldur von Schirach told the Nazi leader that he had to end the war. Hitler commented to his adjutant Below: "How could he imagine that? He knows as well as I do that there is no longer any way except to put a bullet in my brain."[106] Henriette von Schirach even claims in her memoir (which is, however, thoroughly self-justifying from start to finish) that she brought up the "deportation of Jewish women" from Holland during one of the evening gatherings at the Berghof; Hitler supposedly screamed, "You are being sentimental! What do you care about Jewish women in Holland!"[107]

The end of the decades-long and almost familial connection between Hitler and the Schirachs, however it actually came about, shows the increasing tension within the inner circle in light of the desperate course the war was taking. "The Führer, on the other hand," Goebbels dictated on August 10, 1943, "points out most forcefully Eva Braun's calm, intelligent, and objective way of being." He called her "a clever girl who means a lot to the Führer," whereas Hitler was "through with Schirach, both personally and politically."[108] What had Eva Braun actually done to earn this praise? Apparently she not only stayed loyal but also continued to act unconcerned about external events. Gerda Bormann, for example, reported from the Obersalzberg to her husband in the "Wolf's Lair" that there were constant air raids in Munich but Eva Braun was going swimming in the Königssee with her friends.[109] Apparently, in an oppressive situation where the only military task was to make "the impossible possible" Eva Braun and the carefree attitude she displayed so openly was a relief for Hitler. Just like him, she had subscribed to the motto "All or nothing," and in so doing she impressed Goebbels as well, who indulged in expressions of undying loyalty and felt that the Nazi leader's "closest friends" now had the duty to form "an iron phalanx" around their "Führer."[110]

10

The Events of July 20, 1944, and Their Aftermath

While thus in 1943 and 1944, power struggles were breaking out not only in Hitler's political environment but also in his private circle, which even at the Berghof was showing its first signs of falling apart, resistance to the war was growing among the leading military and diplomatic circles. Many people understood that the war was lost, and they blamed Hitler's political and strategic missteps for the loss. Among the general population, too, the defeat at Stalingrad marked a turning point in the popularity of the Nazi regime. The expectation that the state-run German press had fostered for years—that the war would be swift and victorious—had not been met. The aura of an invincible "Führer" had been shattered.[1]

The climax of this development was the assassination attempt that took place on July 20, 1944. On a hot and humid summer day, Lieutenant Colonel Claus Schenk Graf von Stauffenberg, who was chief of staff to the Commander of the Replacement Army, left behind a briefcase with explosives during a briefing with Hitler in the "Wolf's Lair" headquarters, intending to kill the Nazi leader and help end the war. The attempt failed, and Hitler survived the explosion only lightly wounded.[2] Stauffenberg and three other conspirators were shot the same day, and the other two hundred or so people involved in the plot were then rounded up and hanged after a show trial at the Nazis' so-called People's Court in Berlin.[3] A camera recorded their deaths in Berlin's Plötzensee prison. This film, and photographs of the hanged men, were at the "Wolf's Lair" in August 1944, but no one knows for sure whether Hitler saw them. It is an authenticated fact, however, that one man was delighted by them: SS-Obergruppenführer Hermann Fegelein, Himmler's liaison officer in the headquarters and Eva Braun's brother-in-law.[4]

The Inner Circle's Reaction

Fegelein had married Gretl Braun in Salzburg on June 3, 1944, with Bormann and Himmler as witnesses. The ensuing celebrations took place in Bormann's house and in the teahouse on the Kehlstein peak—the "Eagle's Nest"—and lasted three days, an inappropriately long time for a wedding party during the war. Eva Braun, who apparently brought her sister and Fegelein together, had arranged the party. Fegelein was a highly decorated member of the Waffen-SS and commander of the SS cavalry forces including the First SS Death's-Head Cavalry Regiment. According to Speer, he had paid court to all of the single women at the Berghof, and rumors even circulated that he and Eva Braun had found favor with each other.[5] Eva Braun remarked at the time, according to Christa Schroeder: "I want this wedding to be as beautiful as if it were my own."[6] Her own prospects of one day living with Hitler as his wife in Linz after the so-called final victory were looking slim. On the very night of June 3–4, the Allies took Rome, and on June 6 the long-expected invasion of the Continent began at Normandy.

Thus the end was conceiveable. Nonetheless, life on the Obersalzberg continued to take its "peaceful course." Below, Speer, Brandt, and Goebbels were among the regular guests. Eva Braun showed "a series of color films" that she had shot of Hitler in earlier years at the Berghof. "I have never seen him so relaxed on film," Goebbels remarked.[7] The Minister of Propaganda praised Eva Braun's "critical discernment" in "questions of film and theater," and recorded: "We sit there around the fire until 2 a.m., exchanging memories, taking pleasure in the many beautiful days and weeks that we spent together. The Führer asks about people, now this one, now that one. In short, the atmosphere is like that of the good

*Eva Braun and Hitler
on the Obersalzberg,
probably 1944*

old days."[8] For more than four months—from late February until July
16, 1944, with only brief interruptions—Hitler stayed at the Berghof. It
was his last time there, and he probably suspected it would be. He postponed his departure several times. There had been hints for months that
an attempt on his life from his own military was looming.[9]

Eva Braun heard about the assassination attempt on the afternoon of
July 20. She had once again left the Berghof to go swimming with her
best friend Herta Schneider at Königssee, just five miles away. On the
way back, a chauffeur fetched the women and told them what had happened. Schneider later told the American journalist Nerin E. Gun that
Eva Braun, back at the Berghof, tried to phone Hitler at his headquarters
in Rastenburg, and suffered a nervous crisis when she still could not reach
him after many attempts. When she finally did get through to Hitler, she
reportedly said: "I love you, may God protect you," and cried tears of
joy after hanging up the phone.[10] Hitler had apparently already made
plans with her at the Berghof for the eventuality of his death, given the
rumors that had been circulating for some time of a possible assassination

attempt. Goebbels noted after a discussion with the Nazi leader in Rastenburg on August 24, 1944, for example, that Hitler told him about premonitions he had had even before his departure from the Obersalzberg,
which had weighed on him like a "nightmare," and about having "told
[Eva Braun] precisely" what she "needed to do upon his death." She had
apparently brushed aside "such admonitions," however. Instead, she had
told Hitler that "in such a case, there would be only one thing left for her,
namely to seek her own death as well."[11]

It must certainly have been quite clear to Eva Braun that without Hitler
she would be in a weak and vulnerable position vis-à-vis her many enemies. But would this fear justify suicide? And why would Hitler, otherwise
so silent about private matters, have given Goebbels this advance notice
of his girlfriend's plans? Eva Braun seems to have completely and utterly
bound her life to that of Hitler, early on and quite consciously. She had
already proven many times over that she was prepared to do the utmost for
him. He, in turn, clearly valued this kind of attestation of loyalty, especially
as he saw himself increasingly surrounded by "traitors," and he therefore
must have emphasized his appreciation of her. The whole episode makes
clear that their double suicide nine months later was no accident. Hitler
and Braun had already decided what roles they were to play in the last act.
They may even have made arrangements for it together.

To Hitler's close confidants, the assassination attempt came as a shock.
They all knew, of course, how dependent they were on the "Führer." But
while his girlfriend sat waiting for news at the Berghof, Goebbels and
Speer in Berlin helped crush the revolt. Goebbels took an active role
by putting the "Leibstandarte Adolf Hitler" (Hitler's Personal Bodyguard
Regiment), stationed in the capital, on alert and by arranging for a special
announcement to go out over the German radio: "Assassination Attempt
Failed." Speer, who had come to the Ministry of Propaganda for a meeting on the afternoon of July 20, stood at his side and offered advice.[12] Still,
there was not exactly rock-solid cohesion among Hitler's henchmen in
light of this threat from within, since Speer, for instance, found his name
on a government list of traitors, was exposed to numerous suspicions, and
feared intrigues on the part of his rivals, Goebbels and Bormann.[13]

In any case, the failed attack in no way inspired doubts in Hitler's circle
about the continuation of the war. The members all explicitly declared
their faith in Hitler and their belief in the "final victory." None of Hitler's
longtime companions and convinced National Socialists saw Hitler as the

cause of the human suffering in Europe. Ilse Hess, for instance, had complained of the "destruction of our beautiful, beloved Munich" after the heavy bombardment of the Bavarian capital in spring 1944, and when she heard that "the Führer had stood before the rubble, deeply shaken," she declared:

> I imagine that it must have been terribly difficult for him! To wait relentlessly until eventually the one favorable and right moment comes for the last great strike—and to have to look on as one after another of the things closest to his heart is annihilated—not to mention the loss of life! But it is 1944 and we will never give up hope![14]

Among the German population as well, Hitler grew more popular after the attempt on his life became known, while the subversives reaped widespread disapproval and outrage. In fact, the events of July 20 had been, to quote German historian Hans-Ulrich Thamer, a "resistance without the people." Yet the attack left a deep mark on the Nazi leader himself. More than ever, he saw himself as a hero chosen by Providence, the only man who could save Europe from "Bolshevism." If anything happened to him, he had told his secretary the night before the assassination attempt, there was "no one who would be able to take over as leader."[15]

A *Trophy for Eva Braun*

On the very afternoon of July 20, Christa Schroeder received orders from Hitler to send his uniform, shredded by the explosion, to Eva Braun on the Obersalzberg. The secretary—who said of herself that she "played a greater part [in Hitler's life] than a member of the family"—recalled that Braun was supposed to save the pants, which "were in tatters and threads from top to bottom," and the jacket, whose back was now missing "a square patch." She also remarked that the Nazi leader was "in a way proud of this trophy."[16] In fact, Hitler was euphoric after the incident and transformed the damaged uniform, which at first sight testified to his vulnerability, into a kind of sign of victory with which he tried to emphasize his triumph over his enemies. He might have imagined presenting the uniform to the German public, after a victorious end to the war, as proof of his heroic struggle.

First, though, Hitler was showing his girlfriend that he, too, could not escape injury, but was putting his own life and body on the line like every other soldier in battle. Of course, he stayed in his bunker in the "Wolf's Lair" as though in a fortress, surrounded by several circles of barbed wire fences monitored by the Waffen-SS.[17] But he imagined himself as a warrior, a hero making sacrifices for his People, and he made sure that Eva Braun, whom he spoke about in the headquarters "almost every day," shared his self-image.[18] It is said that she "nearly fainted" when she caught sight of Hitler's uniform.[19] But the claim that Eva Braun received a love letter along with the uniform—Hitler supposedly addressed her, using an Austrian pet name, as "dear Tschapperl" in the letter, added a sketch of the barracks, and signed it with the initials A.H.—is surely a legend. Nerin E. Gun quotes this letter from memory, but its contents and provenance are highly doubtful, and it is extremely unlikely that Hitler, who in general avoided writing personal letters, would have dedicated such a personal document for his secretary to type up in precisely the days after July 20, 1944, in an atmosphere of paranoid mistrust of the people around him.[20]

It is true, though, that Hitler appeared in his East Prussian headquarters right after the attack in an almost giddy mood. (The explosion had killed four people and wounded eleven.) Nicolaus von Below, who took part in the briefing on July 20 and was wounded himself, observed the "lively, almost happy expression on his face" and his "increased sense of mission."[21] Traudl Junge, the secretary Hitler sought out in his bunker immediately after the explosion, recalled that he was walking "upright and ramrod straight as he hadn't for a long time."[22] As before, the Nazi leader rejected all thoughts of capitulation. From his point of view, it must not come to another "November 1918." Even withdrawing from occupied areas so as to deploy the troops stationed there in defense of the Reich itself was never an option for him. The complexities of the war were beyond the dictator's grasp: for him, there was only victory or annihilation. The "downfall was a duty."[23] And so, despite the hopeless military situation—the Red Army was already at the border of the German Reich, while the Allies were making inroads on all fronts—Hitler convinced himself that "Providence" had saved him on July 20, 1944, so that he could complete his "task."[24]

Such convictions aside, Hitler's health, unstable for years, took a dramatic turn for the worse after the assassination attempt. Even during

Hitler's last stay at the Berghof, Goebbels had noticed from Eva Braun's movies that Hitler had "gotten older and older . . . during the war" and now walked "all bent over."[25] His stomach complaints had gotten worse after the war started, despite a strictly vegetarian diet. He also had higher blood pressure and was in the early stages of Parkinson's disease, with involuntary trembling in his arms and legs.[26] Bernd Freytag von Loringhoven, who as a young adjutant of the Chief of the General Staff of the Army first saw Hitler in person at a briefing on July 23, 1944, later recalled a "man of fifty-five with the posture of an old man."[27] Two months after the attack, Hitler suffered a full-blown physical collapse. Morell, his personal physician, noted in his daily calendar that "Patient A" had been feeling increasingly unwell since September 24, and was suffering from heart trouble, stomach aches, and a sore throat. "Finally," Traudl Junge recalls, "the Führer stayed in bed one day. It was sensational news. No one had ever seen Hitler lying in bed."[28] A case of jaundice kept him on strict bed rest into mid-October; he lost a considerable amount of weight, and as a result he seemed haggard and old.[29] The psychological strain increased. But since there was no way out for Hitler, and also no turning back, he devoted himself to the idea of one last great offensive in the west, despite the shortages of fuel and other supplies. He fantasized to Speer that "a single breakthrough on the western front" would "lead to collapse and panic among the Americans."[30]

Eva Braun's Will

At around the same time, on October 26, 1944, Eva Braun drew up her will in Munich.[31] What made her take this step just then? Had Hitler's illness, combined with the visible horrors of war in the destroyed city of Munich, made her aware that the end might be near? This assumption is at least plausible, especially as Gerda Bormann told her husband about a conversation with Eva Braun on the evening of October 23 on the Obersalzberg, in which Braun was deeply concerned that Hitler, who had barely recovered, was so close to the front. The Soviet troops had reached Warsaw and East Prussia in October 1944. Both women therefore hoped that Hitler would return to the Obersalzberg, because that was where, according to Gerda Bormann, it was "safest." Martin Bormann put a damper on their hopes, however, since he knew that Hitler would under no circumstances abandon the "Wolf's Lair." At the same time, Bormann admitted to his wife that "sixty or eighty kilometers" was hardly a sufficient distance; he, too, wanted "more security for the Führer," who needed a more appropriate location to recuperate.[32]

Proximity to the front was not the only problem. Hitler's illness had led to conflicts and power struggles among his attending physicians. Karl Brandt and the other accompanying physicians held Morell responsible for the "Führer's" poor state of health. Brandt accused Morell of having tried to poison Hitler with strychnine. Brandt was unable, though, to supply proof of this charge or to shake Morell's position of trust, and as a result he was himself accused of "treason" and dismissed as accompanying physician on October 10, 1944. Despite losing this post, Brandt, who had been named Reich Commissioner for Health and Sanitation only four weeks earlier, remained one of the most powerful figures in the Nazi regime.[33]

These squabbles and the rumors of Hitler's possible death connected with them could not have remained a secret to Eva Braun. In fact, it is likely that either Hitler himself or Anni Brandt, or Morell, or maybe even Bormann, kept her informed. In any case, the whole situation in the faraway "Wolf's Lair" clearly seemed threatening enough to her that she began to reckon with the possibility of Hitler's death. In her own life, on the other hand, little on the outside had changed. She continued to shuttle between the Obersalzberg and Munich, where she worked in Heinrich Hoffmann's art publishing house and liked the work very much.[34] Since her house in Bogenhausen had suffered serious damage from air attacks, she lived at the Berghof, where materially she lacked for nothing. And yet the thirty-two-year-old woman was preparing for her death.

Her will conscientiously divided up her property—in particular the jewelry, clothes, china, furniture, cash, and paintings—among her family and friends. According to Nerin E. Gun's list, which, he wrote, reproduced the will "verbatim," the paintings included works by Hermann Gradl, Hugo Wilhelm Kauffmann, Theodor Bohnenberger, Oskar Mulley, Heinrich Knirr, and Fritz Halberg-Krauss,[35] all members of the Munich School of genre and landscape painters, Hitler's favorite artists. (Gradl, Mulley, and Halberg-Krauss were represented in the National Socialist "Greater German Art Exhibition" that took place in the "House of German Art" in Munich until 1944.) We can only guess how Eva Braun came into possession of original paintings by these artists—she was certainly close to the source, as a colleague of Heinrich Hoffmann, a major art buyer. Hoffmann's art press, where she now worked, also produced and sold the official postcards of the "Greater German Art Exhibition" exhibits.[36] It is also possible that most of these pictures were gifts from Hitler. He had, for example, personally sought out Hermann Gradl in his studio in 1937, and had had portraits of himself painted by Heinrich Knirr and Theodor Bohnenberger, among others. Eva Braun apparently owned one of each of these "Führer portraits," and was herself painted by Bohnenberger as well.[37] She bequeathed this latter portrait to her sister Ilse, along with the house on Wasserburger Strasse. Gretl Fegelein (née Braun) was to inherit all of Eva Braun's home movies, photo albums, and personal letters.

Eva Braun's will of October 1944 reveals yet again her firm decision to die with Hitler. She would presumably have ended her life in Munich if illness or a Soviet attack had killed Hitler in Rastenburg. A future without him apparently never entered her thoughts. Henriette von Schirach later recalled that during her last visit to the Obersalzberg, in the summer of 1943, she had already discussed the future with Eva Braun—the postwar future—and had suggested that Braun could "go into hiding somewhere." According to Schirach, Braun had answered: "Do you think I would let him die alone? I will stay with him up until the last moment, I've thought it out exactly. No one can stop me."[38]

11

THE DECISION FOR BERLIN

Eva Braun had thus long since set her personal affairs in order in Munich when Hitler and his entourage left the "Wolf's Lair" forever, on Monday, November 20, 1944, at 3:15 p.m., and traveled by special train to the capital, arriving at 5:20 a.m. on November 21.[1] Only a few days earlier, he had categorically refused to change his headquarters—Nicolaus von Below recalls that he personally heard Hitler say the war was lost and he would remain in East Prussia. But Martin Bormann succeeded in changing Hitler's mind.[2] In fact, Hitler was not yet ready to die. The day after his arrival in Berlin, he underwent an operation on his vocal cords— as he had back in 1935—to remove what Goebbels called "an insignificant lump." On the day of the operation, November 22, Eva Braun arrived at the Chancellery. Theodor Morell noted briefly in his daily calendar: "E.B. arrived. I left later."[3]

Once again, Eva Braun stayed with Hitler in the rooms on the second floor of the Old Chancellery. Hitler was not allowed to speak after the operation, and during the daily briefings he could make himself understood only "by writing on slips of paper."[4] A "Führer bunker" had been specially built in the garden behind this building in late September, 1944, about 25 feet underground. It measured just 2,150 square feet and had fifteen rooms, including a living room and bedroom for Eva Braun.[5] For the time being, Hitler and Braun descended into the cramped, damp, and poorly ventilated bunker only during air raids.

The surviving record nowhere mentions when Eva Braun left Berlin again. The secretaries seem not even to have known she was there. However, they had "not been face to face [with Hitler] for three days" after the operation, as Traudl Junge wrote later, and they had no information about whether he was staying in a hospital or in the Chancellery.[6] In all probability, Eva Braun left after only a few days, and had long since returned to Munich when Hitler, on the evening of December 10, left Berlin for the "Eagle's Eyrie" headquarters in Ziegenberg, near the Hessian city of Bad Nauheim.

A week later, the Ardennes Offensive began, with which Hitler intended to take Antwerp and turn the tide of the war. General Heinrich Eberbach—who was interned with other high-ranking German prisoners of war in the British special camp of Trent Park, where British Intelligence eavesdropped on and recorded all of their conversations with each other without their knowledge—commented on Hitler's decision to wage one last offensive: "It's not his last. The man never stops fooling himself. When he's standing at the base of the gallows, he'll still fool himself that he won't be strung up on it."[7] And in fact "Operation Autumn Fog" failed after only ten days. There was no chance it would succeed, and Hitler himself probably didn't believe it would. Late at night in the bunker, Nicolaus von Below recalled, Hitler told him that he knew the war was lost, and what he wanted most was to "put a bullet in his brain right now."[8] But he didn't do it. Not yet.

The Final Offensive

Instead, Hitler returned to Berlin on January 16, 1945. Eva Braun, too, accompanied this time by her pregnant sister Gretl, traveled from Munich to the capital two days later. Both women traveled in the care of Martin Bormann, who had stayed at the Berghof for a few days. Together with his wife, Gerda, and an SS officer, they arrived in Berlin by "special car" on the afternoon of January 19.[9] There is thus no truth to the idea that Eva Braun came to Berlin "unexpectedly and against Hitler's orders," as Julius Schaub later claimed.[10] She was apparently counting on an even earlier reunion, since even before Christmas she had asked Hitler many times to spend the holidays at the Berghof. Hitler told his secretary that "mainly it's Gretl behind that, she wants her Hermann there with her."[11] As he could not fulfill his girlfriend's and her sister's wishes, he had both women come to Berlin as soon as he was back there. Adjutant Bernd Freytag von Loringhoven later wrote in his memoir that he was surprised to see "two elegantly dressed young women with their hair freshly done" coming down the hall of the Chancellery, while he and the other officers were waiting there for the briefing with Hitler to start.[12]

If we believe Goebbels's account, Eva Braun had already decided at that point not to leave Berlin again. The Minister of Propaganda wrote, under the date of February 1, 1945:

> I explain to the Führer that my wife is determined to stay in Berlin, too, and even refuses to let our children leave. The Führer doesn't think this standpoint is the right one, but finds it admirable. He says that Miss Eva Braun has the same view. She also does not want to leave Berlin, especially in this critical hour. The Führer finds words of the deepest recognition and admiration for her. And this is certainly what she deserves.[13]

The small circle of those who linked their fates to Hitler's to the bitter end was thus beginning to form, in the face of the ever-approaching enemy armies. Bormann, who had been Hitler's "shadow" since the start of the war—constantly near him and controlling all access to him to a greater and greater extent—was not, however, among them. True, he did emphasize in a letter to his wife that both of their fortunes and fates were tied to that of the "Führer." At no point, though, did he intend to bring his family to Berlin.[14]

Meanwhile, the Soviet offensive against the German Reich—the attack on Berlin—had started, on January 12, 1945. By the end of the month, the German troops in East Prussia were cut off from the Reich. The Red Army encircled Königsberg and had pushed ahead into Pomerania. Large swaths of the East Prussian population fled their homes. The first battalions under General Georgy Zhukov, Commander of the First Belorussian Front, were already at Frankfurt an der Oder, about fifty-five miles from Berlin.[15] While the situation was thus coming to a head, Eva Braun celebrated her thirty-third birthday in the capital, on the night of February 5–6, 1945. By then, she and Hitler were spending their nights in the

Mohrenstrasse in the center of Berlin, after the bombardment of February 3, 1945

air-raid bunker.[16] Alongside Hitler's "last apartment" in the bunker—two bedrooms, a living room, and a bathroom—a bedroom had also been set up for Eva Braun, which she equipped with her furniture from the Chancellery.[17] They retreated to the bunker more and more often by day as well. Two days earlier, on the morning of February 3, 1945, more than nine hundred American airplanes had attacked Berlin and badly damaged the center of the city, near Potsdamer Platz and Leipziger Strasse, with high-explosive and incendiary bombs. Fires raged everywhere, the government district on Wilhelmstrasse was destroyed, the Old Reich Chancellery was partly reduced to rubble, traffic was at a standstill, and the trains and streetcars no longer ran. Berlin was in ruins. Well over 100,000 people were made homeless and, according to official statistics, 2,895 had died in the air attack, which lasted barely an hour.[18] Goebbels, seeking out Hitler in his bunker one afternoon shortly thereafter, remarked that "access to the Führer" was "totally blocked with mountains of rubble." It was "practically like the chaos of the trenches trying to find the path to him."[19]

In these circumstances, the birthday celebration on the night of February 5 must have been an eerie and ghoulish affair. The small party took place in Eva Braun's living room on the second floor of the Old Reich

Chancellery, which had survived the air raid unharmed while the rooms in the "Führer apartment" had been gutted by fire.[20] Hitler thus now took his midday meals with his girlfriend and the secretaries in the "adjutant wing" of the Old Chancellery, which had likewise survived intact—eating "with the curtains drawn and electric lights," as Christa Schroeder later recalled—and the military briefings were moved to the monumental workroom in the New Chancellery. Only Eva Braun joined him for dinners.[21] Martin Bormann wrote to his wife, who had already returned to Bavaria on January 27 and was back on the Obersalzberg, about the birthday party, that the few guests had included Hitler; Eva Braun's sister Gretl and Gretl's husband, Hermann Fegelein; and Karl and Anni Brandt.[22]

Apparently, Brandt, despite having been fired from his position as Hitler's personal physician, had in no way fallen entirely into disfavor and been expelled from Hitler's innermost circle, as his biographer Ulf Schmidt claims.[23] But the longtime close friend's days were numbered. On April 16, Hitler had Brandt arrested by SS-Gruppenführer Heinrich Müller, the man responsible for carrying out Himmler's orders to send people to concentration camps. The charge was high treason. Brandt had dared to give Hitler an honest report of the catastrophic situation in the Reich regarding medical supplies, and was also accused of having sent his wife and child to Thuringia, already occupied by U.S. troops, so that they and he could defect to the Americans.[24] The following day, Hitler summarily court-martialed him, with Goebbels presiding, and Brandt was sentenced to death. He was to be shot on the morning of April 19. But it never happened—the execution was repeatedly postponed and, in the terrible chaos at the end, was never carried out.[25] Hitler's notion that he was surrounded by traitors who were responsible for the impending defeat thus ended up reaching all the way into his closest circle.

In this regard, Eva Braun was by no means a calming influence on Hitler, as her few statements in the surviving correspondence show. In the case of Karl Brandt, for example, she did not intervene in his favor but rather described his behavior, in a letter to her friend Herta Schneider, as "a real foul trick."[26] In other words, Eva Braun, now in Hitler's innermost trusted circle along with Bormann and Goebbels, only reinforced his delusions. She also seems to have stirred up Hitler's suspicions against people whom she herself did not like; even Albert Speer was now in her sights. When, as Speer wrote later, she asked him in Hitler's name "where my family was," he lied to her and said that they were staying "in the vicinity of Berlin." As a result, Hitler wanted to make sure "that we too [Speer and his family] would go to Obersalzberg when he retreated there."[27] Martin Bormann likewise wrote to his wife on February 6 that Eva Braun had been in a good mood at her birthday party but had criticized various (apparently absent) people with a brusqueness unusual for her.[28] Was Eva Braun now, in the middle of her downfall, lashing out at her former enemies for belittling her role as Hitler's mistress? We will never know, especially since Bormann expressed himself in only vague terms and was, of course, deeply suspicious of her.

After three weeks in Berlin, on the evening of February 9, 1945, Eva Braun and her sister left the destroyed city. Bormann, on Hitler's orders, took care of the women's return trip to Munich.[29] Braun had sat up until six in the morning with Hitler, Speer, Bormann, and the architect Hermann Giesler;[30] presumably, they viewed the gigantic model of Linz after its planned renovations that Giesler's associates had set up that night in one of the basement rooms of the New Reich Chancellery. Giesler later said that, exhausted, he had presented the model to Hitler and his companions "from the angle that his 'City on the Danube' would have been seen at from his retirement residence." In the following days, Hitler returned again and again to this basement room with the architect and other visitors, including the head of the security police, Ernst Kaltenbrunner, who had himself lived in Linz in the late 1920s as a lawyer and was frequently taking part in the briefings. The photographer Walter Frentz's images show a greatly aged Hitler, standing bent over or sitting in a chair and apparently totally withdrawn from the world, staring at this figment of his imagination.[31] Instead of ending the war that had long since been lost, he apparently continued to talk about how the Oder front could be held, and still dreamed of making Linz the most beautiful city in Europe. Speer told his American interrogators in Kransberg, half a year later, that by then Hitler "had left his life behind and descended into an imaginary world that knew no bounds."[32]

Life Underground

On March 7, 1945, Eva Braun returned to Berlin for good. She had already said goodbye to her family and friends in Munich. Only four weeks had passed since her previous visit. Her arrival was not in the least unexpected, as was claimed after the war.[33] Hitler himself had told Goebbels and Bormann that she intended to stay with him in Berlin; Bormann wrote to his wife only a week after Braun's departure for Munich that Hitler had told him Eva Braun wanted to come back to Berlin as soon as possible, but Hitler had told her to stay in Munich for now.[34] Her decision to experience the end with Hitler—if need be, to die with him, wherever that might be—had been made long before. It is unclear, though, whether she traveled to Berlin in early March against Hitler's will or whether they had agreed upon it first. Julius Schaub later said that she came "from Munich by airplane in early March." "She had asked whether she could come," he said, "but Herr Hitler had refused. In spite of that, she appeared one day and then lived in the small room next to his."[35] Bormann, in contrast, wrote that she had arrived one night in a "diplomatic car."[36]

Not only the circumstances of Eva Braun's arrival in Berlin but also her motive for returning to a capital city in flames have unleashed much speculation since her death. Henriette von Schirach wrote, with unconcealed distaste, that Braun wanted to die with Hitler to finally be able "to stand with him for all to see." So she had to "force her way into Hitler's death."[37] Speer, too, wrote in his *Inside the Third Reich* that when she arrived in Berlin "in the first half of the month of April," "everyone in the bunker knew why she had come": she was "figuratively and in reality . . . a messenger of death."[38] But how did he know? As the organizer of the total war effort, he was traveling most of the time between the various armament facilities throughout Germany as well as to the front lines being pushed farther and farther into the Reich. Thus he went, Below noted, "very much his own way during the last three months." Moreover, Speer could rarely gather firsthand information about the mood in Hitler's bunker as he met only occasionally with Hitler then, either there or in the Chancellery. Eva Braun, on the other hand, could have hardly been a "messenger of death" in the bunker since the plan was still, through mid-April, for Hitler to retreat to the Obersalzberg and lead the "final struggle" he had sworn to fight from his Alpine fortress.[39]

On the same day that Eva Braun left Bavaria, March 7, American troops advancing from the west succeeded in taking the Ludendorff Bridge over the Rhine intact, and thus established their first bridgehead on the right bank of the Rhine. Soviet tanks were in Pomerania, directly in front of the city of Kolberg on the Baltic. Even so, Hitler continued to radiate optimism among his followers. He was still playing for time, since he knew perfectly well that there would be no life for him after the defeat. In one way or another, death was awaiting him. Without the slightest regard for the millionfold suffering of others, he extended his own life and dramatized the war in his mind as a life-or-death battle for the existence of the German People. A counteroffensive launched in Hungary on March 6 was once again supposed to halt the Red Army's advance. The production of new weapons, a "miracle weapon" he pinned his hopes on, and internal disagreement in the coalition between the Soviets, the Americans, and the Britons could still bring about a sudden and complete change in the overall course of the war—or so he told himself and those in his circle.[40] At the same time, in his so-called Nero Order of March 19, 1945, he ordered the destruction of every "military transport, news, industrial, and supply facility as well as material of any value within the borders of the Reich" that might fall into the enemy's hands "in the foreseeable future." He intended to leave a "scorched earth" behind him, to weaken the "enemy's strike power." But Speer, who had already declared the war lost in a memo to Hitler, prevented the order from being carried out. By that point, even Himmler—whom Hitler had named Supreme Commander of the Army Group Vistula in January and who was thus responsible, in Hitler's eyes, for the loss of Pomerania—and Ribbentrop as well, had secretly tried to establish contact with the Western powers via Sweden.[41]

While his closest followers were thus slowly drawing away, Hitler continued to receive daily briefings about the military situation in the oppressively close quarters of the workroom in the bunker. The briefings began long after midnight and lasted until 6 a.m., and at the "morning teas" that followed—and took up another two hours—Hitler was, according to Christa Schroeder, "almost constantly on edge" and talked "only about dog training, questions of diet, and how bad and stupid the world is."[42] Eva Braun, on the other hand, remained strangely calm in this tense situation, while the bunker constantly shook under air attacks, lights flickering when bombs hit. Even in March, she occasionally escaped the depressing atmosphere underground to her apartment in the Old Reich Chancellery, where she threw small parties with the young secretaries. "And so, while Hitler was in meetings," Christa Schroeder later wrote, "we played records in her apartment, drank a glass of champagne, and now and then managed a dance with the off-duty officers."[43]

A month later, even this was apparently no longer possible. On April 19,

Eva Braun wrote to her friend Herta Schneider that they could "already
[hear] the artillery fire on the eastern front" and that she "unfortunately"
was "ordered to stand ready at every alarm, in case of flooding," though she
would be spending the rest of her life "only in the bunker" in any case.[44]
The orders came from Hitler personally, who was afraid a bomb hit could
break open the bunker and let groundwater come in. Whenever a report
of enemy planes came over the radio, Hitler now shaved and dressed in
all correctness so as to be able to leave his room immediately when the
air raid started.[45] Eva Braun seems not to have shared his fear of flooding.
Rather, her letter of April 19 gives a carefree, even confident impression.
"The secretaries and I are practicing with the pistol every day," she writes,
adding that she was "very happy to be near *him*, especially now." She
admits that she was constantly being told to save herself at the Berghof,
but "up till now I've always won."[46] How should we understand these
statements? Are they consoling words for the person closest to her, while
she kept her real thoughts and feelings to herself? Or had she accom-
plished her goal in life — to be with Hitler — so that she did not need to pay
attention to threats from without? It is difficult to answer these questions
from a distance. But it does seem to be the case that she was absolutely at
peace about everything, and had arrived where she always wanted to be.
Further evidence is provided by the fact that, according to Nicolaus von
Below — actually, according to everyone who saw her then — Eva Braun
continued "to always take care of herself" in the bunker, to "dress carefully and impeccably," act "as accommodating and gracious as ever," and
show "not the slightest sign of weakness right up to the final hour."[47] She
also seemed to expect from Hitler that he play his part perfectly to the
very end. In fact, her conduct helped him rigidly cling to his insane confidence in victory, and reinforced the delusion that he would still "beat
back the Russians and liberate Berlin." She permitted him no weakness
and reprimanded him even for slight negligence, such as a fleck of dirt on
his uniform. "You can't copy Old Fritz in everything and run around as
unappetizingly as he did," Braun would say, referring to Hitler's worship-
ping of Friedrich the Great, to whom he often compared himself — and
Eva Braun would do so even in the presence of Goebbels, Bormann,
army Adjutant-General Wilhelm Burgdorf, and the secretaries.[48]

On the night of April 20, 1945, Hitler's fifty-sixth birthday, and into the
morning hours, another party took place in Eva Braun's rooms in the
Old Chancellery. Hitler had withdrawn to his bedroom in the bunker,

after accepting since midnight the congratulations of his staff, the military, and leading Nazi politicians including Goebbels, Himmler, Göring, Ribbentrop, and Speer. Many of them had advised Hitler to leave Berlin as quickly as possible and go to the Obersalzberg, because all efforts to halt the Soviet advance had failed. In fact, the first Soviet units reached the southern edge of Berlin that night, April 20–21. The attack on the city center was imminent.[49] The henchmen were thus ready to scatter; they had long since prepared their departures. Even Hitler now seemed undecided whether or not to leave Berlin, according to his adjutant Below. In the briefing on the afternoon of April 20, he had said, according to Speer: "I shall leave it to fate whether I die in the capital or fly to Obersalzberg at the last moment!"[50] And that same day, he had sent his two oldest secretaries to southern Germany, saying that he would need them later and would "follow them in a few days."[51] Erich Kempka, Hitler's driver of many years who supervised the fleet of cars belonging to the Reich Chancellery (forty cars and sixty drivers), then received orders to bring several cars to carry the secretaries and others to various Berlin airports.[52]

Some of those who remained joined Eva Braun and Hitler once more for a glass of champagne in his workroom in the bunker: von Below, Schaub, Heinz Lorenz (adjutant to the Reich Press Chief), the secretaries Gerda Christian and Traudl Junge, and Hitler's dietitian, Constanze Manziarly. But the group broke up before long, since Hitler, as Traudl Junge recalled, was quiet and when asked had replied that he could not leave Berlin, he had to "bring about the decision here—or die!" Then, while the young secretary was shocked by this confession, Eva Braun threw her last little improvised party in the Old Chancellery. It is unclear who was there besides Traudl Junge, Bormann, and Morell. According to Junge, Braun had brought along "anyone she came across." Boisterously, in a "desperate frenzy," they drank champagne, laughed, danced to an old hit record from 1929—Junge quotes the line "Blood-red roses caress you all over"—and tried to forget the fear of the end that was fast approaching.[53]

The next morning, the center of Berlin was under fire from Soviet artillery. Ribbentrop, who until that point had not been allowed in to any meeting with Hitler, apparently pushed once again for Hitler to retreat from the capital in a conversation with Eva Braun.[54] Traudl Junge reports in her memoir that Braun told her about a "discussion" with Ribbentrop, who told her that she was "the only one who could get the Führer to leave"; she should tell him that she wanted to "leave Berlin with him." Eva Braun answered: "I will not speak a word of your suggestion to the Führer. He has to decide alone. If he thinks it is right to stay in Berlin, then I will stay with him. If he leaves, I will, too."[55] In fact, Hitler was hardly responsive to anything anymore. Unhinged to the end, he wanted to keep fighting, and ordered in all seriousness another counterattack, with a hastily thrown-together panzer corps under the command of SS-Obergruppenführer Felix Steiner. Hitler screamed and threatened the air force chief of staff Karl Koller that they had to "deploy every man," and that anyone who kept forces in reserve had "forfeited his life within five hours."[56] He was so beside himself that he did not even let Morell approach him that night, because he was afraid that Morell would sedate him so that he could be taken out of Berlin against his will. The doctor had to leave the bunker and was sent back to the Berghof with Eva Braun's jewelry the following day.[57]

The next day, April 22, saw Hitler's complete psychological breakdown, after he learned in the afternoon briefing that Steiner's counterattack had not taken place. Those present sat through a violent half-hour outburst of rage in which Hitler was especially worked up about the military's "years-long betrayal." He then sank into a chair and said that the war was lost. They should all leave Berlin, but he would stay. That was his "irrevocable decision."[58] He ordered Eva Braun, too, and the hurriedly summoned secretaries, to leave the bunker immediately and evacuate by plane to southern Germany, but Eva Braun, as Traudl Junge recalled, spoke to him as to a "child" and promised to stay, at which point Hitler, in front of the people present, kissed her "on the mouth" while the officers stood outside the conference room "and waited to be dismissed."[59] None of the young secretaries dared to leave. Then Hitler summoned Schaub and ordered him to destroy all his personal files. "Everything must be burned immediately," he ordered, "everything . . . there is in my steel cabinets. Here in Berlin, in Munich, in Berchtesgaden, you have to destroy everything . . . do you hear? . . . everything, everything!" "Not a scrap" must be allowed "to fall into enemy hands."[60]

Hitler had clearly decided to end his life. Eva Braun wrote a rushed letter to her friend Herta that same day, April 22, surrounded by the six Goebbels children, who had just moved into the bunker with their parents, saying that these "are the very last lines and therefore the last sign of life from me." The end was "drawing dangerously near." She could not describe how much she was "suffering personally on the Führer's account"; he had "lost faith." She went on: "Regards to all the friends. I shall die as I lived. It's no burden. You know that."[61] Eva Braun still seemed unsure about how seriously Hitler's intentions were, though, since she added in closing that Herta should keep the letter "until you hear of our fate."

In fact, Hitler postponed his death once again. With the support of Wilhelm Keitel, head of the Supreme Command of the Armed Forces, he now pinned his hopes on the Twelfth Army under General Walther Wenck at the Elbe, which was to march to Berlin from Magdeburg and "fight the Reich Capital free again."[62] In a letter from Eva Braun to her sister Gretl from April 23, 1945, it says: "There is still hope. But obviously we won't let ourselves be taken alive." She had just now "spoken to the Führer" and believed that "the future looked brighter today than it did yesterday" to him, too. Still, she was putting a few last affairs in order, instructing her sister to burn her entire private and business correspondence immediately, except for Hitler's letters, and to pay any outstanding bills.[63] It turned out, of course, that Wenck's assignment could not be carried out. On April 25, the Soviet army completed its encirclement of Berlin.[64]

Meanwhile, Albert Speer, presumably driven by feelings of guilt, had returned to the bunker one last time, on April 23. No one can say with certainty what he and Hitler talked about during their last meeting—no one else was there. In *Inside the Third Reich*, Speer writes that he wanted to "see" Hitler once more and "tell him good-bye."[65] Around midnight, clearly unable to tear himself away from Hitler, Speer sat up for hours with Eva Braun in her small room in the bunker. She revealed, Speer said later, "an almost gay serenity," offered him champagne and sweets, and said: "You know, it was good that you came back once more. The Führer had assumed you would be working against him. But your visit has proved the opposite to him."[66] Even more than Hitler, Braun now seemed to demand loyalty until death from Hitler's closest companions, and seemed not to understand why one after another was vanishing and trying to save his or her own life. Looking back, Traudl Junge described Eva Braun's behavior as a "loyalty complex."[67] Speer, in contrast, obviously admired her for this attitude: during his interrogation in Kransberg a few months later, he said that "Hitler had always emphasized, with resignation, that he had only one person who would stay true to him in the decisive moment, true to the end: Eva Braun. We refused to believe him, but his feelings did not betray him here."[68]

The Wedding and the End in the "Führer Bunker"

It must therefore have come as no surprise to Speer when he later learned that Hitler and Braun had married before taking their lives together in the bunker. On the Obersalzberg, though, where Eva Braun's mother, sisters, and friend Herta Schneider had brought themselves to safety and where Hitler's staff who had fled Berlin after April 20 were gathered, no one suspected anything about the upcoming wedding. At first, the people there, including Morell and the photographer Walter Frentz, hoped that Hitler and Eva Braun would be arriving shortly.[69] Only when Julius Schaub appeared at the Berghof on April 25, a day after it had been badly hit by bombers, to destroy the contents of Hitler's safe, must it have become clear to everyone that Hitler would not be coming and that the end was near. In fact, according to Gretl Fegelein in September 1945, terrible mistrust prevailed when Schaub arrived at the residence, drunk and accompanied by his girlfriend. Christa Schroeder recalls that he burned "letters, files, memos, and books" on the Berghof terrace "without saying a word."[70]

Meanwhile, the "Führer bunker" in Berlin was now under uninterrupted fire and Hitler was handing out poison capsules. These came originally from Himmler and were supplied by Himmler's former personal physician SS-Obersturmbahnführer Dr. Ludwig Stumpfegger, the only doctor who remained in the bunker. Nicolaus von Below reported that he himself was given an "ampule of potassium cyanide" by Hitler in person, on April 27.[71] Hitler had distributed the poison to the women days before. In fact, as a later forensic examination proved, the poison was not potassium cyanide but hydrocyanic acid, a "liquid clear as water" which caused death within seconds and left a scent like that of bitter almonds on the person's clothes and in the room.[72] The conversations over nightly tea in Hitler's living room now turned on only one topic: the best way to die. "I want to be a beautiful corpse, I will take poison," Eva Braun supposedly said on one such occasion. Hitler, on the other hand, told the women that he would shoot himself in the head and then have the body burned.[73] It was an atmosphere of hysteria, according to Bernd Freytag von Loringhoven, who, as the adjutant of General Hans Krebs, whom Hitler had named as his personal adviser, was stationed at his side in the bunker. The

inhabitants of the bunker mostly stood around in the halls, Eva Braun
often with Magda Goebbels, smoking and talking. Their psychological
state continued to swing wildly between hope and despair. Many numbed
their fear with alcohol, of which there was plenty on hand from the Reich
Chancellery.[74]

The mood hit bottom on April 28, when the Reuters news agency
broadcast a report from London that reached Hitler: Himmler had
offered an unconditional surrender to America and England. Talks had
already begun months before between Himmler and the vice president
of the Swedish Red Cross, Count Folke Bernadotte, in which Himmler
had agreed to the release of twenty thousand prisoners from the German
concentration camps. Now the Reichsführer-SS and Interior Minister,
even if late in the day, was trying to use his contact with Bernadotte to
somehow negotiate a way to save his life in the postwar period to come.[75]
The fact is that—like Göring, Speer, Ribbentrop, and Bormann, too, for
that matter—Himmler in no way saw his life as over after the fall of the
"Third Reich." And so, with Hitler's swift death in view, he met with Bernadotte in the Swedish embassy in Lübeck on the night of April 23 and
offered to surrender to the Western powers. He, and the Germans as a
whole, Himmler emphasized, would never surrender to the "Bolshevists"
no matter what happened. But American President Harry S. Truman and
British Prime Minister Winston Churchill refused a partial surrender,
and informed both Stalin and the world media of what had happened.[76]

Hitler exploded with rage that Himmler of all people, one of his most
faithful followers, had betrayed him. Since his liaison officer and protégé
Hermann Fegelein was also nowhere to be found, Hitler ordered an SS
commando to look for him. Eva Braun had apparently looked into
her brother-in-law's whereabouts days before—she wrote to her sister on
April 23: "Hermann isn't here with us! He has left for Nauen to set up a
battalion or something. I am absolutely sure that you will see him again.
He will make it through safely, to maybe carry on the resistance in Bavaria
at least for a while."[77] But obviously Hermann Fegelein was no longer willing to fight—he was ready to get out. Traudl Junge said that Eva Braun,
"disappointed and shaken," had told her about a call from Fegelein in
which, even before Hitler ordered a search for him, he encouraged her
to abandon "the Führer" if she was unable to "get him out of Berlin."
It really was now "a matter of life and death."[78] Gretl Fegelein revealed
to an American secret agent after the war that she had heard from her
father-in-law that Hermann Fegelein had called his father shortly before

the fall of Berlin and explained that he would be coming to Fischhorn the next day. But he never arrived.[79] Instead, he was apprehended in his private apartment in Berlin, wearing civilian clothes, and was taken to the Reich Chancellery, interrogated, and shot for desertion on April 28.[80] At the same time, the Soviet troops were advancing unstoppably toward the center of the city. Hitler and Eva Braun made the final preparations for their double suicide.

Their decision to get married at the very end of their life together was made that same day. There has been a great deal of speculation about their reasons, but the fact is that none of the people who left the bunker alive and survived the war knew about the decision in advance, or heard anything firsthand about Hitler's and Braun's personal motives. Other than the witnesses, Goebbels and Bormann, only Traudl Junge and Nicolaus von Below knew about the upcoming ceremony. Hitler, at around ten thirty at night, had dictated to her his private and political testament.[81] There it says:

> Since I did not believe it would be responsible to found a marriage during the years of struggle, I have now decided, before the termination of this worldly career, to take as my wife the woman who, after many long years of loyal friendship, came to the already almost besieged city of her own free will in order to share her fate with mine. It is my wish that she go with me into death as my wife. Death will replace for us what my work in the service of my People has robbed from us. . . . I and my wife choose death, to avoid the shame of flight or surrender.[82]

We cannot conclude anything about the actual state of Hitler's feelings from this statement about his decision to marry. The phrasing is ambiguous and remains mysterious. The ceremony itself took place on the night of April 28–29. Besides the bride and groom, the only people present were Goebbels, Bormann, and a hastily summoned registrar, Walter Wagner.[83] Afterward, there was a brief champagne reception in Hitler's living room, where others took part, including Magda Goebbels, General Wilhelm Burgdorf, General Krebs, Below, Gerda Christian, Constanze Manziarly, and Artur Axmann, the fanatical National Youth Leader who had moved into the bunker on April 23. They all made an effort, according to Below, "to think happily about the old days." It was a "rather ghostly occasion."[84]

On the afternoon of April 29, Hitler had his favorite German shepherd,

The destroyed Old Chancellery on Wilhelmstrasse, March 1945

Blondi, poisoned. The dog collapsed immediately and was dead on the spot. The Berchtesgaden district court later concluded that "the poison was tested out on the dog with a view to Eva Hitler's death by poison, which had already been decided on."[85] By now there was no longer a telephone connection between the bunker and the outside world. On April 30, the Soviet army reached the Reichstag grounds.[86] Soviet soldiers were expected to force their way into the "Führer bunker" at any moment. That afternoon, between three and four o'clock, Hitler and Eva Braun died by their own hands. While she bit into a cyanide capsule and died before his eyes, he took a poison capsule into his mouth and simultaneously shot himself in the right temple.[87] Their bodies were then taken out to the Chancellery garden, doused in gasoline, and set on fire. The remains were buried that evening in a bomb crater in the garden.

12

AFTER DEATH

Countless legends sprang up after the death of Adolf Hitler and Eva Braun. One reason for this is the fact that the direct witnesses to the burning of the bodies who survived the inferno in Berlin gave contradictory statements later about the exact circumstances of the double suicide. Another reason is that the Soviet Union concealed from its Western allies and the rest of the world, for years, the fact that Soviet troops had found the bodies of Hitler, Braun, and the Goebbels family in early May. Instead of passing the information along, Joseph Stalin, in a conversation with the American special envoy Harry Hopkins on May 26, 1945, spread the rumor that Hitler and Bormann were still alive and hidden abroad, possibly in Japan. It was known to Soviet intelligence, Stalin claimed, "that the Germans had three or four large submarines that traveled back and forth between Japan and Germany." He had "ordered Soviet reconnaissance to locate these submarines, but for now they had not been found." Stalin was trying to exploit the death of Hitler and his wife to suggest to the Western powers that their common struggle was not yet over and had to be continued in the war against Japan. He clearly struck a nerve with the Americans, as Hopkins's reply reveals: he immediately told Stalin, according to the notes of the translator, Vladimir Nikolayevich Pavlov, that "Hitler absolutely must be found and put to death."[1]

Even at the Potsdam Conference, which took place from July 17 to August 2, 1945, in Cecilienhof Palace, Stalin flatly denied to Truman and Churchill knowing anything about Hitler's whereabouts.[2] The Americans were working to shed light on the matter by having everyone who had been close to Hitler questioned by their secret service, including Eva Braun's family and friends. But an undercover agent—apparently disguised as a member of the SS—who tracked down Gretl Braun and Herta Schneider on the evening of September 23, 1945, in Garmisch-Partenkirchen, learned hardly anything from them about the fate of Eva Braun and Hitler. Gretl Braun only repeated various rumors, and finally explained that she did not think it was impossible that Hitler, her sister, and Hermann Fegelein had left Berlin at the last moment.[3]

None of them suspected that the charred remains of Hitler and Eva Braun had been in the Soviets' hands for months. The Red Army had learned of Hitler's suicide as early as April 30, from General Krebs, Hitler's closest military adviser at the end, and had immediately informed Stalin.[4] Additional members of Hitler's staff and employees of the Reich Chancellery were quickly discovered among the prisoners of war and questioned about Hitler's final days. Soviet officers scoured Hitler's air-raid bunker under the garden of the Chancellery, where they found the dead bodies of the six Goebbels children. They discovered the bodies of Joseph and Magda Goebbels in front of the bunker entrance on May 2, and Hitler's and Braun's bodies on May 5. A few days later, an autopsy was performed in the Russian Surgical Army Field Hospital #496 in Berlin-Buch, on the orders of the Soviet secret service, SMERSH counterpropaganda division, and eventually, in February 1946, the bodies were buried at a military site in Magdeburg.[5]

In the West, on the other hand, countless rumors and speculations circulated for years about the Nazi leader's whereabouts. An anonymous letter sent to the American general Dwight D. Eisenhower on November 22, 1948, for example, said that Hitler was living under a false name, together with Eva Braun and Martin Bormann, as the owner of a café in Amsterdam. The U.S. secret service took all such reports extremely seriously and investigated them thoroughly.[6] Former members of Hitler's staff, including Erich Kempka, were also arrested and questioned in the Western occupation zones directly after the end of the war, and they reported Hitler's death and the burning of the bodies, but there was no material evidence to prove these claims.

In 1952, the district court in Berchtesgaden launched "legal proceed-

A wooden chest with human remains, like the one that held Hitler's and Eva Braun's remains until their ashes were burned again and scattered in a river near Magdeburg on April 5, 1970

ings to establish the death and time of death of Adolf Hitler." During the course of the investigation, "all persons still living from Hitler's environment in the last days in Berlin"—forty-two witnesses in total—were interrogated.[7] Among them were his valet, Heinz Linge, and his personal adjutant, Otto Günsche, who had just returned from being Soviet prisoners of war; Harri Mengershausen, a former detective in the Reichssicherheitsdienst (the German secret police); and Käthe Heusermann, who was the last person to work at the dental clinic in the Reich Chancellery and was the assistant to Hitler's dentist in Berlin, Prof. Dr. Hugo Blaschke.[8] In its final report on August 1, 1956, the court concluded that there was "neither concrete evidence" nor any "finding of fact arising" immediately after the "event in the vicinity of the deed," but "merely the statements of numerous persons." Nonetheless, since Hitler's personal dentist, Dr. Blaschke, and his assistant Heusermann "had been shown Adolf Hitler's complete lower jaw and bridge of the upper jaw as well as the artificial bridge from Eva Braun's lower jaw by Russian officers, repeatedly and in various places," and since both Blaschke and Heusermann had "recognized them as coming from Adolf and Eva Hitler without any doubt," "decisive proof" for the identification had been supplied from the Russian side.[9] Adolf Hitler and Eva Braun were therefore officially declared dead in West Germany, in 1956 and 1957 respectively. Thirteen years later, on April 5, 1970, the KGB burned their remains again and scattered their ashes in a river near Magdeburg, in what was then East Germany.[10]

Conclusion

Due to her life and death with Hitler, Eva Braun is forever tied to the National Socialist regime that, driven by radical anti-Semitism and marked by utter contempt for humanity, brought about, in Ian Kershaw's words, "the steepest descent in civilized values known in modern times." Therefore Eva Braun remains a public figure and is present in the media to this day. That is what she wanted, and why she single-mindedly worked toward a joint death with her "Führer" when the Nazi state's downfall and catastrophic defeat in the war were assured. She took her own life with the notion that she died a "hero's death."[1]

In the fourteen years of her intimate relationship with Hitler, Eva Braun developed from an ordinary girl far from the center of power, from a lower-middle-class family whose father believed "to the end" in the "Führer," into a capricious, uncompromising champion of absolute loyalty to the dictator.[2] It is true that she did not belong to the NSDAP, but this fact does not mean that she rejected the Nazi state or was opposed to it in any way. On the contrary: her life, at least as much as those of everyone else around Hitler, was shaped by his worldview, his charismatic attraction (however difficult it may be to explain what that consisted in), and the extent of his power. He, in turn, recognized in her someone from a similar background, and with a similar education, outside of traditional

elites, who was more ready than any of his other fanatical supporters to
live her life on his terms.

Eva Braun's position in Hitler's innermost circle was thus unassailable,
by 1935 at the latest. Many of the people who tried to get close to Hitler,
including Speer, Göring, and Goebbels, thus found it necessary to pay
court to her as well. They even had to be nice to her dog, who crawled
"unnoticed and abandoned" through the rubble of the Berghof after the
death of his mistress. When Eva Braun was still there, "everyone had been
nice to the spoiled, vicious animal," Christa Schroeder later recalled.[3]

In any case, Eva Braun's life was decidedly different from the image of
the woman's world as presented by National Socialist propaganda. In this,
Hitler's girlfriend was like most of the wives of high-ranking Nazi politicians. She led a privileged existence, with trips, expensive clothes, and
occasional professional activities in the service of the NSDAP, in her case
working for Hitler's personal photographer and delivering supposedly private pictures of the "Führer" and his life at the Berghof to him. For that
reason alone, she cannot be seen as someone with no involvement in
the regime, an entirely apolitical young woman, as Albert Speer among
others later claimed. Her collaboration, within the scope of what was possible for her, is unmistakable, and she clearly acted without any sense of
guilt. Furthermore, Eva Braun was neither a housewife nor a mother, and
it is extremely unlikely that she wanted to be. Precisely for that reason,
she fit the needs of a man twenty-three years older than she, afraid of
commitment and with eccentric habits. Since her existence so blatantly
contradicted the officially propagated "Führer image," Eva Braun was not
allowed to appear in public — just as Hitler's other inappropriate proclivities were kept largely hidden, such as his being a teetotaler, a vegetarian,
a nonsmoker, that he did not drink coffee, that he popped an enormous
number of pills, especially before the war, and that, like his girlfriend, he
was obsessed with personal cleanliness.

Eva Braun's life with Hitler thus gives us deep insight into the dictator's personal life, which was carefully concealed in the Nazi state and
whose very existence was officially denied. Contrary to the later protestations from members of Hitler's "royal court," this personal life was not
and could not be separated from his political life. There was no private
sphere in which politics was not discussed and Nazi ideology played no
part. The idea, spread by Speer in particular, that Hitler never touched
on political topics in his private circle and especially when women were

present, has to be considered a myth. Rather, not only the men but also the women around Hitler identified with the anti-Semitic, racist world-view and aggressive expansionist politics of the Nazi regime, laid out in full view during long evening conversations (or monologues) by the fire.

This is especially true for Eva Braun. Why would she, less educated than the others, doubt that Hitler's explanations and arguments were jus-tified when even an officer such as Nicolaus von Below, an educated aristocrat, was convinced by Hitler's explanation of the "constant threat" of "Jewish Bolshevism" hanging over the German People?[4] Every mem-ber of the inner circle was at least familiar with the "Führer's" basic ideas about the world situation, not least the secretaries to whom Hitler often expressed "his innermost fears" after the war started during their "usual coffee breaks," for example that "Russia seemed monstrous and uncanny to him, kind of like the ghost ship in *The Flying Dutchman.*"[5] Finally, the idea that no one could "influence or convince" Hitler of anything—that even Göring, Goebbels, and Himmler were weak and helpless against him—primarily served former committed National Socialists as a tool to exculpate themselves after the war. That does not mean it was true.[6]

Hitler does seem to have prevented his girlfriend from the start from intervening openly in political debates—an attitude that makes him not essentially different from other men of his time. Nor was there any ques-tion of Eva Braun's joining the NSDAP—the same as with any of Hitler's relatives. It is hard to determine from the available sources whether Eva Braun, in these circumstances, "consciously" refrained from expressing herself on political matters, as her sister Ilse claimed before the court after the war, or whether her silence merely indicated a lack of interest on her part.[7] Likewise, the question of whether she knew about the Holocaust remains finally unanswered.

But there can be no doubt that Eva Braun, at twenty years old, pre-sumably with the vigorous support of her boss Heinrich Hoffmann, used self-inflicted violence to fight her way to a place at Hitler's side that many envied her for. She had "very many opponents," according to a later state-ment by her friend Herta Schneider.[8] Indeed, the opinion was widespread among Hitler's followers that Eva Braun was not good enough for the "Führer"—that she lacked the stature to appear publicly at his side. This opinion, which comes up frequently among the memoirs of the surviving parties, later found its way—astonishingly—into the accounts written by professional historians. In truth, it was largely Hitler himself who assigned this thankless role to his girlfriend, a fact that reveals less about her inadequacies than about his own anxieties and lack of self-confidence as a parvenu. Caught between power and powerlessness, but in the end acting decisively—vain and in no way a victim—Eva Braun assured herself of a place, even if a questionable place, in history.

NOTES

PUBLISHER'S NOTE
In the original German edition, Heike Görtemaker cites sources in German, including German translations of English original texts. For this English-language edition, sources originally written in English (e.g., Nerin E. Gun's biography of Eva Braun and Ian Kershaw's biographies of Hitler) are quoted from the English texts. Selected major sources for which there are English translations, such as Speer's memoirs, are also cited from the existing English translations, but no attempt has been made to use an extant translation of every German-language source.

INTRODUCTION

1. See Lew Besymenski, *Die letzten Notizen von Martin Bormann* (Stuttgart, 1974), p. 148; Nerin E. Gun, *Eva Braun: Hitler's Mistress* (New York, 1968), p. 181; Albert Speer, *Inside the Third Reich: Memoirs* (New York, 1970), p. 465; Mario Frank, *Der Tod im Führerbunker* (Munich, 2005), p. 284.
2. Speer, *Inside the Third Reich*, p. 465.
3. Ian Kershaw, *Hitler 1889–1936: Hubris* (New York, 1999), p. xx.
4. These include Alan Bullock, *Hitler: A Study in Tyranny* (New York, 1952); Helmut Heiber, *Adolf Hitler: Eine Biographie* (Berlin, 1960); Hugh R. Trevor-Roper, *Hitlers letzte Tage* (Frankfurt am Main, 1965); Werner Maser, *Adolf Hitler: Legende, Mythos, Werklichkeit*, 6th ed. (Munich and Esslingen, 1974); Joachim C. Fest, *Hitler: Eine Biographie* (Berlin and Vienna, 1973); Ian Kershaw, *Hitler 1936–1945* (New York, 2000).
5. See Maser, *Adolf Hitler*, p. 318.
6. Guido Knopp, *Hitlers Frauen und Marlene* (Munich, 2001), p. 83.
7. See Angela Lambert, *The Lost Life of Eva Braun* (London, 2006); Johannes Frank, *Eva Braun* (Preussisch Oldendorf, 1988); Jean Michel Charlier and Jacques de Launay, *Eva Hitler, née Braun* (Paris, 1978); Glenn Infield, *Eva and Adolf* (New York, 1974). Gun's *Eva Braun: Hitler's Mistress* is regarded by many as the only serious biography. See also "Eva Braun: Die verborgene Geliebte," in Anna Maria Sigmund, *Die Frauen der Nazis* (Vienna, 1998–2002), vol. 1, pp. 235–284.

8. Fest, *Hitler*, pp. 17, 698, and 708.

9. Kershaw, *Hitler 1889–1936*, pp. xxvf. Alan Bullock also claims that Hitler was unable to have a relationship, in *Hitler and Stalin: Parallel Lives* (London, 1991), pp. 502f.

10. Albert Speer, *Albert Speer: Die Kransberg-Protokolle 1945*, ed. Ulrich Schlie (Munich, 2003), p. 12.

11. Ian Kershaw, *The "Hitler Myth": Image and Reality in the Third Reich* (Oxford, 1987), p. 80.

12. See Sigmund, *Die Frauen der Nazis*, p. 248.

13. See Speer, *Inside the Third Reich*, p. 93; Christa Schroeder, *Er war mein Chef*, ed. Anton Joachimsthaler (Munich, 1985), p. 166.

PART ONE: THE MEETING

1. This account is based on a statement from Erich Kempka about Hitler's last days, dated June 20, 1945, from Berchtesgaden, in MA 1298/10, Microfilm, Various Documents DJ-13 (David Irving), Institut für Zeitgeschichte, Munich (hereafter cited as IfZ Munich). Kempka's account differs from that of other sources by approximately one hour.

1. HEINRICH HOFFMANN'S STUDIO

1. Hoffmann's father, Robert Hoffmann, ran a portrait studio in Regensburg with his younger brother Heinrich. This brother had borne the title of "Royal Bavarian Court Photographer" since 1887 and gained international fame with his photographs of Kaiser Wilhelm II and King Edward VII of England. See Rudolf Herz, *Hoffmann & Hitler: Fotographie als Medium des Führer-Mythos* (Munich, 1994), p. 26. See also Joachim Fest and Heinrich Hoffmann, *Hitler—Gesichter eines Diktators* (Munich, 2005), p. 4.

2. Hoffmann's studio in Munich was located first at 33 Schellingstrasse, and later— until 1929—at 50 Schellingstrasse. See Herz, *Hoffmann & Hitler*, pp. 26f.

3. See Heinrich Hoffmann, *Hitler wie ich ihn sah* (Munich and Berlin, 1974), p. 19. See also the original edition of Hoffmann's memoir, *Hitler Was My Friend* (London, 1955), pp. 45f.; Henriette von Schirach, *Der Preis der Herrlichkeit* (Munich and Berlin, 1975), p. 97; Herz, *Hoffmann & Hitler*, p. 34.

4. Heinrich Hoffmann, "Mein Beruf Meine Arbeit für die Kunst-Mein Verhältnis zu Adolf Hitler," unpublished manuscript (presumably from 1947), MS 2049, IfZ Munich, pp. 7f. Cf. Fest and Hoffmann, *Hitler—Gesichter eines Diktators*, p. 4.

5. See Herz, *Hoffmann & Hitler*, p. 34. On Eckart, see Margarete Plewnia, *Auf dem Weg zu Hitler: Der "völkische" Publizist Dietrich Eckart* (Bremen, 1970).

6. See Herz, *Hoffmann & Hitler*, p. 34. On Hoffmann, see also Winfried Ranke, "Bildberichterstattung in den Zwanziger Jahren—Heinrich Hoffmann und die Chronistenpflicht," in *Die Zwanziger Jahre in München*, exhibition catalog (Munich, 1979), pp. 53–73; Philip E. Mancha, "Heinrich Hoffmann: Photographer of the Third Reich," in *Prologue: Quarterly of the National Archives* (1973), pp. 31–40.

7. See Jan Brüning, "Kurzer Überblick zur Technik der Pressefotografie in Deutschland von 1920 bis 1940," in *Fotografie und Bildpublizistik in der Weimarer Republik*, ed. Diethart Krebs and Walter Uka (Bönen/Nordrhein-Westfalen, 2004), pp. 11–28.

8. See Herbert Moldering, *Fotografie in der Weimarer Republik* (Berlin, 1988); José Macias, *Die Entwicklung des Bildjournalismus* (Munich, 1990).

9. "Reichsparteitag der NSDAP in Weimar, 3./4. Juli 1926," in Heinrich Hoffmann Photo Archive, hoff-6750, Bavarian State Library [Bayerische Staatsbibliothek, or BSB], Munich (hereafter cited as BSB Munich).

10. Cf. Herz, *Hoffmann & Hitler*, p. 37. There it says that Hoffmann rose to be Hitler's "medium." Cf. Joachim Fest, *Hitler: Eine Biographie* (Berlin and Vienna, 1973) p. 353; Gerhard Paul, *Aufstand der Bilder: Die NS-Propaganda vor 1933* (Bonn, 1990). See also Mathias Rösch, *Die Münchner NSDAP 1925–1933: Eine Untersuchung zur inneren Struktur der NSDAP in der Weimarer Republik* (Munich, 2002); Werner Bräuninger, *Hitlers Kontrahenten in der NSDAP 1921–1945* (Munich, 2004); also Thomas Tavernaro, *Der Verlag Hitlers und der NSDAP: Die Franz Eher Nachfolger GmbH* (Vienna, 2004).

11. See Hagen Schulze, *Weimar:. Deutschland 1917–1933*, Die Deutschen und ihre Nation, vol. 4, (Berlin, 1982), p. 303.

12. See Herz, *Hoffmann & Hitler*, pp. 36ff. and 49ff. The NSDAP headquarters already located at 50 Schellingstrasse moved into the rooms. Cf. Anton Joachimsthaler, *Hitlers Liste: Ein Dokument persönlicher Beziehungen* (Munich, 2003), p. 432, which states that according to the official notification of a change of address, Hoffmann gave up his studio at 50 Schellingstrasse as early as September 10, 1929. Baldur von Schirach later recalled that he first met Eva Braun in Hoffmann's studio "shortly after" the fourth NSDAP convention in Nuremberg (August 1–4, 1929); see Baldur von Schirach, *Ich glaubte an Hitler* (Hamburg, 1967), p. 118. Heinrich Hoffmann later stated, less precisely, that Eva Braun was "probably" hired in 1929 at the "founding" of his business; see Heinrich Hoffmann, statement from July 1, 1949, at the public hearing of the Munich Hauptkammer for oral arguments in the proceedings against Eva Hitler née Braun, "Öffentliche Sitzung der Hauptkammer München zur mündlichen Verhandlung in dem Verfahren gegen Eva Hitler, geb. Braun," in Denazification Court Records, box 718, State Archives, Munich.

13. See Henriette von Schirach, *Der Preis der Herrlichkeit* (Munich and Berlin, 1975), pp. 23 and 97; and Gun, *Eva Braun*, p. 48.

14. Heinrich Hoffmann, statement from July 1, 1949.

15. See Herz, *Hoffmann & Hitler*, pp. 49f. See also Baldur von Schirach, *Ich glaubte an Hitler*, p. 118.

16. Eva Braun's childhood friend, Herta Schneider, stated after the war that she learned of "Eva Braun's acquaintance with Adolf Hitler in 1928," while Braun "was a trainee at Hoffmann's firm." See Herta Schneider, statutory declaration of May 16, 1948 (typewritten original), in Denazification Court Records, box 1670, State Archives, Munich. Presumably this is a typo, since Schneider stated in the following year that Eva Braun met Hitler "when she was seventeen, in 1929." See Herta Schneider,

statement of June 23, 1949, at the public hearing of the Munich Hauptkammer for oral arguments in the proceedings against Herta Schneider, née Ostermayr, "Öffentliche Sitzung der Hauptkammer München zur mündlichen Verhandlung in dem Verfahren gegen Herta Schneider, geb. Ostermayr," in Denazification Court Records, box 1670, State Archives, Munich.

17. See Gun, *Eva Braun*, pp. 52–53. Anna Maria Sigmund follows his account in *Die Frauen der Nazis*, vol. 1, p. 240. See also Hoffmann, *Hitler wie ich ihn sah*, p. 136, where he states: "Hitler met Eva Braun in my office, just as all my other employees."

18. See Nerin E. Gun, *Red Roses from Texas* (London, 1964); *The Day of the Americans* (New York, 1966). See also "JFK Assassination Documents," CIA, HSCA Segregated CIA Collection, Box 1, Subject Card on Nerin Emrullah Gun, April 2, 1967, Mary Ferrell Foundation Digital Archive. In the CIA files it says: "Gun, born 22 February 1920 in Rome, is a suspected CP member who has been involved in Europe in espionage and falsification of documents."

19. Ilse Hess to Albert Speer, Hindelang/Allgäu, 25. Juni 1968. Albert Speer Papers, N 1340, vol. 27, National Archive [Bundesarchiv, or BA] Koblenz (hereafter cited as BA Koblenz).

20. See Kershaw, *Hitler 1889–1936*, p. 282.

21. See Henriette von Schirach, *Der Preis der Herrlichkeit*, pp. 176f. On Eva Braun's workplace, located above Café Stefanie, see the *Völkischer Beobachter*, Munich edition, November 8, 1929; also Sigmund, *Die Frauen der Nazis*, vol. 1 p. 242.

22. Cf. Henriette von Schirach, *Der Preis der Herrlichkeit*, vol. 1, p. 179; Traudl Junge with Melissa Müller, *Bis zur letzten Stunde: Hitlers Sekretärin erzählt ihr Leben* (Berlin, 2004), p. 115. There, on February 22, 1935, Hitler even organized the wedding of one of the Osteria Bavaria's waitresses: see Rudolf Hess to his father (Fritz Hess), n.p., February 21, 1935 (carbon copy), Rudolf Hess papers, J 1211 1989/148, vol. 12, file 55, folder 5, Swiss Federal Archives [Schweizeriches Bundesarchiv], Bern.

23. See Albert Speer, *Inside the Third Reich*, p. 27. See also Helmut Hess, "Kunstverlag Franz Hanfstaengl," in Historisches Lexikon Bayerns, http://www.historisches-lexikon-bayerns.de/artikel/artikel_44754 (retrieved 3/19/2007); Ernst Hanfstaengl papers, Ana 405, box 26, chronological material from 1927 to 1932, file for 1930, BSB Munich.

24. Kershaw, *Hitler 1889–1936*, pp. 432f. Hanfstaengl considered the following people to be "A.H.'s circle" from 1933 on: Schaub, Brückner, Hoffmann, Amann, Christian Weber. (Ernst Hanfstaengl Papers, Ana 405, box 27, chronological material from 1933 to 1936, file for January–June 1933, BSB Munich). Cf. Fest, *Hitler*, p. 199; also diary entry from November 6, 1925, in Joseph Goebbels, *Die Tagebücher von Joseph Goebbels: Sämtliche Fragmente* (Munich, 1987), Teil I, vol. 1, p. 140.

25. Henriette von Schirach, *Der Preis der Herrlichkeit*, p. 24.

26. See Gun, *Eva Braun*, p. 157.

27. See Jochen von Lang, *Der Sekretär: Martin Bormann—Der Mann, der Hitler beherrschte*, 3rd, fully rev., ed. (Munich and Berlin, 1987); Martin Bormann, *Leben gegen Schatten*, 7th ed. (Paderborn, 2001).

28. See "Eva Braun in the Hoffmann Photohaus," photograph from 1930, in Heinrich Hoffmann Photo Archive, hoff-473, BSB Munich.

29. See Hoffmann, *Hitler wie ich ihn sah*, p. 136. Ian Kershaw, among others, cites this passage as proof that Hitler's relationships with women in general, and with Eva Braun in particular, "lack[ed] emotional bonds" (*Hitler 1889–1936*, p. 354).

30. See Hitler's practicing oratorical poses as photographed by Hoffmann: Heinrich Hoffmann Photo Archive, hoff-1852, BSB Munich.

31. Henriette von Schirach, *Der Preis der Herrlichkeit*, p. 84.

32. Speer, *Inside the Third Reich*, p. 43.

33. See Baldur von Schirach, *Ich glaubte an Hitler*, pp. 122ff.

34. See Otto Wagener, *Hitler aus nächster Nähe*, ed. H. A. Turner Jr. (Frankfurt am Main, 1978), pp. 100 and 242, where it says that Hoffmann's daughter was already "an institution" at the time as "the king's ballerina."

35. See Hoffmann, *Hitler Was My Friend*, pp. 73f. See also "Baldur von Schirach's Wedding, Prinzregentenplatz 16," in Heinrich Hoffmann Photo Archive, hoff-7195, BSB Munich.

36. Hoffmann took over a Berlin press photographer's office at first, before opening a branch of his own company after 1933, first on Friedrichstrasse and later at 10 Kochstrasse in Berlin's newspaper neighborhood. See Herz, *Hoffmann & Hitler*, p. 53.

37. Wagener, *Hitler aus nächster Nähe*, pp. 119f.

38. See Herz, *Hoffmann & Hitler*, p. 42.

39. Ibid.

40. See in this regard Hanns Christian Löhr, *Das braune Haus der Kunst* (Berlin, 2005), pp. 15 ff; Günther Haase, *Die Kunstsammlung Adolf Hitler* (Berlin, 2002), pp. 57ff; Arno Breker, *Im Strahlungsfeld der Ereignisse* (Preussisch Oldendorf, 1972), pp. 132 and 142f.

41. Hoffmann, *Hitler Was My Friend*, p. 104. According to Hoffmann, Hitler told him to bring Stalin Hitler's personal greetings. Kershaw, on the other hand, states that Hoffmann came along "to ensure the historic moment was captured on film" (*Hitler 1936–1945*, p. 210).

42. Ibid., p. 1,147. See also Joachim von Ribbentrop, *Zwischen London und Moskau*, ed. Annelies von Ribbentrop (Leoni am Starnberger See, 1953), p. 83.

43. See Alan Bullock, *Hitler*, p. 63; Herz, *Hoffmann & Hitler*, p. 42.

44. See Hoffmann, *Hitler wie ich ihn sah*, p. 50. See also Joe J. Heydecker, *Das Hitler-Bild* (St. Pölten, 2008), p. 35.

45. See Hoffmann, "Mein Beruf," pp. 20f. See the extensive account of the denazification proceedings in Herz, *Hoffmann & Hitler*, pp. 64ff.

46. See "Heinrich Hoffmann," in *Amtliches Fernsprechbuch für den Reichspostdirektionsbezirk München: Herausgegeben von der Reichspostdirektion München nach dem Stande vom 1. Mai 1934* (July 1934 edition).

47. See Herz, *Hoffmann & Hitler*, pp. 39f. and 333ff. On Hoffmann, see also Anna Maria Sigmund, *Diktator, Dämon, Demagoge* (Munich, 2006), pp. 79ff; Hoffmann, "Mein Beruf," pp. 20f.; Hoffmann, *Hitler Was My Friend*, p. 103.

48. Hoffmann, "Mein Beruf," pp. 21f.

49. See "Gretl Braun and Kurt Berlinghoff's Wedding, 1950," in Heinrich Hoffmann Photo Archive, hoff-61525, BSB Munich.

50. See in this regard Herz, *Hoffmann & Hitler*, p. 41.

2. MUNICH AFTER THE FIRST WORLD WAR

1. See Kershaw, *Hitler 1889–1936*, p. 310; David Clay Large, *Hitlers München* (München, 1998), pp. 212f. See also Anton Joachimsthaler, *Hitlers Weg begann in München*.

2. See Large, *Hitlers München*, pp. 126f. See also Kershaw, *Hitler 1889–1936*, p. 152.

3. See Kurt Eisner, "An die Bevölkerung Münchens!" in *München: Ein Lesebuch*, ed. Reinhard Bauer and Ernst Piper (Frankfurt am Main, 1986), pp. 170ff.

4. Schulze, *Weimar*, p. 329.

5. Thomas Mann, diary entry, Friday, November 8, 1918, in *Diaries: 1918–1939*, sel. Hermann Kesten, trans. Richard and Clara Winston (New York, 1982), pp. 19–20. On January 10 Mann again remarked that "Bavarialand" was neither a "Workers Republic" nor a "domain under the rule of Jewish literati" (this entry is not in the English selection; see his *Tagebücher 1918–1921*, ed. Peter de Mendelssohn [Frankfurt am Main, 1979], pp. 131f.).

6. Ricarda Huch, "Kurt Eisners Todestag: Eine Münchner Erinnerung," in Ricarda Huch, *Erinnerungen an das eigene Leben* (Cologne, 1980), pp. 435ff. See also Bernhard Grau, *Kurt Eisner 1867–1919: Eine Biografie* (Munich, 2001).

7. See Heinrich August Winkler, *Der lange Weg nach Westen*, vol. 1, *Deutsche Geschichte vom Ende des Alten Reiches bis zum Untergang der Weimarer Republik* (Munich, 2000), pp. 396ff. See also Kershaw, *Hitler 1889–1936*, p. 114; Frank Bajohr, *"Unser Hotel ist judenfrei": Bäder-Antisemitismus im 19. und 20. Jahrhundert*, 3d ed. (Frankfurt, 2003), pp. 62ff.

8. See Winkler, *Der lange Weg nach Westen*, vol. 1, p. 378.

9. Thomas Mann, diary entry, Sunday, May 17, 1919, not in the English selection; see *Tagebücher 1918–1921*, p. 239.

10. See Martin Broszat, *Der Staat Hitlers* (Wiesbaden, 2007 [1st ed., 1969]), pp. 13ff.

11. Rösch, *Die Münchner NSDAP 1925–1933*, p. 32.

12. Klaus Mann, *The Turning Point: Thirty-five Years in This Century; The Autobiography of Klaus Mann* (New York, 1984; 1st ed., 1942), pp. 46 and 62.

13. Jules Huret, "Das Hofbräuhaus," in *München: Ein Lesebuch*, pp. 113ff. See also Jules Huret, *Bayern und Sachsen* (Munich, 1910).

14. See Werner Maser, *Der Sturm auf die Republik* (Düsseldorf, 1994), pp. 468ff.

15. See Wilfried Rudloff, "Auf dem Weg zum 'Hitler-Putsch': Gegenrevolutionäres Milieu und früher Nationalsozialismus in München," in *München—"Hauptstadt der Bewegung": Bayerns Metropole und der Nationalsozialismus*, ed. Richard Bauer et al. (Munich, 2002), p. 99. Cf. Kershaw, *Hitler 1889–1936*, pp. 147ff.

16. See Wolfram Pyta, *Die Weimarer Republik* (Wiesbaden, 2004), p. 113; Broszat, *Der*

Staat Hitlers, pp. 42f.; Ernst Hanfstaengl, *Zwischen Weissem und Braunem Haus* (Munich, 1970), pp. 40f.

17. See Joachimsthaler, *Hitlers Liste*, pp. 63ff. See also Andreas Heusler, *Das Braune Haus: Wie München zur "Hauptstadt der Bewegung" wurde* (Munich, 2008), pp. 80ff.

18. See Hanfstaengl, *Zwischen Weissem und Braunem Haus*, pp. 41ff. See also Joachimsthaler, *Hitlers Liste*, pp. 103ff.

19. See Hellmuth Auerbach, "Regionale Wurzeln und Differenzen der NSDAP 1919–1923," in *Nationalsozialismus in der Region: Beiträge zur regionalen und lokalen Forschung und zum internationalen Vergleich*, ed. Horst Möller et al. (Munich, 1996), p. 70.

20. See Carl Zuckmayer, "Der heulende Derwisch," in *München: Ein Lesebuch*, p. 229.

3. The Braun Family

1. See Joachimsthaler, *Hitlers Liste*, pp. 418ff.; Sigmund, *Die Frauen der Nazis*, p. 237.

2. See Eberhard Kolb, *Die Weimarer Republik*, 6th rev. and expanded ed. (Munich, 2002), p. 52; Helmut Kerstingjohänner, *Die deutsche Inflation 1919–1923: Politik und Ökonomie* (Frankfurt, 2004); Ursula Büttner, *Weimar: Die überforderte Republik* (Stuttgart, 2008).

3. See Fritz K. Ringer, *Die Gelehrten: Der Niedergang der deutschen Mandarine 1890–1933* (Stuttgart, 1983), pp. 62f.

4. See Jonathan R. C. Wright, *Gustav Stresemann: Weimar's Greatest Statesman* (Oxford, 2002), pp. 270ff. and 283ff.; Manfred Berg, *Gustav Stresemann und die Vereinigten Staaten von Amerika: Weltwirtschaftliche Verflechtung und Revisionspolitik 1907–1929* (Baden-Baden, 1990).

5. See Joachimsthaler, *Hitlers Liste*, p. 424.

6. See Herta Schneider, Statement of June 23, 1949, "Öffentliche Sitzung der Hauptkammer München zur mündlichen Verhandlung in dem Verfahren gegen Herta Schneider, geb. Ostermayr, in Denazihcation Court Records, box 1670, State Archives, Munich. See also Joachimsthaler, *Hitlers Liste*, p. 423.

7. See Gun, *Eva Braun*, p. 23.

8. Ilse Braun had also received an education at a boarding school of the English Maidens, in Munich-Nymphenburg; see Ilse Fucke-Michels, née Braun, "Meldebogen auf Grund des Gesetzes zur Befreiung von Nationalismus und Militarismus vom 5. März 1946 [Registration Form for the Law for Liberation from National Socialism and Militarism of March 5, 1946]," in Denazification Court Records, box 468, State Archives, Munich. See also Joachimsthaler, *Hitlers Liste*, p. 429.

9. See Herz, *Hoffmann & Hitler*, p. 48.

10. See Schroeder, *Er war mein Chef*, p. 371.

11. See Herz, *Hoffmann & Hitler*, pp. 37ff.

12. Hitler, document of April 1, 1932, in Herz, *Hoffmann & Hitler*, p. 40.

13. See Herz, *Hoffmann & Hitler*, p. 53.

14. See Hoffmann, *Hitler wie ich ihn sah*, p. 136.

15. See Nicolaus von Below, *Als Hitlers Adjutant 1937–1945* (Mainz, 1980), p. 96.

16. Junge, *Bis zur letzten Stunde*, pp. 77 and 132; Schroeder, *Er war mein Chef*, p. 167.

17. Quoted from Joachim Fest, *Die unbeantwortbaren Fragen: Notizen über Gespräche mit Albert Speer zwischen Ende 1966 und 1981* (Hamburg, 2006), p. 143.

18. See Ilse Fucke-Michels to the State Commissioner for Refugees, Ruhpolding, October 2, 1946, in Denazification Court Records, box 468, State Archives, Munich.

19. See Stefanie Harrecker, *Degradierte Doktoren: Die Aberkennung der Doktorwürde an der Ludwig-Maximilians-Universität München während der Zeit des Nationalsozialismus* (Munich, 2008), p. 329.

20. Ilse Fucke-Michels to the State Commissioner for Refugees, Ruhpolding, October 2, 1946.

21. Ibid.

22. See Alex Drecoll, "Die 'Entjudung' der Münchner Ärzteschaft 1933–1941," in *München arisiert: Entrechtung und Enteignung der Juden in der NS-Zeit*, ed. Angelika Baumann and Andreas Heusler (Munich, 2004), pp. 75ff.

23. See Arno Buschmann, *Nationalsozialistische Weltanschauung und Gesetzgebung 1933–1945*, vol. 2, *Dokumentation einer Entwicklung* (Vienna, 2000), pp. 28f.

24. See Ilse Fucke-Michels to the State Commissioner for Refugees, Ruhpolding, October 2, 1946. See also Sigmund, *Die Frauen der Nazis*, p. 244, which states that the "relationship ended only when Marx emigrated to America in the summer of 1938."

25. See Gianluca Falanga, *Berlin 1937: Die Ruhe vor dem Sturm* (Berlin, 2007), p. 39. Speer himself never mentions, in any of his various memoirs, that Ilse Braun was one of his assistants.

26. See Claus-Dieter Krohn et al., eds., *Handbuch der deutschsprachigen Emigration 1933–1945* (Darmstadt, 1998), pp. 782ff.; Ilse Fucke-Michels to the State Commissioner for Refugees, Ruhpolding, October 2, 1946; Harrecker, *Degradierte Doktoren*, p. 329; Renate Jäckle, *Schicksale jüdischer und "staatsfeindlicher" Ärztinnen und Ärzte nach 1933 in München* (Munich, 1988), p. 99.

27. See Joachimsthaler, *Hitlers Liste*, p. 430. See also the photograph of Ilse Braun's wedding dated November 16, 1936 [sic], Heinrich Hoffmann Photo Archive, hoff-14390, BSB Munich.

28. Ilse Fucke-Michels to the State Commissioner for Refugees, Ruhpolding, October 2, 1946.

29. See Peter de Mendelssohn, *Zeitungsstadt Berlin: Menschen und Mächte in der Geschichte der Deutschen Presse* (Berlin, 1959), p. 399; Norbert Frei and Johannes Schmitz, *Journalismus im Dritten Reich*, 3rd ed., revised (Munich, 1999), pp. 59ff.

30. See Elisabeth Noelle-Neumann, *Die Erinnerungen* (Munich, 2006), pp. 82ff.

31. Ursula von Kardorff, *Berliner Aufzeichnungen 1942–1945*, newly edited and annotated by Peter Hartl using the original diaries (Munich, 1997), p. 220.

32. See Ilse Fucke-Michels, née Braun, "Meldebogen auf Grund des Gesetzes zur Befreiung von Nationalismus und Militarismus vom 5. März 1946 [Registration

Form for the Law for Liberation from National Socialism and Militarism of March 5, 1946]," in Denazification Court Records, box 468, State Archives, Munich.

33. See Judith H. Dobrzynski, "Russia Moves to Aid Quest for Art Taken in Holocaust," *New York Times*, December 4, 1998. Hitler gave Hans Posse (1879–1942) the assignment to build the Linz Führer Museum ("Special Assignment Linz") on June 21, 1939. Posse died on December 10, 1942, in Dresden. See Sophie Lille, *Was einmal war: Handbuch der enteigneten Sammlung Wiens* (Vienna, 2003).

34. See "Originalnotizen von P. E. Schramm über Hitler, gemacht während der Befragungen von Hitlers Leibärzten, Haus Alaska, d. h. Altersheim für Lehrerinnen im Taunus, Sommer 1945, in USA-Kriegsgefangenschaft," in Kleine Erwerbung 441–3, BA Koblenz, p. 169.

35. See Ilse Fucke-Michels to the State Commissioner for Refugees, Ruhpolding, October 2, 1946.

4. RISE TO POWER AT HITLER'S SIDE

  1. Wagener, *Hitler aus nächster Nähe*, p. 99.

  2. Hoffmann, "Mein Beruf," pp. 22f.

  3. See Henriette von Schirach, *Frauen um Hitler: Nach Materialien* (Munich and Berlin), 1983, p. 226.

  4. See Gun, *Eva Braun*, p. 62.

  5. See Werner Maser, *Adolf Hitler: Legende, Mythos, Wirklichkeit* (Munich and Esslingen, 1971), p. 318.

  6. See "Ergänzende Erklärung des Herrn Erich Kempka," Berchtesgaden, July 4, 1945, p. 5, in MA 1298/10, Microfilm, Various Documents, DJ-13 (David Irving), IfZ Munich.

  7. See Sigmund, *Die Frauen der Nazis*, p. 245, where Sigmund makes reference to Albert Speer, *Spandauer Tagebücher*, p. 140 (Albert Speer, *Spandau: The Secret Diaries* [New York, 1976], p. 91). Susanne zur Nieden critically examines Sigmund's methods in "Geschichten aus dem braunen Nähkästchen: Der Führer und die Frauen," in *WerkstattGeschichte* 30 (2001), pp. 115–117.

  8. Speer himself noted that "by the winter of 1933" he "had been taken into the circle of Hitler's intimates": Speer, *Inside the Third Reich*, p. 38. In a letter to the head of the Institut für Zeitgeschichte archive, Speer stated that he met Hitler "for the first time in the summer of 1933"; see Albert Speer to Dr. Anton Hoch (Institut für Zeitgeschichte), n.p., March 3, 1981 (carbon copy), Albert Speer Papers, N1340/29, BA Koblenz.

  9. See Speer, *Spandau: The Secret Diaries*, p. 90; Sigmund, *Die Frauen der Nazis*, p. 214; Kershaw, *Hitler 1889–1936*, p. 342.

  10. Henriette von Schirach, *Frauen um Hitler*, pp. 45f. Descriptions of the apartment can also be found in Wagener, *Hitler aus nächster Nähe*, p. 98; Hanfstaengel, *Zwischem Weissem und Braunem Haus*, p. 231; Schroeder, *Er war mein Chef*, p. 153; Kurt Lüdecke, *I Knew Hitler* (1937; London, 1938), p. 454.

11. Speer, *Spandau: The Secret Diaries*, pp. 90. In *Inside the Third Reich*, Speer mentions his first visit to the Prinzregentenplatz apartment in July, 1933 (p. 28).

12. The girl's mother was also named Angela and was born from Alois Hitler's second marriage, to Franziska Matzelsberger, an innkeeper's daughter. See Wolfgang Zdral, *Die Hitlers: Die unbekannte Familie des Führers* (Bergisch Gladbach, 2008 [1st ed., 2005]), pp. 76ff.; Sigmund, *Die Frauen der Nazis*, pp. 196 and 205ff.

13. See "Eine rätselhafte Affäre: Selbstmord der Nichte Hitlers," *Münchener Post*, September 22, 1931. Cf. Adolf Hitler, *Reden, Schriften, Anordnungen*, vol. 4, *Von der Reichstagswahl bis zur Reichspräsidentenwahl, Oktober 1930–März 1932, Teil II, July 1931–December 1931*, ed. Christian Hartmann (Munich, 1996), p. 109. See also Kershaw, *Hitler 1889–1936*, p. 354; Sigmund, *Die Frauen der Nazis*, pp. 218ff.

14. See Sigmund, *Die Frauen der Nazis*, pp. 221, 224. In Kershaw's opinion as well, suicide is "the most likely explanation" (*Hitler 1889–1936*, p. 354). Alan Bullock goes so far as to say that Geli Raubal "committed suicide in protest against [Hitler's] possessiveness"; see *Hitler and Stalin: Parallel Lives* (London, 1991), p. 234.

15. Speech at an NSDAP meeting in Hamburg, September 24, 1931, in Hitler, *Reden, Schriften, Anordnungen*, vol. 4, p. 115.

16. Diary entries from October 27 and November 22, 1931, in Goebbels, *Die Tagebücher von Joseph Goebbels* (Munich, 1987), Teil I, vol. 2/II, pp. 135 and 154. See Sigmund, *Die Frauen der Nazis*, pp. 226ff. and 232, where the author writes that Raubal's death was exploited for propaganda purposes and used to Hitler's advantage "with all possible pathos." Likewise Manfred Koch-Hillebrecht, *Homo Hitler: Psychogramm des deutschen Diktators*, 2nd ed. (Munich, 1999), pp. 309f. In contrast, see Kershaw, *Hitler 1889–1936*, pp. 355, where he claims that Hitler's relationship with Geli Raubal was "more intense than any other human relationship he had before or after." She was "irreplaceable" for him, even if he "soon enough had Eva Braun in tow." There are similar statements in Henriette von Schirach, *Der Preis der Herrlichkeit*, p. 205.

17. Wagener, *Hitler aus nächster Nähe*, pp. 358f., 99.

18. Ibid., p. 358.

19. Hoffmann, "Mein Beruf," p. 14.

20. Hermann Göring joined the NSDAP in 1922 and was a member of Parliament for the Nazi Party since 1928. Hitler named him his "political adviser" in 1930.

21. Hitler had no official nationality at this period, having lost his Austrian citizenship after World War I, when he served in the German army. On February 25, 1932, the Braunschweig secretary of state named Hitler a senior administrative officer with a position at the Braunschweig legation Berlin, which entailed German citizenship ("Schreiben des Vorsitzenden des Braunschweigischen Staatsministeriums an den Reichsratsbevollmächtigten in Berlin, 25. February 1932 [copy]," in Albert Speer Papers, N1340/287, BA Koblenz).

22. See Schulze, *Weimar*, p. 345.

23. Goebbels, entry for January 7, 1932, in *Die Tagebücher von Joseph Goebbels*, Teil I, vol. 2/II, pp. 106f.

24. See Kershaw, *Hitler 1889–1936*, pp. 368f.

25. On the campaign trips see ibid., pp. 455ff.; also Hanfstaengl, *Zwischen Weissem und Braunem Haus*, pp. 262ff.; Fest, *Hitler*, pp. 444f., 455ff.; "Electoral Campaign, 1932," in Heinrich Hoffmann Photo Archive, hoff-7284, BSB Munich.

26. See Joseph Goebbels, *Vom Kaiserhof zur Reichskanzlei: Eine historische Darstellung in Tagebuchblättern (Vom 1. Januar 1932 bis zum 1. Mai 1933)*, 21st ed. (Munich, 1937), p. 104. Cf. Kershaw, *Hitler 1889–1936*, p. 369. On the campaign organization, see Ralph Georg Reuth, *Goebbels* (Munich, 1990), pp. 215ff.

27. See Helmut Heiber, ed., *Goebbels Reden 1932–1945* (Düsseldorf, 1971), pp. xvi, 43.

28. See Heinrich Hoffmann, *Das braune Heer: Leben, Kampf und Sieg der SA und SS*, foreword by Adolf Hitler (Berlin, 1932).

29. See Martin Broszat, *Die Machtergreifung*, p. 151; Kershaw, *Hitler 1889–1936*, p. 370; Sigmund, *Die Frauen der Nazis*, p. 215. See also Henriette von Schirach, *Der Preis der Herrlichkeit*, p. 206, where she says Hitler's half-sister was "competent and power-hungry." See also Florian M. Beierl, *Geschichte des Kehlsteins* (Berchtesgaden, 1994), p. 7.

30. Wagener, *Hitler aus nächster Nähe*, pp. 300 and 485. Cf. Otto Wagener, manuscript vol. 34, pp. 2054f., IfZ Munich: in Wagener's opinion, Eva Braun played "absolutely no role whatsoever" at this point.

31. See Kershaw, *Hitler 1889–1936*, pp. 370ff.

32. See ibid.

33. See Sven Felix Kellerhoff, *Hitlers Berlin: Geschichte einer Hassliebe* (Berlin, 2005), pp. 74f. See also Stephan Malinowski, *Vom König zum Führer* (Berlin, 2003), pp. 554f.

34. See Sigmund, *Die Frauen der Nazis*, p. 245.

35. See Hoffmann, *Hitler wie ich ihn sah*, p. 136.

36. See ibid., p. 137.

37. See Baldur von Schirach, *Ich glaubte an Hitler*, pp. 138ff.; Hoffmann, *Hitler wie ich ihn sah*, p. 137.

38. Goebbels, *Vom Kaiserhof zur Reichskanzlei*, pp. 142ff.

39. See Gun, *Eva Braun*, pp. 64–65. See also Maser, *Adolf Hitler*, p. 317. According to Maser, Ilse Braun personally confirmed this statement to him on March 18, 1969.

40. See Kershaw, *Hitler 1889–1936*, pp. 386ff.

41. Hitler left the Karlsruhe airport for Berlin shortly after 10 p.m.; see *Hitler: Reden, Schriften, Anordnungen*, vol. 4, Teil II, p. 145, document 54.

42. See Kershaw, *Hitler 1889–1936*, p. 388, which claims that Hitler interrupted his election campaign immediately after he heard about Eva Braun's suicide attempt on the night of November 1. Kershaw bases his claim on Maser, *Hitler*, p. 317. Nerin E. Gun, on the other hand, says that Hitler went directly to see Eva Braun in the hospital after he received an "explanatory farewell letter" from her in the morning mail (*Eva Braun*, p. 69).

43. Goebbels, *Die Tagebücher von Joseph Goebbels*, Teil I, vol. 2/III, pp. 49f. For the sequence of campaign speeches, see Adolf Hitler, *Reden und Proklamationen 1932–1945*, ed. Max Domarus, vol. 1: *Triumph, 1932–1938*, (Würzburg, 1962), pp. 141ff.

44. See Gun, *Eva Braun*, pp. 65–66.

45. For example, Ian Kershaw, who speaks of "Eva Braun's presumable suicide attempt," says that she was in despair about Hitler, who "hardly knew she was alive" (*Hitler 1889–1936*, p. 388). Alan Bullock writes that "she had no better idea how to get him to care about her," and that Heinrich Hoffmann "saw through Eva Braun's game from the beginning" (*Hitler and Stalin*, p. 502). For Anton Joachimsthaler, the incident was staged in order "to blackmail Hitler" (*Hitlers Liste*, p. 21).

46. See Gun, *Eva Braun*, p. 65; Sigmund, *Die Frauen der Nazis*, p. 246.

47. Hoffmann, "Mein Beruf," p. 22. Hoffmann claims that Hitler only now started to show "greater interest in Eva Braun," although "there was no question of it being a real relationship." In this regard see also Gun, *Eva Braun*, p. 66.

48. See Sigmund, *Die Frauen der Nazis*, p. 236.

49. See ibid., p. 235.

50. See Margret Boveri, *Tage des Überlebens: Berlin 1945* (Munich, 1968), p. 122.

51. See Hanfstaengl, *Zwischen Weissem und Braunem Haus*, pp. 286f. See also Ernst Hanfstaengl, *Hitler: The Missing Years* (New York, 1994 [1st ed., London, 1957]), pp. 194f., where Hanfstaengl claims that all who took part in that evening believed that Eva Braun was merely "a friend of one of the other girls."

52. See Erika Mann, *Wenn die Lichter ausgehen: Geschichten aus dem Dritten Reich* (Reinbek, 2006).

53. See "Protest der Richard-Wagner-Stadt München," *Münchner Neueste Nachrichten*, April 16, 1933. Quoted from *München: Ein Lesebuch*, pp. 260ff.

54. See Hanfstaengl, *Hitler: The Missing Years*, pp. 194–195.

55. Ibid. All the persons named signed his guest book under the date of January 1, 1933; see Sigmund, *Die Frauen der Nazis*, p. 247. See also Peter Conradi, *Hitler's Piano Player: The Rise and Fall of Ernst Hanfstaengl, Confidant of Hitler, Ally of* FDR (New York, 2004); Ronald Smelser et al., eds., *Die Braune Elite II* (Darmstadt, 1993), pp. 137ff; Wolfgang Zdral, *Der finanzierte Aufstieg des Adolf H.* (Vienna, 2002).

56. See Kershaw, *Hitler 1889–1936*, pp. 395ff.; Karl Dietrich Bracher, "Demokratie und Machtergreifung—Der Weg zum 30. Januar 1933," in *Machtverfall und Machtergreifung: Aufstieg und Herrschaft des Nationalsozialismus*, ed. Rudolf Lill and Heinrich Oberreuter (Munich, 1983), p. 25.

57. See Kershaw, *Hitler 1889–1936*, pp. 396ff. See also Peter D. Stachura, *Gregor Strasser and the Rise of Nazism* (London, 1983); Werner Bräuninger, *Hitlers Kontrahenten in der NSDAP 1921–1945* (Munich, 2004).

58. Quoted from Kershaw, *Hitler 1889–1936*, p. 401. Cf. Hinrich Lohse, "Der Fall Strasser," unpublished typescript [ca. 1960], Forschungsstelle für die Geschichte des Nationalsozialismus, Hamburg, sections 20–22.

59. Adolf Hitler, "Denkschrift über die inneren Gründe für die Verfügungen zur Herstellung einer erhöhten Schlagkraft der Bewegung," NS 22/110, BA Koblenz.

60. Max Weber, "Die drei reinen Typen der legitimen Herrschaft," in *Gesammelte Aufsätze zur Wissenschaftslehre*, ed. Johannes Winckelmann, 7th ed. (Tübingen, 1988), p. 482. Cf. Hans-Ulrich Thamer, *Der Nationalsozialismus* (Stuttgart, 2002), p. 61.

61. Hitler, "Denkschrift über die inneren Gründe für die Verfügungen zur Herstellung einer erhöhten Schlagkraft der Bewegung."

62. Max Weber, "Die drei reinen Typen der legitimen Herrschaft," p. 485.

63. See Kershaw, *Hitler 1889–1936*, pp. 414ff.; Henry Ashby Turner, *Hitlers Weg zur Macht: Der Januar 1933* (Munich, 1997), pp. 199f.

64. According to the latest research, Joachim von Ribbentrop made contact with Adolf Hitler as early as 1927; during the Nuremberg Trials Ribbentrop stated that he first met Hitler in 1931–1932. See Philipp Gassert and Daniel S. Mattern, *The Hitler Library: A Bibliography* (London, 2001).

65. See Kershaw, *Hitler 1889–1936*, pp. 419ff.; Turner, *Hitlers Weg zur Macht*, as cited in note 63, above; Wolfram Pyta, *Hindenburg: Herrschaft zwischen Hohenzollern und Hitler* (Munich, 2007), pp. 791ff.

66. See Kershaw, *Hitler 1889–1936*, p. 433.

67. Goebbels, *Vom Kaiserhof zur Reichskanzlei*, p. 251.

68. Rudolf Hess to Ilse Hess, Berlin, January 31, 1933, in Rudolf Hess, *Briefe 1908–1933*, ed. Wolf Rüdiger Hess (Munich, 1987), pp. 424f.

69. Estimates of the number of participants range from fifteen thousand to one million. Cf. Kershaw, *Hitler 1889–1936*, p. 433; Kellerhoff, *Hitlers Berlin*, p. 89.

70. See Fest, *Hitler*, p. 510; Goebbels, *Vom Kaiserhof zur Reichskanzlei*, p. 253.

71. See Hoffmann, *Hitler wie ich ihn sah*, pp. 48f.; Goebbels, *Vom Kaiserhof zur Reichskanzlei*, pp. 251ff.; Kershaw, *Hitler 1889–1936*, p. 432; Fest, *Hitler*, p. 510.

72. See Gun, *Eva Braun*, p. 95.

73. See Klaus Beck, "Telefongeschichte als Sozialgeschichte: Die soziale und kulturelle Aneignung des Telefons im Alltag," in *Telefon und Gesellschaft: Beiträge zu einer Soziologie der Telefonkommunikation*, vol. 1 of *Telefon und Gesellschaft*, ed. Forschungsgruppe Telekommunikation [The Telecommunications Research Group] (Berlin, 1989).

74. See Junge, *Bis zur letzten Stunde*, p. 121. See also Gun, *Eva Braun*, p. 101: only in 1933, according to Gun, did she request a "private phone" as the "mistress of the Chancellor of the Reich."

75. Herta Schneider, statement of June 23, 1949, "Öffentliche Sitzung der Hauptkammer München zur mündlichen Verhandlung in dem Verfahren gegen Herta Schneider, geb. Ostermayr," in Denazification Court Records, box 1670, State Archives, Munich.

76. *Amtliches Fernsprechbuch für den Reichspostdirektionsbezirk München*, ed. Reichspostdirektion München as of May 1, 1934, part 1, July 1934 edition.

77. Gun, *Eva Braun*, pp. 93ff.; Sigmund, *Die Frauen der Nazis*, p. 248.

PART TWO: CONTRASTING WORLDS

5. WOMEN IN NATIONAL SOCIALISM

1. See Hitler, *Reden und Proklamationen 1932–1945*, vol. 1, *Triumph, First Part: 1932–1934* (Wiesbaden, 1973), pp. 450ff.

2. Ibid.

3. Gertrud Scholtz-Klink, "Meine lieben deutschen Menschen!" (speech given at Nuremberg, September 8, 1934), in Adolf Hitler and Gertrud Schotz-Klink, *Reden an die deutsche Frau: Reichsparteitag Nürnberg, 8. September 1934* (Berlin, 1934), pp. 8–16.

4. See Christiane Berger, "Die 'Reichsfrauenführerin' Gertrud Scholtz-Klink: Zur Wirkung einer nationalsozialistischen Karriere in Verlauf, Retrospektive und Gegenwart" (dissertation, University of Hamburg, 2005), pp. 27f. See also Gertrud Scholtz-Klink, *Die Frau im Dritten Reich* (Tübingen, 1978).

5. See Dörte Winkler, *Frauenarbeit im "Dritten Reich"* (Hamburg, 1977), p. 193.

6. See Matthew Stibbe, *Women in the Third Reich* (London, 2003), pp. 88f.

7. "Reichskanzlei, 4. 5.–25. 7. 1937," in *Akten der Partei-Kanzlei der NSDAP: Rekonstruktion eines verlorengegangenen Bestandes*, ed. Helmut Heiber et al. (Munich, 1983–1992), M 101 04741–45.

8. "Der Führer spricht zur deutschen Frauenschaft," in *Reden des Führers am Parteitag der Ehre 1936*, 4th ed. (Munich, 1936), p. 43.

9. See Stibbe, *Women in the Third Reich*, pp. 85ff.; Thamer, *Der Nationalsozialismus*, pp. 262ff.

10. Gitta Sereny, *Albert Speer, His Battle with Truth* (New York, 1995), pp. 193, 197. Kershaw disposes of the topic by saying that Hitler preferred "obedient playthings" (*Hitler 1889–1936*, p. 284).

11. Joachim Fest, *Das Gesicht des Dritten Reiches: Profile einer totalitären Herrschaft* (Munich, 2006 [1st ed., 1963]), pp. 359f. Fest relies primarily on Hermann Rauschning, *Gespräche mit Hitler* (Zürich, 1940), pp. 240f.

12. Speer, *Inside the Third Reich*, p. 93. "She was not political," Speer curtly informed Sereny when she asked Speer's wife, in Speer's presence, about her own attitude toward the goals of the National Socialists (Sereny, *Albert Speer*, p. 114). See Margret Nissen, *Sind Sie die Tochter Speer?* (Bergisch Gladbach, 2007 [1st ed., Munich, 2005]), pp. 20, 157f., and 182. Speer himself later admitted to Fest that his family did not have a presence in his memoirs "because it didn't have a presence in my life" (quoted in Fest, *Die unbeantwortbaren Fragen*, p. 144).

13. Margret Nissen, *Sind Sie die Tochter Speer?* (Bergisch Gladbach, 2007 [1st ed., Munich, 2005]), p. 182.

14. Sereny, *Albert Speer*, p. 112. See Below, *Als Hitlers Adjutant*, p. 10.

15. Margarete Mitscherlich, "Anti-Semitism—A Male Disease?" in her *The Peaceable Sex: On Aggression in Women and Men* (New York, 1987), pp. 192–208, quotes from p. 203. See also Mitscherlich's "Die befreite Frau: Nachdenken über männliche und weibliche Werte [The Liberated Woman: Reflections on Male and Female Values]," *Frankfurter Rundschau*, September 26, 2000, p. 20.

16. See Knopp, *Hitlers Frauen*, p. 83.

17. See Kathrin Kompisch, *Täterinnen: Frauen im Nationalsozialismus* (Cologne, 2008), pp. 74ff. and 155ff.; Gudrun Schwarz, *Eine Frau an seiner Seite: Ehefrauen in der "SS-Sippengemeinschaft,"* 2nd ed. (Berlin, 2001), pp. 281f.; Karin Windaus-Walser,

"Frauen im Nationalsozialismus," in *Töchter-Fragen. NS-Frauen-Geschichte*, ed. Lerke Gravenhorst and Carmen Tatschmurat (Freiburg im Breisgau, 1990), pp. 59ff.; Sybille Steinbacher, ed., *Frauen in der NS-Volksgemeinschaft*, Beiträge zur Geschichte des Nationalsozialismus, vol. 23 (Göttingen, 2007), p. 18. See also Dieter Schenk, *Hans Frank: Hitlers Kronjurist und Generalgouverneur* (Frankfurt am Main, 2006), pp. 39–45, 179f. and 244–253, where Schenk also analyzes the role of Frank's wife, Brigitte Frank.

18. See Schwarz, *Eine Frau an seiner Seite*, pp. 8ff.

19. Quoted in Sereny, *Albert Speer*, p. 193.

20. Hans-Otto Meissner, *So schnell schlägt Deutschlands Herz* (Giessen, 1951), pp. 100f. On Meissner's biography, see Thomas Keil, "Die postkoloniale deutsche Literatur in Namibia (1920–2000)," (dissertation, University of Stuttgart, 2003), pp. 405ff.

21. Meissner, *So schnell schlägt Deutschlands Herz*, pp. 100f.

22. See Wagener, *Hitler aus nächster Nähe*, pp. 392f. See also Leni Riefenstahl, *Memoiren* (Cologne, 2000 [1st ed., Munich 1987], p. 181.

23. See Wagener, *Hitler aus nächster Nähe*, p. 372. Goebbels, who does not mention the first meeting between his girlfriend and Hitler, describes an evening in Munich together with Magda Quandt and Hitler as early as April 4, 1931 (diary entry of April 4, 1931, in *Die Tagebücher von Joseph Goebbels*, Teil I, vol. 2/I, p. 378). In the opinion of Magda Goebbels's biographer, Anja Klabunde, however, the first meeting between Hitler and Quandt was accidental, and Klabunde dates the event to "a few weeks after Geli's death," i.e., after Sept. 18, 1931. See Anja Klabunde, *Magda Goebbels: Annäherung an ein Leben* (Munich, 1999), pp. 148ff. Also see Joachimsthaler, *Hitlers Liste*, p. 375.

24. See Wagener, *Hitler aus nächster Nähe*, p. 392.

25. In fact, Günther Quandt is said to have met with Hitler at Hotel Kaiserhof on the same day when Quandt's ex-wife tried to make contact with the Nazi leader; Wagener, *Hitler aus nächster Nähe*, pp. 373ff.). Goebbels, on the other hand, first noted on Sept. 12 1931: "Nauseating: Herr Günther Quandt was with the leader. Struck all sorts of poses and showed off, of course" (Goebbels, diary entry, September 12 1931, in *Die Tagebücher von Joseph Goebbels*, Teil I, vol. 2/II, p. 97.)

26. See Rüdiger Jungbluth, *Die Quandts: Ihr leiser Aufstieg zur mächtigsten Wirtschaftsdynastie Deutschlands* (Frankfurt am Main, 2002), pp. 108ff. See also Reuth, *Goebbels*, p. 197.

27. See Heusler, *Das Braune Haus*, pp. 81ff.; Thamer, *Der Nationalsozialismus*, pp. 58f. See also Hagen Schulze, "Democratic Prussia in Weimar Germany, 1919–1933," in *Modern Prussian History 1830–1947*, ed. Philip G. Dwyer (Harlow, England, 2001), pp. 211–229.

28. See Sigmund, *Die Frauen der Nazis*, vol. 1, p. 126.

29. Auguste Behrend, "Meine Tochter Magda Goebbels," *Schwäbische Illustrierte*, March 1, 1952. See also Reuth, *Goebbels*, p. 197; Klabunde, *Magda Goebbels*, pp. 123f. On Magda Goebbels, see in addition Curt Riess, *Joseph Goebbels: Eine*

Biographie (Baden-Baden, 1950); Hans-Otto Meissner, *Magda Goebbels: Ein Lebensbild* (Munich, 1978); Erich Ebermayer and Hans Roos, *Gefährtin des Teufels: Leben und Tod der Magda Goebbels* (Hamburg, 1952); Guido Knopp and Peter Hartl, "Magda Goebbels—Die Gefolgsfrau," in Knopp, *Hitlers Frauen*, pp. 85–147; Anna Maria Sigmund, "Magda Goebbels: Die erste Dame des Dritten Reichs," in her *Die Frauen der Nazis*, pp. 111–150.

30. Speer, quoted in Fest, *Die unbeantwortbaren Fragen* (Hamburg, 2006), pp. 196f.

31. Speer, *Inside the Third Reich*, p. 146.

32. See Sigmund, *Die Frauen der Nazis*, p. 116; Klabunde, *Magda Goebbels*, p. 104. On Arlosoroff, see Golda Meir, *My Life* (New York, 1975), p. 144.

33. See Jungbluth, *Die Quandts*, pp. 49 and 52.

34. Thamer, *Der Nationalsozialismus*, pp. 66ff.

35. See Goebbels, *Die Tagebücher von Joseph Goebbels*, Teil I, vol. II/2, p. 24, according to which Magda Quandt and Viktoria von Dirksen accompanied him. Eva and Gretl Braun as well as Henriette Hoffmann were apparently also present at this event. Friedrich Karl Freiherr von Eberstein, the future Munich police chief, stated that Hitler had sent him to Weimar, where he met Eva Braun for the first time: Eberstein, "Women Around Hitler," in "Adolf Hitler: A Composite Picture," Headquarters Military Intelligence Service USA, OI Special Report 36, April 2 1947, documentation "Adolf Hitler 1944–1953," vol. 4, p. 694, F135/4, IfZ, Munich.

36. See "Bayreuth, Picknick Sommer 1931 [Bayreuth, Summer Picnic, 1931]," in Heinrich Hoffmann Photo Archive, hoff-7060, BSB Munich. Brigitte Hamann does not mention Hitler's presence at the 1931 festival in her *Winifred Wagner oder Hitlers Bayreuth* (Munich, 2002), pp. 209f., and mention of the event is likewise missing from Goebbels's diaries.

37. Hermann Göring's statement quoted in Wagener, *Hitler aus nächster Nähe*, p. 376.

38. See Johannes Hürter, *Wilhelm Groener: Reichswehrminister am Ende der Weimarer Republik 1928–1932* (Munich, 1993), pp. 315f.

39. See "Braunschweig, SA-Aufmarsch vom 17./18. Oktober 1931," in Heinrich Hoffmann Photo Archive, hoff-7094, BSB Munich.

40. See Carlos Widmann, "Magda Goebbels: Die Karriere einer Opportunistin im Führerstaat," in "Hitlers langer Schatten: Die Gegenwart der Vergangenheit," *Der Spiegel*, September 24, 2001; also Klabunde, *Magda Goebbels*, p. 159, which claims: "But what she wanted most of all was power." Klabunde refers here to Meissner, *Magda Goebbels*, p. 119.

41. See Sigmund, *Die Frauen der Nazis*, pp. 126f.

42. Goebbels, diary entry, August 26, 1931, in *Die Tagebücher von Joseph Goebbels*, Teil I, vol. II/2, p. 85. And see Below, *Als Hitlers Adjutant*, p. 178. See also Riefenstahl, *Memoiren*, p. 201, where Riefenstahl claims that Magda Goebbels admitted to her that she had "fallen for the Führer" and divorced Günther Quandt for that reason.

43. Goebbels, diary entry, September 14, 1931, previously cited, p. 98.

44. Wagener, *Hitler aus nächster Nähe*, p. 377.

45. See "Besuch von Magda Goebbels im Teehaus auf dem Kehlstein (Obersalzberg) am 21. Oktober 1938," in Heinrich Hoffmann Photo Archive, hoff-272, BSB Munich.

46. See Sigmund, *Die Frauen der Nazis*, p. 248; Sven Felix Kellerhoff, *Mythos Führerbunker: Hitlers letzter Unterschlupf* (Berlin, 2006), p. 82. Kellerhoff claims that Magda Goebbels tried to "exclude" Eva Braun "even from her own domain on the Obersalzberg." See also Ulrike Grunewald, "Eva Braun und Magda Goebbels," in her *Rivalinnen* (Cologne, 2006), pp. 191–236.

47. See Alfred Kube, *Pour le mérite und Hakenkreuz: Hermann Göring im Dritten Reich*, 2nd ed. (Munich, 1987), p. 202.

48. See Emmy Göring's invitation of Ilse Hess to a "musical Advent's tea," or "garden tea," in Rudolf Hess Papers, J 1211 (–) 1993/300, vol. 5, file 80, Swiss Federal Archives, Bern.

49. Emmy Göring, *An der Seite meines Mannes: Begebenheiten und Bekenntnisse*, 4th ed. (Coburg, 1996), p. 57.

50. Ibid., pp. 148 and 209.

51. Ibid., pp. 66 and 72ff. Cf. Anna Maria Sigmund, "Emmy Göring: Die ‹Hohe Frau›," in her *Die Frauen der Nazis*, pp. 97ff. Emmy Göring does not deny that she knew about the concentration camps, but she claims to have believed that they were for the "political reeducation" of "Jews" and "Communists." Only after the war, she says, did she learn about the crimes there and wondered "if Hitler himself even knew exactly what Himmler was doing at Auschwitz." Margarete Speer makes the exact same argument: see Sereny, *Albert Speer*, p. 195.

52. Ilse Hess, *Gefangener des Friedens: Neue Briefe aus Spandau* (Leoni am Starnberger See, 1965 [1st ed., 1955]), p. 14.

53. Ibid., pp. 26 and 33.

54. Ibid., pp. 18f. and 54.

55. Ibid., pp. 35ff. and 44. See also Rudolf Hess, letter to Klara and Fritz Hess, Munich, September 14, 1920, in Hess, *Briefe 1908–1933*, p. 264. Rudolf Hess joined the NSDAP on July 1, 1920. See Anna Maria Sigmund, "Ilse Hess: Die Frau des 'Führer-Stellvertreters,' " in her *Die Frauen der Nazis*, pp. 737f.

56. Ilse Pröhl to Frau Barchewitz, Munich, February 28, 1921 (carbon copy), in Rudolf Hess Papers, J 1211 (–) 1993/300, vol. 2, file 15, BA Bern. See also in this regard Hitler's speech titled "Warum sind wir Antisemiten? [Why Are We Anti-Semites?]" of August 13, 1920, in Adolf Hitler, *Sämtliche Aufzeichnungen 1905–1924*, ed. Eberhard Jäckel with Axel Kuhn (Stuttgart, 1980), p. 185.

57. Quoted from Othmar Plöckinger, *Geschichte eines Buches: Adolf Hitlers "Mein Kampf" 1922–1945* (Munich, 2006), p. 54.

58. See ibid., pp. 72, 124f. and 151f.

59. Ilse Hess to Heinrich Himmler, n.p., December 9 [1933] (carbon copy), in Rudolf Hess Papers, J 1211 (–) 1993/300, vol. 7, file 98, Swiss Federal Archives, Bern.

60. Eva Braun to Ilse Hess, Obersalzberg, undated [January 2] (handwritten original), in Rudolf Hess Papers, J 1211 (–) 1993/300, vol. 2, file 25, Swiss Federal Archives, Bern.

61. Ilse Hess to Hans Grimm, n. p., November 1, 1943 [must be an error for 1944] (carbon copy), in Rudolf Hess Papers, J 1211 (–) 1993/300, vol. 6, file 84, Swiss Federal Archives, Bern.

62. See Sigmund, *Die Frauen der Nazis*, p. 248.

63. See Joseph Goebbels, *Vom Kaiserhof zur Reichskanzlei: Eine historische Darstellung in Tagebuchblättern (Vom 1. Januar 1932 bis zum 1. Mai 1933)*, 21st ed. (Munich, 1937), pp. 255–271.

64. Anni Winter, Interrogation by Capt. O. N. Norden, Munich, November 6, 1945, in Donovan Nuremberg Trials Collection, vol. 4, subdivision 8/Hitler, Section 8.02, Cornell Law Library, Cornell University.

65. See Thamer, *Der Nationalsozialismus*, pp. 106ff; Kershaw, *Hitler 1889–1936*, pp. 441f.

66. See Goebbels, *Vom Kaiserhof zur Reichskanzlei*, p. 258; Gun, *Eva Braun*, p. 96. Hitler apparently gave her her "first jewels" from him on this day: "a matching ring, earrings, and bracelet."

67. See Goebbels, *Vom Kaiserhof zur Reichskanzlei*, pp. 264ff.

68. See ibid., pp. 269f.

69. Rudolf Hess to Ilse Hess, Berlin, January 31, 1933, in Hess, *Briefe 1908–1933*, p. 425.

70. See Kershaw, *Hitler 1889–1936*, pp. 433f and 613f. Cf. Fest, *Hitler*, p. 352.

71. Speer, *Inside the Third Reich*, p. 34.

72. See Beierl, *Geschichte des Kehlsteins*, p. 7. See also Fest, *Hitler*, p. 353.

73. See the public placard for the Reichstag election of 3/5/1933, district and parliamentary electoral nominations, Upper Bavaria/Swabia electoral district.

74. David Clay Large, *Hitlers München: Aufstieg und Fall der Hauptstadt der Bewegung* (Munich, 2001 [1st ed., 1998]), p. 299.

75. Tony van Eyck, "Adolf Hitler spricht zu einer Schauspielerin: 'Der echte Künstler kommt von selbst zu uns,' " n.p., March 21, 1933, in Ernst Hanfstaengl Papers, Ana 405, box 27, file for Jan.–June 1933, BSB Munich.

76. See Goebbels, *Vom Kaiserhof zur Reichskanzlei*, p. 264. See also Ernst K. Bramsted, *Goebbels und die nationalsozialistische Propaganda 1925–1945* (Frankfurt, 1971), pp. 288f.; Fritz Redlich, *Hitler: Diagnose des destruktiven Propheten* (Vienna, 2002), p. 92.

77. See Kellerhoff, *Hitlers Berlin*, pp. 107f. Kellerhoff says there that Berlin was "Hitler's most important stage."

78. See Goebbels, *Vom Kaiserhof zur Reichskanzlei*, pp. 280ff.

79. Ibid., p. 289. Extensive information on the topic may be found in Kershaw, *Hitler 1889–1936*, pp. 472f.

80. For the debate about Hitler's leadership style and his personal position of power within the Nazi state, see Gerhard Hirschfeld and Lothar Kettenacker, eds., *Der "Führerstaat": Mythos und Realität; Studien zur Struktur und Politik des Dritten Reiches*, Veröffentlichungen des Deutschen Historischen Instituts London, vol. 8, (Stuttgart, 1981). Ian Kershaw says about Hitler in this context: "He took the key

decisions; he alone determined the timing. But little else was Hitler's own work" (*Hitler 1889–1936*, p. 542). On Hitler's style of governing see also Ian Kershaw, *Der NS-Staat: Geschichtsinterpretationen und Kontroversen im Überblick*, rev. and expanded ed. (Reinbek, 1994), pp. 112–147.

81. Gesetz zur Wiederherstellung des Berufsbeamtentums, April 7, 1933, Reichsgesetz-blatt 1933 I, pp. 175–177, in documentArchiv.de, at http://www.documentArchiv.de/ns/beamtenges.html.

82. Kershaw, *Hitler 1889–1936*, pp. 470 and 535.

83. See Goebbels, *Vom Kaiserhof zur Reichskanzlei*, pp. 292ff.

84. Otto Dietrich, *12 Jahre mit Hitler* (Munich, 1955), pp. 149f. See also Thamer, *Der Nationalsozialismus*, p. 184.

85. Goebbels, *Vom Kaiserhof zur Reichskanzlei*, p. 301. See Thamer, *Der Nationalsozialismus*, pp. 231ff. See also Kershaw, *Der Hitler-Mythos*, pp. 53ff.

86. See Rolf Düsterberg, *Hanns Johst—"Der Barde der SS": Karriere eines deutschen Dichters* (Paderborn, 2004).

87. Joseph Goebbels, "Unser Hitler," radio broadcast of April 20, 1933, in Goebbels, *Signale der neuen Zeit: 25 ausgewählte Reden* (Munich, 1934), pp. 141 and 149.

88. Kershaw, *Hitler 1889–1936*, p. 485.

89. See Friedrich Sieburg, *Napoleon: Die hundert Tage*, 9th ed. (Stuttgart, 1964), p. 95, where the author compares Napoleon's relationship with France to a relationship with a lover, and analyzes the lover's status in this context. What is missing, he says, are "natural bonds," since the lover is "there for exceptional cases."

90. See Gun, *Eva Braun*, p. 95; Sigmund, *Die Frauen der Nazis*, p. 248.

91. See "Hitlers Urlaub 20.–22. April 1934," in Heinrich Hoffmann Photo Archive, hoff-10486, BSB Munich.

92. Johanna Wolf had already worked for Dietrich Eckart. See Adolf Hitler, *Monologe im Führerhauptquartier 1941–1944: Die Aufzeichnungen Heinrich Heims*, ed. Werner Jochmann (Hamburg, 1980), p. 465.

93. Speer, *Inside the Third Reich*, pp. 46–47. In contrast, Nerin E. Gun claims that Hitler, "always mindful of appearances," did not have Eva Braun spend nights in Haus Wachenfeld; instead, she stayed at first at the Hotel Post or the Berchtesgadener Hof ("according to the evidence of the manageress of one of these hotels," Gun writes), and later at the Platterhof, a mountain inn (Gun, *Eva Braun*, pp. 101–102).

94. Speer, *Inside the Third Reich*, pp. 46f.

95. Ibid., pp. 59ff. See also Fest, *Die unbeantwortbaren Fragen*, p. 59.

96. Zentralkommando d. Kriegsgefangenenlager Nr. 32/DI-21, 2. Juli 1945, Sonder-haftzentrale "ASHCAN." Detailed report on the interrogation of Dr. Karl Brandt: Answers to the Questionnaire. Ref.: SHAEF Interrogation Documents from June 15, 1945, in Rep. 502, KV-Anklage, Umdrucke deutsch, NO-331, State Archives, Nuremberg.

97. This seems to be confirmed as well by the Heinrich Hoffmann photographs dated 1934, according to which Eva Braun stayed on the Obersalzberg on both April 20–22

and in August–September, 1934, along with Heinrich and Erna Hoffmann, the adjutant Wilhelm Brückner and his girlfriend Sofie Stork, Reich Press Chief Otto Dietrich, and others. See Heinrich Hoffmann Photo Archive, hoff-49683, BSB Munich.

98. See Johannes Fried, "Erinnerung im Kreuzverhör: Kollektives Gedächtnis, Albert Speer und die Erkenntnis erinnerter Vergangenheit," in the Festschrift for Lothar Gall, *Historie und Leben. Der Historiker als Wissenschaftler und Zeitgenosse,* ed. Dieter Hein et al. (Munich, 2006), pp. 343ff. See also Matthias Schmidt, *Albert Speer: Das Ende eines Mythos; Speers wahre Rolle im Dritten Reich* (Bern and Munich, 1982), pp. 21ff.

99. Heinrich Breloer, *Unterwegs zur Familie Speer: Begegnungen, Gespräche, Interviews* (Berlin, 2005), pp. 115f.

100. Albert Speer to Rudolf Wolters, n.p., July 6, 1975 (carbon copy), in Albert Speer Papers, N1340/76, BA Koblenz.

101. Speer, *Inside the Third Reich,* p. 32.

102. Albert Speer, quoted in Fest, *Die unbeantwortbaren Fragen,* p. 196. See also Speer, *Inside the Third Reich,* pp. 32–33.

103. See Speer, *Inside the Third Reich,* p. 31: "I had found my Mephistopheles." This reference to the devil from Goethe's *Faust* emphasizes the image Speer likes to present of Hitler's superiority—Hitler representing the root of all evil as a "destroyer" and "liar" (the etymology of the word "Mephistopheles").

104. Joachim Fest, meanwhile, doubts the value of Speer's testimony with respect to the nature of the relationship between Hitler and Braun; see his *Die unbeantwortbaren Fragen,* pp. 60f.

105. "Besprechung zwischen Herrn Albrecht und Frl. Schroeder, früher Sekretärin von Hitler," Berchtesgaden, May 22, 1945, in MA 1298/10, microfilm, Various Documents, DJ-13 (David Irving), IfZ Munich.

106. See Schroeder, *Er war mein Chef,* pp. 213f. See also Julius Schaub, *In Hitlers Schatten: Erinnerungen und Aufzeichnungen des persönlichen Adjutanten und Vertrauten Julius Schaub 1925–1945,* ed. Olaf Rose (Stegen am Ammersee, 2005).

107. See David Irving, "Notes on an Interview of Johannes Göhler at his home, Stuttgart-Nord, Feuerbacher Weg 125, from 12:30 to 4 pm, 27 March 1971," in ZS 2244 (Johannes Göhler), IfZ Munich. See also Schroeder, *Er war mein Chef,* p. 216.

108. David Irving, interview with "a certain Frau Gö" on November 4, 1973 (entry under the date of May 12, 1975), in David Irving Collection, ED 100/44, IfZ Munich.

109. Eva Braun to Gretl Fegelein, Berlin, April 23, 1945, in Gun, *Eva Braun,* pp. 253–254. On April 30, 1945, Eva Braun gave Hanna Reitsch, the pilot who had flown General Robert Ritter from Greim to Hitler in Berlin and had stayed for a week in the bunker, a last letter to her sister Gretl. The whereabouts and content of the letter are unknown. (Anna Maria Sigmund, "Hanna Reitsch: Sie flog für das Dritte Reich," in her *Die Frauen der Nazis,* pp. 559ff.)

110. Gun, *Eva Braun,* pp. 289–290; Schroeder, *Er war mein Chef,* p. 216; Wolfgang Benz and Barbara Distel, *Der Ort des Terrors: Geschichte der nationalsozialistischen*

Konzentrationslager, vol. 2, *Frühe Lager, Dachau, Emslandlager* (Munich, 2005), pp. 324ff. See likewise the statements of SS-Hauptsturmführer Erwin Haufler questioned by American officers in the Bad Aiblingen camp, December 27, 1945, and of SS-Hauptsturmführer Franz Konrad, questioned in Zell am See on January 6–8, 1946, in David Irving Collection, "Adolph Hitler 1944–1953," vol. 2, F 135/2, IfZ Munich.

111. See Speer, *Albert Speer. Die Kransberg-Protokolle 1945: Seine ersten Aussagen und Aufzeichnungen (Juni–September)*, (Munich, 2003), p. 31.

112. See Gun, *Eva Braun*, p. 82. The letter, Ilse Fucke-Michels to Nerin E. Gun, Munich, April 8, 1967, is reproduced in the German edition, *Eva Braun-Hitler: Leben und Schicksal* (Velbert, 1968), pp. 67 and 69. Gun claims that Eva Braun kept "a more intimate diary later," which, "bound in green leather," was locked in the "armored safe at the bunker" when she left the Berghof in 1945. See also Joachimsthaler, *Hitlers Liste*, pp. 443ff.

113. Werner Maser, *Adolf Hitler: Legende, Mythos, Wirklichkeit*, 6th ed., expanded (with Eva Braun's Diary), (Munich and Esslingen, 1974), pp. 236 and 325ff. The original of the diary-fragment is located at the National Archives of the United States, in Washington, DC.

114. See Douglas L. Hewlett, *Hitler et les Femmes: Le journal intime d'Eva Braun* (Paris, 1948); Paul Tabori, ed., *The Private Life of Adolf Hitler: The Intimate Notes and Diary of Eva Braun*, (London, 1949). See also Alison Leslie Gold, *The Devil's Mistress: The Diary of Eva Braun, the Woman Who Lived and Died with Hitler—A Novel* (Boston, 1997); Alan Bartlett, *The Diary of Eva Braun* (Bristol, 2000).

115. Eva Braun, diary, February 6, 1935, in Gun, *Eva Braun*, p. 83.

116. Goebbels, diary entries of January 31 and February 4, 1935, in *Die Tagebücher von Joseph Goebbels*, Teil I, vol. 3/I, pp. 177 and 179.

117. See Eva Braun, diary, February 15, 1935, in Gun, *Eva Braun*, pp. 84–85.

118. Paul Ludwig Troost (b. 1878) died on January 21, 1934, in Munich. Gerhardine "Gerdy" Troost (1904–2003), who joined the NSDAP in 1932, and Leonhard Gall were in charge of renovating Hitler's apartment. Gerdy Troost was named a professor by Hitler on April 20, 1937, and in 1938 published a work with the title *Das Bauen im Neuen Reich [Construction in the New Reich]*.

119. Eva Braun, diary, February 15, 1935, in Gun, *Eva Braun*, p. 84. These dates agree with Goebbels's diary, where he records under February 10 and 18 that Hitler left Berlin for Munich (*Die Tagebücher von Joseph Goebbels*, Teil I, vol. 3/I, pp. 182f. and 186).

120. See Goebbels, diary entry, March 2, 1935 ("Hitler in Munich"), in *Die Tagebücher von Joseph Goebbels*, Teil I, vol. 3/I, p. 193.

121. Eva Braun, diary, March 4, 1935, in Gun, *Eva Braun*, pp. 85–86. See also Goebbels, diary entry, March 4, 1935 ("We are not going to the Munich city ball"), in *Die Tagebücher von Joseph Goebbels*, Teil I, vol. 3/I, pp. 193f.

122. Eva Braun, diary, March 4, 1935, in Gun, *Eva Braun*, pp. 85–86. See also Goebbels,

diary entry, March 4, 1935 ("Midnight together in Berlin"), in *Die Tagebücher von Joseph Goebbels*, Teil I, vol. 3/I, pp. 193f. According to Goebbels, Hitler sat with him at the hotel before his departure.

123. Paul Schmidt, *Statist auf diplomatischer Bühne 1923–1945* (Bonn, 1953), pp. 295f.

124. See Kershaw, *Hitler 1889–1936*, p. 550.

125. See Eva Braun, diary, March 16, 1935, in Gun, *Eva Braun*, p. 87. See also Goebbels, diary entry, March 16, 1935, in *Die Tagebücher von Joseph Goebbels*, Teil I, vol. 3/I, p. 200, which says Hitler "suddenly" returned to Berlin that morning.

126. See Eva Braun, diary, March 11, 1935, in Gun, *Eva Braun*, pp. 86–87. The Czech-German movie star Anny Ondra presumably stopped in Munich to promote her movie *Knock-out*, produced by Bavaria Film AG (with Ondra-Lamac-Film GmbH).

127. Max Schmeling, *Erinnerungen* (Frankfurt am Main, 1977), pp. 275ff.

128. Ibid., pp. 293f. In the same year, Bavaria Film AG in Munich produced the documentary film *Schmeling gegen Hamas* [Schmeling vs. Hamas]: see Dorothea Friedrich, *Max Schmeling und Anny Ondra: Ein Doppelleben* (Berlin, 2001). In the Nazi state, the "trained, healthy body fit for service" became the "epitome of the German, Aryan person"; see Ralf Schäfer, "Fit für den Führer," in *Vorwärts-Zeitblende* 3 (April 2007).

129. William L. Shirer, *Berlin Diary: The Journal of a Foreign Correspondent, 1934–1941* (Baltimore, 2002 [1st ed., New York, 1941]), p. 31; Eva Braun, diary, March 16, 1935, in Gun, *Eva Braun*, p. 87. See also Kershaw, *Hitler 1889–1936*, pp. 550f.

130. Earlier, the hotel was home to meetings of the "Germanenorden," an anti-Semitic group founded in 1912. The hotel still stands at 17 Maximilianstrasse, under the name Kempinski Four Seasons. See "Projekt eines NS-Dokumentationszentrums in München," http://www.stmuk.bayern.de/blz/gutachten.pdf.

131. Eva Braun, diary, April 1, 1935, in Gun, *Eva Braun*, p. 87. According to Goebbels, Hitler arrived in Munich only on that Sunday (diary entry, April 1, 1935, in *Die Tagebücher von Joseph Goebbels*, Teil I, vol. 3/I, pp. 210f.)

132. Albert Speer, quoted in Fest, *Die unbeantwortbaren Fragen*, pp. 84f.

133. Schmidt, *Statist auf diplomatischer Bühne*, p. 307.

134. See Thamer, *Der Nationalsozialismus*, pp. 286ff.

135. See Richard Walther Darré, *Aufzeichnungen 1945–1948*, vol. 3, Bl. 407f., ED 110, IfZ Munich. Darré's statements cannot be verified and are clearly based on rumor. He even says that "Eva Braun's star" began to rise only in 1935, after Laffert turned Hitler down (Bl. 408).

136. See Stephan Malinowski, *Vom König zum Führer: Deutscher Adel und Nationalsozialismus* (Berlin, 2003), pp. 554f. See also Heinz Höhne, *Der Orden unter dem Totenkopf: Die Geschichte der SS* (Bindlach, 1990 [1st ed., Munich, 1984]), p. 127; Joachimsthaler, *Hitlers Liste*, pp. 203ff.

137. See Sigrid v. Laffert, NSDAP-Questionnaire, Gau Berlin, May 9, 1938, BA PK [formerly Berlin Document Center], G0424, Bl. 2370/71. The place of residence is given there as 11 Margaretenstrasse in Berlin W. 9.

138. See Heinz Linge, *Bis zum Untergang: Als Chef des Persönlichen Dienstes bei Hitler*, ed. Werner Maser (Munich, 1982), p. 97; "Kundgebung 1. Mai 1934, Berlin, Tempel-hofer Feld," in Heinrich Hoffmann Photo Archive, hoff-9030, BSB Munich.

139. In 1940, Sigrid von Laffert married the diplomat Johannes Bernhard Graf von Wel-czek, who became the attaché of the German Embassy in Madrid in 1941.

140. See Dr. Dieter Leithäuser, "Der Stimmbandpolyp des A. H. Patient A., zwischen Tinnitus und Heiserkeit," http://www.zieleit.de/artikel/spurensuche/0001.html (last update: 8/20/2000). Eicken received an honorarium of 260,000 reichsmarks for the procedure. Cf. "Hitler's Throat," *Time*, November 14, 1938, which quotes Eicken as saying: "The Chancellor had convinced that he had cancer." See also Speer, *Inside the Third Reich*, p. 104; Kershaw, *Hitler 1889–1936*, pp. 549f.

141. Eva Braun, diary, May 28, 1935, in Gun, *Eva Braun*, p. 90.

142. See Goebbels, diary entry of May 29, 1935, in *Die Tagebücher von Joseph Goebbels*, Teil I, vol. 3/I, p. 239. Henriette von Schirach mentions only one suicide attempt by Eva Braun, in *Der Preis der Herrlichkeit*, p. 25.

6. The Myth of the "Führer," or Herr Hitler in Private

1. See Gun, *Eva Braun*, p. 102; Schroeder, *Er war mein Chef*, p. 164. See also Eva Braun, registration card, August 24, 1935, Az. 3012/3231.0/2009, State Archives, Munich.

2. Hitler's sister Paula, however, admitted after the war that she met Eva Braun for the first time at the 1934 NSDAP convention ("Besprechung zwischen Herrn Albrecht und Frl. Paula Hitler," Berchtesgaden, May 26, 1945, in MA 1298/10, microfilm, Various Documents DJ-13 [David Irving], IfZ Munich).

3. See Peter Reichel, *Der schöne Schein des Dritten Reiches: Faszination und Gewalt des Faschismus*, 3rd ed. (Munich and Vienna, 1996), pp. 116ff. See also Siegfried Zelnhefer, *Die Reichsparteitag der NSDAP* (Nürnberg, 1991), likewise Markus Urban, *Die Konsensfabrik: Funktion und Wahrnehmung der NS-Reichsparteitag 1933–1941* (Göttingen, 2007), pp. 64ff.

4. "Gesetz über das Reichsbürgerrecht" and "Gesetz zum Schutz des deutschen Blutes und der deutschen Ehre," in Reichsgesetzblatt 1935 I, pp. 1,146–1,147. See Kershaw, *Hitler 1889–1936*, pp. 566ff.

5. See Heinrich Hoffmann Photo Archive, hoff-11588, BSB Munich.

6. On the expansion of Hoffman's business, see Rudolf Herz, *Hoffmann & Hitler*, pp. 52ff.: "On March 1, 1943, there were more than three hundred people employed in the main office and ten sub-offices." Sales reached over 15 million reichsmarks in 1943.

7. See Hanfstaengl, *Zwischen Weissem und Braunem Haus*, pp. 359f. See also an-nouncement for the "Begrüssungsansprache des Auslandspressechefs der NSDAP," in Hanfstaengl Papers, Ana 405, box 27, file 1935, BSB. See also Sigmund, *Die Frauen der Nazis*, p. 254. Cf. *Reichsparteitag 1935: Programm, Polizeiliche Anord-nungen, Sonstiges*, ed. Polizeidirekton Nürnberg-Fürth, State Archives, Nuremberg, pp. 1ff.

8. See *Reichsparteitag 1935*, p. 6.

9. However, Speer wrote to George L. Mosse on March 5, 1973: "The cathedral of light was displayed for the first time during the 1935 convention, at the rally of Party functionaries, after an earlier attempt on Bückeberg the previous year (at the harvest festival) failed due to insufficient resources. There were only movie spotlights available." Albert Speer to George L. Mosse, n.p., March 5, 1973 (carbon copy), including "Anmerkungen zu [Notes to] George L. Mosse," p. 4, in Albert Speer Papers, N 1340/39, BA Koblenz. See also Kershaw, *Hitler 1889–1936*, p. 568.

10. Herbert Döhring's statements appear in *Der Berghof—Hitler privat*, parts 1 and 2 (DVD), ZeitReisen Verlag (Bochum, 2009).

11. Schroeder, *Er war mein Chef*, pp. 164f. Cf. Zdral, *Die Hitlers*, pp. 112ff.

12. Schroeder, *Er war mein Chef*, p. 165. See also Hanfstaengl, *Hitler: The Missing Years*, pp. 273–274. Hanfstaengl there claims, in the context of Eva Braun's appearance at the 1935 convention: "Magda Goebbels, who thought she was the one woman to whom Hitler ought to pay attention, was ill-advised enough to make some disparaging remark [about Eva], which aroused Hitler to a fury. Magda was forbidden to enter the Chancellery for months. . . . In the end she was received again, but there was always a rivalry between the two women. . . . Each of them [stayed] in the besieged Führer-bunker as long as the other: to the end." Joachimsthaler says as well, referring to Julius Schaub, that Eva Braun sat with Magda Goebbels among others on the VIP platform (*Hitlers Liste*, p. 456). In Anja Klabunde's biography, however, there is no indication that Magda Goebbels was even at the convention, since she was very pregnant at the time; she checked into a Berlin hospital clinic even before the end of the convention, on September 15, 1935 (*Magda Goebbels*, p. 229).

13. Angela Hammitzsch [née Raubal] to Rudolf Hess, Oberlössnitz-Dresden, May 22, 1936 (original), in Rudolf Hess Papers J 1211 (–) 1993/300, vol. 6, file 90, BA Bern.

14. For example, it has been claimed that Hitler threw his half-sister out of the house because she advocated for one of the victims after the "Röhm Putsch" of June 30, 1934. See Henrik Eberle and Matthias Uhl, eds., *Das Buch Hitler: Geheimdossier des NKWD für Josef W. Stalin, zusammengestellt aufgrund der Verhörprotokolle des Persönlichen Adjutanten Hitlers, Otto Günsche, und des Kammerdieners Heinz Linge* (Bergisch Gladbach, 2005 [1st ed., Moscow, 1948/1949]), pp. 101f., and Linge, *Bis zum Untergang*, p. 79.

15. See the "Führer's" invitation to Marga Himmler for the NSDAP convention of September 10–16, 1935, in Nuremberg, in Himmler Papers, N1126/20, Fol. 1, BA Koblenz; Hotel Kaiserhof Guest List, in Himmler Papers, N1126/20, Fol. 1, BA Koblenz. Eva Braun's name does not appear on the list, nor does Magda Goebbels's. See also Joachimsthaler, *Hitlers Liste*, p. 456, which says that Angela Raubal met Eva Braun at the Hotel Kaiserhof.

16. See "Adjutantur des Führers, 20. Juni 1936," H 124 00 363 (54), in *Akten der Partei-Kanzlei der NSDAP*.

17. See "Eva Braun im Kreise der Mitarbeiter und Freunde Heinrich Hoffmanns auf einer Fotografie anlässlich seines Geburtstages am 12. September 1935," in Heinrich Hoffmann Photo Archive, hoff-11583/hoff-11588, BSB Munich.
18. Ilse Hess to Helene Hess, Hohenlychen, August 28, 1935 (carbon copy), in Rudolf Hess Papers, J 1211 (–) 1993/300, vol. 17, file 226 (H–Z), Swiss Federal Archives, Bern.
19. Hanfstaengl, *Zwischen Weissem und Braunem Haus*, p. 359.
20. Lambert, *The Lost Life of Eva Braun*.
21. Hanfstaengl, *Zwischen Weissem und Braunem Haus*, pp. 243 and 359.
22. See Plöckinger, *Geschichte eines Buches*, pp. 30 and 36; Ernst Hanfstaengl, *Hitler: The Missing Years* (London, 1957), p. 127. See also Conradi, *Hitler's Piano Player*, pp. 77ff.
23. Ernst Hanfstaengl to State Secretary Lammers, London, December 9 [and 24], 1937, in R 43 II/889b, Bl. 20 and 22, National Archive [Bundesarchiv, or BA], Berlin (hereafter cited as BA Berlin); Ernst Hanfstaengl to Julius Streicher, London, December 19, 1937, in R 43 II/889b, Bl. 25–31, BA Berlin. See also Conradi, *Hitler's Piano Player*, pp. 241ff.
24. See Conradi, *Hitler's Piano Player*, pp. 341ff. See also Office of Strategic Services, "Adolf Hitler," December 3, 1942, p. 4, in CIA Special Collections, National Archives of the United States, Washington, DC; and Michael S. Bell, "The Worldview of Franklin D. Roosevelt: France, Germany, and the United States Involvement in World War II in Europe" (dissertation, University of Maryland, College Park, 2004), pp. 333 and 393.
25. See here Leonidas E. Hill, "The Published Political Memoirs of Leading Nazis, 1933–1945," in *Political Memoir: Essays on the Politics of Memory*, ed. George Egerton (London, 1994), pp. 225ff.
26. See Gun, *Eva Braun*, p. 103; Fritz [Friedrich] Braun, statement of December 1, 1947, Öffentliche Sitzung der Spruchkammer München, in Denazification Court Records, box 188, State Archives, Munich.
27. See Gun, *Eva Braun*, p. 103.
28. Henrietta von Schirach, *Frauen um Hitler*, pp. 227f. The date of the incident cannot be determined from Schirach's account.
29. See Gun, *Eva Braun*, pp. 101–104.
30. See Richard J. Evans, *David Irving, Hitler, and Holocaust Denial: Pressures on Hitler's Entourage After the War*, electronic edition http://www.holocaustdenialontrial.org/trial/defense/evans/530bB.
31. See Gun, *Eva Braun*, p. 104.
32. "Hitlers Schwiegereltern vor Gericht: Vater Braun war gegen das 'schlampige Verhältnis,' " *Die Welt*, August 2, 1947, p. 3.
33. "Der öffentliche Kläger bei der Spruchkammer, Munich, 9. Juli 1947, Klageschrift gegen Franziska Katharina Braun," in Denazification Court Records, box 188, State Archives, Munich.
34. "Hitlers Schwiegereltern vor Gericht"

35. Fritz Braun, statement of December 1, 1947. A Czech newspaper had published a picture of Eva Braun, describing her as "Hitler's Madame Pompadour." See Joachimsthaler, *Hitlers Liste*, p. 426.

36. "Hitlers Schwiegereltern vor Gericht."

37. Fritz Braun, statement of December 1, 1947.

38. See Gun, *Eva Braun*, p. 105; Joachimsthaler, *Hitlers Liste*, pp. 424f. See also Sigmund, *Die Frauen der Nazis*, pp. 252f.

39. See the photograph of Königsplatz, Munich, September 5, 1935, in Heinrich Hoffmann Photo Archive, hoff-11463, BSB Munich.

40. See Speer, *Inside the Third Reich*, pp. 88.; Kershaw, *Hitler 1889–1936*, p. 574.

41. See Sigmund, *Die Frauen der Nazis*, p. 252.

42. Adolf Hitler, "Mein privates Testament, 29. April 1945," in Werner Maser, *Hitlers Briefe und Notizen: Sein Weltbild in handschriftlichen Dokumenten* (Düsseldorf, 1988), pp. 213ff. See also Gun, *Eva Braun*, pp. 266, where the will is mentioned, but not the passage referring to Franziska Braun.

43. Fritz Braun, statement of December 1, 1947. See also Eberle and Uhl, *Das Buch Hitler*, p. 352.

44. See Zdral, *Die Hitlers*, p. 207. See also Jürgen Hillesheim, *Hitlers Schwester Paula Wolf und das "Dritte Reich"* (Berlin, 1992).

45. Thus she wrote to Ilse Hess that Gauleiter Bürckel must "not disregard the laws and regulations still in effect. I know that Bürckel is in a difficult position, but his relations with his Austrians will not improve if incidents like this continue to arise." Angela Hammitzsch to Ilse Hess, Dresden, January 22, 1940 (original), in Rudolf Hess Papers, J 1211 (–) 1993/300, vol. 6, file 90, BA Bern.

46. See Winfried Müller, *Schulpolitik in Bayern im Spannungsfeld von Kultusbürokratie und Besatzungsmacht 1945–1949* (Munich, 1995), p. 74.

47. See *PG—Zum Mitgliedschaftswesen der NSDAP* (no year), BA Koblenz; Christoph Wagner, *Entwicklung, Herrschaft und Untergang der nationalsozialistischen Bewegung in Passau 1920–1945* (Berlin, 2007), pp. 151f.

48. See Müller, *Schulpolitik in Bayern*, pp. 74f. In 1937, Wagner ordered that every teacher must participate "in every cooperative effort and every community organization in the Party or the State." Fritz Braun himself later said that he faced increasing difficulties at his technical school (Fritz Braun, written declaration of July 21, 1947, in Denazification Court Records, box 188, State Archives, Munich). See Gun, *Eva Braun*, p. 149, according to which Fritz Braun had "obstinately refused" until then to join the party.

49. See Gun, *Eva Braun*, p. 159.

50. Kershaw, *Hitler 1936–1945*, p. 273.; Peter Steinbach and Johannes Tuchel, "Georg Elser," http://www.georg-elser.de/Steinbach_Tuchel_Elser_Politische_Koepfe.pdf. A novel by Wolfgang Brenner, *Führerlos* [Führerless] (Berlin, 2008), addresses the question of what Hitler's death at this point in time might have meant for the Nazi state and for the fate of Eva Braun.

7. THE MISTRESS AND THE INNER CIRCLE

1. Speer, *Inside the Third Reich*, pp. 91, 94. See also Joachim Fest, *Speer: Eine Biographie* (Berlin, 1999), p. 14; Susanne Willems, *Der entsiedelte Jude: Albert Speers Wohnungsmarktpolitik für den Berliner Hauptstadtbau* (Berlin, 2002), pp. 20ff.

2. Margret Nissen, *Sind Sie die Tochter Speer?*, p. 25.

3. Ibid.

4. Ibid., pp. 23f.

5. See ibid., p. 26.

6. Margarete Speer, quoted in Sereny, *Speer*, p. 193.

7. Margarete Speer, quoted in Fest, *Die unbeantwortbaren Fragen*, pp. 142 and 171.

8. See Speer, *Inside the Third Reich*, pp. 88 and 100. See also Speer, *Spandau: The Secret Diaries*, p. 132.

9. Speer, *Inside the Third Reich*, p. 88.

10. Speer, *Albert Speer: Die Kransberg-Protokolle 1945*, p. 119.

11. Speer, *Inside the Third Reich*, p. 93. See also Speer, quoted in Sereny, *Albert Speer*, p. 109: "I liked her right away and later we became good friends; she could use a friend."

12. Fest, *Speer*, pp. 14f. and 462f.

13. Margarete Speer, quoted in Sereny, *Albert Speer*, p. 193.

14. See Sereny, *Albert Speer*, p. 405. Unlike Magda Goebbels, Margarete Speer—like Eva Braun—was not a member of the NSDAP.

15. See Sereny, *Albert Speer*, p. 235. See also Speer, *Inside the Third Reich*, pp. 146 and 257.

16. See Ulf Schmidt, *Karl Brandt: The Nazi Doctor; Medicine and Power in the Third Reich* (London, 2007), p. 88.

17. Albert Speer explained that Hitler, although he never participated in sports, "thought it was very important that youth be thoroughly trained athletically." This corresponded to the ideal he drew from his understanding of ancient Greek culture See Speer, *Albert Speer: Die Kransberg-Protokolle 1945*, p. 118. See also Schroeder, *Er war mein Chef*, pp. 173f. and 265.

18. See Schmidt, *Karl Brandt*, pp. 50 and 51.

19. See Schroeder, *Er war mein Chef*, pp. 173f. and 265; Schmidt, *Karl Brandt*, p. 51.

20. See Albert Schweitzer, *Die Ehrfurcht vor dem Leben: Grundtexte aus fünf Jahrzehnten*, 8th ed. (Munich, 2003), pp. 50ff. See also Schmidt, *Karl Brandt*, pp. 76ff. and 83f.

21. Karl Brandt, "Das Problem Hitler, Nr. 2," September 27, 1945, p. 6, in Kleine Erwerbung 441–3, BA Koblenz, pp. 75 and 80. See also Ulrich Herbert, *Best: Biographische Studien über Radikalismus, Weltanschauung und Vernunft 1903–1989*, 2nd ed. (Bonn, 1996), pp. 42–45.

22. See Volker Hess, "Die Medizinische Fakultät im Zeichen der 'Führeruniversität,'" in *Die Berliner Universität in der NS-Zeit*. vol. 1, *Strukturen und Personen*, ed. Christoph Jahr (Stuttgart, 2005), pp. 46f.; Schmidt, *Karl Brandt*, p. 73.

23. See "Gruppenbild der Hochzeitsgesellschaft mit Hitler in Uniform, Göring, Wilhelm Brückner und dessen Freundin, der Münchner Künstlerin Sofie Stork," in Heinrich Hoffmann Photo Archive, hoff-8918, BSB Munich.

24. See Schmidt, *Karl Brandt*, pp. 95ff. The decision to make Brandt his accompanying physician came after Hitler's visit to Italy to see Mussolini in 1934. From that point on, Brandt accompanied Hitler's travels. See U.S. Strategic Bombing Survey, APO 413, Interview No. 64, Dr. med. Karl Brandt, 17./18. Juni 1945, p. 456, in Irving Collection, ED 100, vol. 1002, USSBS: Interrogation Reports, vol. 2, IfZ Munich.

25. See Speer, *Albert Speer: Die Kransberg-Protokolle 1945*, p. 145; Schmidt, *Karl Brandt*, p. 131.

26. See ibid., pp. 104f. Later, Brandt moved into the Bechstein Villa in the spring of 1935 and Speer moved there that summer. At the end of May 1937, Speer moved into a studio building near the Berghof that he had designed himself (*Inside the Third Reich*, p. 84). See Ulrich Chaussy und Christoph Püschner, *Nachbar Hitler: Führerkult und Heimatzerstörung am Obersalzberg*, 5th ed. (Berlin, 2005), p. 91.

27. Speer later commented that he was "happy to have been granted so obvious a distinction and been admitted to the most intimate circle," even if life in a fenced-in compound was not to his taste (*Inside the Third Reich*, pp. 84 and 149). See also Hamann, *Winifred Wagner oder Hitlers Bayreuth*, pp. 424 and 557f.

28. See Karl Brandt, "Das Problem Hitler, Nr. 2," September 27, 1945, p. 5, in Kleine Erwerbung 441-3, BA Koblenz. See also Winfried Süss, *Der "Volkskörper" im Krieg: Gesundheitspolitik, Gesundheitsverhältnisse und Krankenmord im nationalsozialistischen Deutschland 1939–1945* (Munich, 2003), p. 93; Fest, *Die unbeantwortbaren Fragen*, p. 200. In *Spandau: The Secret Diaries* Speer says, in an entry dated July 28, 1949, that Hitler had "forfeited all claim on [his, i.e., Speer's] loyalty; loyalty to a monster cannot be" (p. 134).

29. See Schmidt, *Karl Brandt*, pp. 118ff.

30. Ibid., pp. 154ff. and 159ff.

31. Ibid., pp. 177ff. According to Schmidt, there are practically no documents about the conversations between Brandt and Hitler; almost all Hitler's instructions were given verbally (p. 224).

32. See Rüdiger Hachtmann and Winfried Süss, eds., *Hitlers Kommissare: Sondergewalten in der nationalsozialistischen Diktatur*, Beiträge zur Geschichte des Nationalsozialismus, vol. 22 (Göttingen, 2006), pp. 12f. and 19ff. See also Willems, *Der entsiedelte Jude*, pp. 77ff. 182ff.

33. Cf. Schmidt, *Karl Brandt*, p. 72: "they chose to be" unaware of the truth. According to Schmidt, "ignorance was at the core of" both Eva Braun's and Karl Brandt's "relationships with Hitler."

34. See Fest, *Speer*, p. 65; Fest, *Die unbeantwortbaren Fragen*, pp. 54 and 86. But even Fest, in the end, cannot avoid remarking that Speer was clearly "among Hitler's most radical followers" (p. 28).

35. See "Brandt. Report on Hitler," in Headquarters Military Intelligence Service Cen-

ter, U.S. Army, APO 757, OI Special Report 36, "Adolf Hitler: A Composite Picture (2 April 1947)," F135/4, p. 6, in David Irving Collection, "Adolph Hitler 1944–1953," vol. 4, IfZ Munich, p. 692. Speer quotes this sentiment of Hitler's, which he supposedly also expressed in Eva Braun's presence, in *Inside the Third Reich*, where he says Hitler told him: "A highly intelligent man should take a primitive and stupid woman" (*Inside the Third Reich*, p. 92).

36. Karl Brandt, quoted in Schmidt, *Karl Brandt*, p. 72.

37. See "Originalnotizen von P. E. Schramm über Hitler, gemacht während der Befragungen von Hitlers Leibärzten, Haus 'Alaska,' d. h. Altersheim für Lehrerinnen im Taunus, Sommer 1945 in USA-Kriegsgefangenschaft," p. 169, in Kleine Erwerbung 441–3, BA Koblenz. Under "Eva Braun," Schramm notes: "Annoyance among entourage"; "has got nothing in life"; "had to be there"; "taste, discreet"; "absolutely no pol[itical] influence"; "runs people down"; "she hated Hoffmann"; "disapproved of Morell."

38. See "Gruppenbild auf einer Tribüne: Anni Brandt, Eva Braun, Erna Hoffmann, Viktoria von Dirksen (in der Reihe dahinter Unity Mitford), Reichsparteitag der NSDAP 6.–13. September 1937, Hauptmarkt Nürnberg," in Heinrich Hoffmann Photo Archive, hoff-16020, BSB Munich.

39. See Lang, *Der Sekretär*, pp. 49ff.

40. See ibid., p. 52.

41. See Martin Bormann, *Leben gegen Schatten* (Paderborn, 1996), pp. 12f.

42. For example, there is the following passage in a book by her father (Walter Buch, *Des nationalsozialistischen Menschen Ehre und Ehrenschutz*, 5th ed. [Munich, 1939], p. 15): "The National Socialist has recognized that the Jew is not a human being. The Jew is a putrid sign of decay."

43. Fest, *Das Gesicht des Dritten Reiches*, p. 366. See in this regard Gerda Bormann to Martin Bormann, Obersalzberg, February 7, 1945, in Martin Bormann, *The Bormann Letters: The Private Correspondence between Martin Bormann and His Wife from January 1943 to April 1945*, ed. Hugh Trevor-Roper (London, 1954), pp. 176f.

44. See Speer, *Albert Speer: Die Kransberg-Protokolle 1945*, pp. 136ff.

45. See *Akten der Partei-Kanzlei der* NSDAP, Teil I, Regesten, vol. 1, pp. viii ff.

46. See Schmidt, *Karl Brandt*, p. 298.

47. Darré, *Aufzeichnungen*, p. 295.

48. Schroeder, *Er war mein Chef*, pp. 30ff.

49. See "Aufzeichnungen des Reichspressechefs Dr. Dietrich" (copy), in Kleine Erwerbung 441–3, p. 16, BA Koblenz.

50. See Robert Ley, "Abschied," in "Aufzeichnungen in Nürnberg 1945," p. 1, Robert Ley Papers, N 1468/4, BA Koblenz. See also Kershaw, *Hitler 1889–1936*, p. 476.

51. See Robert Ley, "Gedanken um den Führer," in "Aufzeichnungen in Nürnberg 1945," pp. 13ff, Robert Ley Papers, N 1468/4, BA Koblenz.

52. See Hoffmann, "Mein Beruf," p. 59.

53. See Robert Ley, "Gedanken um den Führer," pp. 13ff.

54. Cf. Speer, *Inside the Third Reich*, pp. 87 and 93; Gun, *Eva Braun*, p. 136; Lang, *Der Sekretär*, pp. 108f.

8. LIFE ON THE OBERSALZBERG

1. See Reinhard Spitzy, *So haben wir das Reich verspielt: Bekenntnisse eines Illegalen*, 4th ed. (Munich, 1994), pp. 128f.
2. See Henriette von Schirach, *Frauen um Hitler*, p. 227.
3. See Horst Möller et al., eds., *Die tödliche Utopie: Bilder, Texte, Dokumente, Daten zum Dritten Reich* (Munich and Berlin, 1999), pp. 62f.; Chaussy and Püschner, *Nachbar Hitler*, p. 45.
4. See Schroeder, *Er war mein Chef*, p. 166. The rumor circulated among the staff that Eva Braun's and Hitler's rooms were connected by a "hidden door": Eva Braun "had a room that was connected to Hitler's bedroom by a secret door" (Therese Linke, unpublished handwritten memoir, no year [from the 1950s], in ZS 3135, vol. 1, IfZ Munich, p. 9).
5. Albert Speer to Werner Maser, n.p., January 30, 1967 (carbon copy), in Albert Speer Papers, N 1340/37, BA Koblenz. Cf. Speer, *Albert Speer: Die Kransberg-Protokolle 1945*, p. 146.
6. Martin Bormann to Dr. Friedrich Wolffhardt, Führer Headquarters, December 27, 1941, U.S. National Archives, Washington National Records Center, Suitland, MD, quoted in Beierl, *Geschichte des Kehlsteins*, p. 8.
7. Ibid., p. 9.
8. Starting in 1934, Department 1 of the Reich Security Service (Reichssicherheitsdienst, RSD) and the SS-Begleitkommando under SS-Standartenführer Johann Rattenhuber were responsible for Hitler's security. See Möller, ed., *Die tödliche Utopie*, p. 67; Chaussy and Püschner, *Nachbar Hitler*, p. 130. See also Peter Hoffmann, *Die Sicherheit des Diktators: Hitlers Leibwachen, Schutzmassnahmen, Residenzen, Hauptquartiere* (Munich and Zürich, 1975).
9. See Schroeder, *Er war mein Chef*, pp. 16 and 171.
10. Therese Linke, unpublished handwritten memoir, p. 9.
11. See Chaussy and Püschner, *Nachbar Hitler*, pp. 146ff.
12. Speer, *Albert Speer: Die Kransberg-Protokolle 1945*, p. 100.
13. Christa Schroeder to Johanna Nusser, Führer Headquarters, August 30, 1941 (original), in ED 524, IfZ Munich. Fritz Wiedemann similarly states: "There were always the same people, proof of the consistency of the company at table" (undated notes, including "Obersalzberg," (transcription), in Fritz Wiedemann Papers, Kleine Erwerbung Nr. 671, vol. 4, BA Koblenz.
14. Fritz Wiedemann, as cited in note 13, above. Hitler, according to Wiedemann, never worried about his own personal security. He repeatedly used to "rush off on a drive somewhere or another, or even to a play, without telling his security staff."
15. Fritz Wiedemann, undated notes, as cited in note 13, above.
16. See Schroeder, *Er war mein Chef*, p. 186.

17. Fritz Wiedemann, undated notes, as cited in note 13, above.

18. Ibid. Wiedemann first mentioned Eva Braun as well only in his memoir published in 1964: *Der Mann, der Feldherr werden wollte: Erlebnisse und Erfahrungen des Vorgesetzten Hitlers im 1; Weltkrieg und seines späteren Persönlichen Adjutanten* (Velbert, 1964), p. 79.

19. See Below, *Als Hitlers Adjutant,* pp. 50f.

20. State Secretary and Head of the Chancellery (Lammers) to the Minister of Finance (Lutz Graf Schwerin von Krosigk), Berchtesgaden, September 11, 1936 (copy), in R 43/4326, Bl. 5 u. 6, BA Berlin.

21. See Thamer, *Der Nationalsozialismus,* pp. 183f. See also *Akten der Reichskanzlei, Regierung Hitler 1933–1945,* vol. 5, *Die Regierung Hitler 1938,* ed. Historischen Kommission bei der Bayerischen Akademie der Wissenschaften und dem Bundesarchiv (Munich, 2008).

22. See Kershaw, *Hitler 1936–1945,* p. 32. The "Private Chancellery of the Führer and Chancellor," run by Albert Bormann, Martin Bormann's brother, was Chief Department 1 of the "Chancellery of the Führer." It lost its significance, as did the "Chancellery," when the "Party Chancellery" run by Martin Bormann (a renaming of the "Deputy Führer's" staff after Rudolf Hess's disappearance) was established in 1941.

23. See State Secretary and Head of the Chancellery (Lammers) to Retired Captain Wiedemann (adjutant to the Führer), Berlin, August 18, 1938 (copy), in Rep. 502, NG-1465, Bl. 739, State Archives, Nuremberg. Lammers writes that he has ordered payment of the "41 receipts" that Weidemann sent over from the Munich art dealer Maria Almas, totaling 284,550 reichsmarks. See also Hanns Christian Löhr, *Das Braune Haus der Kunst: Hitler und der "Sonderauftrag Linz"* (Berlin, 2005), p. 35; and Lutz Graf Schwerin von Krosigk, *Staatsbankrott: Die Geschichte der Finanzpolitik des Deutschen Reiches von 1920 bis 1945, geschrieben vom letzten Reichsfinanzminister* (Göttingen, 1974), pp. 241f.

24. See *Völkischer Beobachter,* January 19, 1937, in R 43 II/1036, Bl. 103, BA Berlin. See also Franz Alfred Six, ed., *Dokumente der deutschen Politik: Das Reich Adolf Hitlers,* vol. 5 (Berlin, 1940).

25. State Secretary and Head of the Chancellery (Lammers) to the Minister of Finance (Lutz Graf Schwerin von Krosigk), Berchtesgaden, September 11, 1936 (copy), in R 43/4326, Bl. 6, BA Berlin.

26. See Chaussy and Püschner, *Nachbar Hitler,* p. 132.

27. See Wiedemann, *Der Mann der Feldherr werden wollte,* pp. 68f. This was also a try for Party work, according to Otto Dietrich (*12 Jahre mit Hitler,* p. 45).

28. Reichsminister and Head of the Chancellery to the personal adjutant of the Führer and Chancellor (SA-Obergruppenführer Brückner), Berchtesgaden, October 21, 1938 (copy), in R 43 II/888b, F 1, Bl. 42, BA Berlin.

29. Reichsminister and Head of the Chancellery to Economic Minister Walther Funk, Berchtesgaden, October 24, 1938 (copy), in R 43 II/888b, F 1, Bl. 43, BA Berlin.

30. Reichsminister and Head of the Chancellery to the personal adjutant of the Führer

and Chancellor (SA-Obergruppenführer Brückner), Berchtesgaden, October 21, 1938.

31. See Jörg Osterloh, "Nationalsozialistische Judenverfolgung im Reichsgau Sudetenland 1918–1945" (dissertation, Munich, 2006), p. 13.

32. See Reichsminister and Head of the Chancellery to the personal adjutant of the Führer and Chancellor (SA-Obergruppenführer Brückner), Berchtesgaden, October 25, 1938 (copy), in R 43 II/886a, F 3, Bl. 128f., BA Berlin. On Bl. 129, there is a handwritten note mentioning resubmission on October 27 and 31. Lammers, who clearly still had not received an answer from Brückner after two days, let his assistants remind him twice, presumably to try to get an answer by phone.

33. See Kershaw, *Hitler 1889–1936*, p. 535; *Hitler 1936–1945*, p. 186; *The "Hitler Myth": Image and Reality in the Third Reich* (Oxford, 1987), p. 121. Kershaw writes that Hitler, from 1935–1936 on, withdrew more and more from domestic government activities and turned over political business to "chancelleries, ministries, and special plenipotentiary organizations." Cf. Martin Moll, ed., *"Führer-Erlasse" 1939–1945* (Stuttgart, 1997), p. 11. Moll maintains that this claim is based not least on a "giant gap in the sources with respect to civilian matters."

34. See Wilhelm Treue, "Das Dritte Reich und die Westmächte auf dem Balkan," *Vierteljahrshefte für Zeitgeschichte* 1 (1953), no. 1, p. 61. Cf. Dilek Barlas, *Etatism & Diplomacy in Turkey: Economic & Foreign Policy Strategies in an Uncertain World, 1929–1939, The Ottoman Empire and Its Heritage*, vol. 14, (Leiden, 1998), pp. 188f.

35. See Moll, *"Führer-Erlasse,"* pp. 26ff.

36. See Gun, *Eva Braun*, p. 126.

37. Wiedemann, *Der Mann, der Feldherr werden wollte*, p. 69.

38. Speer, *Albert Speer: Die Kransberg-Protokolle 1945*, p. 100. How this process of reaching a decision and converting it to action actually played out remains unexplained. See in this regard Moll, *"Führer-Erlasse,"* p. 26.

39. See Hans Mommsen, "Hitlers Stellung im nationalsozialistischen Herrschaftssystem," in Hirschfeld and Kettenacker, eds., *Der "Führerstaat,"* pp. 43–72; Carl Schmitt, "Der Zugang zum Machthaber: Ein zentrales verfassungsrechtliches Problem," in *Verfassungsrechtliche Aufsätze aus den Jahren 1924–1954*, 2nd ed. (Berlin, 1973), pp. 430ff.

40. See Fest, *Hitler*, p. 718; Knopp, *Hitlers Frauen*, p. 45.

41. Speer, *Albert Speer: Die Kransberg-Protokolle 1945*, p. 144.

42. See Peter Longerich, *Heinrich Himmler: Biographie* (Munich, 2008), pp. 760ff. Longerich likewise attributes to Himmler an "emotional void" due to insecurity and a deficient emotional life (p. 763).

43. See Kershaw, *Hitler 1936–1945*, p. 104; Speer, *Albert Speer: Die Kransberg-Protokolle 1945*, pp. 233f.

44. See Peter Longerich, *Hitlers Stellvertreter: Führung der Partei und Kontrolle des Staatsapparates durch den Stab Hess und die Partei-Kanzlei Bormann* (Munich, 1992), p. 109.

45. See Evans, *David Irving, Hitler, and Holocaust Denial*, electronic edition.
46. Kershaw, *Hitler 1936–1945*, p. 34.
47. Speer, *Albert Speer: Die Kransberg-Protokolle 1945*, p. 144: "This strict separation between politics and private life on the Obersalzberg" lasted until the end of the war. Meanwhile, Speer claims in his memoir that the other "close associates" of the Nazi leadership stayed away from the Obersalzberg (*Inside the Third Reich*, p. 92).
48. See "Anni Esser, Hanni und Theodor Morell sowie Eva Braun auf einer Tribüne am Nürnberger Marktplatz, 10. Reichsparteitag der NSDAP (5.–12. September 1938)," in Heinrich Hoffmann Photo Archive, hoff-20423 and hoff-20447, BSB Munich.
49. See Heinrich Hoffmann Photo Archive, hoff-14083 and hoff-50118, BSB Munich.
50. Below, *Als Hitlers Adjutant*, p. 35.
51. Ibid., pp. 22f.
52. Hitler named Below Speer's "liaison man to Hitler" on May 22, 1944. Below's assignment was "to keep [Speer] constantly informed about the Führer's remarks" (*Inside the Third Reich*, p. 350n).
53. Below, *Als Hitlers Adjutant*, p. 81.
54. Ibid., pp. 166ff. Below admitted after the war that he heard about the Einsatzgruppen security forces' murder of Jews in 1942, in Hitler's Ukrainian headquarters in Vinnytsia; see KV Anklage, Interrogations, Rep. 502 VI B51, Nicolaus von Below, Interrogation 2786a of Nicolaus von Below, March 24, 1948, p. 10, State Archives, Nuremberg.
55. Below, *Als Hitlers Adjutant*, p. 96. See also Maria von Below, quoted in Sereny, *Albert Speer*, pp. 113ff., and Kershaw, *Hitler 1936–1945*, p. 33. Another woman in Hitler's private circle, Winifred Wagner, expressed similar outrage over Speer's *Inside the Third Reich*. No "opponent of Hitler's" could have written worse things, she said; Hitler was "always [portrayed] as a despot along petit-bourgeois lines" while Speer "completely overlooked his genius—what was in my view his demonic side as well" (quoted in Hamann, *Winifred Wagner oder Hitlers Bayreuth*, p. 592).
56. Below, *Als Hitlers Adjutant*, p. 95. See in this regard Kershaw, *Hitler 1936–1945*, pp. 136f. and 65f.
57. Below, *Als Hitlers Adjutant*, p. 370.
58. Junge, *Bis zur letzten Stunde*, p. 74.
59. Schroeder, *Er war mein Chef*, p. 196.
60. See Sofie Stork, questionnaire from May 17, 1946, as well as Sofie Stork's testimony from August 11, 1947, before the Munich Fourth District Court, in Denazification Court Records, box 1790, State Archives, Munich.
61. See the biographical details from the "Akten des Polizei-Präsidiums zu Berlin" of July 21, 1931 (copy), in N 26/2504, BA Berlin.
62. Wagener, *Hitler aus nächster Nähe*, pp. 198f.
63. Kershaw, *Hitler 1889–1936*, pp. 432f.
64. See Albert Bormann to Rudolf Hess, Berlin, June 9, 1938 (original), in Rudolf Hess Papers, J 1.211 (–) 1993/300, vol. 7, file 98, BA Bern.

65. See Conradi, *Hitler's Piano Player*, p. 231.
66. Below, *Als Hitlers Adjutant*, p. 248.
67. Wiedemann, *Der Mann, der Feldherr werden wollte*, p. 72.
68. Ibid.
69. See Lang, *Der Sekretär*, p. 97. Wilhelm Brückner's interrogation by R.M.W. Kempner on August 26, 1947, KV-Anklage, in Interrogations B 173 (Wilhelm Brückner), State Archives, Nuremberg.
70. Albert Speer, quoted in Fest, *Die unbeantwortbaren Fragen*, p. 40.
71. Below, *Als Hitlers Adjutant*, pp. 29f. Gitta Sereny concludes, in contrast, that Anni Brandt, Maria von Below, and Margarete Speer "constituted a circle of their own, unconnected with the women on Hitler's personal staff" (*Albert Speer*, p. 194).
72. See "Hitler, Otto Dietrich, Sofie Stork und Eva Braun u. a. im Freien an einem Tisch sitzend, 1934," in Heinrich Hoffmann Photo Archive, hoff-49671, BSB Munich.
73. See Sofie Stork, testimony from October 13, 1948, before the Munich Fourth District Court, quoted in Joachimsthaler, *Hitlers Liste*, pp. 500f. See also Schroeder, *Er war mein Chef*, pp. 38 and 216.
74. See daily planner, Sunday, June 19, 1938 (copy), in Albert Speer Papers, N 1340/288, BA Koblenz.
75. Below, *Als Hitlers Adjutant*, p. 248. Kannenberg's first name is given here as "Willy" (p. 440).
76. See Hamann, *Winifred Wagner oder Hitlers Bayreuth*, pp. 322 and 590.
77. Schroeder, *Er war mein Chef*, pp. 38 and 57. See also Below, *Als Hitlers Adjutant*, p. 248.
78. See Georg Birnstiel to Albert Bormann, Munich, October 27, 1939, in Denazification Court Records, box 1790 (Sofie Stork), State Archives, Munich. See also Adalbert Keis, tax advice for the H. Stork company in a document from April 17, 1947, in Denazification Court Records, box 1790, State Archives, Munich. According to this document, Sofie Stork contributed 45,000 reichsmarks to her father's business in 1937. See also in this regard Joachimsthaler, *Hitlers Liste*, pp. 502ff. By way of comparison, a skilled laborer earned an average of approximately 1,900 reichsmarks a year at the time.
79. *Akten der Partei-Kanzlei der NSDAP*, W 124 00093. A remark dated May 27, 1937, reads: "Receipt of a check from Bormann's Chancellery via Sofie Stock [sic] Munich." See also Georg Birnstiel to Albert Bormann, Munich, October 27, 1939, in Denazification Court Records, box 1790 (Sofie Stork), State Archives, Munich; similarly, "Brieftagebuch des NSKK-Brigadeführers Albert Bormann, 29. Juli 1939 bis 14. Juli 1941," in NS 24/327, BA Berlin.
80. "Brieftagebuch des NSKK-Brigadeführers Albert Bormann, 29. Juli 1939 bis 14. Juli 1941," in NS 24/327, BA Berlin.
81. Schroeder, *Er war mein Chef*, p. 38.
82. See Frank Bajohr, *Parvenüs und Profiteure: Korruption in der NS-Zeit* (Frankfurt am Main, 2001), pp. 37f.; Kershaw, *Hitler 1889–1936*, p. 674.

83. See Heinrich Hoffmann's questioning on November 13, 1946, p. 5, in Rep. 502, KV-Anklage Interrogations, H 180 (VI), State Archives, Nuremberg.

84. See Marianne Schönmann, statement from April 16, 1947, Munich District Court, quoted in Joachimsthaler, *Hitlers Liste*, p. 508. According to Schönmann's own statement, she first met Hitler after Heinrich Hoffmann's second wedding on April 18, 1934, in the photographer's house; she was still named Petzl at the time.

85. Ibid., p. 510. Hitler included Marianne Schönmann (under the name Marion Perard-Theisen) on his "gift list" as early as Christmas 1935 (ibid., p. 14).

86. See "Hochzeit Marion Schön[e]manns, 7. August 1937," in Heinrich Hoffmann Photo Archive, hoff-15850, BSB Munich.

87. Marianne Schönmann, statement from April 16, 1947, p. 510. A U.S. Army military intelligence service report determined that, according to statements from Karl Friedrich von Eberstein (member of the NSDAP and SS; Munich chief of police from 1936 to 1942), Eva Braun couldn't stand "Marion Schoenemann" and finally succeeded in getting her banned from Hitler's environment: Eberstein, "Women around Hitler," in Headquarters Military Intelligence Service Center, U.S. Army, APO 757, OI Special Report 36, "Adolf Hitler: A Composite Picture (2. April 1947)," p. 9, F135/4, in David Irving Collection, "Adolph Hitler 1944–1953," vol. 4, IfZ Munich, p. 695. Nicolaus von Below, on the other hand, recalled that Schönmann was one of Eva Braun's friends whom she brought along from Munich to the Berghof (*Als Hitlers Adjutant*, pp. 96f.).

88. See Office of U.S. Chief of Counsel for War Crimes, APO 124 A, Evidence Division, Interrogation Branch, Interrogation Summary No. 413, 4 November 1946, Nuremberg (Dr. Karl Brandt), State Archives, Nuremberg.

89. See Kershaw, *Hitler 1936–1945*, pp. 66f.

90. Walter Schellenberg, *Aufzeichnungen: Die Memoiren des letzten Geheimdienstchefs unter Hitler*, ed. Gita Petersen, newly annotated by Gerald Fleming (Wiesbaden and Munich, 1979), p. 52.

91. Schroeder, *Er war mein Chef*, p. 85.

92. See Gun, *Eva Braun*, pp. 152f.

93. See Below, *Als Hitlers Adjutant*, pp. 96f.

94. See Gerhard Paul, "Joseph Bürckel—Der rote Gauleiter," in Smelser et al., eds., *Die braune Elite II*, pp. 59ff.

95. Decree of Josef Bürckel's from March 22, 1938, quoted in Alexander Mejstrik et al., *Berufsschädigungen in der nationalsozialistischen Neuordnung der Arbeit: Vom österreichischen Berufsleben 1934 zum völkischen Schaffen 1938–1940*, Veröffentlichungen der Österreichischen Historikerkommission, Vermögensentzug während der NS-Zeit sowie Rückstellungen und Entschädigungen seit 1945 in Österreich, vol. 16 (Munich, 2004), p. 299.

96. Below, *Als Hitlers Adjutant*, p. 97. Cf. Baldur von Schirach, *Ich glaubte an Hitler* (Hamburg, 1967), pp. 267f.

97. Speer, *Inside the Third Reich*, p. 94.

98. See Doris Seidel, "Die jüdische Gemeinde Münchens 1933–1945," in *München*

arisiert: Entrechtung und Enteignung der Juden in der NS-Zeit, ed. Angelika Baumann and Andreas Heusler for the state capital of Munich (Munich, 2004), pp. 34f. On Fiehler, see Helmut M. Hanko, "Kommunalpolitik in der 'Hauptstadt der Bewegung' 1933–1935: Zwischen 'revolutionärer' Umgestaltung und Verwaltungskontinuität," in Martin Broszat et al., eds., *Bayern in der NS-Zeit: Herrschaft und Gesellschaft im Konflikt,* part 3 (Munich, 1981), pp. 334ff. and 417ff.

99. See Julia Schmideder, "Das Kaufhaus Uhlfelder," in *München arisiert,* pp. 130ff.

100. Speer, *Inside the Third Reich,* p. 94; for "sworn to silence," see the German original: Speer, *Erinnerungen,* (Frankfurt am Main and Berlin, 1993 [1st ed., 1969]), p. 108.

101. See Mejstrik et al., *Berufsschädigungen in der nationalsozialistischen Neuordnung der Arbeit,* pp. 131f.

102. See Thamer, *Der Nationalsozialismus,* p. 306. See also Lynn H. Nicholas, *Der Raub der Europa: Das Schicksal europäischer Kunstwerke im Dritten Reich* (Munich, 1995), pp. 57ff.

103. Hans Heinrich Lammers to Heinrich Himmler, Berlin, June 18, 1938, in R 43 II, 1296a, Bl. 5, BA Berlin. Cf. Löhr, *Das Braune Haus der Kunst,* pp. 22f.

104. See Haase, *Die Kunstsammlung Adolf Hitler,* pp. 16ff.; Brigitte Hamann, *Hitlers Wien: Lehrjahre eines Diktators,* 5th ed. (Munich, 2002), pp. 11ff.; Speer, *Inside the Third Reich,* p. 99.

105. See Löhr, *Das Braune Haus der Kunst,* p. 129.

106. For example, Hitler's art dealer Karl Haberstock gave Hitler's secretary Christa Schroeder an "Italian Renaissance storage bench" and a "mirror from the year 1510" with a frame "by the Italian sculptor Sanvoni," which she proudly displayed in her Berlin apartment. See Christa Schroeder to Johanna Nusser, Berlin, April 28, 1941, in ED 524, IfZ Munich; likewise Spitzy, *So haben wir das Reich verspielt,* p. 211.)

107. Heinrich Hoffmann's questioning on November 13, 1946.

108. Ibid.

109. Office of U.S. Chief of Counsel for War Crimes, APO 124 A, Evidence Division, Interrogation Branch, Interrogation Summary No. 413, 4. November 1946, Nuremberg (Dr. Karl Brandt), State Archives, Nuremberg.

110. See Nicholas, *Der Raub der Europa,* pp. 47 and 213; also Gerhard Engel, *Heeresadjutant bei Hitler 1938–1943,* ed. and annotated by Hildegard von Kotze, Schriftenreihe der Vierteljahrshefte für Zeitgeschichte, vol. 29 (Stuttgart, 1974), pp. 33f.

111. See Löhr, *Das Braune Haus der Kunst,* p. 127; Haase, *Die Kunstsammlung Adolf Hitler,* pp. 52ff. These two authors do not agree on the question of whether Maria Almas-Dietrich was a member of the NSDAP.

112. See State Secretary and Head of the Chancellery (Lammers) to Retired Captain Wiedemann (adjutant to the Führer), Berlin, August 18, 1938 (copy), in Rep. 502, NG-1465, Bl. 739, State Archives, Nuremberg.

113. See Gabriele Anderl and Alexandra Caruso, eds., *NS-Kunstraub in Österreich und die Folgen* (Innsbruck, 2005), p. 41.

114. See Ernst Günther Schenck, *Patient Hitler: Eine medizinische Biographie* (Augsburg, 2000), p. 163. Schenck dates the meeting to December 25, 1936, relying on

a statement by Heinrich Hoffmann's son. See also Speer, *Inside the Third Reich*, p. 105. According to Speer, the first meeting between Hitler and Morell took place long before the end of 1936, possibly even by late 1935. Speer admits to having sought out Morell's services himself in 1936, on Hitler's suggestion. See also U.S. Strategic Bombing Survey, APO 413, Interview No. 64, "Dr. med. Karl Brandt, 17–18. Juni 1945," p. 457, in David Irving Collection, ED 100, USSBS: Interrogation Reports, vol. 2, IfZ Munich. Brandt states that Hoffmann brought the future "personal physician" with him to Berlin in 1936, as his own doctor. Morell even lived in Hoffmann's Berlin apartment at first, which is how he met Hitler.

115.   See Heinrich Hoffmann Photo Archive, hoff-15850 and hoff-16378, BSB Munich.

116.   See Heinrich Hoffmann Photo Archive, hoff-20423/hoff-50275/hoff-20676, BSB Munich.

117.   See Kershaw, *Hitler 1936–1945*, p. 121.

118.   See Speer, *Inside the Third Reich*, p. 105: "From then on, Morell belonged to the intimate circle." See also Below, *Als Hitlers Adjutant*, p. 97, according to which the Morells were invited to the Berghof for Easter 1938, along with the Bormanns, the Speers, and the Brandts. Also Schroeder, *Er war mein Chef*, p. 206: "Hitler named him his personal physician and later also made him a professor." In this regard, see Schenck, *Patient Hitler*, p. 163. Schenck, who analyzed the "Morell Papers" from the U.S. National Archives, held the view that Morell became part of Hitler's innermost circle only after the beginning of the Second World War, i.e., in 1941.

119.   Speer, *Inside the Third Reich*, pp. 105.

120.   Franz von Sonnleithner, *Als Diplomat im "Führerhauptquartier"* (Munich and Vienna, 1989), p. 59.

121.   See Hamann, *Winifred Wagner oder Hitlers Bayreuth*, pp. 374f.

122.   See Kershaw, *Der Hitler-Mythos*, pp. 162f. and 167; Schroeder, *Er war mein Chef*, p. 206.

123.   Cf. Speer, *Inside the Third Reich*, p. 105; Schellenberg, *Aufzeichnungen*, p. 75. According to Schellenberg, head of domestic counterespionage in the Reich Security Main Office (Reichssicherheitshauptamt, or RSHA) in 1939, Himmler assigned him to keep Morell under surveillance after the outbreak of war, since he found Morell suspicious on numerous grounds; however, "a connection with enemy secret services" on Morell's part could "not be proven."

124.   Schenck, *Patient Hitler*, pp. 163f.

125.   Hanfstaengl, *Zwischen Weissem und Braunem Haus*, p. 185. He referred here to Morell's wife, Hanni Moller, who allegedly said that bodily examinations of Hitler were impossible for this reason. See Schenck, *Patient Hitler*, pp. 162 and 180ff.

126.   See Reich Minister and Head of the Chancellery, Lammers, to Professor Dr. med. Morell, Berlin, January 31, 1943 (copy), in F 123, Sammlung Prof. Morell 1937–1945, IfZ Munich (original documents in the possession of Dr. Justin MacCarthy, 608 S. Granite St., Deming, NM 88030, USA).

127.   See Schroeder, *Er war mein Chef*, p. 206.

128. See Hamann, *Winifred Wagner oder Hitlers Bayreuth*, p. 374; Riefenstahl, *Memoiren*, p. 394.

129. Below, *Als Hitlers Adjutant*, p. 87.

130. Speer, *Inside the Third Reich*, pp. 105–106.

131. See ibid., p. 106.

132. Cf. Katz, *Theo Morell*, pp. 169 and 287. Katz declares that this claim is one of the "many stupid stories" in Speer's *Inside the Third Reich*.

133. Ilse Hess to Carla Leitgen, n.p., February 3, 1938 (carbon copy), in Rudolf Hess Papers, J 1211 (–) 1993/300, vol. 9, file 111, Swiss Federal Archives, Bern.

134. See Theodor Morell, 1944 calendar (entry of January 8: "Call [. . .] Miss Eva"), in Theodor Morell Papers, N 1438/2, BA Koblenz.

135. See Katz, *Theo Morell*, p. 253.

136. Thus Morell, while staying on the Obersalzberg on April 20, 1943, noted that Hitler had begun an evening "Enterofagos treatment" and "Eva Braun likewise"; see David Irving, *Die geheimen Tagebücher des Dr. Morell: Leibarzt Adolf Hitlers* (Munich, 1983), p. 123).

137. Junge, *Bis zur letzten Stunde*, p. 133. The historian Percy Ernst Schramm also noted, during the questioning of Hitler's doctors after the war, under the keyword "Eva Braun": "disapproved of Morell." "Originalnotizen von P. E. Schramm über Hitler, gemacht während der Befragungen von Hitlers Leibärzten. Haus 'Alaska', d. h. Altersheim für Lehrerinnen im Taunus, Sommer 1945 in USA-Kriegsgefangenschaft," in Kl. Erwerb. 441–3, p. 169, BA Koblenz.

138. Brandt emphasized after the war his "disapproving sense of Morell as a person and as a doctor." Morell was, in Brandt's view, incompetent as a scientist and "himself practically uninvolved" in such procedures; see Karl Brandt, "Theo Morell," September 19, 1945 (Haus "Alaska" in Taunus as an American prisoner of war, summer 1945), in Kl. Erwerbungen 441–3 (copy), pp. 61f., BA Koblenz.

139. See Schmidt, *Karl Brandt*, pp. 492ff.

140. Hanfstaengl, *Zwischen Weissem und Braunem Haus*, p. 50.

141. Below, *Als Hitlers Adjutant*, p. 81.

142. Quoted from Kershaw, *Hitler 1889–1936*, p. 180. See also Hans-Ulrich Thamer, *Verführung und Gewalt: Deutschland 1933–1945* (Berlin, 1986), pp. 69 and 95. In any case, there was already talk of "our Führer" since the fall of 1921 in the *Völkischer Beobachter*.

143. See Plöckinger, *Geschichte eines Buches*, pp. 329f.; Mathias Rösch, *Die Münchner NSDAP 1925–1933: Eine Untersuchung zur inneren Struktur der NSDAP in der Weimarer Republik* (Munich, 2002), p. 513.

144. Speer, *Spandau*, p. 442.

145. See Interrogation Summary No. 666, Office of U.S. Chief of Counsel for War Crimes, APO 124 A, Evidence Division, Interrogation Branch, "Interrogation of Hermann Esser, Staatssekretär, Interrogated by Mr. Fehl, 6 December 1946, Nuremberg," p. 2, in ZS 1030 (Hermann Esser), IfZ Munich. Esser as president of the Reich Tourism Association (*Akten der Partei-Kanzlei der NSDAP*, p. 287).

146. See Rösch, *Die Münchner NSDAP 1925–1933*, p. 193; Ernst Piper, *Alfred Rosenberg: Hitlers Chefideologe* (Munich, 2005), pp. 124f.

147. Interrogation Summary No. 666, pp. 3f.

148. Ibid.

149. Hermann Esser and Johann Jacob Bierbrauer, *Die jüdische Weltpest: Judendämmerung auf dem Erdball*, 6th ed. (Munich, 1941).

150. See Interrogation Summary No. 666, p. 2. The National Socialist Party platform of 1920 was, according to Esser, completely different from those of 1939 and 1940 with respect to the "Jewish question." Esser also claimed that he had nothing to do with the decision at the 1935 convention (p. 3). The fact is, Rosenberg himself denied to the end that he knew about the extermination policies of the Nazis, despite being very precisely informed about the "Final Solution" and despite his own involvement in the extermination actions as the Reich Minister for the Occupied Eastern Territories. See Piper, *Alfred Rosenberg*, pp. 579ff. and 634f.

151. In 1950, Esser was sentenced to five years in prison in the denazification proceedings; he was released early, after two years.

152. See Speer, *Albert Speer: Die Kransberg-Protokolle 1945*, p. 144. Speer counted Esser—along with Eva Braun, Bormann, Brandt, Morell, Sepp Dietrich, Botschafter Hewel, and himself—as members of the Berghof circle. See also Junge, *Bis zur letzten Stunde*, p. 94: Junge, who traveled along to the Obersalzberg for the first time in March 1943, mentions "Minister of State Esser and his wife" as guests.

153. See "Gruppenbild vor Modell Haus des Fremdenverkehrs in Berlin, Berghof, 10. Januar 1937," in Heinrich Hoffmann Photo Archive, hoff-14728, BSB Munich.

154. The ruins were torn down in 1964.

155. See Piper, *Alfred Rosenberg*, p. 12.

156. For example, Esser read aloud the "Führer's Proclamation" at the annual "Celebration of the Founding of the Party" in Munich's Hofbräuhaus on February 24, 1943, while Hitler was residing "in the east" at his "Wolf's Lair Führer Headquarters" ("Wortlaut der Führerproklamation," in Franz Ritter von Epp Papers, N 1101/86, BA Koblenz).

157. See Thilo Nowack, "Rhein, Romantik, Reisen: Der Ausflugs- und Erholungsreiseverkehr im Mittelrheintal im Kontext gesellschaftlichen Wandels (1890–1970)" (dissertation, University of Bonn, 2006), pp. 117ff.

158. See in this regard Bajohr, *"Unser Hotel ist judenfrei,"* pp. 16ff.; Alfred Bernd Gottwaldt and Diana Schulle, *"Juden ist die Benutzung von Speisewagen untersagt": Die antijüdische Politik des Reichsverkehrsministeriums zwischen 1933–1945* (Teetz, 2007).

159. See Susanne Appel, *Reisen im Nationalsozialismus: Eine rechtshistorische Untersuchung*, Schriften zum Reise- und Verkehrsrecht, vol. 3 (Baden-Baden, 2001); Kristin Semmens, *Seeing Hitler's Germany: Tourism in the Third Reich* (University of Victoria, Palgrave, Canada, 2005).

160. See Prof. Dr. von Hasselbach, "Hitlers Mangel an Menschenkenntnis," September 26, 1945 (copy), p. 5, in Kl. Erwerbungen 441–3, BA Koblenz.

161. See Michael Humphrey, *Die Weimarer Reformdiskussion über das Ehescheidungs-
recht und das Zerrüttungsprinzip: Eine Untersuchung über die Entwicklung des
Ehescheidungsrechts in Deutschland von der Reformation bis zur Gegenwart unter
Berücksichtigung rechtsvergleichender Aspekte* (Göttingen, 2006), p. 74.

162. Minister of Justice to Reich Minister and Head of the Chancellery, Berlin, October
29, 1938 (copy), in Fa 199/47, IfZ Munich.

163. Marriage Act (*Gesetz zur Vereinheitlichung des Rechts der Eheschliessung und der
Ehescheidung im Lande Österreich und im übrigen Reichsgebiet* [Law for the Stan-
dardization of Marriage and Divorce Rights between the State of Austria and the
Other Territory in the Reich]) of July 6, 1938, Section 55, in Reichsgesetzblatt I 1938,
pp. 807ff.

164. Ibid. The actual words of Section 9, Ehebruch (Adultery), are: "(1) *Eine Ehe darf
nicht geschlossen werden zwischen einem wegen Ehebruchs geschiedenen Ehegatten
und demjenigen, mit dem er den Ehebruch begangen hat, wenn dieser Ehebruch im
Scheidungsurteil als Grund der Scheidung festgestellt ist. (2) Von dieser Vorschrift
kann Befreiung bewilligt werden.*"

165. Reich Minister and Head of the Chancellery to Minister of Justice Gürtner, Berchtesgaden, November 23, 1938 (copy), in Fa 199/47, IfZ Munich.

166. Ibid.

167. See in this regard Lothar Gruchmann, *Justiz im Dritten Reich 1933–1940: Anpas-
sung und Unterwerfung in der Ära Gürtner*, 3rd ed. (Munich, 2002).

168. Transcript of the judgment of the Berlin district court from December 23, 1938, ref.
no. 220. R.303.38, in Fa 199/47, IfZ Munich.

169. Hermann Esser to Reich Minister Dr. Lammers, Berlin, December 23, 1938 (copy),
in Fa 199/47, IfZ Munich.

170. Minister of Justice to Reich Minister and Head of the Chancellery Dr. Lammers,
Berlin, February 6, 1939 (copy), in Fa 199/47, IfZ Munich.

171. See photographs of the wedding party, April 5, 1939, in Heinrich Hoffmann Photo
Archive, hoff-24169, BSB Munich.

172. See "Eva Braun während der Taufe im Hause Hermann Essers in München,"
undated, in Heinrich Hoffmann Photo Archive, hoff-363, BSB Munich. According to a statement by Hedwig Hoffmann, a former employee at Esser's house, Eva
Braun was invited to the celebration as a godmother because she "was an acquaintance of Frau Esser." (Aussage der Zeugin Hedwig Hoffmann, 18. Oktober 1949,
Öffentliche Sitzung der Berufungskammer, München, VI Senat, zur mündlichen
Verhandlung über den Nachlass der verstorbenen Eva Hitler, geb. Braun [Witness
statement from Hedwig Hoffmann, October 18, 1949, official session of the appellate
chamber, Munich, Sixth Senate, for oral arguments concerning the estate of the
deceased Eva Hitler, née Braun], in Denazification Court Records, box 718, State
Archives, Munich.) Hanfstaengl also stated that Eva Braun was friends with Esser's
second wife since their schooldays: *Zwischen Weissem und Braunem Haus*, p. 359.

173. The Brandts' son, born on October 4, 1935, was given the name Karl-Adolf. Speer's

son, born 1937, was named Friedrich Adolf. Ribbentrop also named his son Adolf. Rudolf Hess, in turn, took on the role of godfather to one of Bormann's sons, who was named Rudolf (Gerhard) after him.

174. See Adolf Hitler, "Rede vor der NS-Frauenschaft am 8. September 1934," in Hitler, *Hitler: Reden und Proklamationen 1932–1945*, p. 451.

175. See Michael Rissmann, *Hitlers Gott: Vorsehungsglaube und Sendungsbewusstsein des deutschen Diktators* (Zürich and Munich, 2001), p. 80.

176. Ferdinand Hoffmann, *Sittliche Entartung und Geburtenschwund*, Schriften für naturgesetzliche Politik und Wissenschaft, H. 4, 2nd, expanded, ed. (Munich, 1938), pp. 6 and 14.

177. See Speer, *Inside the Third Reich*, p. 92; Henriette von Schirach, *Frauen um Hitler*, p. 228. See also Gerda Bormann to Martin Bormann, Obersalzberg, December 25, 1943, in Bormann, *The Bormann Letters*, p. 38.

178. Note from the Führer Headquarters, October 21/22, 1941, in Hitler, *Monologe im Führerhauptquartier 1941–1944*, p. 99.

179. Kershaw, *Hitler 1936–1945*, p. 30.

180. Hitler, quoted in Speer, *Inside the Third Reich*, p. 92. See also Hamann, *Hitlers Wien*, pp. 536ff. The Italian fascist leader Benito Mussolini, in contrast, did not share this attitude. He is quoted as having said the following: "I'm not married to Italy, after all, the way Hitler is with Germany." See Rachele Mussolini, *Mussolini ohne Maske: Erinnerungen*, ed. Albert Zarca (Stuttgart, 1974).

181. "Der Führer spricht zur deutschen Frauenschaft," in *Reden des Führers am Parteitag der Ehre 1936*, 4th ed. (Munich, 1936), p. 44.

182. Kurt Sontheimer, *Antidemokratisches Denken in der Weimarer Republik: Die politischen Ideen des deutschen Nationalismus zwischen 1918 und 1933*, 4th ed. (Munich, 1994), pp. 214ff.

183. Hitler, *Monologe im Führerhauptquartier 1941–1944*, p. 230.

184. Speer, *Inside the Third Reich*, p. 92. Kershaw adopts this evaluation of Braun. "For prestige reasons, he kept her away from the public eye" (*Hitler 1936–1945*, p. 34).

185. "Besprechung zwischen Mr. Albrecht und Frl. Paula Hitler," Berchtesgaden, May 26, 1945. See also Zdral, *Die Hitlers*, p. 207; Alfred Läpple, *Paula Hitler—Die Schwester: Ein Leben in der Zeitenwende*, 2nd ed. (Stegen am Ammersee, 2005), pp. 147ff.

186. Rudolf Hess to Ilse Pröhl, Landsberg Castle, June 8, 1924, in Hess, *Briefe 1908–1933*, p. 332. Otto Dietrich, formerly Reich Press Chief and in Hitler's innermost circle, remarked on Hitler's "aversion to everything familial" (*12 Jahre mit Hitler*, p. 235). See also Hamann, *Hitlers Wien*, p. 516, which says that Hitler experienced inhibitions and fear of contact with women even in his early years. He apparently confided to Reinhold Hanisch, whom he knew from his time in the homeless shelter for men in Vienna, that he was afraid of the "possible consequences" of an intimate relationship.

187. Speer, *Inside the Third Reich*, pp. 86 and 92.

188. Speer, *Albert Speer: Die Kransberg-Protokolle 1945*, p. 119.

189. See Schroeder, *Er war mein Chef*, pp. 166f. Henry Picker, in contrast, claims that Braun was the "lady of the house" and "in charge of running the Berghof"; see Henry Picker, *Hitlers Tischgespräche im Führerhauptquartier: Entstehung, Struktur, Folgen des Nationalsozialismus* (Berlin, 1997), pp. 352ff.

190. See Hanskarl von Hasselbach, "Hitler," in Headquarters Military Intelligence Service Center, U.S. Army, APO 757, OI Special Report 36, "Adolf Hitler: A Composite Picture (2 April 1947)," F135/4, p. 6, in David Irving Collection, "Adolph Hitler 1944–1953," vol. 4, IfZ Munich, p. 714. Albert Speer, on the other hand, emphasized that Eva Braun was "very shy and very modest" and "much maligned" by others' backbiting (Sereny, *Albert Speer*, pp. 192f.). See also Spitzy, *So haben wir das Reich verspielt*, p. 129: Ribbentrop's adjutant here describes Braun as "a child of the petit bourgeoisie," with no "class." An "educated, intelligent wife at Hitler's side," in contrast, would have been able to be a "moderating influence at his side."

191. See Ian Kershaw, *Hitlers Macht: Das Profil der NS-Herrschaft* (Munich, 1992), pp. 31ff.

192. Ley, "Gedanken um den Führer," p. 22.

193. See Emmy Göring, *An der Seite meines Mannes: Begebenheiten und Bekenntnisse*, 4th ed. (Coburg, 1996), pp. 148f.

194. See Kube, *Pour le mérite und Hakenkreuz*, pp. 71ff. and 202. See also Werner Maser, *Hermann Göring: Hitlers janusköpfiger Paladin; Die politische Biographie* (Berlin, 2000); James Wyllie, *The Warlord and the Renegade: The Story of Hermann and Albert Goering* (Sutton, 2006).

195. Emmy Göring, *An der Seite meines Mannes*, p. 149.

196. On Hermann Göring's declining significance, see Kube, *Pour le mérite und Hakenkreuz*, p. 359. It is noteworthy that Göring applied for membership in the NSDAP for his wife in January 1939 (ibid., p. 203). The issue with Emmy Göring's invitation of Eva Braun was certainly not the supposed "faux pas" of "inviting Eva Braun to tea together with the staff of the Berghof," as Anna Maria Sigmund claims (*Die Frauen der Nazis*, p. 264).

197. See Speer, *Albert Speer: Die Kransberg-Protokolle 1945*, p. 119.

198. See Kershaw, *Hitler 1936–1945*, pp. 19f.; Fest, *Die unbeantwortbaren Fragen*, p. 240. See also Speer, *Inside the Third Reich*, pp. 100–101: he describes an "unbreakable wall" and writes that Hitler "was never completely relaxed and human" in others' presence—not even with Eva Braun. Earlier, Speer claimed that Hitler tried to come across "as a good 'paterfamilias' " in the private realm (*Albert Speer: Die Kransberg-Protokolle 1945*, p. 112).

199. Speer, *Inside the Third Reich*, pp. 92 and 123.

200. Speer, *Albert Speer: Die Kransberg-Protokolle 1945*, pp. 69ff., 112, and 118.

201. Seventh Army Interrogation Center, APO/758, May 26 1945, "Amann's Control of German Press," in David Irving Collection, "Adolph Hitler 1944–1953," F 135/3, IfZ Munich, p. 490.

202. Walther Darré, *Aufzeichnungen von 1945–1948*, vol. 2, p. 369.

203. See "Biographical Report, Nurnberg, 26 October, 1945." Office of U.S. Chief of Counsel APO 403, U.S. Army, Interrogation Division, in ZS 1452 (Franz Xaver Schwarz), IfZ Munich.

204. Interrogation of Reich Treasurer Schwarz, 21 July 1945, 1600 Hours, in ZS 1452 (Franz Xaver Schwarz), IfZ Munich. An interview record from the same day reports: "Hitler seemed to him [i.e., to Schwarz] an honest, intelligent man of great strength of character. He maintained that his relations with women were on a high plane. Stating that Hitler became a close friend of Eva Braun as early as 1931, he insisted that the relationship was purely platonic since Hitler had decided to forgo matrimony in the interest of his country; Eva Braun frequented the Schwarz household."

205. Report on Historical Interrogations of German Prisoners of War and Detained Persons, 20 December 1945 (Lt. Col. Oron J. Hale), War Department Historical Commission, War Department Special Staff, Historical Division, in Fh 51, IfZ Munich.

206. "Besprechung zwischen Herrn Albrecht und Frl. Schröder, früher Sekretärin von Hitler," Berchtesgaden, May 22, 1945, p. 3, in MA 1298/10, Microfilm, Various Documents DJ-13 (David Irving), IfZ Munich.

207. Schroeder, *Er war mein Chef*, pp. 155f.

208. Hoffmann, "Mein Beruf," pp. 22f.

209. Ibid., pp. 18ff. and 21f.

210. "Vernehmung des Julius Schaub am 12. 3. 1947 von 15.30 bis 16.00 durch Dr. Kempner," pp. 6f., in ZS 137 (Julius Schaub), IfZ Munich. See also Julius Schaub, *In Hitlers Schatten: Erinnerungen und Aufzeichnungen des Chefadjutanten 1925– 1945*, ed. Olaf Rose (Stegen am Ammersee, 2005), p. 278.

211. See Kershaw, *The "Hitler Myth,"* p. 121.

212. Karl Brandt stated in September 1945 that Schaub certainly had a "very exact picture" of "Hitler's private life." He described the adjutant as a petty and self-important schemer who spread "gossip of the pettiest kind" and often created conflicts in Hitler's circle with his "sneaky dealings" and "dreaded deviousness." Schaub influenced "Hitler's judgment of people" and therefore "even men of high and dignified office very much paid court to him" (Karl Brandt, "Julius Schaub," September 20, 1945, "Oberursel/Alaska,", p. 71, in Kl. Erwerbungen 441–3 [copy], BA Koblenz). On Schaub's role see also Angela Hermann, "Hitler und sein Stosstrupp in der 'Reichskristallnacht,' " *Vierteljahrshefte für Zeitgeschichte* 56 (2008), pp. 603–619.

213. Herta Schneider, "Aussage vom 23. Juni 1949, Öffentliche Sitzung der Hauptkammer München zur mündlichen Verhandlung in dem Verfahren gegen Herta Schneider, geb. Ostermayr," in Denazification Court Records, box 1670, State Archives, Munich.

214. Heinrich Hoffmann, "Aussage vom 1. Juli 1949, Öffentliche Sitzung der Hauptkammer München zur mündlichen Verhandlung in dem Verfahren gegen Eva Hitler, geb. Braun," in Denazification Court Records, box 718 (Eva Hitler, geb. Braun), State Archives, Munich. Braun's sister, Ilse Fucke-Michels, stated that Eva Braun

"worked in Herr Hoffmann's sales office until 1945 and also took photographs for the love of it"; Eva Braun "earned a net monthly salary of 400 reichsmarks in the later years." Her "special photographs" were paid for "separately" by Hoffmann. See Ilse Fucke-Michels, Aussage vom 31. Mai 1949, Öffentliche Sitzung der Hauptkammer München, in Denazification Court Records, box 718 (Eva Hitler, geb. Braun), State Archives, Munich. See also Joachimsthaler, *Hitlers Liste*, p. 466. Eva Braun shot movies with a 16 mm Agfa-Movex camera.

215. See the reproduced receipt in the German edition of Gun, *Eva Braun* (*Eva Braun-Hitler*, p. 128 [g]). See also Herta Schneider, statement of June 23, 1949 (previously cited): Braun, Schneider said, still "worked" in Munich "during the first year of the war."

216. Heinrich Hoffmann, statement of July 1, 1949, previously cited. See also Sigmund, *Die Frauen der Nazis*, p. 254: "Eva stopped working at the end of 1935."

217. On corruption among Hitler's entourage, see Bajohr, *Parvenüs und Profiteure*, pp. 58ff.

218. Speer, *Inside the Third Reich*, p. 93. In late June 1939, Eva Braun traveled with her mother and younger sisters on a cruise through the Norwegian fjords, aboard the KdF ship the MS *Milwaukee* (Lambert, *The Lost Life of Eva Braun*, p. 372; see also Gun, *Eva Braun*, p. 179). The fact that Eva Braun traveled independently contradicts Speer's claim that Eva Braun had no freedom or latitude and always had to be present whenever Hitler was on the Obersalzberg.

219. See Speer, *Inside the Third Reich*, p. 82. Speer claims that he himself suffered under the need to always be at Hitler's beck and call.

220. Statement from Adolf Widmann, "Protokoll der Öffentlichen Sitzung vom 15. Oktober 1948 zur mündlichen Verhandlung in dem Verfahren gegen Eva Anna Paula Hitler, geb. Braun," Munich District Court 1, in Denazification Court Records, box 718 (Eva Hitler, geb. Braun), State Archives, Munich. See also in this regard Joachimsthaler, *Hitlers Liste*, pp. 459ff.

221. "Berufungskammer für München, Abteilung Ermittlung an den Generalkläger beim Kassationshof im Bayerischen Ministerium für Sonderaufgaben, München, 13. September 1948," in Denazification Court Records, box 718 (Eva Hitler, geb. Braun), State Archives, Munich.

222. See Munich District Court, land register of Bogenhausen, vol. 90, Bl. 2574, p. 6. A sales contract no longer exists, and the original files were also destroyed, in an air raid on December 17, 1944. Munich District Court, Div. 3, to the General Prosecutor at Kassationshof in the State Ministry for Special Tasks, Munich, March 11, 1948, in Denazification Court Records, box 718 (Eva Hitler, geb. Braun), State Archives, Munich.

223. Hoffmann, "Mein Beruf," p. 22. See also Heinrich Hoffmann's statement of July 1, 1949—he was in prison at the time, and classified as a Class 1 Major Offender—for the "Öffentliche Sitzung der Hauptkammer München zur mündlichen Verhandlung in dem Verfahren gegen Eva Hitler, geb. Braun, in Denazification Court Records, box 718 (Eva Hitler, geb. Braun)," State Archives, Munich.

224. See Gun, *Eva Braun*, p. 140. See also Eva Braun's registration card dated August 24, 1935, State Archives, Munich.

225. See Walter Wönne and Falko Berg, *Halte, was Du hast: Erinnerungen* (n.p., 2000), p. 404.

226. Adolf Hitler, "Reichstagsrede vom 7. März 1936," in Johannes Hohlfeld, ed., *Dokumente der Deutschen Politik und Geschichte von 1848 bis zur Gegenwart*, vol. 4, *Die Zeit der nationalsozialistischen Diktatur 1933–1945: Aufbau und Entwicklung 1933–1938* (Berlin, n.d.) pp. 275ff. See also Kershaw, *Hitler 1889–1936*, pp. 532f.

227. Speer, *Albert Speer: Die Kransberg-Protokolle 1945*, p. 219.

228. Joseph Goebbels, quoted in Frank Omland, *"Du wählst mi nich Hitler!" Reichstagswahlen und Volksabstimmungen in Schleswig-Holstein 1933–1938* (Hamburg, 2006), p. 132.

229. "Besprechung zwischen Mr. Albrecht und Frl. Paula Hitler," Berchtesgaden, May 26, 1945, as cited in note 185, above.

230. Hitler, *Monologe im Führerhauptquartier 1941–1944*, p. 158. See also Rissmann, *Hitlers Gott*, pp. 176ff., and Dietrich, *12 Jahre mit Hitler*, pp. 168f. Hitler, according to Dietrich, believed in "the existence of a higher being and the prevailing of a higher purpose, in a sense that he never explicitly defined."

231. See "Gruppenbild, u. a. mit Helene Bechstein, Erna Hoffmann und Eva Braun in der zweiten Reihe hinter Otto Dietrich, Adolf Wagner und Hitler sitzend," in Heinrich Hoffmann Photo Archive, hoff-12309, BSB Munich.

232. Hitler, *Monologe im Führerhauptquartier 1941–1944*, p. 356.

233. Title page, *Berliner Illustrirte Zeitung*, August 24, 1919, in *Weimar in Berlin: Porträt einer Epoche*, ed. Manfred Görtemaker and Bildarchiv Preussischer Kulturbesitz (Berlin-Brandenburg, 2002), p. 186.

234. Hitler, *Monologe im Führerhauptquartier 1941–1944*, p. 356.

235. RMdI, 7. Juni 1935, H 101 13805–09, in *Akten der Partei-Kanzlei der NSDAP*, p. 59.

236. "Der Chef des Reichssicherheitsdienstes, Himmler, an die Aussenstelle Garmisch-Partenkirchen der Bayerischen Politischen Polizei, z. Hd. Herrn Hauptmann der Schutzpolizei Staudinger, Berlin, 29. Januar 1936. Betr. 'Sicherungsdienst bei Besuchen der Olympischen Winterspiele durch den Führer' [Head of the Reich Security Office, Himmler, to the Garmisch-Partenkirchen Branch of the Bavarian Political Police, attn. Capt. of the Uniformed Police Staudinger, Berlin, January 29, 1936. Re: Security for the Führer's Visit to the Winter Olympic Games]" (original), in ED 619/vol. 1, IfZ Munich. See also Wolfgang Fuhr, ed., *Olympische Winterspiele 1936: Die vergessene Olympiade von Garmisch-Partenkirchen* (Agon, 2006).

237. See David Clay Large, *Nazi Games: The Olympics of 1936* (New York, 2007); Arnd Krüger and William Murray, eds., *The Nazi Olympics: Sport, Politics and Appeasement in the 1930s* (Urbana and Chicago, 2003).

238. See Heinrich Hoffmann and Ludwig Hayman, *Die Olympischen Spiele 1936* (Diessen, 1936).

239. Rudolf Hess to his father, n.p., June 8, 1936 (carbon copy), in Rudolf Hess Papers, J 1211, 1989/148, vol. 13, file 57, folder 18, Swiss Federal Archives, Bern. Only Angela

Lambert claims the opposite, without providing any proof, in her unreliable, basically novelistic Braun biography (*The Lost Life of Eva Braun*, pp. 278f.).

240. See Gun, *Eva Braun*, p. 152.

241. Schroeder, *Er war mein Chef*, pp. 84ff.; Below, *Als Hitlers Adjutant 1937–45*, pp.
      92f.; Dietrich, *12 Jahre mit Hitler*, pp. 52f.; Speer, *Inside the Third Reich*, p. 109. Gitta
      Sereny, in contrast, writes that Speer told her upon questioning about his stay in
      Vienna in March 1938, at the Hotel Imperial (*Albert Speer*, p. 191).

242. See Richard J. Evans, *David Irving, Hitler, and Holocaust Denial*, electronic edi-
      tion. See also Ron Rosenbaum, *Explaining Hitler: The Search for the Origins of His
      Evil* (New York, 1999), pp. 228ff. According to Rosenbaum, Christa Schroeder was
      for David Irving the "key" to the "magic circle."

243. For example, Goebbels noted under the date March 20, 1938: "The Führer is mag-
      nificent: generous and constructive. A true genius. Now he sits for hours at a time
      brooding over his maps. It is moving when he says that he wants to see the Greater
      German Reich again with his own eyes" (*Die Tagebücher von Joseph Goebbels*,
      Teil I, vol. 5, p. 222).

244. See Heinrich Hoffmann Photo Archive, hoff-12309, BSB Munich.

245. Julius Schaub, statement at Nuremberg, June 8, 1948, KV Trials, Document 1856,
      Case 11, File G15, Dietrich Document No. 279, Julius Schaub Affidavit, State
      Archives, Nuremberg. Karl Brandt, too, addressing the "question of guilt" in the tract
      "The Hitler Problem #2" that he wrote in an Allied prison after the war, avoided all
      mention of the fate of the German Jews. He spoke only of Bolshevism, the "danger
      threatening Europe from the Asian sphere" against which Hitler had to secure "the
      Lebensraum of the German People" ("Das Problem Hitler, Nr. 2," September 27,
      1945, p. 8, in Kleine Erwerbung 441-3, BA Koblenz).

246. Paul Schmidt, *Statist auf diplomatischer Bühne 1923–45* (Bonn, 1953), p. 390.

247. See Below, *Als Hitlers Adjutant*, p. 98. See also Maser, *Adolf Hitler*, pp. 374f.

248. Adolf Hitler, "Mein Testament," Berlin, May 2, 1938 (copy), in Adolf Hitler Papers,
      N 1128/22, BA Koblenz.

249. See Gun, *Eva Braun*, pp. 169–170. Nicolaus von Below mentions the will, but does
      not say whether he knew about it at the time (*Als Hitlers Adjutant*, p. 98).

250. See Walther Darré, *Aufzeichnungen 1945–1948*, vol. 2, p. 377. It is possible that Bor-
      mann, as alternate executor, and Schaub also knew about the will. The latter was to
      examine private "books and correspondences" and decide whether or not to destroy
      them (Hitler, "Mein Testament," as cited in note 248, above).

251. See Schmidt, *Statist auf diplomatischer Bühne*, p. 390; Below, *Als Hitlers Adjutant*,
      p. 98; Wiedemann, *Der Mann, der Feldherr werden wollte*, pp. 133f.; Spitzy, *So haben
      wir das Reich verspielt*, pp. 260ff. See also Kube, *Pour le mérite und Hakenkreuz*,
      p. 72.

252. See "Auswärtiges Amt an Marga Himmler, 'Vorläufiges Fahrtprogramm für die
      Damen' vom 1. bis zum 11. Mai 1938, anlässlich des Staatsbesuches in Italien [For-
      eign Office to Marga Himmler, 'Provisional Travel Schedule for the Ladies for May

1–11, 1938, during the state visit in Italy]," in Himmler Papers, N 1126/20, Fol. 1, BA Koblenz. See also Wiedemann, *Der Mann, der Feldherr werden wollte*, p. 135.

253. Hitler, *Monologe im Führerhauptquartier*, p. 247.

254. See "Auswärtiges Amt an Marga Himmler," as previously cited. See also Wiedemann, *Der Mann, der Feldherr werden wollte*, p. 139.

255. See Gun, *Eva Braun*, pp. 161f; Henriette von Schirach, *Frauen um Hitler*, p. 228. Christa Schroeder, the only secretary "to travel with the Führer in his special train," as it says in her memoir, never mentions Eva Braun's presence (see *Er war mein Chef*, pp. 86f. and 345f.). See also Jürgen Ehlert, *Das Dreesen: 100 Jahre Geschichte und Geschichten im Rheinhotel* (Bonn, 1994).

256. See Heinrich Hoffmann Photo Archive, hoff-18577, BSB Munich.

257. See Kershaw, *Hitler 1936–1945*, pp. 150f.

258. See Gun, *Eva Braun*, p. 162. Gun repeats the rumor that an unknown assassin tried to stab Eva Braun in Naples, instead wounding her companion, Maria Dreesen.

259. Henriette von Schirach, *Frauen um Hitler*, p. 230. Schirach also says that Mussolini, after hearing that "Hitler's lover was coming along on the trip," had a "small crocodile-leather suitcase containing every imaginable kind of toiletry" brought to Eva Braun.

260. See Wiedemann, *Der Mann, der Feldherr werden wollte*, p. 127. See also Otto Meissner, *Staatssekretär unter Ebert—Hindenburg—Hitler: Der Schicksalsweg des deutschen Volkes von 1918–1945, wie ich ihn erlebte*, 3rd ed. (Hamburg, 1950), p. 460. Cf. Joachim von Ribbentrop, *Zwischen London und Moskau*, pp. 136, 139 and 150.

261. See Hamann, *Hitlers Wien*, p. 15; Fest, *Hitler*, p. 726.

262. See Speer, *Inside the Third Reich*, pp. 99–100; cf. pp. 297–298, where Speer says: "in those days, I suspect, all that was mere coquettishness." See also Speer, *Albert Speer: Die Kransberg-Protokolle 1945*, pp. 112f. Speer thought at the time that Hitler wanted to retire after the war, since he was "not happy with his mission" and would "rather be an architect." Nicolaus von Below, who stayed with Hitler at the Berghof in both April and August 1938, mentions nothing of this sort (see Below, *Als Hitlers Adjutant*, pp. 112ff.).

263. See Fest, *Die unbeantwortbaren Fragen*, p. 52. Cf. Speer, *Inside the Third Reich*, p. 99, where he says that "the design for the picture gallery and the stadium was to be assigned to me."

264. Photographs of Roderich Fick and Albert Speer's visit to the Berghof on May 9, 1939, are in Heinrich Hoffmann Photo Archive, hoff-25259, BSB Munich.

265. See Ingo Sarlay, "Hitlers Linz: Planungsstellen und Planungskonzepte," http://www .linz09.info. See also Below, *Als Hitlers Adjutant*, pp. 81 and 83; Michael Früchtel, *Der Architekt Hermann Giesler: Leben und Werk (1898–1987)* (Tübingen, 2008); Hermann Giesler, *Ein anderer Hitler: Bericht seines Architekten Hermann Giesler*, 2nd ed. (Leoni am Starnberger See, 1977), pp. 213ff.

266. See Giesler, *Ein anderer Hitler*, p. 406.

267. See Hubert Houben, *Kaiser Friedrich II: Herrscher, Mensch, und Mythos* (Stuttgart, 2008); Karl Ipser, *Der Staufer Friedrich II: Heimlicher Kaiser der Deutschen* (Berg, 1977), pp. 144ff. and 214ff.

268. See Oskar Hugo Gugg, *Castel del Monte* (1942), oil on board, German Historical Museum, Berlin. See also Ipser, *Der Staufer Friedrich II*, p. 230.

269. Giesler, *Ein anderer Hitler*, pp. 213ff.

270. Ibid., p. 407. On April 4, 1943 Hitler traveled with Giesler, Speer, Fick, Eigruber, Karl Brandt, Heinrich Hoffmann, and Bormann to Linz, to review the progress of the project. See Heinrich Hoffmann Photo Archive, hoff-47460, BSB Munich.

271. See Henriette von Schirach, *Frauen um Hitler*, p. 233.

272. See Fest, *Die unbeantwortbaren Fragen*, p. 183.

PART THREE: DOWNFALL

9. ISOLATION DURING THE WAR

1. Adolf Hitler, *Mein Kampf*, 173rd ed. (Munich, 1936), pp. 732 and 742. See also Christian Zentner, *Adolf Hitlers Mein Kampf: Eine kommentierte Auswahl*, 19th ed. (Berlin, 2007), pp. 131f.

2. See the minutes of army adjutant Colonel Friedrich Hossbach, printed in Thilo Vogelsang, "Neue Dokumente zur Geschichte der Reichswehr, 1930–1933," *Vierteljahrshefte für Zeitgeschichte* 4 (1954), pp. 434f.; Andreas Wirsching, " 'Man kann nur den Boden germanisieren': Eine neue Quelle zu Hitlers Rede vor den Spitzen der Reichswehr am 3. Februar 1933," *Vierteljahrshefte für Zeitgeschichte*, 49 (2001), pp. 518f. 526ff., and 540ff.; Kershaw, *Hitler 1889–1936*, pp. 559ff.

3. See Friedrich Hossbach, "Niederschrift über die Besprechung in der Reichskanzlei am 5. November 1937, Berlin, 10. November 1937," in Bernd-Jürgen Wendt, *Grossdeutschland: Aussenpolitik und Kriegsvorbereitung des Hitlerregimes* (Munich, 1987); Kershaw, *Hitler 1936–1945*, p. 60.

4. See Goebbels, diary entry, February 3, 1939, in *Die Tagebücher von Joseph Goebbels*, Teil 1, vol. 6 (Munich, 1998), p. 247.

5. See Reuth, *Goebbels*, pp. 395f.

6. "Hitlers Rede vor Truppenkommandeuren am 10. Februar 1939," in Klaus-Jürgen Müller, *Armee und Drittes Reich 1933–1939* (Paderborn, 1987), pp. 365ff.

7. Below, *Als Hitlers Adjutant*, p. 147.

8. Adolf Hitler, "Rede vor dem Reichstag am 30. Januar 1939," in *Verhandlungen des Reichstags, 4. Wahlperiode 1939, Band 460. Stenographische Berichte 1939–1942. 1. Sitzung, Montag, 30. Januar 1939*, pp. 1–21.

9. Below, *Als Hitlers Adjutant*, p. 147.

10. See Sereny, *Albert Speer*, p. 236.

11. Speer, *Inside the Third Reich*, p. 130; Gun, *Eva Braun*, p. 173; Breloer, *Unterwegs zur Familie Speer*, p. 96. Speer's oldest son showed Breloer a chest with snapshots and architectural photographs including images of "Eva Braun Furniture" and "Old Chancellery, Eva Braun's Ladies' Room, Living Room, and Bedroom."

12. Speer, *Inside the Third Reich*, p. 102. Cf. Speer, *Albert Speer: Die Kransberg-Protokolle 1945*, pp. 223f.; Kellerhoff, *Hitlers Berlin*, pp. 132f.; Dietmar Arnold, *Reichskanzlei und "Führerbunker": Legenden und Wirklichkeit* (Berlin, 2006), pp. 69ff.

13. Speer, *Inside the Third Reich*, p. 130. It says there that Eva Braun's bedroom was located next to Hitler's. See also Gun, *Eva Braun*. "Room and boudoir communicated with Hitler's library." Eva Braun is there said to have entered her room "through the servants' entrance," since "officially her position was [as] one of the numerous secretaries in the offices." Christa Schroeder, very familiar with the "Führer household" in the Old Chancellery since 1933, due to her "on-call duties," stated that Hitler's "work room, library, and bedroom, and later Eva Braun's apartment next door" were located there (*Er war mein Chef*, pp. 6of.).

14. "More About Evi," *Time*, December 18, 1939. See also "Hitler's Girl Evi Braun Takes His Picture," *Life*, November 6, 1939; Richard Norburt, "Is Hitler Married?" *Saturday Evening Post*, December 16, 1939.

15. "Spring in the Axis," *Time*, May 15, 1939. It says there: "To her friends Eva Braun confided that she expected her friend to marry her within a year."

16. Bella Fromm, *Blood & Banquets: A Berlin Social Diary* (New York, 1990 [1st ed., London, 1943]), pp. 255 and 303. Bella Steuerman Fromm wrote for Ullstein Verlag (including for *B.Z. Am Mittag*) and *The Times* (London) since the mid-1920s. Her contacts extended all the way to Schleicher and Papen. See Stephan Malinowski, *Vom König zum Führer: Deutscher Adel und Nationalsozialismus* (Berlin, 2003), p. 556; also Louis P. Lochner, *Always the Unexpected: A Book of Reminiscences* (New York, 1956). Another source for such inside information was Sigrid Schultz (pseudonym "John Dickson"), Berlin correspondent for the *Chicago Daily Tribune*, who knew Hermann Göring personally and interviewed Hitler many times. On the monitoring and censorship of foreign reporters, see Peter Longerich, *Propagandisten im Krieg: Die Presseabteilung des Auswärtigen Amtes unter Ribbentrop* (Munich, 1987), pp. 290ff.

17. See "Weisung des Führers und Obersten Befehlshabers der Wehrmacht, Geheime Kommandosache, Berlin, 21. Oktober 1938," in Michael Freund, *Weltgeschichte der Gegenwart in Dokumenten: Geschichte des Zweiten Weltkrieges*, vol. 1 (Freiburg, 1954), pp. 302ff.

18. See Kershaw, *Hitler 1936–1945*, p. 172.

19. See Rainerf Schmidt, *Der Zweite Weltkrieg: Die Zerstörung Europas* (Berlin, 2008), p. 13.

20. See Hans-Ulrich Thamer, *Der Nationalsozialismus*, pp. 319ff.

21. See Below, *Als Hitlers Adjutant*, pp. 169f.

22. Below, *Als Hitlers Adjutant*, p. 169. The circle around Hitler was thus neither "unsuspecting" nor "morally indifferent to his real plans," as Sereny writes in her biography of Speer (*Albert Speer*, p. 223).

23. See Speer, *Albert Speer: Die Kransberg-Protokolle 1945*, pp. 224f. and 227. While the "negotiations with Russia progressed," Speer claimed at that point, there were

"vague rumors" on the Obersalzberg "that something was going on with Russia" (p. 227). In *Inside the Third Reich*, p. 162, Speer writes that Hitler had already, for "weeks before" in "long talks with his four military adjutants tried to arrive at definite plans." In the German edition of his memoir, Speer specifies that talks "often went on for hours" [*Erinnerungen*, pp. 176–177]—"Hitler tried to arrive at definite plans." See also Kershaw, *Hitler 1936–1945*, pp. 283 and 290: Speer, according to Kershaw, "did not discuss foreign-policy details" with Hitler. See also Lars Lüdicke, *Griff nach der Weltherrschaft: Die Aussenpolitik des Dritten Reiches 1933–1945* (Berlin, 2009), pp. 124f.

24. Speer, *Inside the Third Reich*, p. 162.

25. Goebbels, diary entry, August 24, 1939, in *Die Tagebücher von Joseph Goebbels*, Teil I, vol. 7, p. 75.

26. Dietrich, *12 Jahre mit Hitler*, pp. 60f.

27. See snapshots from Eva Braun's photo diary, reproduced in Gun, *Eva Braun*, after p. 176. However, Gun falsely claims that these scenes took place in the Chancellery. Eva Braun apparently sold the negatives to Hoffmann, since all of the images can be found in the inventory of the Hoffmann Photo Archive in the Bavarian State Library [Bayerische Staatsbibliothek]; they are not labeled there as photographs by Eva Braun. In this regard see also Below, *Als Hitlers Adjutant*, pp. 182f.

28. Press statement in Fritz Sänger, *Politik der Täuschungen: Missbrauch der Presse im Dritten Reich: Weisungen, Informationen, Notizen 1933–1939* (Vienna, 1975), p. 360.

29. Quoted from Kershaw, *Hitler 1936–1945*, pp. 293ff. Cf. Franz Halder, *Kriegstagebuch: Tägliche Aufzeichnungen des Chefs des Generalstabes des Heeres 1939–1942*, ed. Hans-Adolf Jacobsen, vol. 1 (Stuttgart, 1963f.), p. 25.

30. See Lüdicke, *Griff nach der Weltherrschaft*, p. 127.

31. See Sigmund, *Die Frauen der Nazis*, p. 273.

32. See Joseph Goebbels, "Ansprache an die Danziger Bevölkerung anlässlich der Danziger Gaukulturwoche am 17. Juni 1939, Danzig, Balkon des Staatstheaters," in *Goebbels Reden 1932–1945*, ed. Helmut Heiber (Bindlach, 1991 [1st ed., Düsseldorf, 1971/1972]), pp. 334f. See also Below, *Als Hitlers Adjutant*, p. 182. According to Below, Hitler expressed himself in similar terms on the afternoon of August 23. See likewise Jeffrey Herf, " 'Der Krieg und die Juden': Nationalsozialistische Propaganda im Zweiten Weltkrieg," in *Das Deutsche Reich und der Zweite Weltkrieg*, vol. 9.2, ed. Jörg Echternkamp for the Militärgeschichtliches Forschungsamt (Munich, 2005), pp. 173f.

33. See Speer, *Inside the Third Reich*, pp. 163–164. Speer gives no departure date here ("a few days later"). Cf. Below, *Als Hitlers Adjutant*, p. 184, which says that Hitler flew to Berlin on the afternoon of August 24; Goebbels, diary entry, August 25, 1939, in *Die Tagebücher von Joseph Goebbels*, Teil I, vol. 7, p. 76: ". . . to Ainring by car. Flight to Berlin. The Führer in very high spirits." On Eva Braun's presence, see Gun, *Eva Braun*, pp. 180f.

34. See Below, *Als Hitlers Adjutant*, p. 192 (image on the following page).

35. Adolf Hitler, "Erklärung der Reichsregierung," in *Verhandlungen des Reichstages, 4. Wahlperiode 1939, Band 460. Stenographische Berichte 1939–1942, 3. Sitzung, Freitag, 1. September 1939.* Cf. Gun, *Eva Braun,* p. 181.

36. See Kershaw, *Hitler 1936–1945,* p. 221; "Weisung für den Angriff auf Polen vom 31. August 1939," in Hitler, *Reden und Proklamationen 1932–1945; Kommentiert von einem deutschen Zeitgenossen* (Wiesbaden, 1973), pp. 1,299f.

37. Hitler, "Erklärung der Reichsregierung, 1. September 1939," p. 48.

38. Quoted from Gun, *Eva Braun,* p. 181. On Hitler's appearance, see Below, *Als Hitlers Adjutant,* p. 195.

39. Christa Schroeder to Johanna Nusser, Berlin, September 3, 1939 (original), in ED 524, Institut für Zeitgeschichte (IfZ) Munich. Cf. Andreas Hillgruber, "Zum Kriegsbeginn im September 1939," in *Kriegsbeginn 1939. Entfesselung oder Ausbruch des Zweiten Weltkriegs?* ed. Gottfried Niedhart; Wege der Forschung, vol. 374 (Darmstadt, 1976), pp. 173ff. Hitler, Speer recalled, "tersely took his leave of the 'courtiers' who were remaining behind" (*Inside the Third Reich,* p. 167).

40. See Franz W. Seidler and Dieter Zeigert, *Die Führerhauptquartiere: Anlagen und Planungen im Zweiten Weltkrieg,* 2nd ed. (Munich, 2001), pp. 260 and 271.

41. See Dietrich, *12 Jahre mit Hitler,* p. 223; Rochus Misch, *Der letzte Zeuge: "Ich war Hitlers Telefonist, Kurier und Leibwächter"* (Munich and Zürich, 2008), p. 96.

42. Speer, *Albert Speer: Die Kransberg-Protokolle 1945,* p. 102.

43. See Seidler and Zeigert, *Die Führerhauptquartiere,* pp. 205f.

44. On the number of people the "Führer train" could hold (around 140), see Speer, *Spandauer Tagebücher,* illustration to the left of p. 305 (not reproduced in the English translation).

45. See Heinrich Hoffmann Photo Archive, hoff-27509, BSB Munich.

46. See Uwe Neumärker et al., *Wolfsschanze: Hitlers Machtzentrale im Zweiten Weltkrieg* (Berlin, 2007), p. 20.

47. Christa Schroeder to Johanna Nusser, Führer Headquarters, September 11, 1939 (copy), in ED 524, IfZ Munich. Cf. Kershaw, *Hitler 1936–1945,* p. 328.

48. See ibid.

49. See Heinrich Hoffmann Photo Archive, hoff-27282, hoff-27283, hoff-27398, hoff-27445, BSB Munich. Hoffmann's employees included the photographers Hermann Ege, Otto Schönstein, and Hugo Jäger, among others.

50. See Heinrich Hoffmann Photo Archive, hoff-27394; hoff-27779, BSB Munich. See also Heinrich Hoffmann, ed., *Mit Hitler in Polen* (Berlin, 1939). This photo-illustrated book eventually had 325,000 copies in print (Herz, *Hoffmann & Hitler,* pp. 372f.). Hoffmann later justified himself by saying that his images and books were not propaganda, merely a "record of contemporary history" (Hoffmann, "Mein Beruf," p. 36).

51. See Kershaw, *Hitler 1936–1945,* pp. 246f.; Schmidt, *Der Zweite Weltkrieg,* pp. 40ff.

52. See Heinrich Hoffmann Photo Archive, BSB Munich: arrest of Polish Jews by the SD, hoff-28297; Polish Jews in the Ghetto, hoff-28315; Polish Jews at forced labor,

hoff-28325; members of the security forces cutting off Jews' beards, hoff-28303; Polish Jews wearing yellow star, hoff-69249.

53. See Kershaw, *Hitler 1936–1945*, pp. 246f; Schmidt, *Der Zweite Weltkrieg*, pp. 40ff.

54. See Kershaw, *Hitler 1936–1945*, p. 522. See also Hildegard von Kotze, ed., *Heeresadjutant bei Hitler 1938–1943. Aufzeichnungen des Majors Engel*, Schriftenreihe der Vierteljahrshefte für Zeitgeschichte, no. 29 (Stuttgart, 1974), p. 65.

55. See Gun, *Eva Braun*, p. 199. Hoffmann says that Eva Braun's visits to Berlin were "always limited to a few days" (Hoffmann, "Mein Beruf," p. 23).

56. Below gives this date in *Als Hitlers Adjutant*, p. 219. See also Karl-Heinz Frieser, *Blitzkrieg-Legende: Der Westfeldzug 1940* (Munich, 2005), pp. 22ff.

57. See Below, *Als Hitlers Adjutant*, p. 212.

58. Hoffmann, *Hitler wie ich ihn sah*, p. 113.

59. Ibid. Cf. Dietrich, *12 Jahre mit Hitler*, p. 97.; Schroeder, *Er war mein Chef*, pp. 101f. Kershaw follows their account (*Hitler 1936–1945*, p. 276).

60. Below, *Als Hitlers Adjutant*, p. 229. Cf. Lang, *Der Sekretär*, p. 157. The decision to go to war against France was made immediately after the Poland campaign, and the commanders of the army, navy, and air force were informed of it on September 27, 1939 (Schmidt, *Der Zweite Weltkrieg*, pp. 49f.).

61. See Below, *Als Hitlers Adjutant*, pp. 214ff.; Speer, *Inside the Third Reich*, p. 169.

62. See Schmidt, *Der Zweite Weltkrieg*, pp. 62f.; Schroeder, *Er war mein Chef*, p. 106.

63. Breloer, *Unterwegs zur Familie Speer*, p. 247. Cf. Fest, *Die unbeantwortbaren Fragen*, pp. 80f.

64. On Hitler's travels, see Below, *Als Hitlers Adjutant*, pp. 239ff.

65. Misch, *Der letzte Zeuge*, pp. 110f.

66. Ibid.

67. See Below, *Als Hitlers Adjutant*, p. 249; Misch, *Der letzte Zeuge*, pp. 111f. There is an extensive account of the meeting in southern France in Kershaw, *Hitler 1936–1945*, pp. 441ff.

68. See Seidler and Zeigert, *Die Führerhauptquartiere*, p. 260.

69. See *Kriegstagebuch des Oberkommandos der Wehrmacht (Wehrmachtsführungsstab)*, ed. Percy Ernst Schramm, vol. I.1, *August 1940–31. Dezember 1942* (Frankfurt am Main, 1965), pp. 257f.; Kershaw, *Hitler 1936–1945*, p. 419.

70. See Schmidt, *Der Zweite Weltkrieg*, p. 100.

71. See in this regard Seidler and Zeigert, *Die Führerhauptquartiere*, pp. 193ff.

72. Below, *Als Hitlers Adjutant*, p. 256.

73. Ibid., p. 290. See also Schroeder, *Er war mein Chef*, pp. 278f.

74. Christa Schroeder to Johanna Nusser, Führer Headquarters, June 28, 1941, in ED 524, IfZ Munich. See also "Lagebesprechung im Kartenraum der 'Wolfsschanze' im Juni/Juli 1941," Heinrich Hoffmann Photo Archive, hoff-36340, BSB Munich.

75. Christa Schroeder to Johanna Nusser, Führer Headquarters, July 13, 1941, in ED 524, IfZ Munich.

76. Christa Schroeder to Johanna Nusser, Führer Headquarters, August 20, 1941, in ED 524, IfZ Munich.

77. See Below, *Als Hitlers Adjutant*, pp. 292 and 295; Kershaw, *Hitler 1936–1945*, pp. 444f., 466, and 485. See also Seidler and Zeigert, *Die Führerhauptquartiere*, pp. 205 and 208, according to which Hitler first, at the beginning of December, paid a visit to Army Group South in Mariupol on the Azov Sea in southeastern Ukraine, accompanied by Schmundt, Linge, and Morell.

78. See Henriette von Schirach, *Frauen um Hitler*, p. 235.

79. See Schmidt, *Der Zweite Weltkrieg*, pp. 104ff., 116ff., and 150. On Hitler's arrival at the Berghof, see Below, *Als Hitlers Adjutant*, p. 310, where he reports that he traveled with Hitler on April 24 to Berlin, where Hitler spoke before the Reichstag two days later.

80. See August Eigruber, "Besprechung in München am 27. April 1942" (p. 2) and "Vortrag beim Führer am 28. April 1942 in München" (p. 4) in "Vorträge des Gauleiters Eigruber vor dem Führer in Angelegenheiten der Planung der Stadt Linz," Political Files, Box 49, Upper Austria State Archives, Linz. Cf. Kershaw, *Hitler 1936–1945*, p. 516.

81. See Seidler and Zeigert, *Die Führerhauptquartiere*, pp. 261ff. See also Sigmund, *Die Frauen der Nazis*, p. 273, who writes: "The war's proceeding so badly for Germany meant the end of the idyllic life on the Obersalzberg."

82. See Hans Georg Hiller von Gaetringen, ed., *Das Auge des Dritten Reiches: Hitlers Kameramann und Fotograf Walter Frentz*, 2nd ed. (Munich and Berlin, 2007), p. 125. Photographs from the same black-and-white series can also be found in the Heinrich Hoffmann Photo Archive, hoff-584; hoff-579, BSB Munich.

83. See Heinrich Hoffmann Photo Archive, BSB Munich: Hitler with Speer's children, Braun with a camera in the picture (hoff-578); Hitler on the terrace, Uschi Schneider getting up (hoff-312); Hitler in the great hall with Gitti and Uschi Schneider (hoff-2177).

84. See Hiller von Gaetringen, *Das Auge des Dritten Reiches*, p. 125.

85. See Junge, *Bis zur letzten Stunde*, p. 80. Eva Braun, Junge writes, was the only person who was allowed to photograph Hitler "whenever she wanted." See also Danielle Costelle, *Eva Braun: Dans l'intimité d'Hitler* (Paris, 2007).

86. Schroeder, *Er war mein Chef*, p. 182.

87. Baldur von Schirach, *Ich glaubte an Hitler*, p. 267. See also Schroeder, *Er war mein Chef*, p. 182.

88. Baldur von Schirach, *Ich glaubte an Hitler*, p. 267.

89. Lang, *Der Sekretär*, pp. 166ff. Cf. Kershaw, *Hitler 1936–1945*, pp. 371ff. On Bormann's behavior, see Lang, *Der Sekretär*, p. 167.

90. See Ilse Hess to Albert Speer, Hindelang, June 25, 1968, in Speer Papers, N 1340, vol. 27, BA Koblenz.

91. Ilse Hess to Steffi Binder, n.p., August 7, 1941 (carbon copy), in Rudolf Hess Papers, J 1211 (–) 1993/300, vol. 2, file 21, BA Bern. Cf. Speer, *Inside the Third Reich*, p. 175.

92. See *Akten der Partei-Kanzlei der NSDAP: Rekonstruktion eines verlorengegangenen Bestandes*, Teil I, *Regesten*, vol. 1, p. viii (introduction).

93. Speer, *Inside the Third Reich*, p. 297.

94. See Seidler and Zeigert, *Die Führerhauptquartiere*, p. 260; Gun, *Eva Braun*, p. 212, and the reproduction of the passport issued April 3, 1942, with entry stamp of June 21, 1942, after p. 176.

95. See Schroeder, *Er war mein Chef*, p. 196.

96. See reproduction of Eva Braun's passport and visa in Gun, *Eva Braun*, after p. 176. Gun writes that Eva Braun traveled to Portofino for a month every year (p. 212).

97. See in this regard Bruno Frommann, *Reisen im Dienste politischer Zielsetzungen: Arbeiter-Reisen und "Kraft durch Freude"-Reisen* (Stuttgart, 1993).

98. See Rüdiger Overmans, "Das Schicksal der deutschen Kriegsgefangenen des Zweiten Weltkrieges," in *Das Deutsche Reich und der Zweite Weltkrieg*, vol. 10.2 (Munich, 2008), p. 404. Kershaw gives the figures of 90,000 captured and around 146,000 fallen German soldiers (*Hitler 1936–1945*, p. 550).

99. Traudl Junge Memoir, David Irving Collection, ED 100/106, pp. 11 and 17, IfZ Munich.

100. See Kershaw, *Hitler 1936–1945*, p. 726.

101. See Martin Bormann to Gerda Bormann, n.p., July 21, 1943, in Bormann, *The Bormann Letters*, pp. 12f.

102. Cf. Goebbels, diary entry, June 25, 1943, in *Die Tagebücher von Joseph Goebbels*, Teil II, *Diktate 1941–1945*), vol. 8, p. 537; Kershaw, *Hitler 1936–1945*, pp. 728 and 736ff.

103. Kershaw, *Hitler 1936–1945*, pp. 739ff. On Goebbels's role, see Aristotle A. Kallis, "Der Niedergang der Deutungsmacht: Nationalsozialistische Propaganda im Kriegsverlauf," in *Das Deutsche Reich und der Zweite Weltkrieg* (Stuttgart, 1979–2008), vol. 9.2, pp. 235ff.

104. See Schmidt, *Der Zweite Weltkrieg*, pp. 155f.

105. Goebbels, diary entry, August 10, 1943, in *Die Tagebücher von Joseph Goebbels*, Teil II, vol. 9, p. 267.

106. Below, *Als Hitlers Adjutant*, p. 340.

107. Henriette von Schirach, *Der Preis der Herrlichkeit*, pp. 214f. See also Kershaw, *Hitler 1936–1945*, p. 768.

108. Goebbels, diary entry, August 10, 1943, in *Die Tagebücher von Joseph Goebbels*, Teil II, *Diktate 1941–1945*, vol. 9 (Juli–September 1943), p. 267.

109. See Gerda Bormann to Martin Bormann, Obersalzberg, August 13, 1943, in Bormann, *The Bormann Letters*, p. 19.

110. See Goebbels, diary entry, March 2, 1943, in *Die Tagebücher von Joseph Goebbels*, Teil II, *Diktate 1941–1945*, Band 7 (Januar–März 1943), p. 454. See Below, *Als Hitlers Adjutant*, p. 340.

10. THE EVENTS OF JULY 20, 1944, AND THEIR AFTERMATH

1. See Kallis, "Der Niedergang der Deutungsmacht," in *Das Deutsche Reich und der Zweite Weltkrieg*, vol. 9.2, pp. 232f.

2. Hitler suffered bruises and burns on his head, arms, and legs; both arms were severely swollen, according to the doctor's report (Theodor Morell, July 20, 1944, Patient A., in Theodor Morell Papers, N 1348, BA Koblenz).

3. See Tobias Kniebe, *Operation Walküre: Das Drama des 20. Juli* (Berlin, 2009); Bernhard R. Kroener, *Generaloberst Friedrich Fromm: Eine Biographie* (Paderborn, 2005), pp. 700ff.

4. See Kershaw, *Hitler 1936–1945*, p. 797; Speer, *Inside the Third Reich*, p. 395. See also Below, *Als Hitlers Adjutant*, p. 385: Hitler looked at the pictures "so little . . . the way he reluctantly paid attention to the pictures of destroyed cities." Fegelein, though, "generously" showed around "the photos of the hangings." Bernd Freytag von Loringhoven, in contrast, reports (*Mit Hitler im Bunker: Die letzten Monate im Führerhauptquartier Juli 1944-April 1945* [Berlin, 2006], pp. 65f.) that Hitler "eagerly" seized "the macabre pictures" and examined them "for a long time with practically lascivious pleasure."

5. See Fest, *Die unbeantwortbaren Fragen*, p. 143. On Fegelein, who played a leading part in "combatting partisans" and in "cleansing actions" and had the lives of thousands of civilians on his conscience, see Peter Longerich, *Heinrich Himmler: Biographie* (Munich, 2008), pp. 316f., 331f., and 549ff.

6. Quoted in Schroeder, *Er war mein Chef*, pp. 167f. Schroeder was convinced that Eva Braun's feelings for Fegelein "exceeded that of purely a sister-in-law" but that nonetheless "nothing happened between them."

7. Goebbels, entry of March 14, 1944, in *Die Tagebücher von Joseph Goebbels*, Teil II, vol. 11, p. 472.

8. Goebbels, entry of June 6, 1944, in *Die Tagebücher von Joseph Goebbels*, Teil II, vol. 12, p. 414.

9. See Below, *Als Hitlers Adjutant*, pp. 370 and 379.

10. Account by Herta Ostermayr, quoted in Gun, *Eva Braun*, p. 213.

11. Goebbels, entry of August 24, 1944, in *Die Tagebücher von Joseph Goebbels*, Teil II, vol. 13, pp. 305f.

12. See Schmidt, *Albert Speer*, p. 123; Reuth, *Goebbels*, pp. 549ff.

13. See Schmidt, *Albert Speer*, p. 125; Speer, *Albert Speer: Die Kransberg-Protokolle 1945*, pp. 47f.

14. Ilse Hess to Lucian W. Reiser, n.p., May 16, 1944 (carbon copy), in Rudolf Hess Papers, J 1211 (–) 1993/300, vol. 12, file 148, Swiss Federal Archives, Bern.

15. "Besprechung zwischen Herrn Albrecht und Frl. Schröder, früher Sekretärin v. Hitler," Berchtesgaden, May 22, 1945, in MA 1298/10, Mikrofilm, Various Documents, DJ-13 (David Irving), IfZ Munich. See also Kershaw, *Hitler 1936–1945*, p. 798.

16. Schroeder, *Er war mein Chef*, p. 148. Cf. "Besprechung zwischen Herrn Albrecht und Frl. Schröder, früher Sekretärin v. Hitler," previously cited. See also Junge, *Bis zur letzten Stunde*, p. 151, where Junge writes that Eva Braun wrote Hitler an "anxious and despairing letter," so that he, "utterly moved by her devotion," sent "his shredded uniform to [her in] Munich as a keepsake."

17. See Loringhoven, *Mit Hitler im Bunker*, pp. 7ff.

18. Junge, *Bis zur letzten Stunde*, p. 155.

19. See Gun, *Eva Braun*, p. 213. Gun is here quoting Braun's friend Herta Schneider. In the Heinrich Hoffmann Photo Archive are pictures of a soldier presenting a

uniform destroyed in the attack, presumably Hitler's (hoff-53923, hoff-53921, BSB Munich).

20. See Gun, *Eva Braun*, pp. 214–215. This alleged document is cited uncritically by Sigmund (*Die Frauen der Nazis*, p. 274).

21. See Below, *Als Hitlers Adjutant*, pp. 382 and 384.

22. Junge, *Bis zur letzten Stunde*, p. 146.

23. See John Zimmermann, "Die deutsche Kriegführung im Westen 1944/55," in *Das Deutsche Reich und der Zweite Weltkrieg*, vol. 10.1, ed. Rolf-Dieter Müller for the Militärgeschichtliches Forschungsamt (Munich, 2008), p. 277.

24. See Kershaw, *Hitler 1936–1945*, p. 722.

25. Goebbels, entry of March 14, 1944, in *Die Tagebücher von Joseph Goebbels*, Teil II, vol. 11, p. 472.

26. See Schenck, *Patient Hitler*, pp. 44ff. and 78f.

27. Loringhoven, *Mit Hitler im Bunker*, p. 10.

28. Junge, *Bis zur letzten Stunde*, p. 160.

29. See Theodor Morell, 1944 pocket calender, in Theodor Morell Papers, N 1348–2, BA Koblenz. See also Schenck, *Patient Hitler*, p. 57; Schroeder, *Er war mein Chef*, p. 149; Below, *Als Hitlers Adjutant*, pp. 387 and 389; Junge, *Bis zur letzten Stunde*, p. 152; Kershaw, *Hitler 1936–1945*, p. 726. Karl Brandt and Hanskarl von Hasselbach ceased to be Hitler's accompanying physicians on October 10, 1944; the role was taken on by SS-Obersturmbannführer Dr. Stumpfegger (Reichsleiter Martin Bormann [Secretary to the Führer] to Reich Press Chief Dr. Dietrich, Führer Headquarters, October 10, 1944 (original), in Theodor Morell Papers, N 1348–4, BA Koblenz).

30. See Speer, *Inside the Third Reich*, p. 415; *Albert Speer: Die Kransberg-Protokolle 1945*, p. 394; Kershaw, *Hitler 1936–1945*, p. 731. This idea of Hitler's was strengthened by Alfred Jodl, Artillery General and Chief of the Operations Staff of the Army, who had been convinced since fall 1943 that the war would be "decided" in the west (Werner Rahn, "Die deutsche Seekriegführung 1943 bis 1945," in *Das Deutsche Reich und der Zweite Weltkrieg*, vol. 10.1, p. 21).

31. See reproduction of the last page of her handwritten directions from October 26, 1944, in Gun, *Eva Braun*, after p. 176. Eva Braun noted in her last letter to her friend Herta Schneider, April 22, 1945, that she had left her last "testament at Wasserburgerstrasse" (see reproduction in Gun, *Eva Braun*, after p. 192).

32. See Gerda Bormann to Martin Bormann, Obersalzberg, October 24, 1944, and Martin Bormann to Gerda Bormann, Führer Headquarters, October 25, 1944, in Bormann, *The Bormann Letters*, pp. 138, 139.

33. See Schmidt, *Karl Brandt*, pp. 495ff.

34. See Hoffmann, "Mein Beruf," p. 67. See also Gerda Bormann to Martin Bormann, Obersalzberg, October 24, 1944, in Bormann, *The Bormann Letters*, p. 138. On August 28, Gerda Bormann still wrote that Eva Braun very much hoped to be able to work with Hoffmann in Munich or Reichenhall, but that nothing was yet decided

(Gerda Bormann to Martin Bormann, August 28, 1944, in *The Bormann Letters*, pp. 91f.).

35. See Gun, *Eva Braun*, pp. 145ff. Also named are paintings by Karl Rickelt, Johann Fischbach, and Adalbert Wex. Eva Braun is said to have owned a picture of Hitler and another of herself by Theodor Bohnenberger, a painter of portraits and nudes.

36. See Hans Sarkowicz, ed., *Hitlers Künstler: Die Kultur im Dienst des Nationalsozialismus* (Frankfurt am Main, 2004).

37. See Eva Braun testament of October 26, 1944, in Gun, *Eva Braun*, pp. 233f.

38. Quoted in Henriette von Schirach, *Frauen um Hitler*, p. 235.

11. The Decision for Berlin

1. Theodor Morell, 1944 pocket calendar, in Theodor Morell Papers, N 1348–2, BA Koblenz. On November 22, Goebbels noted in his diaries: "The Führer has now arrived in Berlin, thank God" (entry of November 22, 1944, in *Die Tagebücher von Joseph Goebbels*, Teil II, vol. 14, p. 258.

2. See Below, *Als Hitlers Adjutant*, p. 395.

3. Theodor Morell, 1944 pocket calendar, in Theodor Morell Papers, N 1348–2, BA Koblenz. Morell also notes in his calendar under the same date: "Met Miss E." Again, a few lines later: "Met E. when leaving." See also Lambert, *The Lost Life of Eva Braun*, p. 511.

4. Goebbels, entry of November 24, 1944, in *Die Tagebücher von Joseph Goebbels*, Teil II, vol. 14, p. 269.

5. See Ulrich Völklein, ed., *Hitlers Tod: Die letzten Tage im Führerbunker* (Göttingen, 1998), pp. 23ff.

6. See Junge, *Bis zur letzten Stunde*, p. 167.

7. See Sönke Neitzel, *Abgehört: Deutsche Generäle in britischer Kriegsgefangenschaft 1942–1945* (Berlin, 2007), p. 166.

8. See Kershaw, *Hitler 1936–1945*, pp. 743; Below, *Als Hitlers Adjutant*, p. 398.

9. See Besymenski, *Die letzten Notizen von Martin Bormann*, p. 64: "1/18 19.10 departure with Sonderwagen to Bln. Dad with Mom, with E. B., Frau Fegelein, and Bredow."

10. Dr. Hans-Otto Meissner, "Der letzte Befehl," undated manuscript, p. 11, in Ms 291, IfZ Munich. See also Schroeder, *Er war mein Chef*, p. 168, which says that Eva Braun arrived "in Berlin at the Chancellery in February 1945, against Hitler's will."

11. Junge, *Bis zur letzten Stunde*, p. 169.

12. See Loringhoven, *Mit Hitler im Bunker*, pp. 72f. The encounter is here erroneously dated to "shortly before Christmas," at which time Hitler was at his headquarters on the western front.

13. Goebbels, entry of February 1, 1945, in *Die Tagebücher von Joseph Goebbels*, Teil II, vol. 15, p. 296.

14. See Martin Bormann to Gerda Bormann, Führer Headquarters, December 28, 1944, in Bormann, *The Bormann Letters*, pp. 154f.

15. See Richard Lakowski, "Der Zusammenbruch der deutschen Verteidigung zwischen Ostsee und Karparten," in *Das Deutsche Reich und der Zweite Weltkrieg*, vol. 10.1, pp. 588ff. See also Below, *Als Hitlers Adjutant*, p. 400.

16. See Seidler and Zeigert, *Die Führerhauptquartiere*, p. 324; Kershaw, *Hitler 1936–1945*, p. 793. Gun, on the other hand, claims that Eva Braun celebrated her last birthday on February 8 in Munich (*Eva Braun*, p. 239).

17. See Meissner, "Der letzte Befehl," p. 11: "The bedroom next door, originally intended as just a cloakroom was furnished with a bed, table, and chair only in February 1945 so that it could serve as a place to sleep, and then occupied by Eva Braun when she showed up in Berlin unexpectedly and against Hitler's orders." See also Junge, *Bis zur letzten Stunde*, p. 177, and Speer, *Inside the Third Reich*, p. 484: Eva Braun "had had some one the expensive furniture which I had designed for her years ago brought from her two rooms in the upper floors of the Chancellery."

18. These figures are taken from the following: Horst Boog, "Die strategische Bomber-offensive der Alliierten gegen Deutschland und die Reichsluftverteidigung in der Schlussphase des Krieges," in *Das Deutsche Reich und der Zweite Weltkrieg*, vol. 10.1, p. 790. See Kershaw, *Hitler 1936–1945*, p. 792. See also Antony Beevor, *Berlin: The Downfall 1945* (London, 2002), pp. 74f.

19. Goebbels, diary entry of February 6, 1945, in *Die Tagebücher von Joseph Goebbels*, Teil II, vol. 15, p. 320.

20. See Martin Bormann to Gerda Bormann, February 6, 1945, in Bormann, *The Bormann Letters*, pp. 174f. See also Besymenski, *Die letzten Notizen von Martin Bormann*, p. 106.

21. Schroeder, *Er war mein Chef*, p. 196. Schroeder says nothing in her memoir about Eva Braun's presence in Berlin in February 1945. See also "Besprechung zwischen Herrn Albrecht und Frl. Schröder, früher Sekretärin v. Hitler," Berchtesgaden, May 22, 1945, in MA 1298/10, Microfilm, Various Documents, DJ-13 (David Irving), IfZ Munich.

22. See Martin Bormann to Gerda Bormann, February 6, 1945, in Bormann, *The Bormann Letters*, pp. 174f.

23. See Schmidt, *Karl Brandt*, p. 499.

24. Ibid., pp. 500f.

25. Ibid., pp. 501ff.

26. Eva Braun to Herta Schneider, Berlin, April 19, 1945, in Gun, *Eva Braun*, pp. 247–248. Transcript in Speer Papers, N 1340, vol. 287, BA Koblenz. Walter Schellenberg, head of the secret service since 1944, even claimed in his postwar memoir that the death sentence passed on Brandt really had to do with "an intrigue in Hitler's closest circle, including Eva Braun and her sister, Frau Fegelein" (Schellenberg, *Aufzeich-nungen*, p. 361).

27. Speer, *Inside the Third Reich*, p. 465.

28. See Martin Bormann to Gerda Bormann, February 6, 1945, in Bormann, *The Bormann Letters*, pp. 174f.

29. See Martin Bormann to Gerda Bormann, February 9, 1945, in Bormann, *The*

Bormann Letters, pp. 180. See also Besymenski, *Die letzten Notizen von Martin Bormann*, p. 107.

30. See Martin Bormann to Gerda Bormann, February 9, 1945, in Bormann, *The Bormann Letters*, pp. 180. See also Besymenski, *Die letzten Notizen von Martin Bormann*, p. 107; Heinz Linge, *Bis zum Untergang: Als Chef des Persönlichen Dienstes bei Hitler*, ed. Werner Maser (Munich, 1982), pp. 69f. According to Linge, Bormann's wife and children went with Eva Braun and her sister to Munich.

31. See Kershaw, *Hitler 1936–1945*, pp. 821f.; Giesler, *Ein anderer Hitler*, pp. 479f. Neither Bormann, named by Giesler as one of the people present, nor Speer makes reference to this event in his notes. Cf. Hiller von Gaetringen, ed., *Das Auge des Dritten Reiches*, pp. 86f.; Below, *Als Hitlers Adjutant*, p. 403.

32. Speer, *Albert Speer: Die Kransberg-Protokolle 1945*, p. 133. See also Wilhelm Höttl, *Einsatz für das Reich* (Koblenz, 1997), p. 117.

33. See Besymenski, *Die letzten Notizen von Martin Bormann*, p. 147; Speer, *Erinnerungen*, p. 468.

34. Martin Bormann to Gerda Bormann, February 18, 1945, in Bormann, *The Bormann Letters*, p. 183. See also Linge, *Bis zum Untergang*, p. 70.

35. Julius Schaub, quoted from Meissner, "Der letzte Befehl," p. 34.

36. Besymenski, *Die letzten Notizen von Martin Bormann*, p. 148. Cf. Gun, *Eva Braun*, p. 181.

37. Henriette von Schirach, *Frauen um Hitler*, p. 236.

38. Speer, *Inside the Third Reich*, p. 465. See also Artur Axmann, "*Das kann doch nicht das Ende sein*": Hitlers letzter Reichsjugendführer erinnert sich (Koblenz, 1995), p. 434. Axmann, who moved into the "Führer bunker" on April 23, reports that Eva Braun told him there "that the Führer had sent her to Munich in early March, but that she had returned to Berlin against his will on April 15."

39. Speer, *Inside the Third Reich*, p. 465; Below, *Als Hitlers Adjutant*, p. 404.

40. See Kershaw, *Hitler 1936–1945*, p. 731. Joachim von Ribbentrop, *Zwischen London und Moskau*, p. 268.

41. See the extensive discussion in Kershaw, *Hitler 1936–1945*, p. 732. See also Michael Bloch, *Ribbentrop: A Biography* (New York, 1993), pp. 421ff.; Schmidt, *Albert Speer*, pp. 151ff.; Fest, *Speer*, pp. 314ff.; Longerich, *Heinrich Himmler*, pp. 745ff.

42. Schroeder, *Er war mein Chef*, p. 198.

43. Ibid., p. 168.

44. Eva Braun to Herta Schneider, Berlin, April 19, 1945, in Gun, *Eva Braun*, pp. 247–248.

45. See Schroeder, *Er war mein Chef*, p. 199.

46. Eva Braun to Herta Schneider, Berlin, April 19, 1945, previously cited. Junge also reports that there were gunshots (*Bis zur letzten Stunde*, p. 182). Hitler had apparently tried again and again to persuade her to leave the bunker and get herself to safety. Heinrich Hoffmann reports that Hitler asked him to bring Eva Braun to Munich with him in early April 1945 (Hoffmann, *Hitler wie ich ihn sah*, pp. 230f.).

47. Below, *Als Hitlers Adjutant*, p. 408. Speer similarly writes (*Inside the Third Reich*,

p. 484) that Eva Braun was "the only prominent candidate for death in this bunker who displayed an admirable and superior composure." Likewise Schroeder, *Er war mein Chef*, p. 169, and Axmann, *"Das kann doch nicht das Ende sein,"* p. 434, who wrote that Eva Braun appeared to him "like an unreal apparition."

48. See Junge, *Bis zur letzten Stunde*, p. 183; Below, *Als Hitlers Adjutant*, p. 417.

49. See Lakowski, "Der Zusammenbruch der deutschen Verteidigung zwischen Ostsee und Karpaten," p. 648.

50. See Below, *Als Hitlers Adjutant*, p. 411; Speer, *Inside the Third Reich*, pp. 474; Loringhoven, *Mit Hitler im Bunker*, p. 145; Kershaw, *Hitler 1936–1945*, p. 823; Frank, *Der Tod im Führerbunker*, pp. 34ff. Eva Braun had written to Herta Schneider on the previous day that "getting through with a car" was probably "no longer an option." But "a way for us *all* to see you again would surely" turn up (Eva Braun to Herta Schneider, Berlin, April 19, 1945, previously cited).

51. Schroeder, *Er war mein Chef*, pp. 200ff.

52. Statement of Erich Kempka about Hitler's last days, Berchtesgaden, June 20, 1945, MA 1298/10, Microfilm, Various Documents, DJ-13 (David Irving), IfZ Munich.

53. Cf. Junge, *Bis zur letzten Stunde*, p. 177, gives the line as "Blood-red roses tell you of my joy." But this line does not appear in the 1929 song "Bluterote Rosen" ["Blood-Red Roses"]; music by Hans Hünemeyer, lyrics by Alfred Krönkemeier).

54. See Bloch, *Ribbentrop* p. 425. See also Speer, *Inside the Third Reich*, p. 483, which however does not mention a meeting between Eva Braun and Ribbentrop.

55. Eva Braun, quoted from Junge, *Bis zur letzten Stunde*, p. 178.

56. Hitler, quoted from Kershaw, *Hitler 1936–1945*, p. 1,032.

57. See Junge, *Bis zur letzten Stunde*, p. 189; Loringhoven, *Mit Hitler im Bunker*, p. 150. See also Schroeder, *Er war mein Chef*, p. 205. Eva Braun wrote to her sister Gretl on April 23, 1945: "I hope Morell has safely arrived with my jewelry. It would be terrible if something had happened." (Eva Braun to Gretl Fegelein, Berlin, April 23, 1945, in Gun, *Eva Braun*, p. 254.)

58. See Kershaw, *Hitler 1936–1945*, pp. 824f. Cf. Below, *Als Hitlers Adjutant*, p. 411. See also Frank, *Der Tod im Führerbunker*, pp. 63ff.

59. Junge, *Bis zur letzten Stunde*, p. 180.

60. See Meissner, "Der letzte Befehl," pp. 2 and 16. These notes are based on what Schaub, who shared "time and a cell" with Meissner "in the witness wing of the Nuremberg prison," apparently told Meissner about "his last days with Adolf Hitler." Schaub mentioned Hitler's "last command": the "order to destroy the secret Führer archive" (p. 6). Hitler allegedly said: "No scrap of it must fall into enemy hands" (p. 2). Cf. Below, *Als Hitlers Adjutant*, p. 411.

61. Eva Braun to Herta Schneider, Berlin, April 22, 1945, in Gun, *Eva Braun*, 252. See also Speer, *Inside the Third Reich*, p. 476: According to Speer Eva Braun had told him during his last visit to the bunker that Hitler "had wanted to take his own life on April 22."

62. See Kershaw, *Hitler 1936–1945*, p. 826.

63. Eva Braun to Gretl Fegelein, Berlin, April 23, 1945, in Gun, *Eva Braun*. Eva

Braun mentions here an additional letter that Hitler's servant Wilhelm Arndt had been given to bring to the family at the Berghof, together with a suitcase. They had heard, Braun writes, that his airplane was "overdue." In fact, the plane, having taken off from Berlin-Staaken on April 22, crashed in Börnersdorf. Arndt lost his life. See Schroeder, *Er war mein Chef*, p. 362. Decades later, a reporter for the *Stern*, Gerd Heidemann, reported that "Diaries" by Adolf Hitler had been salvaged from the wreckage in Börnersdorf. See Michael Seufert, *Der Skandal um die Hitler-Tagebücher* (Frankfurt am Main, 2008), p. 15.

64. See Lakowski, "Der Zusammenbruch der deutschen Verteidigung zwischen Ostsee und Karpaten," pp. 664f.; Besymenski, *Die letzten Notizen von Martin Bormann*, p. 230.

65. Speer, *Inside the Third Reich*, p. 476.

66. Ibid., p. 484.

67. Junge, *Bis zur letzten Stunde*, p. 187.

68. Speer, *Albert Speer: Die Kransberg-Protokolle 1945*, p. 119.

69. "Report of Conversation among Gretl Braun Fegelein, Frau Herta Schneider, and Walter Hirschfeld (undercover), 25 September 1945," in F 135/2, vol. 2, p. 367, IfZ Munich. See also Riefenstahl, *Memoiren*, p. 405; Hiller von Gaetringen, *Das Auge des Dritten Reiches*, p. 32.

70. "Report of Conversation among Gretl Braun Fegelein, Frau Herta Schneider, and Walter Hirschfeld (undercover), 25 September 1945," p. 368. See also Schroeder, *Er war mein Chef*, pp. 213f.

71. Below, *Als Hitlers Adjutant*, p. 414.

72. Expert assessment in the matter of Adolf Hitler, Berchtesgaden District Court, August 1, 1956 (Ref.: Z.: II 48/52), copy, Gb 05.01/2, pp. 30ff., IfZ Munich. See also Kershaw, *Hitler 1936–1945*, p. 1038.

73. See Junge, *Bis zur letzten Stunde*, p. 196.

74. See Loringhoven, *Mit Hitler im Bunker*, pp. 157ff.; Gerhard Boldt, *Die letzten Tage der Reichskanzlei* (Hamburg, 1964), pp. 128ff.

75. See Boldt, *Die letzten Tage der Reichskanzlei*, pp. 135f. Extensive discussion in Schellenberg, *Aufzeichnungen*, pp. 355ff.

76. See Longerich, *Heinrich Himmler*, pp. 750f.; Folke Bernadotte, *Das Ende: Meine Verhandlungen in Deutschland im Frühjahr 1945 und ihre politischen Folgen* (Zürich and New York, 1945).

77. Eva Braun to Gretl Fegelein, Berlin, April 23, 1945, previously cited. Thus Fegelein in no way "left the Chancellery unnoticed" on April 26, as Gerhard Boldt claims (*Die letzten Tage der Reichskanzlei*, p. 133). Boldt was a member of General Wilhelm Krebs's staff and spent the last weeks in the bunker.

78. Junge, *Bis zur letzten Stunde*, p. 197. Below and Loringhoven also report that they received a call from Fegelein from his Berlin apartment (Below, *Als Hitlers Adjutant*, p. 415; Loringhoven, *Mit Hitler im Bunker*, p. 167).

79. "Report of Conversation among Gretl Braun Fegelein, Frau Herta Schneider, and Walter Hirschfeld (undercover), 25 September 1945," p. 367.

80. See Below, *Als Hitlers Adjutant*, p. 415. Below dates these events to April 28, whereas Traudl Junge writes that Fegelein was already being sought on the previous day and was brought to the Chancellery on the evening of April 27 (*Bis zur letzten Stunde*, pp. 197ff.).

81. See Kershaw, *Hitler 1936–1945*, p.823

82. Adolf Hitler, "Mein privates Testament," Berlin, April 29, 1945, 4 o'clock (transcription of a copy of a notarized testament), in Adolf Hitler Papers, N 1128/38, BA Koblenz. On the testament, see Kershaw, *Hitler 1936–1945*, p. 823

83. See Below, *Als Hitlers Adjutant*, p. 415; Henrik Eberle and Matthias Uhl, eds., *Das Buch Hitler: Geheimdossier des NKWD für Josef W. Stalin, zusammengestellt aufgrund der Verhörprotokolle des Persönlichen Adjutanten Hitlers, Otto Günsche, und des Kammerdieners Heinz Linge* (Bergisch Gladbach, 2005 [Moscow, 1948–1949]), p. 436. Hitler's servant Heinz Linge gave the impression in his memoir, published in 1980, that he had been present (Linge, *Bis zum Untergang*, pp. 281f.). A few years after the fact, Otto Meissner recalled that Hitler had had "the authorized registrar" brought on April 28 in an "armored car" (*Staatssekretär*, p. 610).

84. See Below, *Als Hitlers Adjutant*, p. 416. See also Kershaw, *Hitler 1936–1945*, p. 823

85. Expert assessment in the matter of Adolf Hitler, Berchtesgaden District Court, August 1, 1956 (Ref.: Z.: II 48/52), copy, Gb 05.01/2, pp. 34f., IfZ Munich.

86. See Lakowski, "Der Zusammenbruch der deutschen Verteidigung zwischen Ostsee und Karpaten," p. 671.

87. See "Ergebnisse der gerichtsmedizinischen Untersuchung durch sowjetische Ärzte," in *Hitlers Tod*, ed. Völklein, pp. 121ff.

12. AFTER DEATH

1. Notes by the translator, Pavlov, on the conversation between Stalin and Harry Hopkins, May 26, 1945, in the Russian Presidential Archives, Moscow, quoted from Völklein, *Hitlers Tod*, p. 60.

2. See Charles L. Mee Jr., *Meeting at Potsdam* (New York, 1975), p. 94.

3. "Report of Conversation among Gretl Braun Fegelein, Frau Herta Schneider, und Walter Hirschfeld (undercover), 25 September 1945," p. 368.

4. Personal telegram from the Commander of the First Belorussian Front, Marshall Georgy Zhukov, May 1, 1945, Dossier No. 41-Sh/2-w/I, Russian Presidential Archives, Moscow, quoted in Völklein, *Hitlers Tod*, p. 47. See also Lew Besymenski, *Der Tod des Adolf Hitler* (Hamburg, 1968).

5. See autopsy records for Adolf Hitler (File 12) and Eva Braun (File 13), Archive of the President of the Russian Federation in the Archive of the Federal Counterintelligence Service, Moscow, quoted in Völklein, *Hitlers Tod*, pp. 126ff.

6. Anonymous letter to Dwight D. Eisenhower, Amsterdam, November 22, 1948. (Glenn H. Palmer, Chief, Intelligence & Security Branch) in David Irving Collection, "Adolph Hitler 1944–1953," vol. 1, pp. 16ff., F 135/1, IfZ Munich.

7. "Presse-Information des Bayerischen Staatsministeriums der Justiz, Betreff: Ver-

fahren zur Feststellung des Todes Hitlers, München, 25. Oktober 1956 [Press release from the Bavarian State Ministry of Justice, re: Proceedings to Determine Hitler's Death, Munich, October 25, 1956]" (copy), Gb 05.01/1, IfZ Munich.

8. See expert assessment in the matter of Adolf Hitler, Berchtesgaden District Court, August 1, 1956 (Ref.: Z.: II 48/52), copy, Gb 05.01/2, pp. 2f., IfZ Munich.

9. Ibid., pp. 71ff.

10. See Völklein, ed., *Hitlers Tod*, pp. 194f.

Conclusion

1. Junge, *Bis zur letzten Stunde*, p. 196.

2. Fritz Braun, statement of December 1, 1947, public hearing of the Munich District Court for oral arguments in the case of Braun, Fritz Wilhelm, in Denazification Court Records, box 188, State Archives, Munich.

3. Schroeder, *Er war mein Chef*, p. 215.

4. See Below, *Als Hitlers Adjutant*, pp. 166ff.

5. Christa Schroeder to Johanna Nusser, Führer Headquarters, June 28, 1941, in ED 524, IfZ Munich.

6. See Walther Darré, *Aufzeichnungen.*

7. See Ilse Fucke-Michels to State Commissioner for Refugees, Ruhpolding, October 20, 1946, in Denazification Court Records, box 468, State Archives, Munich.

8. Herta Schneider, statement of June 23, 1949, "Öffentliche Sitzung der Hauptkammer München zur mündlichen Verhandlung in dem Verfahren gegen Herta Schneider, geb. Ostermayr," in Denazification Court Records, box 1670, State Archives, Munich.

Selected Bibliography

I. Primary Sources

1. *Archival Sources*

Bavarian State Library [Bayerische Staatsbibliothek, or BSB], Munich

Ernst Hanfstaengl Papers

Heinrich Hoffmann Photo Archive

Cornell Law Library, Cornell University

Donovan Nuremberg Trials Collection

Institut für Zeitgeschichte (IfZ), Munich

Besprechung zwischen Herrn Albrecht und Frl. Paula Hitler [Conversation between Mr. Albrecht and Miss Paula Hitler], Berchtesgaden, May 26, 1945, microfilm, Various Documents DJ-13 (David Irving)

Richard Walther Darré, Notes 1945–1948, ED 110

Hermann Esser, ZS 1030

Johannes Göhler, ZS 2244

Documentation "Adolph Hitler 1944–1953," F 135, vols. 1–4

Gutachten in der Angelegenheit Adolf Hitler, Amtsgericht Berchtesgaden, 1. August 1956, Kopie, Gb 05.01/2

Heinrich Hoffmann, "Mein Beruf," undated manuscript [1947?]

David Irving Collection, ED 100

Statement from Erich Kempka about Hitler's last days, Berchtesgaden, June 20, 1945, microfilm, Various Documents DJ-13 (David Irving)

Therese Linke, unpublished handwritten memoir, no year, ZS 3135

Dr. Hans-Otto Meissner, "Der letzte Befehl," undated manuscript, Ms 291

Julius Schaub, ZS 137

Christa Schroeder letters to Johanna Nusser, April 21, 1939–August 14, 1942, ED 524

Franz Xaver Schwarz, ZS 1452

Mary Ferrell Foundation Digital Archive, www.maryferrell.org/wiki/index .php.JFK_assassination

CIA Collection, JFK Assassination Documents

Municipal Archives [Stadtarchiv], Munich

Meldekarte Eva Anna Paula Braun

NATIONAL ARCHIVE [BUNDESARCHIV, OR BA], BERLIN

Albert Bormann, diary of correspondence from July 29, 1939, to July 14, 1941, NS 24/327

Reich Chancellery ("New Reich Chancellery"), R43

NATIONAL ARCHIVE [BUNDESARCHIV, OR BA], KOBLENZ

Brammer Collection, Zsg. 101 / Nr. 93

Karl Brandt, "Das Problem Hitler, Nr. 2," September 27, 1945, Kleine Erwerbung 441–3

Karl Brandt, "Julius Schaub," September 20, 1945, Kleine Erwerbung 441–3

Notes of Reich Press Chief Dr. Dietrich, Kleine Erwerbung 441–3

Franz Ritter von Epp Papers, N1101

Fritz Hesse Papers, N1322

Heinrich Himmler Papers, N1126

Adolf Hitler Papers, N1128

Robert Ley Papers, N1468

Theodor Morell Papers, N1438

"Originalnotizen von P. E. Schramm über Hitler, gemacht während der Befragung von Hitlers Leibärzten," summer 1945, Kleine Erwerbung 441–3

Albert Speer Papers, N1340

Fritz Wiedemann Papers, Kleine Erwerbung Nr. 671

NATIONAL ARCHIVES OF THE UNITED STATES, WASHINGTON, DC

CIA Special Collections: Office of Strategic Services, Adolf Hitler, December 3, 1942

STATE ARCHIVES [STAATSARCHIV], MUNICH

Spruchkammerakten Eva Hitler, geb. Braun

Spruchkammerakten Herta Schneider, geb. Ostermayr

Spruchkammerakten Ilse Fucke-Michels

Spruchkammerakten Sofie Stork

STATE ARCHIVES [STAATSARCHIV], NUREMBERG

KV-Anklage, Documents

KV-Anklage, Interrogations (Nicolaus von Below, Dr. Karl Brandt, Wilhelm Brückner, Heinrich Hoffmann

KV-Anklage, Organisation (Theodor Morell)

Reichsparteitag 1935. Programm, Polizeiliche Anordnungen, Sonstiges [1935 Party Convention: Program, Police Orders, Other Material], ed. Polizeidirektion Nürnberg-Fürth

SWISS FEDERAL ARCHIVE [SCHWEIZERISCHES BUNDESARCHIV], BERN

Rudolf Hess Papers

UPPER AUSTRIA STATE ARCHIVE [OBERÖSTERREICHISCHES LANDESARCHIV], LINZ

"Vorträge des Gauleiters Eigruber vor dem Führer in Angelegenheiten der Planung der Stadt Linz," Politische Akten, Schachtel 49

2. *Printed Sources*

Akten der Partei-Kanzlei der NSDAP: Rekonstruktion eines verlorengegangenen Bestandes. Edited by Helmut Heiber et al. Munich, 1983–1992.

Besymenski, Lew. *Die letzten Notizen von Martin Bormann: Ein Dokument und sein Verfasser.* Stuttgart, 1974.

Bormann, Martin. *The Bormann Letters: The Private Correspondence Between Martin Bormann and His Wife from January 1943 to April 1945.* Edited by H. R. Trevor-Roper. Translated by R. H. Stevens. London, 1954.

Braun, Eva. "Diary, February 6–May 28, 1935." In German in Werner Maser, *Adolf Hitler: Legende, Mythos, Wirklichkeit*, 6th ed., expanded (with Eva Braun's Diary), Munich and Esslingen, 1974, pp. 325–369. Also in Nerin E. Gun, *Eva Braun: Leben und Schicksal*, Velbert, 1968, pp. 70–78. In English in Gun, *Eva Braun: Hitler's Mistress*, New York, 1968.

Eberle, Henrik, and Matthias Uhl, eds. *Das Buch Hitler: Geheimdossier des NKWD für Josef W. Stalin, zusammengestellt aufgrund der Verhörprotokolle des Persönlichen Adjutanten Hitlers, Otto Günsche, und des Kammerdieners Heinz Linge.* Bergisch Gladbach, 2005. (Originally in Russian; Moscow, 1948/1949.)

Goebbels, Joseph. *Die Tagebücher von Joseph Goebbels: Sämtliche Fragmente; herausgegeben von Elke Fröhlich im Auftrag des Instituts für Zeitgeschichte und in Verbindung mit dem Bundesarchiv.* 20 vols. Munich, 1987–1996.

———. *Vom Kaiserhof zur Reichskanzlei: Eine historische Darstellung in Tagebuchblättern (Vom 1. Januar 1932 bis zum 1. Mai 1933).* 21st ed. Munich, 1937.

Hess, Ilse. *Gefangener des Friedens. Neue Briefe aus Spandau.* Leoni am Starnberger See, 1965. (Original edition, 1955.)

Hess, Rudolf. *Briefe 1908–1933.* Edited by Wolf Rüdiger Hess. Introduction and annotations by Dirk Bavendamm. Munich, 1987.

Hitler, Adolf. *Mein Kampf.* 173rd ed. Munich, 1936.

Hitler, Adolf. *Monologe im Führerhauptquartier 1941–1944: Die Aufzeichnungen Heinrich Heims.* Edited by Werner Jochmann. Hamburg, 1980.

Hitler, Adolf. *Reden und Proklamationen 1932–1945.* Vol. 1, *Triumph, First Part: 1932–1934.* Edited by Max Domarus. Wiesbaden, 1973. First published in Würzburg, 1962–1963.

Hitler, Adolf. *Sämtliche Aufzeichnungen 1905–1924.* Edited by Eberhard Jäckel with Axel Kuhn. Stuttgart, 1980.

Hitler, Adolf. *Reden, Schriften, Anordnungen.* vol. 4, *Von der Reichstagswahl bis zur Reichspräsidentenwahl, Oktober 1930–März 1932. Teil II, Juli 1931–Dezember 1931.* Edited by Christian Hartmann. Munich, 1996.

Hitler, Adolf, and Gertrud Scholtz-Klink. *Reden an die deutsche Frau: Reichsparteitag Nürnberg, 8. September 1934.* Berlin, 1934.

Mann, Thomas. *Diaries: 1918–1939.* Selected by Hermann Kesten. Translated by Richard and Clara Winston. New York, 1982. Translation of *Tagebücher 1918–1921*, edited by Peter de Mendelssohn, Frankfurt am Main, 1979.

Militärgeschichtliches Forschungsamt. *Das Deutsche Reich und der Zweite Weltkrieg.* 10 vols. Stuttgart and Munich, 1979–2008.

Picker, Henry. *Hitlers Tischgespräche im Führerhauptquartier: Entstehung, Struktur, Folgen des Nationalsozialismus.* Berlin, 1997.

Speer, Albert. *Albert Speer: Die Kransberg-Protokolle 1945; Seine ersten Aussagen und Aufzeichnungen (Juni–September).* Edited by Ulrich Schlie. Munich, 2003.

3. Memoirs

Axmann, Artur. *"Das kann doch nicht das Ende sein": Hitlers letzter Reichsjugendführer erinnert sich.* Koblenz, 1995.

Below, Nicolaus von. *Als Hitlers Adjutant 1937–1945.* Mainz, 1980.

Boldt, Gerhard. *Die letzten Tage der Reichskanzlei.* Hamburg, 1964.

Bormann, Martin. *Leben gegen Schatten: Gelebte Zeit, geschenkte Zeit; Begegnungen, Erfahrungen, Folgerungen.* 7th ed. Paderborn, 2001.

Breker, Arno. *Im Strahlungsfeld der Ereignisse: Leben und Wirken eines Künstlers; Porträts, Begegnungen, Schicksale,* Preussisch Oldendorf, 1972.

Dietrich, Otto. *12 Jahre mit Hitler.* Munich, 1955.

Engel, Gerhard. *Heeresadjutant bei Hitler 1938–1943.* Edited and annotated by Hildegard von Kotze. Schriftenreihe der Vierteljahrshefte für Zeitgeschichte, vol. 29. Stuttgart, 1974.

Fromm, Bella. *Blood & Banquets: A Berlin Social Diary.* New York, 1990. (Original edition, London, 1942).

Giesler, Hermann. *Ein anderer Hitler: Bericht seines Architekten Hermann Giesler.* 2nd ed. Leoni am Starnberger See, 1977.

Göring, Emmy. *An der Seite meines Mannes: Begebenheiten und Bekenntnisse,* 4th ed. Coburg, 1996.

Hanfstaengl, Ernst. *Hitler: The Missing Years.* London, 1957.

Hanfstaengl, Ernst. *Zwischen Weissem und Braunem Haus: Erinnerungen eines politischen Aussenseiters.* Munich, 1970.

Hoffmann, Heinrich. *Hitler wie ich ihn sah: Aufzeichnungen seines Leibfotografen.* Munich and Berlin, 1974. (Originally published as *Hitler Was My Friend;* London, 1955.)

Junge, Traudl, with Melissa Müller. *Bis zur letzten Stunde: Hitlers Sekretärin erzählt ihr Leben.* 3rd ed. Berlin, 2004.

Kardorff, Ursula von. *Berliner Aufzeichnungen 1942–1945.* Newly edited and annotated by Peter Hartl using the original diaries. Munich, 1997.

Kempka, Erich. *Die letzten Tage mit Adolf Hitler.* 3rd ed. Rosenheim, 1991.

Linge, Heinz. *Bis zum Untergang: Als Chef des Persönlichen Dienstes bei Hitler.* Edited by Werner Maser. Munich, 1982.

Loringhoven, Bernd Freytag von. *Mit Hitler im Bunker: Die letzten Monate im Führerhauptquartier Juli 1944–April 1945.* Berlin, 2006.

Lüdecke, Kurt. *I Knew Hitler.* New York, 1937; London, 1938.

Meissner, Hans-Otto. *So schnell schlägt Deutschlands Herz.* Giessen, 1951.

Meissner, Otto. *Staatssekretär unter Ebert—Hindenburg—Hitler: Der Schicksalsweg des deutschen Volkes von 1918–1945, wie ich ihn erlebte.* 3rd ed. Hamburg, 1950.

Misch, Rochus. *Der letzte Zeuge: "Ich war Hitlers Telefonist, Kurier und Leibwächter."* Munich and Zürich, 2008.

Nissen, Margret. *Sind Sie die Tochter Speer?* Bergisch Gladbach, 2007. (Original edition, Munich, 2005.)

Ribbentrop, Joachim von. *Zwischen London und Moskau: Erinnerungen und letzte Aufzeichnungen.* Edited by Annelies von Ribbentrop. Leoni am Starnberger See, 1953.

Riefenstahl, Leni. *Memoiren.* Cologne, 2000. (Original edition, Munich, 1987.)

Schaub, Julius. *In Hitlers Schatten: Erinnerungen und Aufzeichnungen des Chefadju-tanten 1925–1945.* Edited by Olaf Rose. Stegen am Ammersee, 2005.

Schellenberg, Walter. *Aufzeichnungen: Die Memoiren des letzten Geheimdienstchefs unter Hitler.* Edited by Gita Petersen. Newly annotated, using previously unpublished documents, by Gerald Fleming. Wiesbaden and Munich, 1979.

Schirach, Baldur von. *Ich glaubte an Hitler.* Hamburg, 1967.

Schirach, Henriette von. *Der Preis der Herrlichkeit: Erlebte Zeitgeschichte.* Munich and Berlin, 1975.

———. *Frauen um Hitler: Nach Materialien.* Munich and Berlin, 1983.

Schmeling, Max. *Erinnerungen.* Frankfurt am Main, 1977.

Schmidt, Paul. *Statist auf diplomatischer Bühne 1923–1945.* Bonn, 1953.

Schroeder, Christa. *Er war mein Chef: Aus dem Nachlass der Sekretärin von Adolf Hitler.* Edited by Anton Joachimsthaler. Munich, 1985.

Sonnleithner, Franz von. *Als Diplomat im "Führerhauptquartier."* Foreword by Reinhard Spitzy. Munich and Vienna, 1989.

Speer, Albert. *Inside the Third Reich: Memoirs.* New York, 1970.

———. *Spandau: The Secret Diaries,* New York, 1976.

Spitzy, Reinhard. *So haben wir das Reich verspielt: Bekenntnisse eines Illegalen.* 4th ed. Munich, 1994.

Wagener, Otto. *Hitler aus nächster Nähe: Aufzeichnungen eines Vertrauten 1929–1932.* Edited by H. A. Turner Jr. Frankfurt am Main, 1978.

Wiedemann, Fritz. *Der Mann, der Feldherr werden wollte: Erlebnisse und Erfahrungen des Vorgesetzten Hitlers im 1; Weltkrieg und seines späteren Persönlichen Adjutanten.* Velbert, 1964.

II. Selected Secondary Literature

Bullock, Alan. *Hitler: A Study in Tyranny.* New York, 1952.

———. *Hitler and Stalin: Parallel Lives.* London, 1991.

Charlier, Jean Michel, and Jacques de Launay. *Eva Hitler, née Braun.* Paris, 1978.

Conradi, Peter. *Hitler's Piano Player: The Rise and Fall of Ernst Hanfstaengl, Confidant of Hitler, Ally of FDR.* New York, 2004.

Costelle, Danielle. *Eva Braun: Dans l'intimité d'Hitler.* Paris, 2007.

Evans, Richard J. *David Irving, Hitler, and Holocaust Denial: Pressures on Hitler's Entourage After the War.* Electronic edition, http://www.holocaustdenialontrial.org/trial/defense/evans/530bB.

———. *The Third Reich at War, 1939–1945.* London and New York, 2008.

Fest, Joachim C. *Hitler: Eine Biographie.* Berlin and Vienna, 1973.

———. *Die unbeantwortbaren Fragen: Notizen über Gespräche mit Albert Speer zwischen Ende 1966 und 1981.* Hamburg, 2006.

Frank, Johannes. *Eva Braun: Ein ungewöhnliches Frauenschicksal in geschichtlich bewegter Zeit.* Preussisch Oldendorf, 1988.

———. *Speer: Eine Biographie.* Berlin, 1999.

Frank, Mario. *Der Tod im Führerbunker: Hitlers letzte Tage.* Munich, 2005.

Gaetringen, Hans Georg Hiller von, ed. *Das Auge des Dritten Reiches: Hitlers Kamera-mann und Fotograf Walter Frentz.* 2nd ed. Munich and Berlin, 2007.

Gun, Nerin E. *Eva Braun: Hitler's Mistress.* New York, 1968.

Hamann, Brigitte. *Winifred Wagner oder Hitlers Bayreuth.* Munich, 2002.

Herz, Rudolf. *Hoffmann & Hitler: Fotografie als Medium des Führer-Mythos.* Munich, 1994.

Heusler, Andreas. *Das Braune Haus: Wie München zur "Hauptstadt der Bewegung" wurde.* Munich, 2008.

Heydecker, Joe J. *Das Hitler-Bild: Die Erinnerungen des Fotografen Heinrich Hoffmann.* St. Pölten, 2008.

Infield, Glenn. *Eva and Adolf.* New York, 1974.

Joachimsthaler, Anton. *Hitlers Liste: Ein Dokument persönlicher Beziehungen.* Munich, 2003.

Kellerhoff, Sven Felix. *Mythos Führerbunker: Hitlers letzter Unterschlupf.* Berlin, 2006.

Kershaw, Ian. *Hitler 1889–1936: Hubris.* New York, 1999.

———. *Hitler 1936–1945: Nemesis.* New York, 2000.

———. *The "Hitler Myth": Image and Reality in the Third Reich.* Oxford, 1987.

Klabunde, Anja. *Magda Goebbels: Annäherung an ein Leben.* Munich, 1999.

Knopp, Guido. *Hitlers Frauen und Marlene.* Munich, 2001.

Kompisch, Kathrin. *Täterinnen: Frauen im Nationalsozialismus.* Cologne, 2008.

Lambert, Angela. *The Lost Life of Eva Braun.* London, 2006.

Lang, Jochen von. *Der Sekretär: Martin Bormann—Der Mann, der Hitler beherrschte.* 3rd, fully rev., ed. Munich and Berlin, 1987.

Maser, Werner. *Adolf Hitler: Legende, Mythos, Wirklichkeit.* 6th ed., expanded (with Eva Braun's Diary). Munich and Esslingen, 1974.

———. *Hitlers Briefe und Notizen: Sein Weltbild in handschriftlichen Dokumenten.* Düsseldorf, 1988.

Nicholas, Lynn H. *Der Raub der Europa: Das Schicksal europäischer Kunstwerke im Dritten Reich.* Munich, 1995.

Schmidt, Ulf. *Karl Brandt: The Nazi Doctor; Medicine and Power in the Third Reich.* London, 2007.

Sereny, Gitta. *Albert Speer: His Battle with Truth.* New York, 1995.

Sigmund, Anna Maria. *Diktator, Dämon, Demagoge: Fragen und Antworten zu Adolf Hitler.* Munich, 2006.

———. *Die Frauen der Nazis.* 3 vols. Vienna, 1998–2002.

Thamer, Hans-Ulrich. *Der Nationalsozialismus.* Stuttgart, 2002.

Völklein, Ulrich, ed. *Hitlers Tod: Die letzten Tage im Führerbunker.* Göttingen, 1998.

Winkler, Heinrich August. *Der lange Weg nach Westen.* Vol. 1, *Deutsche Geschichte vom Ende des Alten Reiches bis zum Untergang der Weimarer Republik.* Munich, 2000.

Zdral, Wolfgang. *Die Hitlers. Die unbekannte Familie des Führers.* Frankfurt am Main, 2005; Bergisch Gladbach, 2008.

INDEX

Eva Braun posing on a desk: bpk/Bavarian State Library /Heinrich Hoffmann

Hitler practicing oratorical poses: bpk/Bavarian State Library/Heinrich Hoffmann

The Braun family: bpk/Bavarian State Library/Heinrich Hoffmann

Eva Braun with ribbon in hair: bpk/Bavarian State Library/Heinrich Hoffmann

Hitler with his stepniece: Ullstein Bild

Hitler and Eva Braun at the center of a group photo: Bavarian State Library/Hoffmann Photo Archive

Harald Quandt next to Goebbels: bpk/Bavarian State Library/Heinrich Hoffmann

Hitler, Magda Goebbels, and Eva Braun: bpk/Bavarian State Library/Heinrich Hoffmann

Ilse Hess and Rudolf Hess: bpk/Bavarian State Library/Heinrich Hoffmann

Letter from Eva Braun to Ilse Hess: Swiss Federal Archives, Rudolf Hess Papers, J 1.2118-, 1993/300, vol. 2, file 25

Eva Braun with Hitler in front of the chimney stove: Bavarian State Library/Hoffmann Photo Archive

Eva Braun in blackface: Gallerie Bilderwelt/Getty Images

Hitler on the Obersalzberg: bpk/Bavarian State Library/Heinrich Hoffmann

Hitler and Sigrid von Laffert with Joseph and Magda Goebbels: Ullstein Bild

Eva Braun in Florence: Taken from: N. E. Gun, *Eva Braun Hitler: Leben und Schicksal*, Blick + Bild Verlag, 1968

Margarete Speer: Ullstein Bild / LEONE

Eva Braun, ice-skating: bpk/Bavarian State Library/Heinrich Hoffmann

Eva Braun and Albert Speer: bpk/Bavarian State Library/Heinrich Hoffmann

Karl Brandt and Eva Braun: bpk/Bavarian State Library/Heinrich Hoffmann

Eva Braun and Martin Bormann: bpk/Bavarian State Library/Heinrich Hoffmann

Hitler on the Obersalzberg: bpk/Bavarian State Library/Heinrich Hoffmann

The Berghof: bpk/Bavarian State Library/Heinrich Hoffmann

The terrace of the Berghof: Ullstein Bild/Roger Violet/Eva Braun Album

Soirée in the great hall: Ullstein Bild/Walter Frentz

The Morells with Eva Braun: bpk/Bavarian State Library/Heinrich Hoffmann

Hitler between Eva and Gretl Braun: bpk/Bavarian State Library/Heinrich Hoffmann

Eva Braun on the Berghof terrace: Ullstein Bild/Walter Frentz

Eva Braun photographing Hitler: Ullstein Bild/Roger Violet/Eva Braun Album

Eva Braun sitting behind Hitler: bpk/Bavarian State Library/Heinrich Hoffmann

Hitler and a model of the city of Linz: Ullstein Bild/Walter Frentz

Heinrich Hoffmann taking a photograph: Walter Frentz/Hanns-Peter Frentz

Hitler's arrival on the Obersalzberg: Süddeutsche Zeitung Photo/p. M

Eva Braun on the Obersalzberg: bpk/Bavarian State Library/Heinrich Hoffmann

Hitler and Eva Braun with Herta Schneider's children: Ullstein Bild/Walter Frentz

Hitler and Eva Braun at the dining table: bpk/Bavarian State Library/Heinrich Hoffmann

Hitler in his airplane: Ullstein Bild/Walter Frentz

Eva Braun and Hitler on the Obersalzberg: AP

Mohrenstrasse in the center of Berlin: German Federal Archive and Koblenz Scherl/183-
     J31347

The destroyed Old Chancellery: Walter Frentz/Hanns-Peter Frentz

Wooden chest with human remains: akg-images

A NOTE ABOUT THE AUTHOR

Heike B. Görtemaker, born in 1964, is a German historian and author. She studied history, economics, and German literature in Berlin and in Bloomington, Indiana. In 2005, she published a biography of Margret Boveri, a prominent German journalist from the 1930s to the 1970s. Görtemaker lives with her husband near Berlin. She is currently working on a project dealing with the legacy of Hitler's inner circle in postwar Germany.

A NOTE ABOUT THE TRANSLATOR

Damion Searls is a writer and award-winning translator of more than a dozen books, most recently Mirjam Pressler's *Treasures from the Attic: The Extraordinary Story of Anne Frank's Family* and Hans Keilson's rediscovered World War Two novel *Comedy in a Minor Key*, which was a *New York Times* Notable Book and National Book Critics Circle Award finalist. He lives in New York City.

A NOTE ON THE TYPE

The text of this book was set in Electra, a typeface designed by W. A. Dwiggins (1880–1956). This face cannot be classified as either modern or old style. It is not based on any historical model, nor does it echo any particular period or style. It avoids the extreme contrasts between thick and thin elements that mark most modern faces, and it attempts to give a feeling of fluidity, power, and speed.

Composed by North Market Street Graphics, Lancaster, Pennsylvania

Printed and bound by Berryville Graphics, Berryville, Virginia

Designed by Maggie Hinders